The Conversion of Herman the Jew

THE MIDDLE AGES SERIES

Ruth Mazo Karras, *Series Editor*

Edward Peters, *Founding Editor*

A complete list of books in the series
is available from the publisher.

The Conversion
of Herman the Jew

Autobiography, History, and Fiction in the Twelfth Century

Jean-Claude Schmitt

Translated by
Alex J. Novikoff

PENN

UNIVERSITY OF PENNSYLVANIA PRESS

PHILADELPHIA · OXFORD

This work is published with the cooperation
of the French Ministry of Culture, Centre National du Livre

Originally published as *La Conversion d'Hermann le Juif*
by Editions du Seuil

Published by
University of Pennsylvania Press
Philadelphia, Pennsylvania 19104–4112

Printed in the United States of America on acid-free paper
10 9 8 7 6 5 4 3 2 1

Library of Congress Cataloging-in-Publication Data
Schmitt, Jean Claude.
    [Conversion d'Hermann le juif. English]
    The conversion of Herman the Jew : autobiography,
history, and fiction in the twelfth century / Jean-Claude
Schmitt ; translated by Alex J. Novikoff.
        p.   cm.— (The Middle Ages series)
    Includes bibliographical references and index.
    ISBN 978-0-8122-4254-6 (hardcover : alk. paper)
    1. Herman, of Scheda, 12th cent. Opusculum de
conversione sua.   2. Christian converts from Judaism—
Germany—Biography—History and criticism.I. Gottfried,
von Cappenberg, ca. 1097–1127.   II. Herman, of Scheda, 12th
cent. Opusculum de conversione sua. English.   III. Title.
    BX4668.H4S3613 2010
    248.2′46092—dc22   2010004925

I learned something essential for my work: the difference between fiction and reality and how reality must be completed by fiction in order to make life easier.
—Pedro Almodovar
Le Monde, 17 September 1999

Contents

Map of Rhineland-Westphalia.

Introduction

This book invites a double displacement; one in time, by rolling back the centuries to the beginning of the twelfth century, the other in space, by focusing the reader on what is probably an unfamiliar region—the northwest of Germany, and more precisely the present-day region of Rhine-Westphalia, between Cologne and Munster, further to the east (see map). The occasion for this journey backward through time and across space is a text—the *Opusculum de conversione sua* attributed to *Hermannus quondam Judaeus*, "Herman the former Jew"—written in Latin in the twelfth century. This text has been transmitted to us in two manuscripts dating from around 1200. Their sizes are modest: several dozen manuscript leaves, exactly fifty-eight pages in Gerlinde Niemeyer's modern critical edition of the text published in 1963 in the *Monumenta Germaniae Historica*. The editor's commentary alone is a good ten pages longer than the text itself. Previous to this the text had appeared in three separate editions between the end of the seventeenth century and the middle of the nineteenth century, the last appearing in 1854 in volume 170 of Jacques-Paul Migne's *Patrologia Latina*, a series which remains to this day one of the pillars of historical research.

The two oldest manuscripts (others exist, but not from before the seventeenth century) do not come from Rhine-Westphalia but from further east in the regions of Saxony and Bohemia. They belonged not to the abbots or priories of the Order of Canons Regular of Prémontré, with which the text is directly concerned, but to monastic libraries of the Cistercian Order. The distant location of these manuscripts attests to the rapid dissemination of the text made possible by the network of religious houses. The oldest manuscript, now preserved in the Vatican Library in Rome (ms. lat. 504, f. 71v–93r), dates from the end of the twelfth century. The volume in which the text is found contains, among other works, theological writings of Saint Jerome and a history of Troy. The second manuscript dates from the beginning of the thirteenth century and is now housed in the university library of Leipzig (ms. 200, f. 178r–185v). Marks of ownership indicate that the manuscript once belonged to the library of the Cistercian monastery of Altzelle, near Nossen in Saxony. In addition to the *Opusculum*, this manuscript contains various writings by Saint Jerome, including a commentary on Isaiah, a description of the heavenly Jerusalem, and a letter from Pope Innocent III addressed to the participants of the Fourth Crusade (1204). By the end of the seventeenth century at the latest, this manuscript was located in the library of the Paul Academy in Leipzig where a scholar by the name of Johann Benedikt Carpzov had the text transcribed in preparation for its first printed edition.

We know of other later copies of the text. They come from its region of origin, Westphalia, and more precisely the Premontratensian houses of Cappenberg and Scheda. They date from the seventeenth century and inform us, as we shall see, about the later reputation of the supposed author of the document: the Jewish convert Herman.

Nothing in this text so far would merit our special attention were it not for a peculiarity that, for its time, signifies an uncommon originality. The text, as it turns out, is presented in a form that we today call an autobiography. What is more, it is the autobiography of a converted Jew: "Herman the former Jew."

It was more than fifteen years ago, while reflecting on the problems of self-representation in the eleventh and twelfth centuries and its relation to dreams and images, that I first encountered this text. Slowly it began to occur to me that there converged here several problems crucial to the framing of a historical anthropology of the medieval era: the questions of subjectivity and the "writing of the self," of the dream and the image, and at the same time the issue of conversion, the status of "the other," and the position of historical writing vis-à-vis the question of truth. The importance and diversity of these questions impelled me not to restrict the interpretation of this document to a single field of analysis, a sole historiographical domain, neither to the isolated history of the order of Prémontré (source of both the document and the first studies about it), nor to the history of autobiography (which led the great specialist Georg Misch to be among the first to examine this text), nor even to the history of Judaism and the relations between Jews and Christians in the Middle Ages (a historiographical field which has produced considerable debate over this text for some time). I try to incorporate all these approaches, as well as others, in the hopes of achieving some cross-fertilization. For I am certain that not one of these approaches alone can offer an interpretative framework sufficient to do justice to the unique richness of the *Opusculum*.

I wish first to investigate the status of the text, its style of writing and method of organization; in other words, its rhetorical nature. Then I shall investigate its presentation of historical truth before going further into the examination of its content. In posing these questions the historian cannot help but reflect on the conditions in which he himself writes history, on the relation between what he writes and what and who he writes about, and what he thinks may "really have happened" in the past. Having to reflect two realities, the historian must shift from the situation of producing a historical document that he has before his eyes to the situation of producing the history that he purports to write for his contemporaries. It is precisely there that doubt takes hold of him. Consider this modest *Opusculum*: how does one know to what extent Herman, in his autobiographical writings, reconstructed the story of his life for the purpose of passing it on to posterity in the best light? And indeed, was it really he who wrote this story preserved in the text as most historians who have handled it claim? Might not "Herman" be an alias, and if so, for whom and for what purpose? And if one believes that he was not the "author" of the *Opusculum*, how can one be sure that he really existed? Was Herman but a convert made on parchment? Similar questions relate not only to this text, but to all scholars who practice the "historical profession," whatever may be their precise object of study. However, it seems to me that the singular case presented here permits us to pose these questions in an exemplary manner, perhaps because of the very uniqueness of the text.[1]

The goal of this study, however, is not to provide a word-for-word expli-cation of the text. I will not get into all the aspects of the document, particu-larly when previous scholars have already treated them. Let me reiterate that my primary focus is on the grander anthropological questions: questions of fiction, of the dream, of autobiography, of images, of conversion as an indi-vidual experience and as a cultural paradigm.[2] In asking these questions I will begin with the testimony attributed to Herman the Jew, but test it against a rich contemporary literature to which Herman's work is sometimes explicitly related. The debate that has raged these last few years over the interpretation of this very enigmatic text has resulted in scholars either focusing their atten-tion solely on the text or comparing it only to other contemporary texts relating to Jewish-Christian polemics. But other very different documents that relate to the regional and local milieu that produced the *Opusculum* must be taken equally into account. This is the case, in the first instance, of the

Vita of Count Godfried of Cappenberg, which Gerlinde Niemeyer knew very well but which historians of medieval Jewish history systematically ignore.[3] I on the other hand think that this text is essential if we wish to define the status of the *Opusculum*.

Finally, we will notice that modern historiography has, between the sixteenth and the seventeenth centuries, appeared very slowly out of the very history in which the *Opusculum* was for centuries the focus of attention. This focus has varied in the past, but it consists nowadays most especially in the interpretation of the history of Christian-Jewish relations. The "longue durée" as well as the implication of historiography as a goal in itself shall be at the heart of my investigations. But before going any further it is appropriate to summarize the contents of the text, a full translation of which is provided at the end of this book.

Two Accounts for One Conversion

Following a title written in the third person and not preserved in all of the manuscripts, thus suggesting that it may not have been present in the original version ("Herman the Former Jew. Short Account of His Own Conversion"), there comes a letter of dedication; here Herman writes in the first person and writes to his "very dear son Henry" in order to tell him that he has given in to his entreaties, as well as those of a great many of his brothers and sisters in religion, and agreed to put in writing the account, which he had already made orally, of his long and difficult conversion. This "brother Henry" cannot be identified with certitude. Let us note, however, that in the *Vita* of the founder of Cappenberg, Count Godfried of Cappenberg, composed about 1150, mention is made of a certain "brother Henry" and that his blood brother, Encruvinus, tried to remove him by force from the community; the arguments of "Saint" Godfried forced Encruvinus to renounce such a baneful project.[4] But the name Henry is in fact too common for this period and in this region of the Empire for it to be worth the while to inquire any further about the identity of this person. For now let us note that he was a cleric.

There then follows an introductory formula (*incipit*) written in the third person and making it known that Herman the former Jew (*quondam Judaeus*) was already dead (*bone memorie*) at the time the manuscript was written.

Like the general title and the incipit, the twenty-one chapter-titles of the account of the conversion use the third person. We can see in the title and subtitles a framework no doubt given to the account after the story of conversion was related. The account itself, however, is written in the first person: it thus constitutes "the autobiography of conversion" written by a Christian, Herman, offering a retrospective look back on his Jewish past.

In the first chapter Herman recalls his childhood within a Jewish family in Cologne. His name at the time, if one wishes to read the Jewish nomenclature behind its Latin version, was Judas ben David ha-Levi. He had a father named David and a mother named Sephora, and he belonged to the tribe of Levi (Levi, the third son of Jacob and Leah, is the ancestor of the Levite tribe). The place of his birth is also given: Cologne, a city that in the twelfth century possessed the most important Jewish community in the Rhine valley. In his thirteenth year he had a dream: he dreamt that the reigning emperor, Henry V (1105–1125), bestowed upon him a white horse, a purse of gold, a silk baldric, and the possessions of a very powerful prince who had suddenly died. Then the emperor invited him into his palace, to sit at his table at his right and to partake of his meal of "herbs and roots." Awakening full of joy, the young Jew asked his uncle Isaac to interpret his dream. But Isaac saw only a "carnal" meaning in this dream—the foretelling of a rich marriage and a great fortune—an interpretation that did not satisfy the young Herman.

The second chapter brings us seven years forward in time. Judas is now twenty years old and living, along with several other merchants, in Mainz where King Lothar (r. 1125–1133) is temporarily residing along with other important members of his court, including Bishop Eckbert of Munster (1127–1132). Judas agrees to lend a sum of money to the bishop without security, thus going against the common practice among Jewish money-lenders of asking for a collateral of double the loan amount. When his parents find this out they are very unhappy and force their son to follow the bishop all the way to Munster in order to claim the debt. He lives there for twenty weeks in the household of an elderly Jewish man by the name of Baruch who is charged with looking after him. To disguise his untimely presence he attends the bishop's sermons where he is seduced by the "spiritual" commentaries on Scripture. One day he goes so far as to penetrate into the cathedral, which seems to him like a "pagan temple" (*delubrum*). Once inside, he is horrified by the presence of a great crucifix that he views as a "monstrous idol" (*monstruosum quoddam ydolum*). Deaf to the reproaches of Baruch, he begins visiting Christian schools where his talents are noticed. Soon thereafter his first contacts with the Christian world give way to real conversations with clerics.[5] Judas finds himself unable to refute the "reasons and authorities" that the clerics pose against the literal interpretation of the Old Testament practiced by Jews.

In chapter 3 these debates reach a higher level. Judas does not hesitate to take on one of the most respected theologians in Germany of this time, the Benedictine Abbot Rupert of Deutz (born in 1075, Abbot of Deutz from 1120 until his death in 1129/30). Judas complains to Rupert about the contempt in which Christians hold Jews, whom they call "dead dogs," and he also complains about the reprehensible liberty that Christians take in interpreting the Law, that is, the Old Testament. The Christian cult of images, which Judas likens to the worship of idols, is the only example he gives of such liberties. In chapter 4 Rupert replies in an equally direct manner saying that Christians too abhor idolatry: he argues that Christians do not worship the wood of the cross but rather the Christ that it represents. Images are useful to those who cannot read the sacred books. Moreover, justification can be found in the Old Testament, as is demonstrated by, among other examples, the altar on the banks of the Jordan River ordered by Joshua in memory of the entrance into the promised land by the Chosen People. In a similar fashion, the image of the crucifix is a "witness" to Christ's passion. The "reasons and authorities" put forth by Rupert sweep aside Judas's objections, although he persists in his "Jewish blindness."

He is then revisited (chapter 5) by the memory of an episode that he judges worthy of recording in his narrative, for it offered him "a great incitement to convert" and may offer the reader "a dazzling and forceful example of love and unfeigned faith worthy of imitation." From theological arguments insufficient for Judas to convert, the narrative then moves on to a lived moral example that is judged more effective. This consists of the virtuous behavior of Bishop Eckbert's bursar, a very religious man named Richmar. The latter offered to Judas, who was seated at his side, a slice of white bread and a roast joint that the bishop had a squire bring him. The generous bursar then made do with just bread and water. Herman here spins out the food metaphor, already present in his childhood dream and that will follow him on the road to conversion all the way to the "table" of the Lord. The bursar's charitable deed and his words of affection capture the admiration of Judas. But they do not suffice to change his mind. This is why Richmar, knowing that "Jews require signs" (1 Cor. 1:22), offers him a deal: he will subject himself to an ordeal by red-hot iron; if he escapes unhurt Judas will agree to convert; if the contrary proves true Richmar will renounce his attempts to convert him. But Bishop Eckbert does not permit his bursar to tempt God by a test of fire. He instead advises him to call upon divine mercy in order to obtain the salvation of man. An exterior and visible sign is superfluous: it is enough that God, if He so wishes, send his invisible grace into the hearts of man. And thus Herman agrees: numerous are those, he says, who convert without need of "signs," but innumerable are those who have persisted in their error even after having seen miracles. The words of Christ bear witness to this: happy are those who have faith in things unseen. Herman then raises some general considerations by having the readers of his small work bear witness to the important example of faith and charity that was once given him by a man such as Richmar.

In chapter 6 Herman recalls how he was given yet another example of Christian piety. While seeking the reimbursement of his debt, he accompanied the bishop on his visit to the Premonstratensian canons of the Abbey of Cappenberg, newly founded by counts Godfried (d. 1127) and Otto (who was the second provost until his death in 1171), two brothers who took vows and converted their castle into an abbey in 1121. There, Judas observed the austerity of the Rule, the diet, the habit of the canons, as well as their humility and piety. At first he pitied them without yet understanding the grandeur of their self-imposed sacrifice. Then he doubted the legitimacy of his own faith, since the dispersion and the trials of the Jews seem to show that God prefers Christians. The account of the conversion of Saint Paul, heard from the mouths of both clerics and laymen, comes to his memory. And so he addresses God and asks that he too be shown, by means of a secret inspiration, a vision or some other visible sign indicating which path to follow.

But it is the opposite that ensues. In chapter 7, Judas once again falls under the influence of his own people. At Easter, now that the bishop has repaid his debt, the young Jew returns to Cologne in the company of Baruch, who publicly accuses the young man of being a secret Christian. For this, God punishes Baruch by having him die a pitiful death just fifteen days later. Impressed by this divine chastisement, Judas doubles his prayers and implores God to show him the true path through a "nocturnal vision" (chapter 8). Following the example of the prophet David, he fasts for three days and, out of precaution, follows the observances of both Christians (who during days of fasting eat at the hours of None—in the middle of the day—but abstain from meat) and Jews (who fast until evening but permit the eating of meat). Nevertheless, three days of fasting, praying, and shedding tears yield nothing: God sends him no vision. The only result of his abstinence is a heightened suspicion on the part of his fellow Jews.

In order to avert total treason, his parents decide to wed him to a young Jewish girl, about whom we learn only that her father was named Alexander (chapter 10). Judas tries to delay his marriage by pleading his desire to go study in France. Brought before the council of the community, he is accused of apostasy and is threatened with being driven from the synagogue. Isolated and in despair, he finally gives in, ignoring the pleas of his Christian friends, and engulfs himself in the pleasures of marriage.

After three months, however, he decides to pull himself together (chapter 11). Henceforth no mention is made of his wife, who remains as ephemeral as she is anonymous. He renews contact with the clerics and asks them to enlighten him, but his soul remains blind. He tries to drive away the temptations of the Devil by repeatedly crossing himself, but it is in vain since he still has no faith.

He understands that the intervention of the church alone will allow him to obtain the grace of Christ (chapter 12). Remembering the names of two recluses from Cologne, Berta and Glismut, he heads off to ask them to pray to God for his enlightenment. Soon thereafter, a sudden clarity comes and chases from his heart "the darkness of all doubt and of all earlier ignorance." The prayers of two simple women produce results that the reasoning of the clerics and even their examples of virtue could not.

He immediately devotes himself to strengthening his burgeoning faith (chapter 13). Barely stopping to eat, he hastens to churches to listen with delight to the word of God. Increasingly he desires baptism.

Judas wishes to lure his seven-year-old paternal half-brother down the same path. The boy, whose name is not given, is living with his mother in Mainz, where Judas goes to fetch him (chapter 14). But the Jews of Cologne keep a watchful eye on Judas and threaten him with punishment. Through the intermediary of Wolkwin, a chaplain to Queen Richenza (d. 1141, the wife of emperor Lothar), they send a letter in Hebrew characters to their coreligionists in Mainz denouncing Judas's apostasy. By the greatest of coincidences Judas meets this messenger on the road to Mainz and convinces him to show him the letters. Once he discovers their contents, Judas throws the letters into the fire (chapter 15).

Encouraged by his success, he travels to Worms where a "blood-brother" named Samuel lives (chapter 16). In the synagogue Judas argues against David, the head of the community, and contests the "carnal" interpretation of Scripture. For this Judas is branded a "half-Christian." In an effort to appease the Jews, he assures them that he is only defending Christian arguments in order to enrich the debate.

Arriving in Mainz (chapter 17), he succeeds in taking his half-brother away from his mother. But, led astray by the Devil, he fails to find the way out of town. Yet as soon as he makes the sign of the cross on his forehead, he miraculously finds himself in front of the city gates. Outside, a servant awaits him with horses. Meanwhile, the Jews of Cologne arrive by boat and denounce him as an apostate before the Jews of Mainz. The mother of the child presses charges in front of the city's magistrates, who search unsuccessfully for the child. Judas finds refuge with his half-brother in the Abbey of Flonheim. So as not to render the holy men complicit in his flight, Judas entrusts them with the child, so that they can give the boy a Christian education, and then flees secretly to the Augustine Abbey of Ravengiersburg. On the third day of the calends of November (November 30), he becomes a catechumen.

In chapter 18, three weeks later, the Wednesday preceding the Sunday fixed for his baptism, Judas dreams of Christ seated in the majesty of the Father, carrying his triumphal cross as a scepter on his right shoulder. In his vision Judas also recognizes the two sons of his aunt, Nathan and Isaac, who pass behind his back. They, too, see the vision, but this only adds to their torment, for they are dead, confirmed in their lack of faith. Judas reminds them that he had tried in vain to convince them that Christ was the Messiah announced by Isaiah. At present, they suffer in Hell without hope of redemption. Shortly afterward they disappear from Judas's view and he wakes up. He then remembers that he had often hoped for such a vision, one that he had hitherto been unworthy of receiving.

The following Sunday he is at last baptized in the church of Saint Peter of Cologne, in the presence of all the clergy of the city (chapter 19). At the hours of Terce he confesses his belief in the Trinity and is immersed in the baptismal fonts that have been prepared for the ceremony. The Devil makes a last attempt to prevent his baptism by triple immersion, but despite this, he completes the rite of baptism and receives his Christian name: Herman.

Not satisfied with merely being baptized, he decides to leave the world and to join the Augustinian Order in Cappenberg (chapter 20). He learns Latin with a speed judged to be miraculous and, five years later, after having climbed one by one the ranks of the ecclesiastic orders, he accedes to the priesthood. Only then is he capable of understanding and offering an interpretation of the dream he once had as a child.

Chapter 21 thus concludes the *Opusculum* where it began: with the dream of chapter 1, which had remained without satisfactory explanation. Christian and baptized, a canon of Prémontré and a priest, Herman is now in a position to explain the "spiritual" meaning hidden in his childhood dream. Each of the elements of the dream symbolize a Christian figure or value: the emperor who invites the child to his table is the King of Heaven; the prince who dies prematurely is the Devil; the white horse offered to the child by the emperor is the grace of baptism; the baldric symbolizes the strength to resist the temptation of the flesh; the seven deniers are the seven gifts of the Holy Ghost; the palace is the abbey where he would eventually enter; the royal table is the altar for sacrifice; the banquet is the Eucharistic meal; the dish of herbs is the gospel of Christ; the plate he shared with the king symbolizes the unity of the Catholic faith. Concluding with thanks to God for his kindness, Herman addresses himself once more to his "readers and listeners," so that they may rejoice in his conversion and praise the Lord on his behalf.

I have said above that the *Opusculum* was the sole document that I have to work with. This is not entirely true. There is in fact another contemporary account that also describes Herman's conversion. The events are mentioned, though much more summarily, in a text of a quite different nature—not an autobiography, but a hagiography: the *Life of Godfried of Cappenberg*, the oldest version of which was written around 1150–1156 by an anonymous brother of Cappenberg.[6] After a first chapter on the noble origins of count Godfried, the *Vita* relates how, in 1121, he and his brother Otto gave their castle to Norbert of Xanten (who had just recently founded Prémontré) for the purpose of establishing a religious community there. The text continues with the merits and miracles accomplished by Norbert and of which the author of the *Vita* was a direct witness: on more than one occasion he speaks in the first person by noting all that he had seen and heard. On the occasion of a visit to Cappenberg by Norbert, the author overheard Norbert saying that this abbey was his favorite. Norbert explained to the brothers the dreams he had had about the abbey: he saw the Holy Ghost descend upon it, and on another occasion he saw the abbey radiating a celestial light. Norbert also told the brothers that Saint Augustine had appeared to one of them in order to recommend the observance of his Rule, which will be their best defense when the day of the last judgment comes. He also performed "great miracles" on the spot for the benefit of the community and he thanked one of the brothers for assiduously praying for the dead, thus compensating for the negligence of their carnal parents.[7] Without any transition, the author of the

Vita then cites Psalm 68 (67):24 on the tongue of the "dogs of God" who have "their share of enemies," and just as quickly offers his interpretation: the Jews "today" are these "enemies" against whom the "dogs of the Lord" bark, that is, "the many Jews who have converted."[8] Indeed these recent conversions are the result of divine grace. In Cappenberg there lives a "Jewish brother" (*frater hebraeus*) whose story is immediately summarized.

The convert, now a member of the community of brothers, is not named. But the vicissitudes of his conversion—most notably the disputes between him and the clerics, his waiting for a divine sign, his vision of Christ carrying his cross on his shoulder, his crossing himself repeatedly, his younger brother whom he led into baptism and (although the two accounts differ on this point) into the order of Prémontré—can leave no doubt that this anonymous Jewish convert and Judas/Herman are one and the same person.

Scholars are divided over whether this brief passage in the *Life* of God-fried was a summary of the *Opusculum a posteriori*, or whether, on the contrary, the *Opusculum* was a later amplification of this anonymous and brief first account. It is difficult to say, and, to tell the truth, the question does not seem to me of primary importance in so far as the two texts are contemporaneous. They seem to me rather to be two *versions* of the same account, in the same way in which ethnologists speak of different versions of the same myth. It is more important to analyze the differences of form, structure, and function of these versions than to debate at length and with no final verdict on the precedence of one or the other.

These two texts are central to my analysis in the pages that follow. I will continuously blend two planes of reflection: reflection on documents (especially, though not exclusively, textual documents), and reflection on the work of historians, myself and others. This study is followed by the English translation of the two principal Latin texts: an extract of the *Life of Godfried of Cappenberg* and, above all, a fresh translation of *Short Account of His Own Conversion*, attributed to "Herman the former Jew."

Chapter 1

Fiction and Truth

Three Centuries of Erudition

The first printed edition of the *Opusculum* appeared during the formative period of Christian anti-Jewish apologetics: in Leipzig in 1687 Johann Benedikt Carpzov took to reediting the famous *Pugio fidei* (or *Dagger of Faith*), a treatise composed in 1278 by the Dominican Raymond Martini, a lecturer on the *studium* in Barcelona. Born there around 1210–1215, Raymond Martini joined the Dominican order in around 1237–1240, and in 1250 was sent to Tunis by Raymond of Peñaforte as part of the new *studium arabicum* dedicated to evangelizing Muslims. Upon his return Raymond Martini wrote the *Dagger of Faith*, which marks the culmination of his work and is distinguished by its firsthand knowledge of Hebrew texts. He died in 1285–1290.[1] Carpzov (1639–1699), for his part, belonged to a long line of Lutheran theologians and ministers. He himself worked in both capacities in his native city of Leipzig where he finished his career as minister of Saint Thomas (1689) and a professor of theology (1684). He is the author of several exegetical works, a translation of Maimonides and studies of the Talmud, as well as sermons and letters. His edition of the *Pugio fidei* features a frontispiece of an armed hand representing the eponymous dagger of Raymond Martini's work; the dagger reaches out from a celestial cloud and threatens a terrified old rabbi, flanked by an acolyte in oriental costume who throws himself to the ground. Following the title page comes Carpzov's four-page dedication to Jacobus Bornius, a lawyer and advisor to the prince elector of Saxony. This is followed by a series of different texts: a 126-page *Introductio in theologiam Judaicam* by Carpzov himself; then, the six-page separately paginated prologue (*Proemium*) of Raymond Martini; after this, the *Observationes in proemium pugionis fidei* by Joseph de Voisin (184 pages); and then finally the full text of the *Pugio fidei* (pp. 191–961), also edited by Joseph de Voisin and published for the first time in Paris in 1651. This Joseph de Voisin, a native of Bordeaux (1610–1685) and protected by the prince of Conti, was a famous Hebraist, the translator of several Kabalistic texts, and also the author of a *Theologia Judaeorum* (1647). His French translation of the *Missel romain* (1660), immediately placed on the index of forbidden books, was the occasion of a great ecclesiastical-political polemic.

It is following this new edition of the *Pugio fidei* that one arrives in Carpzov's work at the *editio princeps* of the *Opusculum de sua conversione*, complete with a distinct pagination of thirty-two pages. Carpzov dedicates this edition to the theologian Theophilus Spizel, whom he describes as "a most vigilant minister of orthodoxy." Born in Augsburg, where he ended his career as doyen of the Lutheran church, Spizel (1639–1691) must have met Carpzov while studying theology at Leipzig. He is the author of controversial anti-Jewish and anti-Anglican writings. After this dedication, Carpzov explains, in the space of two pages, the circumstances under which he came to publish this previously unedited text: the manuscript was brought to his attention by the librarian of the Academy in Leipzig, the poet Joachim Feller (1628–1691),[2] who told him that it was the work of a "proselyte." Carpzov was actually searching desperately to find among the holdings of the library the work of Raymond Martini, which he had thought lost. He says that he immediately admired the elegance of the written form of the manuscript and he specifies that he had hitherto never come across the name Herman among anti-Jewish polemicists. The friends he consulted confirmed to him that the *Opusculum* remained unedited. Carpzov finds particularly noteworthy the account Herman gives of his meeting with the Abbot Rupert of Deutz, a well-known author of the early twelfth century, and the information that he gives about his own period, which also happens to be that of Bernard of Clairvaux.

It is under the banner of an anti-Jewish polemic, then, that the *Opusculum* reaches a scholarly audience at the end of the seventeenth century. The work is considered a personal account meant to confound Jews and push them toward conversion through the edifying example of a convert who himself recounted the story of his progression toward grace. It is Carpzov's edition, let us remember, that Migne would reedit in the nineteenth century in the *Patrologia Latina* and that historians would use exclusively until the second half of the twentieth century.

The second edition of the *Opusculum* appears in Johann Dietrich von Steinen's *Brief Description of the Noble "Houses of God" in Cappenberg and Scheda* (Dortmund, 1741). This edition has a completely different purpose from the first. The issue is no longer proving the superiority of Christianity over Judaism, but describing the first stages of the history of the order of Prémontré in Germany, and especially in Rhineland-Westphalia. The history of these "Houses of God" in Cappenberg and Scheda affords an opportunity to consult all the available local sources, including the *Opusculum*. It is the ecclesiastical and religious history, and more especially the history of Prémontré, that defines this second wave of interpretation of our text. In the historiographical fate of Herman the Jew, the history of the order of Prémontré plays a role of primary importance. The foundation of this order of canons regular in 1119–1121 is part of the great eleventh- and twelfth-century Gregorian movement of reform and owes itself to a single priest, Norbert of Xanten. Like many of its contemporary orders, the new order of Prémontré adopts the less rigid Rule of the Augustinians and spreads rapidly, especially in the north of Europe. The order's first appearance in Germany is in Cappenberg in 1121. The story of this foundation is related in the *Vitas* of Godfried of Cappenberg and Norbert of Xanten.

We have already said that the *Vita* of Godfried mentions the entrance into Cappenberg of a *frater hebraeus*; the *Opusculum* also mentions Cappenberg in connection with the wondrous visit the young Jew made in the company of Bishop Eckbert of Munster. Curiously, it is not the name of Cappenberg that history has attached to Herman's, but that of a filial priory called Scheda in Westphalia. According to tradition the author of the *Opusculum* calls himself "Herman of Scheda" and not "Herman of Cappenberg." Two writs of the archbishop of Cologne dated 1170 justify this displacement: one mentions a provost of Scheda by the name of Herman (*Herimannus Schedensis prepositus*), but without qualifying that he is a Jewish convert; the other specifically mentions the provost Herman the Jew (*Herimanno Israelita preposito*), but also says nothing of his connection to Cappenberg. There are no further sources until 1619 when the prior of Scheda Johannes Caesar compiles a list of provosts and abbots who preceded him. At the top of that list he places *Hermannus Israelita*, but once again no connection is established between him and the author of the *Opusculum*. The link is only formally established several years later by the abbot of Scheda Wilhelm Grüter and the vicar general for the archbishop of Cologne, Johannes Gelenius, for on 23 and 24 June 1628 they proceed to open the tombs of two people whom they believe played a distinguished role in the founding of Scheda. Gelenius left a detailed written report of the exhumation. In the first tomb were found the bones of the preacher Echardus, who according to tradition convinced a widow by the name of Wiltrudis and her children to contribute to the founding of Scheda. Located seven feet below the ground, the second tomb contained a skeleton in good condition, with a "large and deep" cranium and thirty-two teeth. A tombstone covered the remains. It lacked any inscription, but there was an effigy of a brother from Prémontré in a long robe wearing a cross and with his hands clasped on his chest. This effigy had one peculiarity: at his feet lay "a pointed hat similar to the one Jews wear publicly in paintings" (*superne acuminatum ea forma qua judaei pinguntur*).[3] For Grüter and Gelenius there is no doubt about their finding: this tomb can only be that of the first "abbot" of Scheda. They are all the more familiar with his history since the library of the priory possessed a manuscript of the *Opusculum*. The abbot and the vicar general order the exhumation of Herman's remains and present the act as the elevation and transportation of the relics of a saint. Gelenius composes an epitaph in commemoration of the event and to celebrate the one who, following the example of Saint Paul (the universal model for Jewish converts), is a "fox" who has transformed himself into a "lamb."[4] The fifth of July 1628 saw the transportation of Herman's remains into the sacristy. The vicar general removes some relics for the chapel of Saint Margaret in the cathedral of Cologne, the sepulcher chosen by his parents and himself.

Thus by the seventeenth century at the latest Scheda, the "daughter" house of Cappenberg, had posited for itself a founding "saint" in the person of Herman the Jew, a "first abbot" rather than an actual founder. Objective criteria such as the presence in this priory of a twelfth-century brother named Herman, indeed Herman the Jew, with the same name as the supposed author of the *Opusculum* whose link to Cappenberg is known, no doubt helped to confirm his identification. More generally, another factor also needs to be borne in mind: starting in the twelfth century a rivalry develops between Scheda and her "mother" house of Cappenberg, the latter complaining of the "daughter" house's desire for independence. Cappenberg thus "commits the imprudent move of repudiating her daughter's subject status" (*filiam subjectionem [. . .] minus prudenti diu denegaverunt*).[5] It is therefore possible that the brothers of Scheda wished to find in Herman, so glorified by his reputation as a convert, the figure of the original saint they needed. My hypothesis is that Herman, whether he was indeed the provost of Scheda, or, as is more likely the case, he was confused with a later person of the same name (the abbot Herman of Scheda who is attested to at the end of the twelfth century), has played a role in the collective memory of this priory close to that of the two major "founders" of the Order: Norbert of Prémontré and Godfried of Cappenberg. The incompleteness of medieval sources unfortunately does not permit exact knowledge of when and how the role of "original saint" was created and assigned to Herman the Jew.

The terrible destructions of the Thirty Years War (1618–1648) in Rhine-Westphalia following the Council of Trent prompted those responsible for the immense ecclesiastical province of Cologne to bring about a "religious reordering" (*Religionsordnung*) in the style of a Catholic reconquest. One of the principal promoters of this reconquest is none other than the vicar general Johannes Gelenius, whom we have just met at Scheda in the context of unearthing the "relics" of Herman the Jew. From 1626 until 1631 he assists the archbishop Ferdinand of Bavaria (1612–1650) in his work of reform and reconstruction. A series of synods, pastoral visits, and Episcopal mandates testifies to their joint efforts. They pay close attention to the cult of saints as a support for their reformist activities as well as the persecution of witchcraft, which was experiencing renewed fervor during these same years. This may well explain the presence of Gelenius at the side of Abbot Grüter at Scheda in June 1628.

At the very same time, the canons of Prémontré were preoccupied with carrying Herman the Jew, or of Scheda (for them it is all the same), to the altar. In 1625 Johann Christof Van der Sterre of Antwerp gives him a place in the catalogue of saints of the Order of Prémontré (*Natales Sanctorum candidissimi Ordinis Praemonstratensis*). The initiative comes from the priory of Saint-Michael of Anvers. Herman is named "first abbot and provost" of Scheda and is given as a feast day on 23 December. In the historiography of the order it seems that the prestige of another Herman far more famous and with better saintly credentials, abbot Herman-Joseph of Steinfeld (1150–1241), did not in fact eclipse the reputation of his modest namesake at Scheda, but rather was projected upon the earlier Herman. In the catalogues of illustrious persons in the Order of Prémontré, the alphabetic classification made it possible for Herman of Scheda to come directly before blessed Herman-Joseph. It was therefore difficult not to merge the two. Herman-Joseph was born in 1150 (also in Cologne) to a poor but once affluent family. He entered Steinfeld young, was sent to study in Frisia, and returned to enter into the priesthood. His many visions of the Virgin Mary, with whom he contracted a "mystical marriage," established his reputation.[6] The conflation of the two Herman "saints" of Prémontré is made explicit in the *Lilium inter spinas*, a work which Van der Steere consecrated in 1627 to the "blessed Herman Joseph, priest and canon of Steinfeld of the Order of Prémontré." Only in this work is the feast date of Herman of Scheda fixed on 6 August and not 23 December. In the dedicatory note Van der Steere cites a passage from the *Opusculum*.[7] In 1645 the canon Aegidius Gelenius, historiographer of the archbishop of Cologne and relative of Johannes Gelenius, cites Van der Streere and mentions the presence in Cologne of the relics of Herman of Scheda, whose autobiographical *Vita* he transcribes.[8]

In carrying out the exhumation of Herman's remains, Abbot Grüter aims at recovering the relics of a "saint." But hagiography is not his only motive. His abbey falls victim to a violent internal conflict. Driven by the provost Caspar von der Hees, certain canons wish to limit the recruitment of brothers to the nobility. Others, under the direction of Abbot Wilhelm Grüter, want to retain the possibility of recruiting among common people. In this campaign, the memory of Herman is high stakes: if a simple Jewish convert managed to become the first "abbot" of Scheda, and indeed a saint, are Grüter's claims against privileging the nobility not fully justified? The discovery of Herman's tomb did not, however, thwart a victory for the opposing party. In 1647, after a string of events, Caspar von der Hees is reestablished in his prerogatives and the third successor of Grüter, Johannes Hansaeus, is forced to quit the abbey with his non-noble brothers. But he is not ready to give in just yet. In Brussels he hands over to the Bollandistes a file containing one copy of the *Opusculum* that was preserved at Scheda (the original is now lost), the text of a morning prayer also attributed to Herman the Jew, the written report by Johannes Gelenius describing the exhumation in 1628, and the epitaph that Gelenius composed in honor of Herman. This turned out to be a providential gift since the greatest part of the archives of Scheda would disappear in the midst of this troubled period and then later during the French Revolution. Even the abbey itself would not survive the turbulences of the Napoleonic era: it was shut down in 1809 and the church destroyed in 1817. Today only a nineteenth-century manor and a large farm occupy the site. At best, only a few ivy-covered rocks scattered nearby recall the old priory. In the dining room of the manor house, a mediocre eighteenth-century painting illustrates the founding of Scheda by the priest Echardus, the widow Wiltrudis, and her sons.

No further attempts were made to sanctify Herman the Jew. In the middle of the seventeenth century, while the local defeat and departure of the low-born canons ruined the cause for the Jewish convert, the hagiographic critics of the Bollandists (who on the other hand had no hesitation in honoring Godfried of Cappenberg in 1643 with a place in the *Acta Sanctorum*) defeated the arguments favorable to recognizing Herman the Jew as a saint. Nevertheless, the scruples of the literate Jesuits led them to prepare an edition of the *Opusculum* based on Hansaeus's copy. But only the 1735 edition of the *Acta Sanctorum* mentions, by the title of *praetermissus* ("failed"!), the name of Herman.

In the meantime, as we have seen, the suspicions of the Bollandists did not prevent the publication in Dortmund in 1741 of a new edition of the *Opusculum*, distinct from that of Carpzov. The goal here was neither to frame an anti-Jewish polemic nor to bring to light a saint from Prémontré. For Johann Dietrich von Steinen, author of the new edition, the intended purpose is an ecclesiastical history of Westphalia and in particular the history of its "noble abbeys" of Cappenberg and Scheda. Thus it is to the mid-eighteenth century that one may date the beginning of the "laicization" of the historiography of Herman the Jew, or put another way, its entrance in scientific history.

The editions of 1687 and 1741 did not enjoy the sort of circulation that would have been guaranteed by publication in the *Acta Sanctorum*. One has to wait for the priest Jacques-Paul Migne and volume 170 of the first edition of his *Patrologia Latina* (1854) for the *Opusculum* to at last catch the attention of modern scholarship. Let us note that this edition is given in the last of the four volumes (167–170) devoted to the monumental work of Rupert of Deutz, one of the most prolific of the "patristic" authors since Saint Augustine. By the end of the nineteenth century (the second edition of volume 170 of the *Patrologia Latina* dates to 1894), German scholars were grabbing hold of this curious document newly placed at their disposal: writing for the Institute of Jewish Studies in Leipzig in 1891, Reinhold Seeberg grounds his analysis in the Migne edition in order to privilege the "Jewish aspect" of the work, devoting a short study (and the title is revealing) to "Herman of Scheda: A Jewish Proselyte of the Twelfth Century." Nor is the regional aspect of the history neglected: in 1920, A. Zak gives to the journal of the history and archaeology of Westphalia a piece on "the biography of the provost Herman of Scheda," and in 1929 a well-known philologist named Joseph Greven also turns to the *Opusculum* in the journal of the history of the lower Rhine.

The publication in 1959 of Georg Misch's ambitious *History of Autobiography* (*Geschichte der Autobiographie*) marks a break with these earlier studies. In several volumes, and beginning with late antiquity and the *Confessions* of Saint Augustine, Misch explores the vagaries of "autobiography" as a genre in Christian culture. He sees it as almost completely disappearing during the early Middle Ages, only to be revived and renewed in various milieus (i.e., in monasteries, among secular clergy) in about 1100 and with spiritual and intellectual goals carefully delineated by the author. Thus the "era of Abelard" appears to him to be characterized by a "troubled interior" and "tensions between philosophy and theology." It is in this context that he places two "histories of conversion" each seeking "to resolve by two different paths the ethical-religious problem of existence": the "personal confessions" (*Selbstbekenntnisse*) of the Cistercian Abbot Ailred of Rievaulx (author of various letters and the *Speculum caritatis*) and the "autobiography of the Abbot of Prémontré Herman of Scheda." What follows is devoted entirely to Abelard. Misch's main contribution lies not in his analysis of the *Opusculum*, which consists of hardly more than a paraphrase of the text, but in giving this work a new contextual horizon by drawing it closer to other comparable autobiographical accounts, such as the ones written by the monks Otloh of Saint-Emmeran and Guibert of Nogent. In doing this, he leaves a major question unanswered: what to make of Herman's "Jewishness"? Is it legitimate to place the *Opusculum* only in the company of Christian autobiographies?

In 1960 Bernhard Blumenkranz was the first to approach the *Opusculum* as a medieval Jewish autobiography. But he was also the first, to my knowledge, to raise doubts about the reality of Herman's Jewish past and even of his very existence; in other words, he was the first to question the authenticity of the account as it is presented. Could the *Opusculum* be no more than a piece of Christian "propaganda"? However, in a later article (1966) that appeared after Gerlinde Niemeyer's (1963) new edition of the *Opusculum*, Blumenkranz reverses his position and no longer doubts that Judas/Herman the Jewish convert really existed.

In 1963 Gerlinde Niemeyer's critical edition appeared under the title *Hermannus quondam Judaeus: Opusculum de conversione sua*. It is thus that the *Opusculum* receives a title that does not appear in the manuscripts. Most notably there is an author: "Herman the former Jew." The editor's long introduction aims to establish Herman's identity based on the clues provided by the text and other clues carefully gleaned from the archives. The chronology of Herman's life, as Niemeyer establishes it, is as follows:

Around 1107–1108: Born in Cologne.

Around 1120–1121: Dream during his "thirteenth year."

1127–1128: At the age of twenty, a short stay in Mainz with Bishop Eckbert of Munster; dispute with Rupert of Deutz.

1128–1129: Return to Cologne, and trips to Mainz and Worms.

25 November 1128 or 1129: Baptism in Cologne, and entry into Cappenberg.

1129–1134/1135: Learns Latin in the five years in Cappenberg.

1137–1138: Having risen the ecclesiastical orders and attained the minimum age of thirty, Herman becomes a priest.

Niemeyer's research does not end where the *Opusculum* does. She further endeavored to reconstruct Herman's biography from his entrance into the priesthood and his death:

1149–1153: He leaves Cappenberg in order to complete his education at Saint-Cassius of Bonn, where there is mention during these two years of a canon and priest by the name of *Herimannus Judeus*. The identity of this person as being our Herman is judged "probable" by Niemeyer.[9]

1170: He becomes provost of the priory of Prémontré of Scheda, where the presence of a *Herimannus Schedensis prepositus* and a *Herimannus Israhelita prepositus* is confirmed. But a conflict between Scheda and Cappenberg may have obliged him to abandon his post and leave the priory.

1172 and again 1181: He was named during these two years—but without the title of provost—as canon of Saint-Marie *ad Gradus* of Cologne under the name *Herimannus Judeus*.

1181 or shortly thereafter: The probable date of Herman's death, at the age of approximately seventy-four.

On the basis of this chronology, Niemeyer places the composition of the *Opusculum* during the 1150s at the earliest, and more probably during the 1160s. Consequently, she excludes Cappenberg and even Bonn as places of composition, suggesting Scheda or even Cologne as more likely locations.[10] The *Opusculum* would consist, then, not of memories written down at the end of one's life and gathering together a lifetime's recollections, but of an autobiographical account written by someone in the prime of life some twenty or thirty years after the major event that gave that entire life its meaning—a conversion.

Recent Reinterpretations of the *Opusculum*

Niemeyer's critical edition of the *Opusculum* awakened the attention of historians even outside the circle of medievalists. In 1984, the celebrated Italian historian of Judaism and late antiquity Arnaldo Momigliano turned to the new edition in an effort to take up and expand upon the analyses of Misch and Blumenkranz. Herman's existence is not once called into question. It is the text as the work of a convert that interests Momigliano: Herman does not write as the events are taking place, but when everything has happened, and it is for this reason that he ponders who this person was *before* his conversion. Herman is not a proselyte who writes to convert his former coreligionists. He writes for Christians with whom he shares his life and faith. Momigliano is the first to highlight the crucial importance of the dream in the account attributed to Herman. What is its connection with conversion? The connection is an important one if we wish to judge it in comparison to other medieval texts: one finds a similar role assigned to the dream in Dante's *Vita Nuova*, and even more so in two accounts of Christians who converted to Judaism. Both narratives were found in the archives of the Cairo Geniza. One was written in the first person by an anonymous former priest, the other, dating from around 1121, is a third-person account attributed to a Norman in southern Italy, John of Oppido, who converted in 1102 and took on the name Obadiah. As a child in his father's house, he dreams that he is in a cathedral where a "man" (an angel?), standing near the altar, admonishes him and puts him on the road to conversion. This text enjoyed a large dissemination among Jews along the Mediterranean and in the West, and Momigliano goes so far as to ask whether Herman might have known it. This is unlikely in my opinion.

Two years after Momigliano, Sander L. Gilman (1986) takes up Niemeyer's edition of the *Opusculum* and sees in the text one of the oldest examples of what he calls Jewish "self-hatred" (a term that could equally be applied to other minorities such as blacks and homosexuals). For him this consists, in a manner unchanging across the centuries, of one group adopting the negative stereotypes projected upon them by the dominant class. Once converted, Herman adds to the negative image of his former brethren and to their charge of "blindness."[11] The following year Jeremy Cohen offers a much more informed and convincing article on "the mentality of the medieval Jewish apostate."[12] He compares the case of Judas/Herman to two other Jewish converts to Christianity: the first is Petrus Alfonsi (converted in Huesca in 1106 at the age of forty-four) and who wrote, if not an autobiography, certainly a polemical work, the *Dialogues Between Moses and Peter*, in which he casts himself in the role of the two adversaries: the Jew he once was, Moses, and the Christian he has become, Peter, in honor of his godfather King Peter of Aragon. The second is Pablo Christiani, formerly Saul of Montpellier, who converted in 1209 and, once a member of the Dominican Order, opposed the rabbi Moses ben Nahman (Nachmanides) in the famous *Disputation of Barcelona*, which Raymond Martini, as we have already seen, echoed during the same period in his *Pugio fidei*. Even if all these cases concern Mediterranean Judaism, the case of Herman the Jew is no longer as isolated as it may have first seemed.

In 1988 Avrom Saltman, a professor at Bar Ilan University in Jerusalem, published a radical refutation of Niemeyer's entire interpretation: "Truth or Fiction?" he asked. For him, the answer is beyond any doubt: the *Opusculum* is not the true history of a real convert, but "a work of fiction, an edifying autobiographical novel." This novel would have been written in and for an exclusively Christian world. The text, he adds, contains no convincing trace of contemporary Judaism. Rather, it reproduces the stereotypes through which Christians of this period see and judge Jews by assimilating them with the Hebrew people of the Bible. For Saltman the names of the hero (Judas) and of his parents and close associates (David, Sephora, Samuel, Isaac, Baruch) resemble biblical names more than they do contemporary Jewish names. What is more, all biblical references follow the translation of the Vulgate. The *Opusculum* repeats among other things the narrative schemes common to other legendary anti-Jewish accounts of the period: the conflict between the young Judas and his father, followed by the young man's conversion, can be compared to the wondrous account in the *Annals of Egmond* in which a young boy also converts after a conflict with his father over an issue of money.

Moreover, the *Opusculum* teems with factual inconsistencies that Saltman delights in pointing out. For example, Judas and Bishop Eckbert could not have arrived at Cappenberg to meet Godfried, the founder of the abbey, since he died 1127, the year in which Eckbert became bishop of Munster.[13] Similarly, it seems unlikely that in Mainz the young Judas summoned the famous Abbot Rupert of Deutz to respond to his objections: it is difficult to imagine the abbot submitting himself to the injunctions of an obscure twenty-year-old Jew! Additionally, Saltman finds no common trait between Rupert's supposed response and the real arguments he develops in his treatise against the Jews, the *Anulus*. Finally, no reliable source mentions Rupert of Deutz's stay in Munster, and one can say the same for King Lothar's stay in the same town, an event mentioned only in the *Opusculum*.

To summarize Saltman's conclusions: the *Opusculum* is a "fiction" that expands and embellishes the corresponding passage in Godfried's *Vita*, a work whose objectivity Saltman does not question. In the *Vita* the name of the convert is omitted. This is either because it was forgotten or because Judas/Herman was "Judaized" and, having "fallen back" into his old "error," it was deemed best to conceal his name while at the same time preserving the edifying part of his story. In the *Opusculum* it was possible to give the name Herman to the hero of the account in honor of the provost Herman of Scheda, attested to in 1170 as a former *Israelita*. In short, Saltman accords the *Vita* and archival documents the authoritativeness he denies the *Opusculum*. He admits the existence of the anonymous convert described in the *Vita* as well as the existence of the provost Herman of Scheda in 1170, but rejects the idea that they are one and the same person identifiable with the protagonist of the *Opusculum*, who is for him a purely imaginary figure.

For Saltman, this text would have been written at the end of the twelfth century by a canon of Cappenberg who drew upon the *Vita* for the conversionary story of a Jew who entered the abbey, but who then let his imagination roam freely. This Prémontré author would then have amplified this account of a conversion by giving it the form of an autobiography.

Saltman's radical position completely changed the terms of the historiographical debate. In 1987 historians were still looking for parallels to Herman. Starting in 1988 the main question became whether Herman really existed and if he indeed is the author of the *Opusculum*. Indicative in these respects is the title Friedrich Lotter gives his 1992 article appearing in *Aschkenas*, the German journal for the history of Judaism: "Is Herman of Scheda's *Opusculum de conversione sua* a fake?" Highly critical of Saltman, Lotter's answer is definitively no. He refutes individually all of Saltman's arguments, and following Niemeyer, whose ideas he vigorously confirms, he even presents some new propositions. For him, nothing proves Saltman's suggestion that the *Opusculum* derives from the *Vita*. Indeed for Lotter the *Opusculum* precedes the *Vita*: it may have been written shortly after 1137–1138 when Herman was thirty years old, the minimum age for becoming a priest. This early date may help explain why, contrary to the *Vita*, the *Opusculum* make no mention of Judas/Herman's younger brother entering Cappenberg: he was still too young to take his vows at the time the *Opusculum* was written down. The *Vita* of Godfried on the other hand, dating to 1150–1157 according to Niemeyer and written about twenty years after the *Opusculum* according to Lotter, was able to cite the entrance into the order as having already happened.

Lotter goes even further in criticizing Saltman: if Saltman sees only "fiction" in the *Opusculum*, it is because he will not admit that Jews could have converted voluntarily and without constraint. But it has to be asked why the canons of Cappenberg would have written this "fake" text in a literary genre so exceptional for its time. Could they not just as easily have written a "dialogue between a Jew and a Christian," or an *adversus judaeos* that conforms to the more standard polemical genres? The unusual nature of the *Opusculum* coupled with the convert's evocation of states of consciousness suggests to Lotter that the text is authentic. Finally, he denounces the danger to historians of suspicions usually thrown onto historical documents. He had already found it deplorable that a scholar as attuned as Gilbert Dahan should have been seduced by Saltman's arguments.[14] Lotter points out that, on his urging, Bernhard Blumenkranz had not long ago reconsidered the doubt he once expressed concerning the authenticity of a fifth-century document dealing with the Jews of Minorca. Saltman therefore should follow his example and humbly admit that he was wrong!

Faced with such extreme and passionate arguments on both sides, one comes to see that the stakes of the debate go beyond strict historical interpretation. Lotter puts his finger on a critical question: could Jews in the past have abandoned the faith of their ancestors consciously and without the usual physical threat? He suspects that Saltman's inability to admit this is the reason why he doubts the authenticity of Herman's account. What strikes me about both sides of the debate is the restricting nature of a poorly framed question: if the same text seems "real" to one and "false" to another, with each side putting forward equally preempting arguments, would it not be better to try and escape from this polarized debate?

Let us see first how Saltman's polemic, once issued, developed steadily in the following years and has gained momentum of late, at the same time keeping in mind the shift toward more complex problems. In 1992, in the same issue of the *Revue des études juives* where Saltman harshly refuted Niemeyer, the Israeli historian Aviad Kleinberg of Tel Aviv University made clear that he, too, like Lotter, believed Herman the Jew's account to be genuine. (Since then several writers, mostly recently William Chester Jordan, have made their arguments either for or against.)[15] Kleinberg refutes all of Saltman's arguments point by point. And if he recognizes several minor inconsistencies in the account, he suggests that he can see in this author a memory affected by the passage of time between his conversion and the writing of his autobiography. For Kleinberg the *Opusculum* and the *Vita* are more or less contemporaneous. But if the latter offers a classic story of conversion, the former presents a convoluted scenario interspersed with "loose ends"; the *Opusculum* is not a well-constructed fiction but rather an account whose incongruities, a sign of spontaneity, speak to its authenticity. Kleinberg notes the paradoxical importance given the Abbot Rupert of Deutz as an interlocutor with the young Jew. But this, too, far from being an argument against its authenticity, is proof-positive of its true authorship, for if the monks of Prémontré had conceived of the account and written it themselves, they would not have accorded Rupert such an important role. After all, they denigrated traditional monastic authority. Kleinberg concludes that the *Opusculum* is "an exceptionally original work," one that "presents the reader with a highly individualistic portrait of the author: arrogant, self-centered, unstable, often dishonest."[16]

Also appearing in 1992, independently of Kleinberg's article, is a work by Karl Morrison entitled "Conversion and Text." Morrison's principle achievement is the part he plays in introducing to medieval studies a kind of reflection inspired by recent work in linguistic and literary criticism. It is the "text itself"—generally a written text, though he does not exclude the artistic and more general visual aspects[17]—which captures his attention, both as a site for "transaction" between transmitters and receivers, and as a response to its audience's "horizon of expectations." Conversion is considered here as a "text" and no longer as an individual event documented by a "source." To this first theoretical advance Morrison adds a second by proposing a comparative analysis of three accounts of conversion from three different periods: those of Saint Augustine (his *Confessions*), the twentieth-century Greek Constantine Tsatos, and also of Herman the Jew, for which he provides the first complete and precise English translation of the *Opusculum*. Herman's existence is not questioned, but what Morrison pays particular attention to are the convert's "hermeneutic strategies" by which he intentionally creates an ambiguous text with a double appearance: sufficiently Jewish to succeed in convincing his former coreligionists to follow him down the path to conversion (indeed, this would be the purpose of the *Opusculum*), and sufficiently Christian to avoid drawing Christian suspicions of "Judaizing." In short, Herman is a master of concealment who hides his game on both sides in order to better assure the proselytizing success of his work. The comparison with Saint Augustine reveals the particularity of his "hermeneutics": in the *Confessions* it is the inner spiritual struggle between good and evil that is at the center of a speculative text. In the *Opusculum* the debate is more external and deals above all else with the opposition between the literal meaning and the spiritual (or symbolic) meaning in the interpretation of scripture. Speculation and introspection are absent. Morrison's hypotheses are most ingenious and have the great advantage of bringing us toward what we have in the first place: a text, not a man. In this respect the turnaround, particularly in view of Niemeyer, is complete. But I remain unconvinced by what Morrison affirms about the new convert's proselytizing: this is not, in my opinion, the function of the text.

By the following year (1993) the British historian Anna Sapir Abulafia had taken a decisive step toward a better comprehension of the theological background of the *Opusculum*. She convincingly demonstrates that its audience consists not of prospective Jewish converts, but of Christians, and more specifically the brothers and sisters of the order of Prémontré. It is from this perspective that one can understand the importance given to the exegetical debate and the idea that the *reasons* essential for Judas/Herman's progression toward baptism do not suffice, but that only *love* and *grace* allow access to the truth of God. This problem was crucial for the new community of Prémontré in which the members lived with intensity the experience of an inner Christian conversion. It is thus not surprising that the text is constructed around it.

Thanks to Karl Morrison, Anna Sapir Abulafia, and also Jeremy Cohen's more recent work,[18] a rapid evolution of the study of the *Opusculum* stimulated by Saltman's article can be detected in the form of a gradual shifting of the problem away from the author and toward the text, its status, and its rhetoric. This gradual shift has already permitted a salutary return critique of Niemeyer's peremptory affirmations: in 1995, Ludger Horstkötter demonstrated the unlikely character reconstruction Niemeyer made of the life of Herman, condensing into one person all the Hermans who qualify as Jew, provost, or canon. Such a condensation is too indiscriminate and one has at the very least to distinguish between Herman the Jewish convert, "author" of the *Opusculum* at the abbey of Cappenberg, and Herman the provost of Scheda, attested to in 1170. According to Horstkötter there is no objective link between these two persons, not to speak of other "Hermans" attested to later, whom Niemeyer doesn't hesitate to assimilate with the "author" of the *Opusculum*, up until his supposed death in 1181. One problem that Horstkötter neglected to consider remains: the assimilation of the two Hermans—the Herman of the *Opusculum* and the provost of Scheda in 1170—dates to well before Gerlinde Niemeyer's work. She was only trying to find a more solid base of scholarship on which to ground a tradition that, in the order of Prémontré, goes back to at least the sixteenth century and which cannot be ignored: why did the priory of Scheda, profiting from the homonym of two separate canons, lay their hands on the Jew of Cappenberg?

So where do we stand as I write this book? Opinions are divided, as is evidenced by the acts of a colloquium that took place in 1996 and which was subsequently published in 2001. This excellent publication assembles contributions of several of the best specialists in twelfth-century Jewish-Christian relations.[19] Among fifteen different contributors, six mention the autobiography of Herman the Jew, a telling indication of the importance this enigmatic figure has acquired in recent studies of the subject. But opinions are divided: some take up without hesitation Niemeyer's conclusions about the "authenticity" of the account, in some cases taking his life up to 1181.[20] In a particularly incisive study William Chester Jordan places Herman in the larger context of Jewish and Christian "adolescents" during the period under consideration. Regarding Judas/Herman, he firmly takes a position against Saltman and for Kleinberg, declaring that "the truth, however, is that the text is authentic."[21] But several lines later he seems to admit, in parentheses, that Herman could not have written this text, which may owe itself to Christians, a fact that would take nothing away from its interest (quite the opposite, I might add) in a history of conversion in the twelfth century.[22] Alfred Haverkamp goes even further in returning to the argument I had advanced in 1994–1995 that the text was written after the death of a convert who entered Cappenberg (Judas/Herman) by a canon (or canons as I am more prepared to say now) of this abbey.[23]

I have only been able to summarize the arguments presented since 1988 (when Saltman's article appeared) without each time going into the detailed critiques offered by these often very admirable scholars, though their arguments are not always convincing. Let us simply note that all the studies cited, which span a very brief period (fifteen years) in comparison to the long historiography of Herman, can be located between the two opposite and equally radical positions of Gerlinde Niemeyer and Avrom Saltman. In 1963 Niemeyer was still following the purest German tradition of Leopold von Ranke: historians must show "how things actually happened" (*wie eigentlich gewesen*). They ought to reconstruct the historical reality starting from fragmentary sources which they then critique and complete with other sources of information. Arising from this effort of reconstruction is an objective portrait of a society whose representation is faithful to the event, or, as in this case, the "real" biography of an author about whom everything is known from cradle to grave. However, wanting to show too much, Niemeyer ends up confusing her hypotheses with reality, for neither the longevity she attributes to Herman (he would be seventy-five at his death in 1181) nor the peripatetic movements of the last period of his life can be judged convincing. Saltman's criticism is thus of a double nature, or rather it targets two "fictions": the "fiction" of the *Opusculum*, which would not be the "authentic" account that Niemeyer claims it to be; and the historiographical "fiction" forged by Niemeyer herself. In wishing to reconstruct year by year the entire biography of the "author" of the *Opusculum*, one could say that Niemeyer had written nothing more than a "fiction of a fiction." If in this document she clings to the reassuring certitude of what is to her eyes a double objective reality—that of the "true" autobiography of Herman and that of her own "positive" reconstruction of the convert's life—then the criticisms that oppose her lead one instead to consider two fictions eight centuries apart: that of a "pseudo-autobiography" forged by medieval canons, and that of a historical reconstruction that, paradoxically, has become adventurous because of positivist zeal.

A double challenge is thus presented to modern historians who are asked to answer at once two essential questions pertaining to their profession: what is nature of their object, the "reality" of the document and of its referent? And, at the same time, what is it about the "writing of history" that makes it possible for the "truth" of an argument that has been constructed with such patience and erudition to be so easily placed in doubt? The question of the relation between history and fiction is presented in two different historical contexts: that of present-day history and of the connection between historians and "truth"; and that of medieval culture and its conception of fiction.

History or Fiction?

How does one demonstrate "how this actually happened"? To do so Gerlinde Niemeyer gleans all the archival documents that she believes concern Herman and places them side by side to previously established timelines, or chronologies that she constructs herself. Her work as a historian consists of assembling in chronological order all the individual pieces of an apparent puzzle. To her eyes the result is a correspondence as perfect as the "sources" permit between a well-ordered chain of documents and the reality of a past life; a correspondence so perfect that no doubt can come and shake her certitudes or those of her readers. Truth is established once and for all: positivist history, the manner of writing it and its perfectly established results, are true and therefore immutable.

The criticisms of Niemeyer, led by Avrom Saltman, are, as we have seen, successful in putting forward reservations about the results of this research. But can we be certain that these criticisms themselves escape the conceptual framework that had constrained Niemeyer? For Saltman too the historian has no other alternative but to find the historical "truth" or, contrarily, "fiction," when, like Niemeyer, he is mistaken about the character of his sources and he even adds to their fictitiousness. Thus we can place Saltman and Niemeyer in the same category even if they arrived at diametrically opposed conclusions. Has the historian no other choice except one that risks missing what seems to me the essential part of the *Opusculum* (like many of the symbolic productions of men in history): its profound ambivalence?

The polemic that concerns us here is fairly representative of a far vaster and older historiographical debate. As Otto Gerhard Oexle has remarked, one does well to "historicize" the old question of history and truth since other solutions have been proposed in the past that are sometimes richer than the ones historians advance today. Historians have not always locked themselves up in the alternate choice—or insoluble contradiction—of truth and fiction. This call to the historiographical conscience also underlines the differences that separate various historical "schools": Oexle distinguishes between an Anglo-Saxon "empiricism" and a "continental rationalism,"[24] at the same time underscoring the extent to which German historiography has remained attached to the founding work of Ranke, whether by following it blindly (for which we have a fine example here) or assuming a radically opposite stance. In entitling his study "Im Archiv der Fiktionen" ("In the Archive of Fictions," 1999), Oexle inverted the terms in order to makes an explicit reference to the polemical article of another German historian, Werner Paravicini: "Rettung aus dem Archiv?" ("Help from the Archive?" 1998).[25] In this article Paravicini denounces all "postmodern" initiatives that exalt the relativity and subjectivity of historical "discourse" and that aim to cast doubt on the possibility that historians can find in their "sources" the "truth" about "facts." In part Paravicini joins Richard J. Evans who in his book *In Defense of History* (1997; translated into German under the surprising title *Fakten und Fiktionen* [*Facts and Fictions*, 1998]), writes: "the stories we tell will be true stories, even if the truth they tell is our own, and even if other people can and will tell them differently, for the fact that no description of anything can be wholly independent of its author's point of view does not mean that no description can be true."[26] Evans thus holds a more nuanced position than does Paravicini, for he points out that every history is exclusive to the historian who writes it, even if he also defends the existence of a "truth about the past" in itself. In doing so Evans distinguishes himself from the more radical followers of the "linguistic turn" for whom history does not differ in any essential way from literature. For followers of the linguistic turn, history has no claims to the scientific objectivity to which it aspired in the nineteenth century; rather it has remained as it was in the seventeenth century: a literary genre. Hayden White, one of the founders of this critique, likens the forms of historical discourse to four rhetorical "styles"—metaphor, metonymy, synecdoche, irony—and highlights the "precritical" stage of historical "knowledge" before concluding that "in history, I have argued, the historical field is constituted as a possible domain of analysis in a linguistic act which is tropological in nature."[27]

O. G. Oexle swiftly demonstrates that this debate is far from being new and that current historians gain nothing in forgetting the past. History shows them that their predecessors often introduced more nuance into the debate than they. The "crisis of history"[28] that we perceive as being of such recent vintage in fact owes its origin to the birth of "historical science" in the nineteenth century. Going against Leopold von Ranke (1824), both Johann Gustav Droysen in 1857 (*Historik*) and Nietzsche in 1881 refused to be constrained by the rigid opposition of fiction and historical facts; in Kantian philosophical fashion, they showed that, quite to the contrary, the task of history was to *transpose* the documentary givens into an *intelligible* presentation for historians and their contemporaries. Facts do not speak for themselves and historians can only arrive at a relative truth. But the historian's exposé is nonetheless not a "fiction" in the sense that a novel is, since s/he always works from *traces* of the past. The historian reconstructs a "world of representations" which is neither a string of "facts" *copying* (*Abbild*) the past, nor a *fiction* about the past. When faced with the insoluble contradiction between facts and fiction, it is better to introduce a third category that assigns to the historian's discourse the place and worth of a "system of signs."

This intuition was already an old one when it was deepened and enriched around 1900 at the great founding moment of the social sciences. The burgeoning fields of history and sociology were simultaneously confronted with a reinforced influence of Kantian epistemology on the one hand and the natural sciences on the other, the latter giving primacy to Albert Einstein's idea of relativity. The important names for the beginning of the century are Georg Simmel, Max Weber, and Ernst Cassirer, and during the 1920s, Ernst Troeltsch for his critical examination of the "crisis of historicity." In France Emile Durkheim and the "French school of sociology" (Marcel Mauss) extending to historians (Marc Bloch)[29] express similar tendencies. Resting on this platform—which I summarize too briefly here—is the proposition of a "third way," one which, for our purposes, both Gerlinde Niemeyer and Avrom Saltman completely misunderstand: history is indeed relative to the context in which it is written, it is a construction, composition, discourse, or better yet, a *system of representation*; it is neither a "copy of reality" nor a "fiction" comparable to novels and poetry since it works with traces of the past (documents) and possesses critical rules of restriction.

One could multiply the examples of historians and epistemologists who in recent years have sought to situate the place of historical discourse between these two radically opposed extremes of fiction and truth. In his *Writing History: Essays on Epistemology* (French original 1971) Paul Veyne affirms the tripartite ancient Aristotelian belief that history is "the relation of true facts, and not seemingly true ones (as in the novel) or unlikely ones (as in the tale)." A "relation of true facts," Veyne reminds us, is how Voltaire defined history by opposing it with the fable, a "relation of facts falsely given." But if we hold legends, tales, fables (and we could add myths) as different forms of fiction, history, however, the "relation of true facts," is not a "copy" of these facts since historians are not able to know everything about the past and must therefore construct a "plot," even if they are duped by the illusion of "complete history."[30]

Basing herself on the very different premises of literary criticism and linguistics, Anne Reboul accurately defines the difference she perceives between history and fiction: "the specificity of fiction is at once the falsity by referential default and the lack of engagement by the speaker."[31] Historians by contrast are constrained to give their references (citations from archives and documents, etc.) and wage battles, so to speak, with their demonstrations, ready to defend them in the polemical wars between specialists. One does well to cite here Michel de Certeau who showed perfectly well how "the writing of history" proceeds from the uncertain relation historians simultaneously have with two forms of the "real": that of the past, which documents deliver up in the form of traces, and that of the historian's own present, which occupies a particular place in contemporary society and culture. Because this double relation is uncertain, the historian may be tempted to privilege one term over another, one type of history over another. But never does the writing of history actually escape this tension:

> One type of history ponders what is comprehensible and what are the conditions of understanding; the other claims to reencounter lived experience, exhumed by virtue of a knowledge of the past. [. . .] Between these two forms there is tension, but not opposition. Historians are in an unstable position. If they award priority to an "objective" result, if they claim to posit the reality of a former society in their discourse and animate forgotten figures, they nonetheless recognize in their composition the orders and effects of their own work. The discourse destined to express what is *other* remains *their* discourse and the mirror of their own labors.[32]

One can hardly overstate the extent to which the insoluble contradiction of "truth against fiction" is devoid of meaning. For indeed, one needs to understand the activity of the historian as a twofold confrontation with the past: through the traces that remain of it on the one hand, and with him or herself thinking and writing in the here and now on the other. It is by understanding this that historians can arrive at and put forth hypotheses and propose, not *the* truth, but their version of the truth.

Medieval Truths and Fictions

Avrom Saltman does not only reproach Gerlinde Niemeyer for taking as a given the historical novel that, according to him, she has patiently worked out. He also asserts that the *Opusculum* is not at all the true autobiography of a converted Jew, but that the convert is himself a "fiction" forged by the canons of Cappenberg. On this point I think Saltman is quite right. On the other hand, it seems to me that he commits an error in attributing the complete creation of this literary fiction to the clerics of Cappenberg without first inquiring into the possibility that such a creation originated in the literate culture of the twelfth century. Without consideration of the historical context, he applies the idea of fiction as novel such as we understand it today to the Middle Ages. He opposes fiction and truth against one another as two impermeable categories without asking whether such a clear boundary separates them, especially during the Middle Ages. For how does one know whether these words have the same meanings and implications in all periods?

For us today a fiction is an imaginative work recognized as such, for example in literature or film. In a bookstore, the sign "Fiction" indicates novels, to be distinguished from books of history or psychology or economics. A subgenre of fiction is science-fiction. This extrapolates from currently accepted facts of science and technology and freely imagines their developments in the future as well as their consequences for lifestyles in future generations. For us fiction is opposed to what is objectively verified and verifiable. Fiction can be unlikely or likely, but in no case is it true.

All these words that we habitually use—false, fictive, true, truthful, likely, etc.—have a history: some have words that have stayed the same over the centuries, but they have acquired new meanings. To be more exact, their relations to one another have altered within the semantic field that they constitute and the dividing lines have shifted.

Following a firm distinction made by Saint Augustine, there was during the Middle Ages, at least for theologians, a clear opposition between a lie, as defined by its intention to mislead, and truth. For as the Bishop of Hippo declared: "'Lying' is to be found in the case of those who lie. They differ from the deceptive in this, that all deceptive creatures have a desire to deceive, but not everyone who lies wishes to deceive" (*non autem omnis vult fallere qui mentitur*).[33] But what is true and what is false in the Middle Ages? The foundation of truth and falseness is of a theological order: the devil is the master of deceit for it is he who seduced our first parents with fallacious words. Everything that touches God, on the other hand, belongs to the domain of truth: the whole Bible, from Genesis to Apocalypse, is God's revealed word and therefore true. Among all His accounts, those of the terrestrial life of Christ are "words of Gospel": all that the Evangelists say, even if there are some points of difference among them, belong to *historia* par excellence, "holy history," because it was revealed. Thus, by definition, it is "authentic." Not authentic in the sense in which we understand it, as when something is subject to an objective verification, such as an expert's "authentication" of an artist's work. "Authentic" in the Middle Ages is that which was *authorized* or approved by an institution that was worthy of faith and a guarantor of truth. It is the Church, in the very first instance, which guarantees truth. Ever since the first centuries the Church, as expressed in the writings of the Church fathers and Church councils, made the distinction between the canonical books of the Bible and the "apocryphal" accounts that were rejected (among them numerous apocalypses): an "apocryphal" text is one that was not approved by ecclesiastical authority. Today the Bible can easily appear to us much like apocryphal writings; a text filled with myths, supernatural occurrences, improbabilities—in a word, *fictions*. However, for the Middle Ages the Bible is "authentic," that is, authenticated by the authority of the Church Fathers, the Popes, and tradition. As for the rest, everything pertaining to the Church, from rites to beliefs, is "authentic": it is thus that we call "authentic" the little strip of parchment that is attached to a relic and bears the name of a saint. Thanks to "authentic," a small piece of bone that would otherwise remain anonymous and might arouse doubt or even derision is at once identified, certified, and offered to the cult of saints with the guarantee of the Church.

The notion of truth in the Middle Ages thus appears far broader and more flexible than the term suggests today. Its only limit is the lie, which is driven by the intention to deceive and harm. But there, too, the boundaries are hazy, for there also exists in the Middle Ages "pious lies" and "written fabrications" devised for a good cause: this is the case for the many false donation charters of all sorts fabricated in the *scriptoria* of the monasteries. Modern historical criticism judges them false, but such was not the opinion of the monks who wrote and used them: did they not, after all, serve the higher interests of their community and of their patron saint? A well-known case is the *Donation of Constantine*, forged in the eighth century in order to guarantee the papacy possession of her Roman inheritance. But by the end of the Middle Ages a more critical examination of historical accounts threw doubt on its authenticity.[34]

Like the monk forgers, ecclesiastic authors proclaimed loud and clear their fidelity to the truth: how could it be otherwise given that truth, as opposed to a lie, is the foundation of Christian morality and a condition for salvation? Indeed, the truth they keep in their minds is far more important than the precision of words and the details of facts. The truth of a text can be constructed based on rendering its contents in conformity to what it should be. From this, what we call fiction enters directly into the discourse of truth. Such is the case with hagiography: the Life of a saint frequently resembles an intricate web of miracles, fantastic accounts, and common locations designed to assimilate the saint to some great model, like Saint Martin, Saint Benedict, or even Christ Himself. For contemporaries, this "fiction"-filled Life could not be more *true*.

Historians of the Middle Ages—the authors of Chronicles and Histories—declare even more powerfully their attachment to telling the truth of past events. As Bernard Guenée writes, "in history [. . .] the truth is essential." Yet judging by *our* criteria of historical truth, their writings leave something to be desired. The reason for this is that they privilege the authority of the witness over the reliability of his account: the prestige of "men worthy of belief"—ancient historians or the Church Fathers for example—compel these historians of the Middle Ages to cite their accounts and even to accumulate them by juxtaposition, thus leaving the reader to make his choice and to believe what he wants. History writers during the medieval period make it a point of honor to cite all sources, but it is rare—at least before the twelfth century—that they attempt to distinguish between what is certain and what is not. What is more, their sources of information are limited to the books—never very many—contained in the library of their monasteries or the chapterhouse of their cathedral. The insistence placed on the *auctoritas* of witnesses is also a way of covering up the inadequacies of their accounts. In any case, the divisions between the library of the monastic historian and the *scriptorium* of his monastery are not watertight:[35] so at Saint Denis, for example, it is the same scribes and men of letters who, for the greater glory of their founding saint, reconstruct history as it should be and forge false documents in order to confer to their community the privileges it should always have held. "In short," Guenée writes, "it must be admitted that often, throughout the Middle Ages, that which we call a fake was the normal product of erudition."[36] Or as Roger Dragonetti remarks: "It is not a question of deception, but of a logic of writing whose fruits were the result of an implementation of the rhetoric of truth."[37]

One can hardly be too attentive to words that, in every period of history and in every language (Latin or vernacular), express the concepts that are here in question. In an exemplary study, the historian of medieval literature Richard Firth Green showed how the Middle English word *trowthe* (the etymological root of *truth*) changed its meaning in England during the course of the fourteenth century, the period of Richard II and Chaucer. It is during this period that the word ceases to signify fidelity or loyalty, as opposed to personal treason, and shifts toward the modern meaning of "conforming to facts" while at the same time "treason" becomes a crime against the State.[38] Green sees in this semantic mutation a major development in the social and cultural transformations of the late Middle Ages: the passage from an oral culture to a culture more and more accommodating to writing, particularly in royal affairs.[39] This is also accompanied by a profound change of attitude regarding proof; the public exercise of justice replaces the unanimous opinion of the community. It is not difficult to recognize in this notion of truth defined as a witness's "good faith" one of the dominant words in narrative literature, including Latin literature (in the *exempla* as much as in historiography), of the central Middle Ages.

It should be clear that medieval categories have meanings and usages other than the ones to which we are accustomed. Should this conceptual relativity surprise us? The anthropologist's consideration of other cultures where oral tradition is as or even more permanent than it was in medieval cultures reveals other affinities and other significant differences to our habits of thought.[40] The British historian and anthropologist Jack Goody clearly showed how irrelevant is our sharp distinction between true and false, or, to borrow his terms, *mythos* and *logos* to oral cultures. In these cultures the boundary between "truth" and "fiction" lies elsewhere. "Among the LoGagaa of northern Ghana there is a firm verbal distinction drawn between *yelmiong* ('proper affaires of telling the truth') and *ziri* (lies), though it is possible to argue that the LoDagaa concept of tales (*sunsuolo*) represents a third category, approximating to that of fiction, where there is no intention to deceive."[41] The fictive account therefore does not resemble a lie (as Saint Augustine also said), but rather offers various affinities with the "true speech" that it supports, embellishes, or extends.

Compared to anthropologists, historians benefit from an enviable temporal distance that permits them to consider investigation into periods conducive to the appearance or semantic displacement of these very notions. G. W. Bowersock detects in the second-century reign of the Roman Emperor Nero a decisive moment in the emergence of "history as fiction." Two authors play a central role. The first is the neo-Platonic philosopher Celsus who writes his *True Discourse*, a pamphlet against the Christian religion, in the year 178. He introduces a rhetorical innovation: the fiction of a Jew who converses with other Jewish converts to Christianity and tries to convince them of their error. If Celsus places arguments in the mouth of an imaginary Jew, Origen (185–254), in his *Contra Celsum*, a Christian refutation of the *True Discourse*, is perfectly conscious of the fictive character of this Jewish figure. For our purposes it is interesting to note that this "fictive Jew" is without a doubt the oldest "ancestor" of the Jewish convert Herman. Being a polemical context, would the thorny question of the relations between Jews and Christians (and pagans) not then constitute a landscape favorable to the writing of similar fiction?

The second author whom G. W. Bowersock considers had other goals: Lucian of Samosata (c. 120–180) wrote a work ironically entitled *True History* which was a collection of invented stories which he knew full well were false. In all of this, he writes ironically, "the only true thing is that I am a liar." In the second century the emergence of literary fiction is confirmed by a whole series of other less important writers. One of these, the physician and skeptic philosopher Sextus Empiricus (late second century) distinguished three categories of accounts: *history* is the account of things that really happened; *fiction* is the account of things that did not happen but resemble those that did (they are not true, but likely); and finally *myths* are accounts of things that have not happened and are false (they are lies). In fact, the dividing lines between these three categories are not as clear-cut as we might wish to believe: if there is a clear denunciation of the falsity of myths, to the point that it is used by the early second-century Christian Hippolytus in a text attributed to him, the *Refutation of All Heresies*, the ancients, Bowersock writes, "draw a thin line between myth and history." The idea that history is fiction would not have surprised them because history was for them a work of rhetoric, an *opus oratorium*. It belongs under this category to an immense collection of fictive accounts or, to use a modern term, novels.

The pagan Hellenistic authors of the second century also plunge us into a world where fiction and history merge in a way already foreshadowing medieval Christian culture. What is more, G. W. Bowersock notes that the emergence of the Hellenistic novel is doubtless not alien to the confrontation between paganism and Christianity. The novel, he writes, playing off the paradox, is presented as "romanced writing" or even a "secular writing," a counterpoint to the writings of the Christians—the Gospels and the Acts of the Apostles—that were for their part "a sort of narrative fiction having the form of history."[42] Finally it is medieval Christian culture which, centuries later, gave impetus to the particular form of truth forged of fictions which we might be tempted to call legends or novels, but which were understood as being part of *historia*. The Lives of saints are the greatest examples for the high Middle Ages, but starting in the twelfth century in Byzantium (and, we might add, the West, accompanying the consecration of vernacular languages as literary languages) secular culture gave birth to distinct forms that are often a mixture of both history and fiction. Indeed it is in the twelfth century, Jacques Le Goff writes, that the "historical novel" is born.[43] So, is the medieval novel not above all, as Roger Dragonetti suggests, a "falsifying art"?

The existence of multiple points of overlap between history and fiction does not prevent medieval authors from being conscious of the differences between levels and genres of writing. In some exceptional cases, they even discuss this theoretically. Perhaps the first attempt to distinguish literary genres precisely on the criterion of truth can be found in the prologue to the *Chanson des Saisnes* (or *Song of the Saxons*) by the trouvère Jean Bodel of Arras (fl. 1165–1210).[44] He is a prolix author to whom is attributed a diverse body of work—in addition to this epic chanson, fabliaux, a *Jeu de saint Nicolas*, pastourelles, and the famous *Congés* in which the poet, now a leper and knowing that he is condemned to a fast-approaching and painful death, returns one last time to the joys of the world which he prepares to leave. The *Song of the Saxons* belongs to the epic cycle of Charlemagne; interlaced in this "historical" account of the emperor's suppression of rebelling Saxons and of their king Witikind (here called Guiteclin) is the amorous intrigue of the queen Sebille and Charlemagne's nephew, Baudoin, the brother of Roland. After the death of Guiteclin, Baudoin will marry Sebille and become king of "Sessoigne." The chanson does not refrain from mixing epic genres, courtly and lyrical genres, or from blending history and fiction. But this is done with perfect mastery of these different types of writing, for the prologue proposes—for the first time—to distinguish "three subjects." The first is the "matter of Brittany," which offers a "light and pleasant" type of narrative and in which the hero par excellence is King Arthur; it is fitting—as is the case for example with the romances of Chrétien de Troyes—for the recreation of princely and chivalric courts. Mentioned next is the "matter of Rome," better known today as the "matter of antiquity" and which narrates the scattering of the Trojans after the fall of their city; this type of account is judged "wise and of a teaching style": it is edifying and pedagogical. Finally there is the "matter of France" which is "true and every day apparent." This is the subject of epic, the history of Charlemagne and his barons in the tradition of the *Chanson de Roland* or even the *Chronicle of Pseudo-Turpin* of which there were no fewer than six translations into French prose at the beginning of the thirteenth century.[45] It is this tradition that Jean Bodel hopes to illustrate in his *Chanson des Saisnes*. This prologue explicitly confirms that medieval authors establish distinctions between types of writing, and that the criterion of truth is at the heart of their preoccupations. History is for them, par excellence, the discourse of truth. But what they understand by history and truth is quite different from our own conceptions: the epic belongs to history and the "historical" Charlemagne is none other than the emperor of the *Chanson de Roland*.

Let us consider a last "literary" example where history and fiction subtly intermingle. Works as diverse as *L'Escoufle* (1200–1202), dedicated to Count Baldwin VI of Hainault, the *Roman de la Rose ou de Guillaume de Dole* (between 1200 and 1228), dedicated to Milon of Nanteuil, the elected bishop of Beauvais (finally consecrated in 1222), and the *Lai de l'Ombre*, written for the same person, unless it was intended for another elected bishop, Hugues de Pierpont, bishop of Liège are all attributed to a single author from the beginning of the thirteenth century, Jean Renart. As early as 1884, Léon Gautier noticed that the romances of Jean Renart, *L'Escoufle* and *Guillaume de Dole*, were teeming with references to contemporary chivalric life and thus supplied the historian with a reliable and immediate "source." Anxious to better acknowledge the specificity of the literary genre, Rita Lejeune (1935) and Anthème Fourrier (1960) prefer to speak of "realistic romances." The literary criticism of Michel Zink and Roger Dragonetti has since brought out in relief the extreme subtlety of the writings of Jean Renart, who plays with language and coyly masks his identity beneath enigmatic and convoluted anagrams. Dragonetti has even defended the strict "auto-referentiality" of Jean Renart's "fictional" writing.[46] But John W. Baldwin, a specialist in the social and intellectual history of the late twelfth and early thirteenth centuries and of the reign of Philip II Augustus, has recently proposed a reading which, while maintaining distance from historicist interpretations of the past, brings to the fore the veiled references that Renart makes to the society and politics of his own time. The idea Baldwin puts forth breaks with earlier antagonistic readings. He discerns in Jean Renart an essential "tension" between romance and history, between fiction and truth. This is evident in the long descriptions of tournaments present in *Guillaume de Dole*, where the hero wins his fame.[47] These passages succeed in reconciling both the characteristic features of tournaments in works of "pure" fiction, like Chrétien de Troyes's *Cligès* or *Érec et Énide* (the hero's combat, the quest for glory, the role of women), and those in texts deemed more "historical," such as the *History of William Marshall* where, by contrast, the battle is led by a squad of closely ordered men and the quest for ransoms and material gain counts at least as much as that of fame, and women are almost completely absent. As if reading a "roman à clef," Baldwin proceeds to decipher all the contemporary references hidden under the names, persons, places, and situations of the two romances.[48] In these works, where all the plots unfold on the Lotharingian marches of the kingdom of France and the empire, Baldwin sees a barely concealed evocation of the great political affair of the time: the crisis that opened up in the empire following the death of Henry VI in 1197, the ensuing struggle for the imperial crown between the claimants of the Staufen party, Philip of Swabia and then Frederick II, each supported by the French king Philip II Augustus, and the Guelf pretender Otto IV of Brunswick, backed by his uncles, and kings of England, Richard the Lionhearted and John Lackland (until his defeat at Bouvines in 1214). Thus all signs point to Jean Renart belonging to the Guelf party: the towns (Liège, Cologne, Mainz) and regions (Flanders and Hainault) that are at the heart of the plot in these romances are also bastions of Otto's coalition. The emperor Conrad in *L'Escoufle* is none other than Otto IV himself, while the "count of Montivilliers, count of Normandy" is by all evidence Richard, the Duke of Normandy and King of England. The same "keys" and games of concealment are manifold in *Guillaume de Dole*. Just as the "chronicles" and "histories," as we have seen, happily include the most marvelous fictions all the while professing their claim to truth, so the romances of Jean Renart and others like him excel in weaving together the thread of their plots with the weft of recent history (Gerbert of Montreuil's *Le Roman de la Violette* supplies another example). And if Jean Renart is interested in giving new proofs of his ability to toy with writing (does his name not evoke the fox?), he is also interested in simultaneously playing with fiction and history, in taking sides or, as we might say, "engaging himself." His romances will offer to this specific audience, and to the larger ministerial public of the empire, a veritable political program designed to find a solution to the endemic evil afflicting the empire: the absence of dynastic succession. The Salians and the Staufen have tried, but in vain. The Guelfs have no solution to offer either. Jean Renart has every reason to deplore this absence, especially when, as an observer from either Hainault or Liège, both francophone territories belonging to the empire, he looked to the success of the Capetian dynasty with envy.

Whether one turns to hagiography, history, or literature, the conclusion, then, is the same with varying degrees: there is never any whole truth or fiction, and an alternative as radical as the one proposed by Avram Saltman for the *Opusculum* is highly unlikely for the literate culture of the twelfth and thirteenth centuries. To be sure, what historians call the Middle Ages extends over a long period, and concepts as well as the practices of truth-telling have evolved over the course of time. This is readily apparent in the domain of rendering justice. There is a striking contrast between the trials by ordeal, which lend themselves to a "truth" both unstable and vulnerable to pressures of all sorts, and the inquisitorial procedures that took shape in the thirteenth century. The establishment of inquisitorial procedures was in fact due to the renewal of Roman law and the consolidation of monarchical powers. Such evolutions affect even the meaning of words, as Richard F. Green has shown with the Middle English word *trowth*. In the rendering of justice, in many ways so modern, that which one is tempted to call fiction—although prudence prevents—still belatedly plays a role. In an elegant book justly entitled *Fiction in the Archives* (1987), Natalie Zemon Davis[49] shows how the formulation of a letter of remission imploring royal grace presupposed the very elaborate construction of a "fictional account" which set forth the extenuating circumstances and sometimes grew until becoming a veritable "life history." She thus correctly places emphasis on the positive and creative character of fiction: "I want to let the 'fictional' aspects of these documents be at the center of analysis. By 'fictional' I do not mean their feigned elements, but rather, using the other broader sense of the root *fingere*, their forming, shaping, and molding elements: the crafting of the narrative."[50]

"To feign," therefore, means to "to create" as much as it does to conceal or to falsify. It is to create for precise ends, for example to save one's life. It is to create not in a vacuum and for the sole pleasure of creating, but in the context of a given social relation, following what Natalie Zemon Davis calls a "transaction narrative": that is, it puts in relation with one another the suppliant, the solicitor who advises him, the notary who copies his petition, the king for whom the petition is intended, and the dignitaries of justice who help the king or substitute for him in the sovereign exercise of grace. Finally, let us remember that outside of justice *stricto sensu*, what Roman law calls a "legal fiction"[51] is likewise a creation, one that shares similarities with the different genres of rhetorical fiction mentioned above.

Fiction and Truth

"*Fiction* or *Truth*?" Better to say: "*Fiction* and *Truth*." In the Middle Ages fiction and truth are always, in some manner, partners. Just as "historical truth" slips into the fiction of a romance, so too does fiction give vigor, flavor, and a profound meaning to hagiography, to the *exempla* of preachers, and even to the accounts of historians who more than any others proclaim to be always telling the truth.

To admit to this ambivalence of "reality" is to also provide today's historians with a manner of reflecting on our own practices: let us beware of seeing history in black and white, and beware of its claims to giving a univocal truth, *the* truth. If Gerlinde Niemeyer's "positivist" reconstruction of the life of the former Jew Herman of Scheda is unconvincing despite its erudition, then Avrom Saltman's idea that the *Opusculum* attributed to Herman could only be a fiction forged by others, while the presumed "author" could never have existed, also falters on the same reasoning. If the "truth" is between the two, or both, it is important to think of it in terms of dynamic relations and tension, and not as an immutable given.

It is remarkable that the *Opusculum* itself invites us to choose this nuanced line of reasoning. In chapter 16, Judas, who can no longer hide his sympathies for Christianity, publicly demonstrates to his coreligionists in the synagogue of Worms that Jewish exegesis of Scripture is erroneous. He openly takes on "Gamaliel," the legendary and polemical personification of the Mishna, and his "stupid old wives' tales" (*stultus et aniles fabulas*).[52] Here the opposition between the "true" exegesis of Christians and the "error" of Jews is clear-cut. Throughout Christian tradition the word "tale" is extremely negative; it has successively meant pagan myths, the accounts of ancient Gods, and the "superstitious" accounts of country folklore. Judas's declarations stir up the feelings of the Jews, who ask of their provocateur if he really believes what he says. To cover his misstep, Judas gives an ambiguous response: he presents himself as a "real false" Jew. It was in order to teach Jews how to respond to their adversaries, whose arguments he still remembers, that he wished to play the role of Christian apologist: "*idcirco eorum in me volui transfigurare personam,*"[53] "I transformed myself into their personage," or even: "I wished to take the guise [*personam*]" of a Christian.

Could not the entire *Opusculum* be a game of masks? But whose face is it that hides beneath the mask? The visible face of the mask is that of "Herman," the converted and baptized Jew who became a canon and priest of Cappenberg. On the other hand, the face beneath the mask—that of "Judas"—remains hidden and enigmatic: is it that of the real Jew spoken of by Gerlinde Niemeyer and other historians after her? Or is it rather, as Avrom Saltman claimed, an edifying scenario made up by a canon of Cappenberg? Or is it still, as I am led to believe, all of this at once? For there is no reason to doubt the existence of one or even several converts at Cappenberg, or even to put in doubt the composition of the *Opusculum* in an autobiographical form by one or more canons, among them perhaps one convert or more. Other works of medieval literature make similar use of an abundance of very plausible details and an autobiographical form, without it being possible to penetrate entirely the identity of the author, even when it is not in question. This is the case, for example, even in the fifteenth century, of Johannes von Templ's *Laborer from Bohemia* (*Ackermann aus Böhmen*). Despite the difference of context, date, and language (the work was written in German), the enigma of this work reminds us of the *Opusculum*: we have archival documents about the author that the work appears to corroborate, as for example concerning the death of his wife during labor. His identity, however, cannot be grasped with certainty.[54]

For Judas/Herman our only certainties are these: the text is of the twelfth century; two manuscripts have been preserved dating indisputably to the end of the century or the beginning of the next; it is a work of Latin Christianity cloaked in the form of an autobiography. That is where one must begin: why this form, why this period, and for what purpose?

Chapter 2

Medieval Autobiography

The *Opusculum de conversione sua* presents itself as an autobiography, and more precisely an autobiography about conversion. It is its form that should concern us, independent of the questions that have already been raised regarding the "authenticity" of the testimony and the Jewish identity of the supposed "author." I insist all the more on this point since the scholarship of the past fifteen years that has been devoted to this text, most of which concerns whether Judas/Herman existed or not and whether he indeed wrote the text, has for the most part neglected the question of its autobiographical form, thus abandoning the path once opened by Georg Misch. The separate but related questions of "autobiography" and "author" cannot be understood in a vacuum, but only in the relevant context of the period. During the Middle Ages "authors" tended to express themselves by hiding behind "authorities," that is, models, arguments, and quotes by which they were "authorized" to write. It is their arrangement in their own texts that often constitutes the main strategy of their writings. On the other hand, this did not prevent an often abundant use of the first person and even the desire on the part of certain "authors" to present themselves to their readers, to tell their life stories, and even to reveal their feelings. It is somewhat paradoxical, then, that the literary culture of the Middle Ages made a place for autobiographical forms of writing.

By all available evidence, the *Opusculum* is a remarkable example of such an autobiography. It has an author who gives his name, explains to a certain "Henry" the reasoning behind his work, and relates the peripities of his conversion from Judaism to Christianity. So far, all seems simple and clear. In fact, however, all these categories as we understand them today—of "author" or "autobiography," no less than the notion of "fiction," of which we have already spoken—must be subjected to a historical critique. These terms must be applied with caution to the realities of the Middle Ages.

An "Author"?

It is for the sake of convenience that we speak of the "author." But even in our day this notion poses many problems for the philosophers, sociologists, and psychologists who study the issue of literary creation.[1] The same is true, perhaps more so, when we turn to the multiple genres of medieval Latin or of vernacular literature. The notion of "author" is not fixed in the vocabulary of the Middle Ages but derives from two distinct ideas, that of *actor*, which denotes the one who conceives of a book, and that of *auctor*, which refers to the authenticity guaranteed by an authority (*auctoritas*).[2] The medieval author, who strictly speaking is the one who "augments" the subject of written knowledge, does not necessarily lay claim to originality as would a modern author. Often enough, his talent consists in a compilation (a term by no means pejorative at this time), that is, in the skillful arrangement of earlier sources and writings, of quotations from the Bible, Church Fathers, and other "authorities" both ancient and recent. Inasmuch as the notions of "signature" and "intellectual property" are unknown during this period,[3] those who write are not interested in asserting their identity. By hiding behind an illustrious name, such as St. Augustine, for example, they guarantee a reputation for their work that it would not otherwise be able to enjoy.[4] As Roger Dragonetti has remarked, the Middle Ages are a time of "pseudonymous writings." With regard to vernacular literature, the concealment of the "author's" name, or the occasional word games based on his name, such as endlessly misleading anagrams, are not necessarily marks of humility (of the sort that can account for the anonymity of monk writers). Rather, such concealment relates to the medieval conception of writing and knowledge, so much so that writers knew how to draw "effects of meaning" from these word games, inversions, pseudonyms, and double meanings. Even such names as "Chrétien de Troyes," the Christian from Troyes, "Jean Renart," John the Fox, or "François Villon" might be symbolic constructions as much as "real" names . . .[5]

But none of this seems to be relevant to the *Opusculum* of Herman the Jew. If the *Life of Godfried of Cappenberg* is indeed anonymous, the *Opuscu-*

lum, on the other hand, is attributed to a named author, Herman, who speaks in the text in the first person. But what has been said above regarding fiction should be enough to give us pause. The idea that a canon named Herman was able to sit down at his desk, alone, in order to write his memoirs, is totally anachronistic. Such an idea ignores an essential dimension of medieval literature to which many recent works, such as those by Paul Zumthor and Michael Clanchy, have called attention: its dimension of orality. For it is this dimension which is put forward in the very first lines of the *Opusculum*, in Herman's letter to his "son Henry": giving in to the repeated demands of the brothers and sisters of Cappenberg who often heard him *tell* his story, Herman finally resolves to put it in writing. Nothing therefore prevents us from imagining an oral circulation in the first instance of such an account by one of the "many Jewish converts" which Cappenberg gloried in welcoming. This could then have been followed by a redaction by an *actor/auctor*, perhaps this still surviving convert, or perhaps, as Avrom Saltman has convincingly suggested, by another Cappenberg canon (or even several), writing after the death of their "Hebrew brother" and sprinkling his story with quotations from the Vulgate which can equally serve as "authorities," even going so far as to give this brother a name, Herman, while leaving us to try and discover its significance.

It thus serves no purpose to try to over-individualize and over-personalize this piece of writing. One has first to consider this text, like many medieval works, in its tension between orality and writing, and consider it more for its *form* (whoever was responsible for it) and less from the point of view of its "author," a notion easily tainted with anachronism. Today we call this form "autobiography," and the real matter before us is to understand of what this form consists and why this form was chosen.

Monodic Writing

One of the first scholars to turn to the *Opusculum*, we have already noted, was the distinguished historian of autobiography Georg Misch.[6] His ambitious enterprise was brought to completion in exile and published immediately following the Second World War. For its magnitude, erudition, and the finesse of his analyses of innumerable texts, one can classify Misch's work as one of the great historiographical landmarks of the twentieth century. It belongs to a long tradition of German philosophy that goes back to Goethe and Herder, passing through to Jakob Burckhardt and Wilhelm Dilthey (d. 1911), Misch's direct master and father-in-law.[7] This tradition puts emphasis on the "development" in the history of the West of what the author calls "sense of identity" (*die Entwicklung des Persönlichkeitsbewusstseins*). To Misch it seemed more important to defend a progressive representation of European history seen from the angle of a history of consciousness—a representation not so different from Norbert Elias's notion of the "progress of civilization" proposed during those same years—when "its loss seemed sealed" by the anti-humanist totalitarianism which was rife in Germany and in Europe at the time Misch conceived of, and carried out, his work.[8] He wrote his work like a great chronological fresco: from pagan antiquity through Judaism (including the prophet Jeremiah in the seventh century B.C.) and Christianity (starting with Saint Paul and then Gregory of Nazianzus and especially Saint Augustine) he aimed to compile a register of all "autobiographical" works produced in the West. As has often been noted, the early Middle Ages shows itself to be rather lacking in works of this genre (with the notable exceptions of Gregory of Tours[9] and Gregory the Great at the end of the sixth century, Valerius in the seventh, Audradus Modicus in the ninth, and Ratherius of Verona in the tenth). The rebirth of the genre comes in the eleventh century with Peter Damian and Otloh of Saint-Emmeran and especially in the twelfth century, with writers from Guibert of Nogent and Bernard of Clairvaux to Peter Abelard, among many others. The flowering of various forms of autobiographical writings is only confirmed by Dante and Petrarch and the Renaissance that followed.[10] Misch's criterion for cataloguing these works and their authors is the personal expression of one's self-consciousness. This expression takes many different forms, and it is far from always having to do with an "autobiography" in the sense of a text written entirely for that purpose and relating to a specific literary genre. The texts that are included are of a most varied kind: letters, visionary accounts, pedagogical dialogues, theoretical treatises, polemical works or works in the form of a "confession," etc. Thus one could reproach Misch for having occasionally cast his net too widely, while in other respects his list presents some lacunae that are difficult to account for.[11] But isn't the question precisely to know how it is possible to speak of an autobiographical "genre," or, more precisely, of autobiographical "forms" as early as the Middle Ages?

Although a specialist on autobiography as eminent as Philippe Lejeune willingly recognizes the existence of a "personal literature" before 1770, as well as outside of Europe, he nevertheless attaches the birth of the autobiographical genre to Western modernity and, more especially, to the *Confessions* of Jean-Jacques Rousseau. Indeed, nothing is more alien to the Middle Ages than Rousseau's egotistical claim about the absolute singularity of his personality and his simultaneous claim about the unique character of his literary project, which is according to him without precedence and without posterity: "I am commencing an undertaking, hitherto without precedent, and which will never find an imitator. I desire to set before my fellows the likeness of a man in all the truth of nature, and that man is myself."[12] Rousseau forgets that the very title of his work is an explicit reference to Saint Augustine and the entire Christian tradition!

Having circumscribed chronologically the object of his study, Philippe Lejeune offers a precise definition for the genre: autobiography is "a retrospective account in prose that an actual person gives of his or her own existence, with the emphasis placed on the individual life, and in particular the development of the personality." He adds that in order to speak of autobiography, "it is necessary that the author, the narrator, and the protagonist be one." For Lejeune this forms the foundation on which the essential matter rests: what he calls the "reader's contract" or the "autobiographical pact" between narrator and reader.[13] One has to begin not so much from the work, he explains, but from the exterior point of view of its reception: "Thus if autobiography is defined by something exterior to the text, it is not because it falls short of an unverifiable resemblance to a real person, but because it is more than the type of reading it gives rise to, the belief it creates, and the belief which can be found in the text itself."[14]

These strong remarks pose a number of problems for medievalists wishing to speak of autobiography in their period. The fact that medieval Latin and vernacular literature makes an abundant use of the grammatical "I" in letters or monastic treaties in order to express the great themes of spiritual friendship, as with Ailred of Rievaulx, or in order to have the listeners of an epic song bear witness to the veracity of the account, does not constitute a sufficient criterion, for it seems often enough that no personality, no "author," stands behind the text. In an article entitled "Autobiography in the Middle Ages?" Paul Zumthor concludes that such a genre does not exist for this period, adding, "there are very few medieval literary texts where one encounters some *I*, the subject of 'direct discourse,' that is to say words for which the referent of this *I* is the enunciator."[15] As the critic par excellence of the resolutely "autoreferential" character of medieval literature, did Paul Zumthor, like Roger Dragonetti, succumb too much to the pervading structuralism of the 1970s and underestimate the subjective value of the "poet's *I*"?[16]

Since then scholars of medieval literature have tried to rehabilitate both the subject and the author. For Michel Zink it is "subjectivity" that signals the birth of "literature" in the thirteenth century. But one has to guard against any anachronism: "literary subjectivity" in the Middle Ages is not "spontaneous display or real expression in a text of an author's personality, opinions, or feelings, but rather what marks the text as the point of view of a consciousness." The text "designates itself as the product of a particular consciousness"[17] and it is in this that subjectivity and literature are inextricably linked. For as Michel Zink rightly notes: all is not new in this double appearance, for "the Middle Ages were a time of subjectivity."[18] The entire ideology of this period, an ideology intimately linked to Christianity, presupposes a personal connection between believer and God. It is thus no accident that the long tradition of *confessio* runs through the majority of the texts that Misch, in his history of autobiography, uses as markers for the medieval period. This concept of *confessio* needs to be understood first in the Augustinian sense of confession of one's faith to God and then in the penitential sense of confession of sins.

It is nevertheless clear that there do not exist for the Middle Ages any autobiographies in the modern sense of the term. But there does exist a "monodic narration" which, under the notion of *confessio*, is devoted to the alliance between Christian subject and God. This consists of "singing oneself alone" (*chanter soi seul*) without distinguishing the subject "self" that addresses its prayer to God and the object "self," which is placed under the watch of one's consciousness and the consciousness of God. In the thirteenth century still, one has to look for "monodic narration . . . within the memoir range of confession. The thirteenth century was the age of memoirs."[19]

While studying the "verse autobiographies" of the two Latin poets of the eleventh and twelfth centuries, Hildebert of Lavardin and Hugh Primat of Oréans, Jean-Yves Tilliette also concluded that it is necessary to handle the word "autobiography" with caution for this period. He first gives the impression of siding entirely with Paul Zumthor regarding the impossibility of knowing anything about the authors behind their texts: in the first case "the poem tells us nothing of the psychological personality of its author," the scenes evoked are only types and "Hildebert's 'I' comes to be identified with *homo*, the human being"; if in the second case Hugh gives his proper name, *Primas*, this move inspires Tilliette to offer the following commentary:

This oblique manner of signing denotes on one hand the assumption of an identity—rather egotistical given the pseudonym—and on the other hand the distancing by the writer (who never signs *Hugo*) from the literary personage whom he stages in the first person, for it is indeed a staging. All Hugh Primat's autobiographical poems, or the ones alleged to be such, converge towards the construction of a *persona* in the sense that psychologists, following Cicero and Horace, use the term, that is the way we choose to appear to others, like a theatrical mask.[20]

One cannot help but think back to chapter 16 of the *Opusculum*. Here, once again, the "author" conceals himself from his readers.

Hildebert and Guibert of Nogent, whom we shall discuss later on, remain in the tradition of *Confessions*, but Hugh *Primas* exceeds them both in introducing for the first time "something new." If I push Tilliette's suggestion, this something might already align itself to what Lejeune has called for the modern period an "autobiographical pact": "The birth of personal expression is marked as much by the appearance of an 'I' as by the acknowledgement that this person exists only in the eyes of the 'other.' The monodic writings settled for appealing to divine judgment. The perspective of others is henceforth part and parcel of autobiographical initiative."[21]

One is clearly not yet dealing with autobiography in the style of Jean-Jacques Rousseau, but perhaps one can witness the first sketch of a "reading contract" (or hearing contract). In any case, the sort of analysis that is proposed here, with its painstaking attention to the specificity of each historical moment and each mode of writing, shows how risky it can be to want to propose a history of "literary subjectivity," let alone autobiography or even the "birth of the individual," conceived of as a linear, regular, quasi necessary "progress" that the historian can enclose in a strict chronology.[22]

The Augustinian Model

Many different approaches confirm the important place Saint Augustine's *Confessions* occupy in a history of autobiography "before autobiography." Thus it is appropriate to ask whether this work may have constituted a sort of underlying pretext for the *Opusculum* attributed to Herman the Jew.

The question is all the more legitimate since the *Confessions* enjoyed an unprecedented position of favor among the literati of the twelfth century.

This is attested to by the growth in the numbers of manuscripts of this work and the increased borrowings and quotations from the text, particularly among Cistercians such as Bernard of Clairvaux and Ailred of Rievaulx. Indeed Saint Augustine is affforded further honor by a good number of newly created orders of canons regular—from Premonstratensians in the beginning of the twelfth century to Preachers and Augustinians at the beginning of the thirteenth century—who place themselves under the much-appreciated flexibility of Saint Augustine's Rule. In addition, no less than three twelfth-century Lives of Saint Augustine come to replace the old Life written by Possidius: the first of these is written by Yves of Chartres (1040–1116) when he is still a canon regular; the second is composed by the Benedictine, Rupert of Deutz (d. 1129) who popularizes a famous dream by Augustine's mother Monica (we meet Rupert in the *Opusculum* in the role of interlocutor with the young Jew Judas); finally, the third is the work of the Prémontré Philip of Harvengt (1100–1182), the declared adversary of Rupert who completes the Life of Possidius with information taken from the *Confessions* and delicately changes it on several important points; for example, he places in direct speech the words of the young man who appears to Monica in the "dream of the rule," words that are so important for Augustine's conversion.[23]

Let us recall that Augustine completed his *Confessions* in 398 at the age of forty-three or forty-four. The work comprises thirteen books, the first nine of which display an autobiographical character that has long been employed: it has been called the "first Christian autobiography" and also an "autobiographical masterpiece."[24] The category of "autobiography" is as problematic when applied to the *Confessions* as when used for medieval works. Peter Brown, whose fascinating biography of Saint Augustine is the authority in the vast field of Augustinian studies, offers the following nuanced view: "It is often said the *Confessions* is not an 'autobiography' in the modern sense. That is true, but not particularly helpful. Because, for a Late Roman man, it is precisely this intense, autobiographical vein in the *Confessions* that sets it apart from the intellectual tradition to which Augustine belonged."[25] Our problem, perhaps, is to determine the nature of the "autobiographical vein" of the *Opusculum*, one that is assuredly different from that of the *Confessions* and one we can only fully grasp by comparing it to all the other "veins" which fed into the rich body of medieval autobiographical writings between the fifth and twelfth centuries.

The first nine books of the *Confessions* make up a retrospective account: Augustine writes from memory twelve years after his baptism and the death

of his mother Monica, this latter event marking, in 387, the end of the autobiographical part of his work. The last four books are composed of philosophical reflections on memory and time and a commentary on the first
verses of Genesis.[26] In the intervening years Augustine has become a priest
(in 391) and then Bishop of Hippo (between 395 and 396), but he does not
speak of these episodes in his life. It is in the light of his present experience
as Bishop, *a posteriori*, that he reinterprets his past, his youth, his attachment
to Neo-Platonist philosophy, and his nine-year-long seduction by the Manic-
haean heresy over the orthodox Christianity his mother preferred. Time in-
terposes between that "then" and this "now."[27] Death and mourning also
slip in: Augustine puts an end to his autobiography when Monica dies.

In the meantime, the flow of external events that punctuate his path
toward baptism constitutes only the surface of an interior drama described
by the *Confessions*, and from which the book draws its remarkable tension. It
is this drama, with its hesitations, temptations, and relapses that Augustine
"confesses" to God—by this title the work is a sort of dialogue with God, a
form of prayer—even if at the same time Augustine speaks to his own conscience in a painful interior monologue. The verb *confiteri* indeed has these
two meanings, whose subtle variations Augustine explores: to confess one's
faith in God while at the same time discovering the Wisdom that allows one
to better "know thyself." And because this inner struggle is full of pitfalls
and remorse, *confiteri* thus also means to confess one's sins, both those of the
past that were inspired by worldly glory (*superbia*), carnal pleasures (*libido*),
and the intellectual pride of pagan philosophy (*curiositas*), as well as those
sins that continue to threaten the Christian's will, for baptism has not put an
end to temptations, especially sexual ones. The Bishop of Hippo is not a
"cured man" but a "convalescent."[28]

Augustine faces both God and his own conscience. He is, however, never
really alone. In Milan he is surrounded by friends who follow the Neo-
Platonist tradition of cenacles. They intensively share with him their inner
experiences. Later in Hippo it is for a similar group of *servi Dei* or *spiritales*
that he writes down his *Confessions*. Among those who have played a deter-
mining role in his conversion, his mother Monica and Saint Ambrose, Bishop
of Milan, must be mentioned above all. Others included his friends, such as
Alypius and Ponticianus. The influence of Ponticianus was critical: it was he
who, in a long account, convinced Augustine to turn away from marriage so
as to dedicate himself solely to God.[29] But at this moment Augustine again

fights a desperate battle, both against himself and against God, which raises him to the summit of spiritual writing:

> This was the story Ponticianus told. But while he was speaking, Lord you turned my attention back to myself. You took me up from behind my own back where I had placed myself because I did not wish to observe myself, and you set me before my face so that I should see how vile I was, how twisted and filthy, covered in sores and ulcers. And I looked and was appalled, but there was no way of escaping from myself. If I tried to avert my gaze from myself, his story continued relentlessly, and you once again placed me in front of myself; *you thrust me before my own eyes so that I should discover my iniquity and hate it*.[30] I had known it, but deceived myself, refused to admit it, and pushed it out of my mind.[31]

The *Confessions* had considerable influence. Yet it did not preclude alternative expressions of the "I" that, unlike Augustine's account, fail to unite life episodes with the hesitant quest of an inner life being divided against itself. It is this dichotomy that perhaps best characterizes the "autobiographies" of the early Middle Ages in contrast to the *Confessions*, and also to a certain array of texts that begin to appear by the end of the eleventh century. Under the influence of the frenzied monastic reform and the thirst for introspection that it kindled among certain clerics, these later texts rediscover the paths traced by Saint Augustine. In the meantime, the "veins" spoken of by Peter Brown have assumed different shapes. Among the more remarkable examples are the *quaerimoniae*, or "complaints," of the Asturian hermit Valerius (c. 630–695). These latter shape his account of forty years in the hermitic life, a work that describes his searching for greater solitude far from the crowds that are attracted to his saintly reputation, from the Cantabrian setting to San Pedro of Montes and the heights overlooking Astorga. A contemporary of two great saints of the Iberian Church—Bishop Isidore of Seville (d. 636) and the monk Fructuosus (d. 665)—Valerius explores a third path to saintliness, the one inaugurated in Egypt by the Desert Fathers. In solitude, which he shares with the few young men who joined him, he is accosted by the devil who symbolizes the perversions of the "world" and tries to block his path to conversion. "For the first time," Georg Misch writes, "the devil enters into the heart of an autobiography."[32] But, to be sure, it is a question here of a struggle against the devil, not of an interior struggle. It is onto the objective reality of the devil, exterior to himself, that Valerius projects the forces menacing him, the terrifying noises provoked by the devil in the night, the stench he exudes during the day, the sight of a monstrous giant that blocked his path one day but who was frightened off by the sign of the cross. Valerius even goes so far as to find the devil lurking in the features of a Moorish priest—an "Ethiopian"!—sent by his adversaries. Here it is no longer a question, as it was with Augustine, of probing the depths of a conscience divided against itself. Instead, as in a hagiographical "auto-legend" written in the first person,[33] Valerius sets out the accounts of miracles marking the intervention of the devil in his daily existence, but which only offer a "weak testimony concerning the consciousness which the narrator might have had of his own personality."[34]

Two centuries later the *Revelationes* of Audradus Modicus arise from a completely different intellectual context, one linked to mid-ninth-century Carolingian power. This is another form of "autobiography," fulfilling other functions. The presentation of the self is here intimately connected to a visionary experience placed in the service of the great political causes of the day. Both a monk and a priest at Saint-Martin of Tours, Audradus may have contributed to the creation of the great bible presented to the Emperor Charles the Bald in 845 by the count Vivien, lay abbot of the great monastery.[35] Shortly thereafter, Audradus was elected "Bishop of the choir" (a sort of aide to the bishop) by the provincial synod of Sens in 847/848. In 849 he went to Rome to present Pope Leo IV with the thirteen "books" of his complete work, of which the twelfth, the only one written in prose, has been partially preserved. This book is devoted to an account of his prophetic visions. But upon Audradus's return the synod of Paris of 849 announced his dismissal as one among the measures taken against the bishops of the choir. In 853 he is summoned to justify himself as a visionary in front of the Emperor Charles the Bald and succeeds in exonerating himself of all fraud. Audradus considers himself a sort of prophet, not in that he can predict the future, but in that he comments on the present as having fallen victim to all sorts of internal and external tensions. Confident of the authority granted to him by his celestial revelations, Audradus advises and even goes so far as to admonish the prince.[36] On the strength of the visions he had experienced during the Norman attacks on Paris in 845 and 851, he warns Charles the Bald against these divine punishments. In a vision that prefigures the last judgment, Audradus sees the saints who are assembled around Christ's majesty accuse the Carolingian kings of the Empire's ruin and the threats that weigh upon it: "*Culpa regum est*," "it is the kings' fault!" they cry out to the celestial sovereign. But it is no longer possible to return to the division of the Empire that, some eight years after the treaty of Verdun, Christ himself seems to accept. . . . In this same vision the heavenly king judges Lothar, brother of Charles the Bald and Louis the German, with severity: Christ has decided that Lothar be deposed because he dared to say "*ego sum*," "I am." One cannot find a better expression of the limits imposed on the expression of the self during the early Middle Ages.

Audradus's visions share the preoccupations of the ecclesiastical elites of the Empire: the Norman raids, the partitioning of the Empire, the danger to the independence of churches and monasteries presented by secular abbots such as Count Vivien who had become Audradus's main adversary and whose death during the campaign in Brittany constitutes yet another sign of divine justice. In another of his books, the *Fountain of Life*, Audradus introduces Hincmar, the archbishop of Reims, who confirms to him the reputation of his "dreams." It is indeed possible that Audradus dreamed a lot, but his visionary accounts are of a completely different genre than the dreamlike accounts of monks from the eleventh and twelfth centuries, of which we shall later speak. They seem rather to resemble those other grand visions that, during the Carolingian period, were a preferred mode for political language. Examples of these include the pronouncement of the monk Wetti of the monastery of Reichenau (d. 824) and the anonymous *Vision of the Poor Woman of Laon* (between 818 and 840).[37]

There are several analogies between the tribulations that drove the sixty-year-old Audradus, deprived of his Episcopal seat, to set down his revelations in writing and those tribulations that, a century later, inspired the very different "autobiographical" writings of Ratherius, the former bishop of Verona who was then approximately of the same age. Ratherius, already driven from Verona, abandoned all hope of asserting his rights to the episcopacy of Liège and had to satisfy himself with the administration of the small abbey of Aulne near Laubach. That is when he wrote his *Dialogus confessionalis* (954). The title simultaneously echoes the *Confessions* of Augustine and the *Dialogues* of Gregory the Great. It also bears witness to the richness of the Augustinian notion of *confessio*, signifying both praise of God and the confession of sins. Indeed this second aspect takes on a special meaning which the dialogue form inflects with a quasi sacramental force: Ratherius of Verona produces an interlocutor who is in fact his double, the result being that there is a constant intermingling of the "I" and the "thou." He recapitulates the misfortunes that have beset him since his childhood, wherever he has lived, "in

Provence, Italy, Germany, and France." He laments his two "divorces" from the churches of Verona and Liège, the first for judicial reasons and the second because of his own vanity. At the heart of his admissions of "perjury," "adultery," "debauchery," and "homicide"—for which, he explains, 265 years of penance should be inflicted upon him!—he feels the urgent necessity for *conversio*, something he understands now in the fully medieval sense. The issue is no longer, as it was in the first few centuries AD, one of a conversion from paganism to Christianity, nor is it question of a conversion from philosophy to Christian faith, as it was for Augustine. Here the issue is a *conversio de malo ad bonum*, the ethical and interior conversion that haunts Christians who, like him, are moved by the ideal of church reform and the anxiety over personal salvation. For Ratherius this demand is countered by the conflicting feeling of his own *inconvertibilitas* to the monastic life, which he nevertheless esteems to be morally superior: because he has not renounced his secular ambitions, he still dreams of the Episcopal seat in Liège.[38]

In another work entitled *Qualitatis conjectura cuiusdam* ("The evaluation of a certain person," which can only be him) Ratherius, now seventy-six years old, tries to paint "the characteristic traits of his personality."[39] Again he speaks of his addressing someone else, here the Emperor Otto I, reminding the emperor of his promise to give him the seat of Verona against the claims of the infamous Count Milo who had expelled him. He tries to flatter the emperor by praising him as the "first great emperor in three hundred years."[40] To further ingratiate himself Ratherius has his enemies speak through the text, including the corrupt clergy. They accuse him of "always having his nose in a book" and of laying down in writing all the events that have happened, calling it by the Greek word *chronographia*, all the while claiming that "he barely knows Latin." Ratherius attributes to them this episode that was supposed to condemn him, but which he actually boasts about all while faking humility: "When someone wants to kiss his foot, he recoils and prevents it. If he could he would stay seated there all day browsing his books. He hates being surrounded by everyone, he likes solitude, does not partake in games of hoops or die, and does not bother with either dogs or hawking." . . . The paradox, or as he himself says very lucidly, the profound *ambiguitas*, is that he portrays himself with the moral traits of a perfect monk which, owing to his frustrated destiny as a bishop, he cannot bring himself to live by.

Rarely does an "autobiography" in the medieval period, or even in later periods, give the impression of being able to approach a real personality so closely. However, as Georg Misch notes, the self-satisfying "portrait" that Ratherius paints of himself does not escape the literary conventions of *psychomachy*, the struggle between vices (those of others) and virtues (principally his own, though he deplores that they are so misunderstood). Conscious of having mastery over all the resources of the Latin language in order to continue the great tradition of ancient satire, he builds a rhetorical smokescreen between himself and his readers that is difficult to penetrate—except perhaps to declare in favor of his detractors, for how can they not recognize the dream of an unquenched thirst for power that still drives the deposed prelate when, seemingly without reason, he goes to great expense to strengthen the small abbey in which he feels trapped? Ratherius reveals himself to us the most when he attempts to defend himself from accusations that he mistakenly believes to be unconvincing. Thus he seems to fall victim to the weaknesses of his own fictions . . .[41]

The Eleventh/Twelfth-Century Renewal

Following Georg Misch, it is at the turn of the eleventh to twelfth century that historians have fixed the moment when Christian writing renews an autobiographical form that had been left somewhat fallow since the time of Augustine.[42] The names and works are well known. Most often they came from black monks, such as Jean of Fécamp (d. 1078), author of a *Confessio theologica*, Otloh of Saint-Emmeran (d. 1070), or Guibert of Nogent (d. 1124). Some left the monastic life in order to assume high positions in the Church, for example Peter Damian (d. 1072), who became cardinal-bishop of Ostia, or Anselm of Bec (d. 1109), who was called to the archiepiscopal seat of Canterbury. Others such as Abbot Suger of Saint-Denis (d. 1151) could also be mentioned. All or most of them are distinguished theologians who belong to traditional currents of monastic theology or break from it in the name of reason: we know the price paid by Peter Abelard (d. 1142) from what he reveals in his *History of My Calamities* (*Historia calamitatum*).[43] Among this generation, mention must also be made of the Cistercians, including Bernard of Clairvaux (d. 1151) and his early English disciple, Ailred of Rievaulx (d. 1167).

The explosion of the *ordo monasticus*, the birth of new orders of monks and canons, their frequent rivalry on the alleged scale of perfection, and the concomitant intensification of the theological debate in the monastic (and later urban) schools encourage expression by individual personalities who are not averse to exposing to their readers or listeners the adversities they have had to confront and the secret anxieties that torment them. Epistolary exchanges and more or less fictive dialogue are privileged forms of expression which, though not excluding other types of autobiographical writing, belong to what father Chenu has described as "the awakening of the conscience" in medieval civilization during the course of this long twelfth century.

The case of Ailred of Rievaulx provided a perfect example for Georg Misch, who discussed him as a counterpoint to Herman the Jew.[44] For Misch these two cases share the common goal of presenting "a history of conversion": the first tells of the young Scottish noble who enters into the Cistercian abbey newly founded at Rievaulx, while the second tells of the newly baptized young Jew from Cologne who enters into the first German Prémontré abbey at Cappenberg. But Misch does not underestimate the difference in form and signification found in the expression of these two comparable experiences: in the manner in which the *Opusculum* describes "the conflict between knowledge and belief and the victory of the latter over the former," Misch sees "the symbol of a historical movement characteristic of this period, a movement which led from the turbulent spiritual expansion to the stability achieved in the Middle Ages."[45] For Ailred this experience is affirmed by spiritual friendship and permits the expression of personal growth, an echo of an even larger historical evolution. Raised at the court of the Scottish King David I, the twenty-five-year-old noble Ethelred converts to the Cistercian ideal, abandoning society for the strict asceticism at Rievaulx. Five years later, on the injunction of Bernard of Clairvaux, he writes his *Mirror of Love* (*Speculum caritatis*), a work devoted to his friendship for a lost brother. This theme is explicitly taken up and again amplified in a second work, *On Spiritual Friendship* (*De spirituali amicitia*), where he addresses God while conversing with several brothers from the monastery, his "boys" Ivo, Walter, etc. But Ailred speaks especially of himself. In a chapter entitled "Example of oneself and one's conversion" (*Exemplum de se ipso et sua conversione*), he explains that it is his reading of the *Confessions* that precipitated his conversion to the monastic life. He recalls the circumstances of his conversion but endeavors above all to expose the effects this had on his interior life. The exterior peripities of his conversion are known solely from his *Vita*, written by his companion Walter David.[46] Ailred addresses God in terms resembling those of Augustine, imploring him for help in abrogating himself from the temptations of classical culture and from Ciceronian rhetoric, from which he borrows the dialogue form. Ailred is especially close to his model when analyzing the depth of his bond uniting him and his friends, for this was the case with Augustine and Ponticianus, the love of God being reflected in the love of the other. As Ailred says, "What more must I say? Is not an important part of happiness to love and be loved? To help and be helped? To be familiar with fraternal love, and to raise oneself to the splendor of God's love? And then soon, on the scale of love, to hoist oneself up to Christ's embrace, to be immediately followed by a return to contrition and a love of others."

Meanwhile, the differences are no less important: if Augustine and Ailred expose the torments of their conversion, the former submits himself in order to arrive at God's only will while the latter, living in a church in the midst of reform, is additionally aware of submitting himself to the yoke of a monastic Rule. The harshness of the monastery's asceticism is for Ailred the condition for discovering the soul's peace. For Ailred as for Herman, autobiography in the twelfth century is thinkable only within the framework of the monastic institution and the community of brothers. It is in the stability of this sacred location that the hurting soul can at last find peace and happiness: *jocunditas, tranquillitas, securitas*—this is Ailred's vocabulary.

Of all the early twelfth-century authors who contributed to reviving the *Confessions*, the Benedictine Abbot Guibert of Nogent (c. 1055–1125) is one of the more remarkable. Guibert wrote several important works including, in around 1110, *De Incarnatione contra Judaeos*, which we shall have to discuss later. He is especially known for three works: his treaty on relics, *De pignoribus sanctorum*, where he questions the authenticity of the purported relic of a baby tooth of Christ, in which the monks of Saint-Médard of Soissons take pride; a history of the first crusade (*Gesta Dei per Francos*); and finally his "autobiography" written between 1114 and 1121, when he was approximately sixty years old. This last work comprises three *libelli*, only the first of which is devoted to the old abbot's retrospective account of his youth in a family of lords in the region of Oise. He recalls how his parents dedicated him to the Virgin and the Church upon his birth, which would otherwise have been fatal to both mother and child. He then describes the education he received from his mother, who was widowed eight months after his birth. Next he evokes his entrance into the monastery and the numerous temptations he encountered. He does not undergo a conversion experience comparable to the ones that led the young pagan philosopher Augustine and Herman the

Jew to baptism, nor even to that which led the young "worldly" Ailred to the doors of the monastery. Like Otloh of Saint-Emmeran, Guibert speaks of the "internal" conversion of one who has been baptized, offered (*oblatus*) into a monastery as a child, and who comes in the cloister to know the price of a fierce interior struggle against temptations, sin, and the Devil.[47]

The second *libellus* is rather different in character: Guibert retraces the history of the monastery of Nogent since its foundation, but he also speaks of himself. By evoking his memories of the monastery of Saint-Germer of Fly where he was once a monk, by recounting his installation as abbot of Nogent, and especially by describing the death of his mother for whom he had boundless affection.[48]

The third *libellus* appears even more distanced from an autobiographical account: Guibert makes himself the witness of the "commune" of Laon, describing with terror the insurrection of the city dwellers and the murder of their lord bishop in the cathedral. Yet he once again returns to himself as he completes his work by telling the story of the healing miracle performed on him as a child in a church dedicated to Saints Leger and Maclou where his mother had taken him.[49]

Modern editors of this apparently composite work have hesitated over what title to give it: *De vita sua* (but this is not Guibert's title), *Autobiographie* in modern French, or *Memoirs* in English?[50] If Guibert did not really give a title to his work, he does nevertheless refer to it using a term derived from the Greek, calling it his *libri monodiarum*, or "books" (in the plural), in which he "sings oneself alone." And as Michel Zink has noted, this "oneself" needs to be understood without making a distinction between subject and object.[51] If the project of a "monodic writing" occupies the first book especially, it is clear that Guibert gives unity to the ensemble of his work since he speaks of himself, his mother, and his relation to God up until the end of the third book. From beginning to end, Guibert, a former student of Anselm, is driven by the will to demonstrate "the need for man to know himself in order to measure the righteousness of his will and thus be able to exercise his freedom, which was nothing but to know God and obey him."[52]

The work is directly inspired by the *Confessions* of Saint Augustine. Guibert cites the *Confessions* six out of the eleven times he mentions a work by the Bishop of Hippo. It is thus no accident that Guibert chooses for the first word of the first book of his *monodiae* the verb *Confiteor* (to confess). One cannot help but observe an explicit allusion to his prestigious model. Starting with the second phrase, the same word returns and is endlessly reused as a motif. Guibert possesses the same semantic wealth as Saint August-ine, even if Guibert further insists on the penitential meaning of the admission of sins, something that is explained by the evolution of religious sensitivity and the sacramental practices of the twelfth century. For Guibert, this involves the need "to confess one's life in order to attain God through knowledge of oneself."[53]

In many respects Guibert's language also recalls the language of August-ine. In fact one is sometimes unsure to whom to attribute a phrase taken out of context: "It follows from this that I try to know you insofar as I know myself; and enjoying the knowledge of you does not mean that I lack self-knowledge. It is a good thing, then, and singularly beneficial for my soul, that confessions of this sort allow my persistent search for your light to dispel the darkness of my reason. With steady lighting my reason will no longer be in the dark about itself."[54] These are Guibert's words, but one can practically hear Augustine.

Guibert of Nogent borrows from Augustine not only his conception of the *confessio* and his monodic style of writing; he also goes so far as to imagine and reconstruct his life in imitation of the Augustinian model. We shall later see the place he, like Augustine, gives to dreams, and in particular the place he gives a long dream that his mother had of him and then recounted to him: indeed Guibert echoes the "dream of the rule" that Monica told her son. Guibert does not give us his mother's name, though he does name his father, Evrard, who is an orphan just like Augustine.[55] But by all evidence he sees in his mother a new "Saint Monica."

Guibert's love for his mother is equaled only by his admiration for her virtue and devotion. In the beginning of the first book he praises her beauty as the reflection of the excellence of her soul. Although no longer alive at the time of his writing, she continues to watch over him from paradise. Guibert owes everything to her: his status as a man of the Church, his education, and the example she has set for him of moral and religious perfection.[56] Further on, Guibert returns to his mother to recount her marital disappointments, her refusal to remarry once widowed, and the vow she takes to remain chaste, and to devote her life to God.[57] He returns to her once more when evoking the works he has undertaken to write. His mother worries that he is priding himself on his intellectual success, she who was the example of the greatest humility. That is where he recalls her long dream concerning him.[58] At the beginning of the second book Guibert again evokes the death of his mother, an occurrence he did not witness. But his former tutor tells him how she manifested her unshakeable faith in the Lord up until the very last moment.[59] The memory of his mother, which returns to him time and again as he writes his autobiography, constitutes the common theme in all three books, a thread of which he never lets go for very long. For Guibert as for Augustine, is not this most intimate writing—*monodiae*—a manner of accomplishing one's "bereavement work"?

The Chronicle of a Conversion?

Does the *Opusculum* attributed to Herman the Jew, roughly contemporaneous with Guibert of Nogent's work, also draw from Saint Augustine's *Confessions*?

The *Opusculum* is well aware of the Bishop of Hippo's reputation, going so far as to praise the excellence of the Augustinian Rule under which the brothers of Cappenberg live.[60] Like the *Confessions*, it is explicitly intended for a group of "friends of God," the brothers and sisters of Cappenberg to whom Herman addresses himself through his "son Henry": to borrow an expression from Brian Stock, it confirms the importance of "textual communities" in the collective thought, and in the debate about philosophical, religious, and devotional writings, in schools and monasteries as well as in the heretical circles of the same period.[61] The community of Cassiciacum, which served as a place of "retreat" for Augustine on the eve of his baptism,[62] may prefigure Cappenberg as another "paradisiac" venue—to use a term from the *Opusculum*—where Herman can come back and stay after his baptism.

In both autobiographies the departure on the path to conversion is found at the end of childhood: Augustine is a sixteen-year-old student in Carthage living a dissolute life when he is shaken by his mother Monica's retelling of the "dream of the rule" she has just recently had; but "almost nine years then followed during which I was in the deep mire and darkness of falsehood."[63] For Judas of Cologne it was in his thirteenth year that he dreamt of the emperor's banquet, which he would later understand announced his conversion; but, in the seven years following his dream, he continued to live with his Jewish family. The *Opusculum* in any case confirms the importance of the dream in autobiographical accounts of this period. We have already begun to see this with Guibert of Nogent, to whom we shall return. The most convincing parallel concerns marriage, which both Augustine and Herman represent as an absolute obstacle to perfect conversion.

Augustine's entourage pressures him to marry. Even his mother hopes that a Christian wife will know how to lead her son to baptism. A union is arranged, but it is only to be consummated two years later, for the anonymous maiden that has been chosen for him is still too young. Augustine is to separate himself from the concubine with whom he is living and with whom he had a child. But, unable to wait two years without satisfying his carnal desires, he takes another mistress.[64] Further on, when feeling ready to accept baptism, Augustine confesses that his only tie binding him to his previous life is "the woman."[65] Finally it is his friend Ponticianus who pushes him to admire the Christian Anchorite's renunciation of the flesh and convinces him to sever this last tie.[66]

In chapter 10 of the *Opusculum* the young Judas also gives in to the pressure of his family and accepts marriage to a Jewess. Like the woman promised to Augustine, she too remains anonymous. In Judas's case the marriage is consummated and Judas even delights in carnal pleasures. Then he recovers and from that moment on, as in the *Confessions*, no further mention is made of the woman. Can one speak of an implicit influence or just a coincidence favored by a common trope in Christian literature, that of the incompatibility of the search for God and the pleasures of the flesh? It seems more prudent not to pursue potential parallelisms since elsewhere the differences between Augustine's *Confessions* and Guibert of Nogent's *monodiae*, on the one hand, and Augustine's *Confessions* and Herman's *Opusculum*, on the other, are quite appreciable. The latter work hardly offers the "veins" of Augustinian autobiography: one finds neither the rhythm of the phrase, nor the vocabulary, nor even the anguished exploration of the unfathomable depths of the soul. Contrary to Guibert of Nogent, who cites the *Confessions* abundantly, the *Opusculum* gives the impression of honoring neither this work nor anything else of Augustine's corpus. The verb *confiteri* or the noun *confessio* are present only three times, and never with the meaning given by Augustine: twice the admission of an ordinary truth is simply rendered as such.[67] And if the third occurrence concerns a "confession of faith," it has nothing to do with the outpouring of the soul's motion toward God, but the recitation of the baptismal formula.[68]

To be sure, it is possible throughout the work to pick out the expressions that traditionally designate the sites of Christian interiority. Among them, the metaphor of the heart occupies a rather remarkable place: touched by the charity of the attendant Richmar, Judas preserves a "hard-heartedness" that nothing can "soften."[69] Indeed, an exterior and visible sign remains empty if it does not operate invisibly with the aid of grace "in the hearts of men."[70] Judas is strongly marked by his visit to the abbey of Cappenberg in the company of Bishop Eckbert. The piety of the brothers who "search for [God] with all their heart"[71] draws "the deepest sighs from his heart."[72] Elsewhere it is again a question of the base spirit that, through baptism, was expelled from "the house of my heart,"[73] and the priest who, at the altar, seems to consider carefully the precepts of the Gospel "as though chewing the cud in the mouth of the heart."[74] Just as frequent are the terms that, with the notable exception of *confessio*, refer to penitential vocabulary: the "contrition" manifested by tears,[75] and the grace of "repentance" promised to a softened heart,[76] all while the young Jew obstinately perseveres on the path of "concupiscence."[77] Finally, Christians have all the reasons to rejoice in the "penitence of a converted sinner."[78]

But these words are nothing more than the conventional strokes of the classical portrait of Christian "psychomachy": despite using the first person and dramatic effects of narration, this psychomachic account—a struggle between vice and virtue—does not echo the personal quest for interior truth found in Augustine's *Confessions* or Guibert of Nogent's "monodic writings." Chapter 11, where Judas breaks the ties of his short-lived Jewish marriage, is perhaps the liveliest example of the voice of a personal "spirituality." By means of rhetorical shifts that somewhat resemble the style of Augustine, Herman aptly describes the contradictions between flesh and spirit, between the past and the promise of salvation, which are tearing him apart. But even there, and this is revealing, the negative forces pulling him back are embodied in a figure exterior to himself, the Devil, and in order to remedy the situation Judas dreams only of appealing to the sign of the cross, which he uses like a talisman.

In his account Herman recounts the past peripities of his conversion and his advances toward baptism as they are thwarted by his relapses into "Jewish superstition." He does speak of his feelings, his temptations, his desires, but always with a sort of distance that prevents us from penetrating into the lived intimacy of subjectivity, into the depths of a tormented soul. Rather than a "singing oneself alone" under the double watch of God's conscience and his own, we encounter the chronicle of a conversion told in the first person. Why the first person?

One can imagine that the very nature of the *Opusculum* imposes this distancing of the subject of narration: Judas/Herman is not the former Neo-Platonic philosopher writing—according to the words of Peter Brown[79]—a "master-piece of strictly intellectual autobiography," nor is he the monk who speaks at the end of his life of the sins that have tormented him for so long. He is allegedly writing as a Christian, but about his Jewish past. For, in the thought of medieval clerics, Judaism is by nature the realm of exteriority (*foris*) that is opposed to the interiority (*intus*) proper to Christianity; Jews can only accede to the exterior, superficial, "carnal" meaning of things while Christians alone have the capacity to grasp the interior, profound, truthful, and "spiritual" meaning. This dichotomy structures the entire opposition between Jews and Christians: it underlies the interpretation of Scriptures which Jews cannot fully understand as well as the interpretation of dreams in which they can only find material and carnal symbolism. It also underlies the representation of the existence of individuals; Judas fits the role well when he is moved by the moral examples offered by Christians, when he waits for a "sign" to convince him of the truth of Christianity, when, in a word, he resides in a surface subjectivity. But he is unable to go further, unable to open his soul completely, and unable to have knowledge of the depths of consciousness reserved for Christian introspection.

Once baptized and a priest, should not Herman at least have revealed the urges that had unconsciously guided his soul when still a Jew, and should he not have had even more reason to reveal the inner workings of his new Christian conscience? One is entitled to ask this of a retrospective autobiography. Yet the opposite occurs. The final interpretation of the childhood dream falls considerably short of sounding the depths of the remarkable personality that should at last be opened up to us (as might be expected of a psychoanalyst's patient who finally comes to understand the relation between his/her dreams and the subconscious scares of early childhood conflict). Instead, this final interpretation erases all signs of individuality by reducing the dream to categories of clerical *interpretatio* and to routine formulations of sacramental and moral discourse.

Herman is not Augustine. Nevertheless, he does share with him (as indeed with many other ecclesiastical authors of the twelfth century) the purpose of recounting in the first person at least a part of his life, or, to put it otherwise, to write his "autobiography." The autobiographical form of his account is the most remarkable aspect of this work, whatever the circumstances of its redaction or the identity of its "author(s)" may have been. Had it been written in the third person, the account would have been only a chronicle or a lengthy *exemplum*: one can indeed encounter, in briefer forms, sketches of a comparable scenario. Here it is a *persona* (with all the ambiguities conveyed by that word) that is brought to the fore, opening (slightly) his heart to his listeners and readers, and engaging them directly. This form of writing produces a remarkably powerful effect of truth. Let us not doubt that this was the objective of the *Opusculum*, and let us also recognize that it achieved its goal.

All things considered, it is more important to inquire about the choice of the autobiographical form than to know *who* is really speaking. Is it a real and unique convert, a Judas/Herman of flesh and blood with his doubts, hopes, fear, and love of God? Or is it the "textual community" of Cappenberg that may remember the oral account of one of its past converted Jews, but who, above all, find in the autobiographical form that highlights the individual destiny of the protagonist the means to proclaim his unique example? The two hypotheses are not mutually exclusive since one or more Cappenberg converts may have contributed to the telling and writing down of such an account. Whoever he may be, Herman cannot be a single individual or "author" in the modern sense of these words, but perhaps a *persona*, a mask, a twofold appearance.

Chapter 3

The Dream and Its Interpretation

Setting the Dream

Herman's conversion account displays at least two exceptional formal characteristics. The first is its autobiographical form, of which we have just spoken. The second lies in the fact that the main part of the autobiography (chapters 2 through 20) is framed between the narration of a dream at the beginning (chapter 1) and its interpretation at the end (chapter 21). The manner in which the last chapter responds to, and illuminates, the first invites us to recognize in the *Opusculum*, if not a literary "fiction," at least the concern for elegant writing and a carefully thought-out plan. The fact that the dream occupies an important place in a medieval autobiography, especially in an autobiography about conversion, is not altogether surprising. As we shall see, this is in fact the rule and, given the number of texts in the category, we might even speak of "dream autobiographies." On the other hand, the *framing* of an entire conversion account within the diptych of a dream and its interpretation is, to my knowledge, unique.

This structure differs even from the well-known *Romance of the Rose*, at the beginning of which Guillaume de Lorris explains under what circumstances he fell asleep and had a long dream: "*Many men say that there is nothing in dreams but fables and lies, but one may have dreams which are not deceitful, whose import becomes quite clear afterward. . . . In the twentieth year of my life, at the time when Love exacts his tribute from young people, I lay down one night, as usual, and slept very soundly. During my sleep I saw a very beautiful and pleasing dream; but in this dream was nothing that did not happen almost as the dream told it.*"[1]

At the end of the romance the author (now Jean de Meun, who has taken over for Guillaume de Lorris) wakes up and plucks at last the rose he has desired: "*Before I stirred from that place where I should wish to remain forever, I plucked, with great delight, the flower from the leaves of the rosebush, and thus I have my red rose. Straightway it was day, and I awake.*"[2]

The difference with the *Opusculum* is twofold: throughout the romance the symbolic commentary merges with the narrative; moreover, the romance blurs the boundaries between that which is supposed to be the dream, and the waking state which the reader (or listener) believes to be reality, forgetting that he/she is a participant in the dream. The *Opusculum*, on the other hand, proceeds following a double and firm distinction: between the dream and the waking state and between the dream and its commentary. What is essential to recognize, however, is that in both cases (as well as in many other works in Latin or the vernacular) the dream occupies an important place. In the case of the romance it is that only from the dream can the poet draw his inspiration and his power to tell the truth (a dream is not necessarily a lie). Throughout the dream the poetic language rises to another order of reality different from the terrestrial and mortal world: the world of dreams from which he claims to speak is celestial and divine, full of singular true images in opposition to the deceptive images of the senses.[3]

The recourse to dreams is not limited to epic, lyric, and courtly works of the Middle Ages. One even finds it in another work concerning the debate between Jews and Christians,[4] for Peter Abelard uses a comparable process to the one found in the *Romance of the Rose* in order to stage his *Dialogue Between a Philosopher, a Jew, and a Christian* (1140): "I saw in the night a vision, and, behold, three men, each coming on a different path, stood before me. As one does in a vision, I asked them immediately what their religion was and why they had come to me."[5] Thus begins, in a direct style, the dialogue between the three characters. Finally, let us note that medieval Jewish literature did not ignore this mode of writing either. At the beginning of the twelfth century, one even finds a Jewish polemical work, Judah Halevi's *Kuzari*, which follows along the lines of Abelard's *Dialogue* and attaches to a dream a debate between a philosopher, a Christian, a Muslim, and a Jew.[6] In the thirteenth century, Jacob Halevy of Marvège (Marvejols) compiles an entire volume of *responsa* on the subject of ritual observances and claims that the revelation came to him in a dream.[7]

Jews and Christians accorded an equal importance to dreams, using them as a means of authenticating an intention or an account. The implicit or explicit appeal to divine revelation was intended to reinforce the strength of the argument. This is no reason to doubt the possibility that the "author" of the *Opusculum* or that of any other contemporary work really had dreams, but what needs to be borne in mind above all is the place symmetrically given to the dream at the beginning and the interpretation at the end. This process resembles the familiar literary conventions of the period, even if its originality is striking. For in contrast to the several literary, philosophical, or legal texts that were cited above (and to which could be added many more), the *Opusculum* does not claim to be only a dream account: indeed the dream is not the scene of the account, but rather its framework.

Do Jews and Christians Dream Differently?

A single dream, according to Herman, was the starting point of his conversion. Along with certain other identifying details about his identity (his name, his lineage, his town of origin), his age at the time is the only precise information he gives concerning the circumstances of this dream: "In my thirteenth year I had a dream." This is immediately followed by the account of the dream in which Herman describes first the visionary encounter with Emperor Henry, who showers the Jewish child with the spoils of a deceased lord, and then the banquet that takes place in the sovereign's palace. Upon waking, and with little confidence in his juvenile ability to understand the meaning of his dream on his own, Judah addresses his wise relative Isaac, but is not satisfied with the "carnal" explanations he is given.

Avrom Saltman claims to have found nothing specifically Jewish in this account. It is true that a dream of receiving one's weapons from the hands of the king or the emperor would better fit a young Christian noble: in Chrétien de Troyes this is the ambition of young Perceval who succeeds in having King Arthur give him the weapons of Knight Vermeil, who offended Perceval. Perceval kills the evil knight and recovers his weapons, which, as the valet Yonet teaches their names to Perceval, the poet lists: "Yonet laced up his mail leggings for him and strapped on the spurs over his rawhide buskins; then he put the hauberk on him—of which there was no finer—and placed the helmet, which fitted him perfectly, over the coif, and showed him how to gird on the sword so that it swung loosely. Then he placed the boy's foot in the stirrup and had him mount the knight's charger."[8]

But why would a Jewish child not also dream of carrying weapons and mounting a charger, of becoming a great lord's equal in close proximity to the emperor?[9] If one admits that one of the functions of a dream is to invent waking reality in a compensatory way, then one should not be so surprised that young Judas's dream evinces desires that seem so unrealistic, but which may express the frustrations related to his condition. Let us admit for a moment that Judas really did exist: constrained to dealing exclusively in the business of money like the rest of his family, could Judas not have dreamt of escaping this life by becoming a great lord, a lord who possessed a charger, the weapons and lands that are precisely prohibited to Jews? In his dream Judas would have unknowingly responded to the vicious reproach made against the Jews by the Abbot of Cluny Peter the Venerable in a letter addressed to King Louis VII of France in the run-up to the second crusade; namely, accusing them of not wanting to bear arms, cultivate lands, or make an honest living, but being interested only in "accumulating coins in their purses, gold or silver in their chests"; "in a word," writes Brigitte Bedos-Rezak, preventing Jews from "participating in the equation formulated by the Benedictines regarding martial responsibilities, land, and salvation."[10]

The dreaming child is now "in his thirteenth year." Arnaldo Momigliano has connected this to the rite of the bar mitzvah which, precisely at the age of thirteen, integrates young boys into the community of pious Jews.[11] Avrom Saltman contests this hypothesis for reason that the child was not yet thirteen, as is required by the ritual. In studying the "rites of childhood" in medieval Judaism, Ivan Marcus notes that bar mitzvahs are not attested to before the fourteenth century.[12] However one does find mention of them in the mid-thirteenth century by Rabbi Avigdor of Vienna, and at the end of the century in the Zohar.[13] But no source, it is true, places the bar mitzvah as early as the twelfth century. Nevertheless, for this period the approximate age of thirteen could well have been a decisive moment in the growth and aspirations of the young Jew. The explicit link established by the text between the "thirteenth year" and the dream which was to shine a light on the rest of his life should grab our attention just as much as the miracle accounts or *exempla* placing the conversion of young Jews (and Jewesses) at the beginning of this critical age we call adolescence—to give the word a psychological force it did not have in the Middle Ages.[14]

The emperor is the central figure of the dream. Did the Jewish child have the opportunity to see the emperor's retinue in Cologne, as is assumed by Gerlinde Niemeyer?[15] Such a memory on the part of Judas does not seem to me necessary given how important the figure of the emperor was to the

Rhineland Jews. Ever since Louis the Pious and the Ottonian emperors had protected Jews, but especially since 1096, when Henry IV had accorded them privileges at the time of the First Crusade, the Rhineland Jews had found in the emperor their principle source of protection.[16] Yet it is during the twelfth century that the notion of *Kammerknechtschaft* (court Jews) takes shape, and it would have a long future. It first appears in the privileges of Frederick Barbarossa, in 1157 (Worms) and 1182 (Regensburg), under the expression *ad cameram nostram attineant*, stating that the Jews "be attached to our treasury." A more explicit expression, *servi camerae nostrae*, "serfs/servants of our chamber/treasury," dates to the emperorship of Frederick II (1236). The situation is unambiguous: the emperor protects Jews so long as he can pressure them financially and at his will. This relationship gained widespread acceptance among medieval monarchies, as is reflected by the concept of "court Jews." In both France and England during this period one speaks of the "King's Jews."

It is a fact that although forced baptisms existed and Jews suffered repeated expulsions starting in the thirteenth century, never did a medieval ruler order a mass killing. The king protects Jews, not out of mercy, but out of interest. In the Bible (Esther 3:13) it is Haman, the evil minister of the Persian king Ahasueras, who nurtures the plot to exterminate the entire Hebrew people, women and children included, and for this he is beaten to death. The Christian kings and their clerical entourage, whatever their sentiments toward Jews may have been, were not ignorant of this story. Genocide does not date from the Middle Ages. It is our "modern" period that invented it, or at least put it into practice.[17]

All of this may have played a role in inspiring the positive figure of Emperor Henry in Herman's dream. But the contents of a dream cannot be reduced to the memories of the night before or to the influence of the dreamer's social environment. Imagination feeds imagination first and foremost. And biblical imagination, above all, strongly weighed on the actions, concepts, and dreams of medieval people, be they Christian or Jewish. Indeed, several biblical dreams concern the relations between the Hebrews and their ruler. In Genesis 37–40 it is thanks to his gift at interpreting dreams that Joseph, who is described as *somniator* (37, 19), or man of dreams, is freed from his prison after he correctly interprets the dreams of the Pharaoh's cupbearer and baker. This same gift of interpretation allows Joseph to win the favor of the Pharaoh himself, for Joseph alone is capable of explaining the premonitory sense of the Pharaoh's dream of seven thin cows devouring seven fat cows and of seven scorched ears of grain that kill the seven healthy ears of grain. This all led to Joseph becoming the Pharaoh's prime minister.

As Arnaldo Momigliano has already noted, Herman is also presented as a "new Mordecai": in Book 6 of Esther (where dreams are not at issue), Mordecai saves the life of Ahasueras, who is married to the Jewess Esther, by informing him of the conspiracy plotted against him by his minister Haman. In return for this deed, Mordecai is paraded around town on the king's horse, while Haman is hanged at the gallows that had been prepared for Mordecai. To further thank Mordecai, the king bestows upon him all of Haman's goods as well as his title of vizir. Mordecai's success in saving his people from extermination is commemorated by Jews each year during the carnival-like festival of Purim.

The biblical model of the Hebrew man who, against all expectations, becomes the principal servant of the king has a long afterlife in the thought and history of the Jewish people, fraught between the search for a privileged, though submissive, status and an escape in eschatology. Nothing indicates that the biblical accounts of Joseph and Mordecai could have influenced Herman's autobiography. They are not even mentioned once. And yet, by its narrative structure, Herman's dream offers some analogies to them: an unexpected reversal of situation permits the hero in each of the cases to benefit from the grace and favor of a pagan (Pharaoh, Ahasueras) or Christian (Emperor Henry V) ruler.

Among the emperor's gifts, a white horse figures prominently. This detail of young Judas's dream was considered by Amos Funkenstein, contra Avrom Saltman, as proof that the *Opusculum* was indeed written by a converted Jew, for the Talmud specifies that a dream of a white horse is a good omen, while a dream of a galloping red horse is an ominous sign.[18] The *Sefer Hassidim* recalls this lesson: "A good Jew is saddened by having dreamt that he mounted a musky horse but finds himself next to an impure animal. His friend explains to him that he will die because of it, but in buying the dream it is the friend who dies shortly thereafter."[19] Jewish tradition thus insists on this image of the white horse. But is it specifically Jewish? The traditions of oneiromancy are quite old, and the detail is common to Jewish, Arab, and Christian cultures. The various medieval *Keys of Dreams* (*Clefs des Songes*), written either in Latin or the vernacular, also state that "to dream of sitting upon a white horse" announces a favorable event, as does for that matter "dreaming of becoming emperor."[20] Pascalis Romanus (d. 1186), a Latin cleric who for a long time resided at the Byzantine court of Manuel II, brought together in his *Liber Thesauri Occulti* (*Book of Secret Treasure*) a solution of these traditions well known in the east. Let us note incidentally that he is also known for his *Disputatio contra Judaeos*, a translation of an eighth-century Greek text that he acquired in Byzantium.[21] In his treatise on dreams he does not speak specifically about horses, but he does of the significance of dreams that have a king or money as a theme, both of which we find in Herman's dream: "If someone who is not of royal lineage dreams that he is crowned by the king, his glory will be exalted, but he will have an unhappy ending." He also cites another *Key of Dreams*: "He who sees in his dream many pieces of money will fall victim to malevolent doings."[22]

The theme of a white horse is present above all in the Book of Apocalypse, a most important source for visionary literature and Christian exegesis. In chapter 6, verses 2–8, the successive irruption of four horses of different colors—white (*albus*), fire red (*rufus*), black (*niger*), greenish or pale (*pallidus*)—made a strong impression on medieval imaginations. In the twelfth century the Premonstratensian Anselm of Havelberg, in conformity with exegetical tradition, sees in this the development of successive stages of the history of the Church: the white horse symbolizes the spark of the primitive Church—its rider none other than Christ, who "governs the Church, humiliating and overturning the arrogant with the arc of apostolic teaching." Following this comes the red horse, the symbol of bloody persecutions and martyrs, then the black horse of heresy, and finally the greenish horse that symbolizes "false brothers."[23] In the final interpretation of his dream (chapter 21), Herman himself also gives a positive significance to the white horse: the spark of its whiteness symbolizes the grace of God, and the use of such a horse is likened to the spiritual exercises that permit God's grace to blossom in oneself. Nothing in this interpretation contradicts Christian exegesis of this period.

One may wish definitively to recognize in the motif of the white horse a trait from Jewish dream lore, but it might equally be connected to Christian culture. Once again, as Jeremy Cohen has pointed out,[24] it is the elements of "convergence" between the two cultures in the same geographic space and at the same time that outweighs their divergences and conflicts. One might otherwise be tempted to attribute unilaterally the entire text in which it appears to one or the other culture if these convergences are too quickly forgotten or if any given expression or image is isolated from its larger context. Indeed there are no arguments put forth claiming the motif for one culture that cannot be reversed to claim it for the other. This being the case, it is this very indetermination that seems to me to be at the heart of the subject.

The dream of young Judas holds an unexpected element: at the imperial table the food served is not venison, as one might have expected, but a vegetable dish (*olus*) of garden herbs or cabbage.[25] Should this detail be interpreted in reference to Jewish dietary prescriptions? Should this vegetable dish be seen as a memory of the *maror*, the ritual Passover dish of horseradish and "bitter herbs"?[26] Every spring, this Jewish holiday commemorates the Exodus of the Hebrew people from Egypt and the end of their enslavement.[27] The meal follows the prescriptions of Numbers 9:11: "They shall eat it [the paschal lamb] with unleavened bread [*mazzah*, plural *mazzot*] and bitter herbs [*maror*, plural *merorim*]." The Talmud prescribes that these herbs not be cooked so that they do not lose their bitterness.[28] But Herman's text says nothing about the taste of the herbs offered to Herman by the emperor and nothing therefore allows us to make any such connection.[29] In following this hypothesis regarding an at least implicit link between young Judas's "thirteenth year" and the ritual of the bar mitzvah, one can also raise the question, following Ivan Marcus, of the importance of symbolism and food consumed at the initiation rites of young Jewish boys in the Middle Ages, except this consists not of "herbs," but of cakes, eggs, honey, wine, and spices.[30]

Let us also recall that Herman's account mentions the vision of these "herbs" during the dream. The treatise of *Lamentations* in the Midrash mentions, among all the dreams of which the wise Rabbi Ishmael is asked to give interpretation, that of a man who says: "I saw in my dream that I was carrying a stick attached to a handful of lettuce." The sage gave the following explanation: "You will know greatness." And adds: "This man has a supply of wine which is in the process of going bad and each person will come and take some in bottles in order to macerate their lettuce."[31] Just as in Herman's dream, the modesty of the food seen in the dream announces, through an inversion of the image, both greatness and wealth. But clearly there is nothing that allows one to assign the least amount of influence from one text to the other.

Does this Christian "path" turn out to be more certain? It can at least be grounded in the study of vocabulary. In Christian literature the word *olus* is sometimes used to designate herbs and salads that nuns grow in their vegetable gardens.[32] It is thus an ascetic food that, when in the form of a gift, can also signify an act of Christian charity. Thus Christina of Markyate (c. 1100–1155/1160) refuses to touch a vegetable (*olus*) that comes from the garden of a neighbor who had refused to give Christina the chervil she had asked for.[33]

Above all, it should be noted that the word *olus* belongs to the vocabulary of the Vulgate in which it appears eight times, four times in each the Old and New Testaments, sometimes in the singular and sometimes in the plural. Some of its biblical occurrences recall the situation of Judas's dream: in 1 Kings 21:2, King Achab offers to give his vine to Nabot so that he may grow a vegetable garden. Proverbs 15:17 offers an ascetic meaning and a gift-giving situation that, by all evidence, brings us close to the meaning that this dish of herbs carries in the dream: "Better a meal of vegetables where there is love than a fattened ox where there is hate." The same word is used for the parable of the wild mustard seed to which the kingdom of the heavens is compared in Matthew 13:32 and Mark 4:31–32: "[it] is less than all the seeds that be in the earth, but when it is sown, it grows, and becomes greater than all herbs." Saint Paul (Romans 14:2) likens a man still weak in his faith to a person who eats only vegetables. This food must therefore be understood in a spiritual sense, since it here refers to the word of God, and recalls Herman's interpretation: "As for the dish of vegetables that I seemed to have eaten at the royal table, I think it designates the gospel of Christ. For just as the dish was made up of various kinds of herbs, so the gospel of Christ is composed of various precepts pertaining to eternal life." This assimilation between herbs and the gospel is particularly relevant for understanding the priest who "chews" the word of God at the altar (Chapter 21).

The dream-inspired figures of the emperor, the white horse, and the dish of vegetables do not allow us to recognize the substratum of Jewish culture hidden behind this dream with any more certitude than the age of the young dreamer. But neither is it possible to discard completely the hypothesis of a Jewish influence. In fact, neither the attitude regarding dreams, nor the modes of interpretation, nor even perhaps the content of dreams differentiates Jews from Christians in any fundamental way. The Latin vocabulary of the *Opusculum* leads us naturally to privilege the Christian path. But the interest in dreams and in certain dream figures with strong symbolic meaning, such as the white horse, was shared by Jews and Christians alike.

By wishing too much to come down on one side or the other of this irresolvable debate of attribution, one risks losing sight of the content of the dream in its broader context. What Judas dreams of is a political ritual, the ceremonial manifestation of royal hospitality in the form of a rite of investiture from which he benefits. What is remarkable is that a political ritual provides a dream expression for the social and religious ambitions of the young man. Beyond its specific function within relations of power, the political ritual is in effect, for the Middle Ages, a narrative model—and, I might add, an imaginary one—that permits thinking about all sorts of social relations.[34] In this way, the two concurrent interpretations which are proposed, first by Isaac the Jew, then, at the end of the *Opusculum*, by Herman himself, should be borne in mind since neither of them is political: the young Jew will not *really* become the great lord whose arms he has received in his dream. For Isaac the Jew, the ritual deployment of royal gifts is the dream version of another ritual which, in the hierarchy of social deeds, is necessarily located one level below: that of the "private" and "carnal" ritual of marriage, a ritual that will indeed take place, but without being able to satisfy the future convert in the long term (chapter 11). For Herman, once a Christian, the political ritual contrarily allows him to think, one level above, of the "spiritual" effects of divine grace, which the ecclesiastical ritual of baptism (chapter 19) will guarantee. The two contrasting interpretations are representative of the whole series of homologous opposing pairings that are the foundations of Christian ideology and can be listed almost *ad infinitum*. Does the entire *Opusculum* not constantly remind one of the oppositions between word and spirit, flesh and soul, feminine and masculine, time and eternity, or more immediately, in the case of the dream, of Jewish "falsity" and the "truth" of Christian interpretation? The dream and its interpretation are thus well inscribed in a coherent system that renders it all the more vain to select, as we have done until now, this or that detail for the sole purpose of demonstrating that an authentic Jewish convert could have—or could not have—had such a dream and written such a work. This system articulates in hierarchy from high to low three levels of ritual, or three "rites of passage":

- Baptism: The rite of integration into a Christian community.
- Investiture by the king: The political secular rite.
- Marriage: The "private" ritual alliance.

The Dream Vision of Christ's Majesty

Judas's dream in the first chapter of the *Opusculum* is both his first and most important visionary experience on the path to conversion. Along the way, he benefits from another vision, one mentioned both in Godfried of Cappenberg's *Vita* and in the *Opusculum*. We have seen that the *Vita* does not speak of the child's dream, while in the *Opusculum* the entire composition is structured around it. Indeed the *Opusculum* speaks of nothing but this vision, though never explicitly qualifying it as a dream. This vision comes at the decisive moment in the "Jewish brother's" conversion, for it comes to satisfy his desire for certitude against the doubts that still haunt him: as a future Christian, he wishes that his "spiritual" eyes be liberated from the Jewish "blindfold" that prevents him from coming to know the truth; and because he is still a Jew, he must receive a manifest sign, a *signum*, that will persuade him. In the *Vita* this wish is immediately satisfied. It comes with the interjection *ecce*, which introduces the vision. This comes as an apparition with the suddenness of a miracle and its effects are no less immediate. The young Jew sees himself in front of the throne of Christ, who is carrying the cross over his shoulder, and thus his decision is made. He goes to Mainz, removes his young brother, flees, and with him receives baptism before rejoining the "militia" of canons at Cappenberg.

This narrative framework is easily recognizable in the *Opusculum* despite the different arrangement of the account. In chapter 8, the young Judas begs for a divine sign, he prays and fasts for three days and three nights, but to no avail. There are no "signs" for those who do not possess grace, and crossing himself repeatedly and fasting yield nothing. Only the prayers of the female saints Berta and Glismut will bring divine grace to him. The "sign" therefore only comes later, in chapter 18, right before the chapter describing his baptism, which is administered to him five days later. Furthermore, contrary to the *Vita*, the *Opusculum* explicitly speaks of a dream ("I saw a dream") by insisting on the "sweetness" he felt when having it and later telling it (*vidi somnium sicut visu ita et relatu dulcissimum*).[35] The description is also more precise, though one can hesitate in translating it, depending on whether we understand the Christ enthroned as radiating *"from* the Father's majesty," or as "seated on an elevated throne, *in* the Father's majesty, [. . .] holding in the guise of a scepter the sign of the cross placed on his right shoulder."[36] According to this second interpretation, which I prefer, Judas sees not only Christ, as the *Vita* affirms, he simultaneously sees the Father in majesty and, *within* the divine majesty, the Son identified by the cross. The dream vision reveals to Judas/Herman an image of the Trinity, even if the dove of the Holy Spirit is absent. It is this image of the Father and the Son alone that is often represented during the twelfth century in the historiated initial of Psalm 109 (Psalm 110), *"Dixit dominus domino meo: sede a dextris meis"* ("The Lord said to my lord: Sit at my right hand"). Historians of art describe this image by the term "dual divinity," to distinguish it from the increasingly frequent images of this period that associate the three persons of the Trinity. The oldest known dual divinity is found in the Utrecht Psalter from the Carolingian period. But it is especially in England, in the Romanesque period, that one observes a rising "tide of dual divinities" between 1125 and 1160.[37] In the initial D of Psalm 109 of an English Psalter of this period, not only is the Son enthroned with the majesty of the Father, but, much as in the vision of Judas/Herman, he also carries the cross (fig. 2). François Boespflug and Yolanta Zaluska insist in their description of this miniature on "the very eloquent opposition of humility and glory" in the figure of Christ, brought down by his nakedness and the expression of his suffering, and at the same time made divine "at the right of the Father."[38] Judas/Herman's vision fits in perfectly with the evolution of spiritual literature and the iconography of the Trinity, for which the twelfth century marks a decisive moment.[39] Rupert of Deutz played a major role in this, as much by his theological writings as by his many visions. On the threshold of his baptism, it is a Trinitarian vision that once again succeeds in convincing Judas/Herman.

The *Opusculum* thus contrasts with the *Vita* in speaking of two dreams: one at the beginning of the autobiography, the other at the end of Judas's catechism. These dreams differ by their position in the arrangement of the account, by the amount of text which is devoted to them, and especially by the fact that the first dream is a symbolic one which requires correct decipherment (which Herman will do himself once he is baptized and made a priest, in chapter 21), while the second dream has a manifest meaning immediately intelligible to the one who is henceforth almost Christian. The function of this second dream is not to convince this soon-to-be Christian, as the vision in the *Vita* miraculously does, but rather to concentrate on God's election of the new convert, which is revealed to him at the moment of his "adoption."

By all measures, the *Opusculum* does not obey the same narrative logic as the *Vita*. Conversion arrives not as a sudden and miraculous event following a vision that could more or less be said to have precipitated it. Instead, conversion is a long process whereby reason (in the debate with the clerics and especially with Rupert of Deutz), good examples (those of the attendant Richmar and the canons of Cappenberg), and especially grace (with the prayers of Berta and Glismut) all contribute to the eventual decision. This is why the baptism is immediately preceded by a dream. It is not the cause of

conversion, but rather the culmination of a long and now irreversible progress. Christ shows by a true and manifest "sign" that in his grace he has
definitively received the catechumen. Thus the long detours, hesitations, and
doubts of the *Opusculum* reinforce the personal and autobiographical tonality
of the account, which seems all the more veracious, while the suddenness and
immediate efficacy of the vision are characteristic of the *Vita's* hagiographical
genre. The two accounts are incontestably linked and it matters little which
came first. To reiterate, they are for me two versions of the same "myth," but
two versions having a different form, a different structure, and by all evidence, a different finality as well.

There are many points in common between the vision of the *Vita* and
the dream of the *Opusculum*. Not only do each describe Christ carrying the
cross on his shoulder, they also both describe a young Jew who discovers that
he is not alone in his dream, but that by his side are two Jews blinded by
error, the cousins that the *Opusculum* goes so far as to name as Nathan and
Isaac, who are incapable of recognizing the Messiah. The citation of Isaiah
9:6 is the same in both cases: they do not recognize that "Him upon whose
shoulders the empire shall be." In the *Opusculum* a dialogue is initiated between the dreamer and the other two, whence we learn that they are dead
and condemned to damnation. The process is the same as in the great dream
of Guibert of Nogent's mother, in which she sees not only her deceased
husband suffering in a sort of purgatory from which she will be able to pull
him with her prayers and her scourging, but also the knight Renaud and a
brother of Guibert, two men she knows well and knows will soon die in a
state of mortal sin. She understands that they will be thrown into the pits of
hell, for in their case all hope is lost.[40] Such dreams concern more than one
individual since their meaning is directed to an entire group. These revelations about an ordinarily invisible hereafter give information about the fate
of dead relatives as well as the fate that awaits those who are still living. They
anticipate the judgment of souls and classify the good and evil ones for the
sake of those living souls that can still learn, emend, and convert.[41] It cannot
be overstated that if in the Middle Ages as in the present dreams constitute
the experience of a single individual, in medieval as well as in other traditional
societies they are also the business of an entire group, be it the small pious
entourage that surrounds Guibert of Nogent and his mother, or a monastic
and canonical community such as that of Cappenberg. And it is no different
in this same period in Jewish communities.

The Jewish Culture of Dreams

For Jews in the Middle Ages, as for Christians, the "culture of dreams"[42] is rooted in the Bible, and particularly in the book of Genesis which is shared by both religions. The great models for "dreamers" are Jacob, with his dream of the heavenly ladder, and Joseph, who himself dreams and interprets the dreams of Pharaoh and his servants.[43] For Jews and Christians alike the evil dreamer par excellence is the King Nebuchadnezzar whose dreams are interpreted by the prophet Daniel. The positive biblical dream is a mode of communication with God, the privilege of God's elect, a prophetic charisma. Certain sites lend themselves to incubation rituals such as the rock of Beth-El on which Jacob sleeps and dreams.[44] Let us note, too, the symbolic importance of numbers: in the dreams of Pharaoh that Joseph interpreted there are two times seven cows, and two times seven ears of grain, which may call to mind the seven deniers given by the emperor in Herman's dream, which in Christian interpretation evokes the seven gifts of the Holy Spirit.

In this respect, ancient Judaism, from the Jerusalem Talmud (the treatise *Ma'aser Sheni*) to the Babylonian Talmud (*Berakhot* 55a–57b) and Midrash (*Lamentations*),[45] holds a more reserved and occasionally more cautious position regarding dreams. The treatise *Berakhot*, compiled between the third and the fifth century C.E., devotes long passages to the questions raised by dreams. Dreams represent but "one sixtieth of prophecy" (57b), a figure that relativizes its importance. The same chapter also aims to reduce the content of certain dreams to remnants of thoughts and perceptions from the day, such dreams being devoid of significance. However, the existence of "true" dreams that emanate from God and whose predictions can be verified is indeed recognized and valorized. Morning dreams, dreams that one person has of another, and dreams whose explanation is provided by other dreams are treated positively. The "fasting of the dream" allows one to guard against "false" dreams and it is possible to address a prayer to God so that he may send "good dreams." The interpretation of dreams indeed holds an important place in Jewish culture: in Jerusalem there had lived twenty-four interpreters of dreams. These interpreters endeavored to decrypt one by one the images of the dream, proceeding by word associations and referring to the biblical verses in which these words were found. Certain Talmudic adages enjoyed a great success, as is testified to by the commentaries dedicated to them in the Middle Ages: "a dream which is not interpreted is like a letter not read," which demonstrates the necessity of interpretation, without which the dream would have no consequence;[46] or even, "all dreams follow the mouth" of the interpreter (*Berakhot* 55a), that is, the dream is realized following the interpretation it is given, or, put another way, the interpretation influences the behavior of the dreamer who thus fulfills the dream; unless one should understand that the well-paid interpreter gives to his client the favorable meaning expected of him! The Talmud also emphasizes that the meaning given to dreams is relative, for the interpreter cannot give the same meaning to the same dream had by two different persons.

Differing currents of thought concerning dreams exist within medieval Jewish culture. Rashi (1030–1104/1105) is the greatest representative of the Jewish intellectual community that extended from the Champagne region to the Rhineland in the period preceding the First Crusade.[47] He received his education under Gershom of Mainz, and in Reims, after 1070, began drawing his own students from Rhineland towns. One may indeed wonder if young Judas's wish to go study "in France" in chapter 10 of the *Opusculum* alludes to the attraction exercised by the Talmudic school in Reims. Rashi's commentary on the Pentateuch departs from Midrash's symbolic and mystical interpretation in order to privilege literal and historical explanations, called *peshat*. Jewish schools thus experience the same internal debate that is taking place within Christian exegesis, which is likewise split between the tradition of symbolic commentary and the novelty of literal and historical commentary.

Rashi's influence even extended beyond Jewish circles. Beginning with Andrew of Saint-Victor in the early twelfth century, the Victorines knew and used his work.[48] Rashi's commentary on Joseph's dreams in Genesis—in which one can even see the local langue d'oïl creeping into the Hebrew text—offers a good example of his method as well as his approach to dreams. For example, regarding the three baskets of baked goods that the baker carries in his dream (Genesis 40), Rashi makes the following comment: "They are baskets made of braided straw. In our country, they are well known; those who sell baked goods called *oublees* in the local language usually place them in this type of basket."[49]

The twelfth-century intellectualist strain of Jewish thought (*tosaphot*) that Rashi represents is quite distinct from the other currents that begin to develop at the same time and that mature in the following century: for instance the mystical currents, like Spanish Kabbalah, or the German Pietist movement (*Ashkenazi Hassidim*). The *hassidim* are an initiates among whom knowledge is transmitted from master to disciple. The Pietist ideal revolved around confession and the expiation of sin. The *Hassidim* were not as interested in taking control of the Rhineland communities as they were in separating themselves from other Jews, by their dress (they wore the prayer shawl, or *talit*, all day and not only for prayer), their manner of prayer (they pick at every letter and attach great symbolic importance to each), their initiation rites, and their endogamy. The first three major figures in this movement are Samuel ben Kalonymus in the middle of the twelfth century, Judah the Pietist, author of the *Sefer Hassidim* (d. 1217), and finally Eleazar ben Judah of Worms (d, c. 1230), author of the *Sode Raza*. While a discrepancy in chronology precludes a direct relation between our mid-twelfth-century text and the later Pietist movement, it is nevertheless worth examining the manner in which Pietism handles the question of dreams, for dreams occupy an important place in the works we have just cited, beginning with the *Sefer Hassidim*. This work contains a lengthy commentary on the Talmud and takes up its principal ideas[50]: namely, dreams that appear during a deep sleep owe their content and their quality to the preoccupations of man. It is in their relation to individuals, their qualities, and their plans that dreams ought to be appreciated. They are distinguished from prophetic dreams, which intercede in a light sleep when the conscious faculties of man are still awake and can receive the message that the angel murmurs in the ear to guide this man to the realization of the divine decree.[51] Finally, one has to guard against the "master of dreams" (*Ba'al-Halom*), a demonic figure of Babylonian origin that inspires dreams whose precepts are not to be followed. Conforming to the Talmud (*Sabbat* 11a), fasting accompanied by repentance is recommended as preparation for a good dream. One should note among the *Hassidim* a particularly strong link between dreams and death or the dead: dreams can announce death and the dead are carriers of revelations. It is necessary to interpret dreams as much to learn their content as it is to rid dreamers of the enigma over which they obsesses from the moment they awaken. On this matter the Talmudic maxims are heavily commented upon: "all dreams follow the mouth" (of the interpreter) here finds an original explanation; the mouth signifies that truth, as in the Torah, is oral; the dream is assimilated to a holy scripture whose meaning a "mouth" must explain. The interpretation privileges the symbolic significance less than it does the content and the very words of the dream. And the correct meaning is not excluded, as is demonstrated by the following example, the marital subject of the dream recalling the "carnal" interpretation that uncle Isaac gave the young Judas:

A man had a dream. He came before a sage and said to him, "I dreamed that I should marry so-and-so; she said to me [after the dream] that she did not want to be married to me. I would take to wife another woman but it appeared to me [evidently, in a subsequent dream] that it would be a sin punishable by death for I must take the one that I dreamed would be married unto me." The sage said to him, "Dreams are of no effect one way or the other." One cannot depend on dreams; it is not a sin for you to marry [another] woman. . . . There are times when one dreams he must marry a woman who has actually died.[52]

With Moses Maimonides (1138–1204) one reaches not only another arena of medieval Jewish culture—the culture of Judeo-Arabic, stretching from Cordoba to as far as Palestine and Cairo where Maimonides died—but also another outlook, a rational and scientific one suffused with Aristotelian thought. The *Guide for the Perplexed* was written in Arabic and only trans-lated into Hebrew in 1204. This work also accords a place to dreams by considering them in their relation to prophecy. Maimonides underscores the superiority of prophecy, stating that it emanates from God's will and exerts itself on the rational and imaginative faculties of men elected as prophets by God. Conforming to *Berakhot* 57b, the dream is only the "sixtieth part of prophecy" or even its "aborted fruit," fallen before having reached maturity. It sometimes happens that God uses dreams to give warnings to ordinary people, but this has not to do with prophecy, for prophecy is reserved for prophets alone.[53]

Our brief review of the different currents of the "Jewish culture of dreams" in the twelfth and thirteenth centuries allows us to note the several main themes they shared in common. In particular, they each held to the weight of the Bible and later religious texts, to the Talmud and Mishna, and more generally to the opinion that the dream, if judged "true," is a form of divine revelation that guarantees its veracity. As for the *Opusculum*, nothing forbids us from calculating its connection to the Jewish culture of dreams. Neither the content of the dream (such as the motif of the white horse), nor the move made toward a relative reputed for his wisdom and his gifts of interpretation, nor even the rather banal meaning that this relative offers in conjuring up the prospect of a beautiful marriage, contradicts this hypothesis. Yet the same elements can just as well relate to the medieval Christian culture of dreams.

Christian Dreams, Conversions, and Autobiographies

Indeed, Christian interest in dreams is no less strong than that of Jews, and it relies very much on the same biblical sources. This interest is also mixed with a certain distrust that is reinforced by the assimilation of the "science of dreams" with Greco-Roman paganism. But Christians also recognize in dreams a mode of divine revelation that benefits martyrs and saints. The role of dreams in the experience of conversion is thus central.

Christian culture inherited from pagan culture, and especially from Macrobius's *Commentary on the Dream of Scipio*, a classification of dreams that helped to resolve this tension. This classification distinguishes five sorts of dreams, from the lowest, or "false," to the highest, or "true": the *insomnium*, the *visum* or *phantasma*, the *oraculum*, the *visio*, and the *somnium*. This classification, however, was more or less forgotten until the twelfth century, when Alcher of Clairvaux revived it in his treatise *De spiritu et anima*, while at the same time William of Conches offered a new commentary of the *Dream of Scipio*.[54] Between late antiquity and the twelfth century, two modes of classification predominated: the system of three types of vision—"corporal," "spiritual" (including dreams), "intellectual"—proposed by Augustine in his *Commentary on the Twelve Books of Genesis*, and Gregory the Great's (540–604) distinction between six classes of dreams, three of them having their origin in the dreamer (within his spirit and his body) and three having their origin outside of him (with God or the Devil).[55] Thus again we have a ternary system, one that is not without resemblance to the system proposed by Jewish culture, for it identifies dreams according to whether they come from God, man himself, or demons.

Throughout the entire Middle Ages the possibility of "false" dreams caused consternation within the Church over diabolical *fantasmata,* which menaced not only the simple folk, but also clerics and even saints—such as Saint Anthony—with temptations and "illusions of the demon." The possibility of dreams of human origin will permit the scholastics of the thirteenth century (such as Albert the Great and Thomas Aquinas), who, like Maimonides before them, were influenced by Aristotle's *De Anima*, to better appreciate the physio-psychological nature of the *imaginatio*.

Starting in the first centuries after Christ, dreams that reveal the will of God play a central role in defining Christian identity—the choice of conversion to the new faith and the road to salvation. Tertullian speaks of these as *somnia vocatoria*, dreams that make a calling to Christianity.[56] Origen (185–

254), while refuting pagan criticisms of Christianity, notes in his *Contra Celsum* (I, 46) the very strong relation between dreams and conversion: "it shall be said that many have come to Christianity as it were in spite of themselves, some spirit having turned their mind suddenly from hating the gospel to dying for it by means of a vision by day or by night."[57] In the fourth century conversions of this type are celebrated everywhere. One could cite the conversions of Arnobe, who, "until then a pagan, was brought to the cross by dreams," or of Gregory of Nazianzus who saw in a dream the conversion of his son. Augustine cites the case of one such pagan of modest means who, interrogated "about miracles and dreams," "responded that if he were admonished or terrified by a divine cause, he would become Christian."[58] Much later, but in referring to the early years of the Church, the fake *Donation of Constantine* would use the pagan emperor's dream as the first stage of his own conversion and, following that, the basis for the conversion of the Roman Empire to Christianity. This document was forged around 760 by a Roman cleric in order to assert papal rights over central Italy. It describes how emperor Constantine, suffering from leprosy, first addressed pagan priests, who advised him to bathe in the blood of innocent children. But, in a dream, Saints Peter and Paul appeared to him telling him to allow the fugitive Pope Sylvester to return home, in exchange for which he would be rid of his suffering. As a price for his healing, the emperor must promise the Pope to abandon idolatry, to worship only God, and to build churches throughout the world. Recognizing in a painting shown to him by the Pope the face of the two apostles, the emperor became convinced of the truth of his dream and accepted to be governed by the will of the Pope. As Paul Edward Dutton has put it, "Constantine entered sleep as a pagan, but left as a man on the road to conversion."[59]

While strongly connected to the idea of conversion, dreams are simultaneously connected to the idea of autobiography. Pierre Courcelle has reminded us how, in the time of Tertullian, the visions that occurred during the course of daily offices were carefully recorded in the form of first-person accounts.[60] The Passions of the first martyrs, such as the *Passio Perpetuae*, give a significant place to dreams in which *juvenes hilares*, or young lads, appear, suffused with heavenly joy and promising eternal glory to the future martyr. These texts are read, known, and cited, most notably by Saint Augustine who, in turn, mentions in his *Confessions* the dreams of his mother whose divine origin he does not doubt. The first among these is the "dream of the rule," which gives his mother the certitude of her son's forthcoming conversion.[61] Finally, he himself benefits from the appearance of a similar *juvenis hilaris* in the garden in which he receives the divine order to abandon the pagan books and to take up Scripture: "*Tolle, lege,*" "Take it and read it."[62] From its earliest origins with Augustine's *Confessions,* or even more Gregory of Nazianzus's *Poemata de se ipso,* translated from Greek into Latin by Rufinus around 399, dreams and conversion find in the autobiographical form a privileged mode of expression from the very beginnings of Christian literature. But we have seen that this type of writing is somewhat eclipsed during the early Middle Ages, at the expense of other literary genres, such as hagiography or the great political visions of the Carolingian period. The mistrust of dreams, always suspected of opening the door to "diabolic illusions," must have dissuaded writers from making too much of personal dreams. Everything changes, however, beginning in the eleventh century.

One of the best witnesses to this change is Otloh, a monk at Saint-Emmeran near Regensburg. Born in Bavaria around 1010 and given as an oblate, he was a monk first at Tegernsee, then at Hersfeld. In 1032, at the age of twenty-two, he experienced a veritable conversion along the model of Saint Jerome, who was accused by a voice from heaven: "You lie! You are a Ciceronian, not a Christian!" Like Jerome before him, Otloh abandons the readings of Lucan and chooses to devote himself completely to meditations on Scriptures. He enters Saint-Emmeran where, several years earlier, the provost Arnold had a similar experience: after the death of a brother who was particularly dear to him, Arnold turned away from the study of pagan authors.[63] Otloh is placed in charge of novices in the monastery. He is also charged with reinforcing the links between Saint-Emmeran and the monastic reform movement that started at Gorze and Hirsau and which had reached Regensburg by the beginning of the century. Otloh himself draws up fraudulent documents that purport to be privileges granted by the emperors Otto III and Henry II and that proclaim the immunity of the monastery from the temporal powers of bishops; in the manner of German monastic reform, this was not, as in Cluny, simply a matter of exemption from the spiritual authority of bishops.[64] It was Otloh, too, who kept the necrology of the monastery: indeed he is charged with the collective memory of Saint-Emmeran, a duty that in all likelihood sharpens his preoccupation with his own memoirs.[65] In 1062 Otloh leaves the monastery after a conflict with its abbot and spends three years in the abbey of Fulda (1062–1066). There he composes his *Liber visionum,* a partially holograph copy of which has been preserved.[66] He returns to Regensburg in 1065 at the age of about fifty-five. By the time of his death, sometime after 1070, he had left a very diverse body of writings, including works of theology (in particular the *De doctrina spirituali*),[67] hagiography (notably a *Life of Saint Boniface*), and autobiography (the *Liber visionum* and the *Liber de temptationibus suis*).

His *Liber visionum* includes the account of twenty-three "visions." Only the first four of these are his own, but they take up a third of the work.[68] The rest of these are taken from witnesses judged worthy of faith, and sometimes from the visionaries themselves. The source for three of these visions (numbers 19, 20, and 21) is literary: Otloh takes them from the Venerable Bede (d. 735). Otloh himself insists in his prologue on the variety of *genera visionum* and the distinction between "visions that we perceive in our peaceful or non-peaceful dreams (*per somnia quieta vel non*)" and the visions that come to us in our waking state (*vigilantes*).[69] Examples of both are given in Scriptures and in the fourth book of Gregory the Great's *Dialogues*: Otloh says he strove to imitate Gregory in the hope that he would not be reproached for his coarseness, or for the "rusticity" of his short work. By "vision" Otloh means all sorts of visionary experiences that Saint Augustine had characterized as "spiritual visions": dreams (*somnia*), visions perceived in a waking state, apparitions, and even what we would call hallucinations suffered in the course of a grave illness or extreme pain. On the other hand, Otloh's four personal "visions" are exclusively dreams: he uses his own authority to guarantee their authenticity, for he himself can bear witness to them. Here there is no need for written or oral mediation by a third party in order to guarantee the truth of dreams or vision.

The dreams that Otloh remembers punctuate the key moments of his existence. The first goes back to 1023 when the young monk was thirteen years old. Otloh recalls this forty years later. In other words, he was marked by it. Thirteen years old: it was at this same age that Judas/Herman was granted the dream that would push him to conversion and illuminate the meaning of his life. Otloh is already Christian, even an oblate, but within the walls of the monastery he lives in doubt. Thirteen is therefore not only the age of bar mitzvah, it is in fact a critical age for all those who leave childhood, an age of doubts and of those "temptations" to which Otloh, in his *De temptationibus*, is suspect. It is the moment at which he makes the choices that launch his life. Having dozed off in the choir of the abbey-church of Tegernsee, Otloh dreams that Christ appears to him and praises him for his singing of the Psalms. Christ consoles him over the attacks of malicious and envious monks, and he encourages Otloh in his path of perfection.

The second personal dream that Otloh remembers occurred "two years later," in 1025, also in Tegernsee. Otloh is again asleep in the choir of the monastery's church. He sees an old man, God, or more likely Jesus, come out from the right-hand corner of the altar at the moment when the young monk was going to spread the incense. Jesus addresses the monks participating in the liturgical ceremony. He reproaches them for their vices, and then, "from above the choir," he encourages the laymen to persevere along the straight path. Upon awaking Otloh decides to amend his ways.

The other personal dreams which Otloh remembers having had several years later, and some thirty years before committing them to writing, are different from his two adolescent dreams. First there is the dream of his conversion. In 1032 Otloh is twenty-two years old and taking refuge at Saint-Emmeran from the hostility of the archpriest of Freising. There, in the middle of Lent, he is assailed by a series of nightmares. It is the first of these dreams that immediately compares to the famous dream of Saint Jerome: an angel appears to him and beats him until he bleeds, leaving him bruised, his skin covered in blisters, until the Thursday of the Passion. Once recovered, he sees his dream as an illusion of the Devil and wishes to flee from the monastery. The monks succeed in holding him back. But he suffers a relapse, his body becomes covered in pustules and is stricken with paralysis. He makes an offer to the monks: if he recovers, he promises to join their community. The monks refuse: this is not how one converts; one converts by the willing acceptance of divine grace. The argument is the same as the one given by Bishop Eckbert in the *Opusculum*, who forbids the attendant Richmar and the young Judas from testing God by an ordeal. New terrifying dreams come and reveal to Otloh the eschatological promises linked to his choice. Thus, he finally acknowledges God's calling and remains at Saint-Emmeran.

Otloh also remembers another personal dream that he had around 1055, at the age of about forty-five, "ten years" before writing the *Liber visionum*. A conflict had just arisen between him and his abbey. He is sick and dreams that his cell is full of smoke, that a pack of demons storm in and take him away across space with the intention of throwing him down a precipice. An angel arrives in time to liberate him at the moment when the bells of prime ring and pull him out from his sleep.

These four personal dreams are the only *somnia* of Otloh's collection of visions. There does not seem to be any reason to doubt that these accounts reflect, many years removed, the memory of real dream experiences that made a strong impression on the author. These accounts depart from the narrative mold of the awakened vision that is transmitted by a written tradition. The place of these personal dreams at the beginning of the work puts them in sharp relief, giving them a greater force of conviction guaranteed by the words of the author, who speaks from personal experience.

The pride of place given to these four dreams, two of childhood and one of conversion, recalls Judas's childhood dream at the very beginning of the *Opusculum*. Both autobiographical works, by Otloh and Herman, tell the tortuous story of a conversion in which dreams play an essential role: in these dreams, the heavens call out to a young man, cause anguish with their mysterious images; they dictate nothing, but incite him to understand. Then their meaning becomes clear: they indicate God's choice of a particular man, who was called to grace and must act accordingly.

Guibert of Nogent also heard this calling through the medium of dreams, as did his mother and others close to him. Like Otloh, it is toward the end of his life, at the age of about sixty, that he recalls these dreams, thus demonstrating once again the importance given to them by monks and clerics during this period.

The whole *monodiae* contains forty-six accounts of visions, fifteen of which are dreams.[70] Among these, eight are Guibert's personal dreams, the only kind of vision to which he lays claim. I see in this the confirmation of a hypothesis: the "waking vision" is above all the vision of someone else, transmitted by an oral and written tradition that gives it authority. If accounts of dreams are equally numerous, as for example in hagiography, the dreams found in autobiographical writings are above all personal experiences that are guaranteed by the words of the author alone, who is also the subject of the dream.[71] This distinction underscores once again the question of *auctoritas*: who is authorized to speak one's dreams and, just as important, who is authorized to write them down. Let us be content to note for the moment that a monk such as Otloh of Saint-Emmeran, a canon such as Herman the former Jew, and an abbot such as Guibert of Nogent can allow themselves to tell their dreams. They possess this authority.

Guibert remembers three childhood dreams in which dead people and terrifying demons appeared to him. Moreover, he recounts two of his mother's dreams that concern him directly: once, she dreamt of him as a monk especially protected by the Virgin; another time, her deceased husband Evrard appeared to her, tortured by the cries of the stillborn child he had illegitimately fathered by another woman before the birth of Guibert. Upon waking, Guibert's mother, who was aware of this episode in Evrard's life, decides to take into her house a child, a living surrogate of the dead child, with the intention of enduring his terrible cries in order to assuage through her own suffering the tortures inflicted on her husband in the hereafter[72] . . . Guibert also recounts the two dreams that his private tutor had of him when as an adolescent he showed himself to be undisciplined. His mother's attendant also dreamed that her mistress would remarry: like Judas/Herman in front of his uncle Isaac, Guibert's mother refuses the "carnal" interpretation of such a dream, seeing instead the sign of her "spiritual marriage" with Christ. Following this dream, she decides to live in proximity to the monastery of Nogent that Guibert directs.

It seems that Guibert, not satisfied with telling the childhood dreams that so profoundly marked him, appropriates for himself the dreams of those who are close to him. He even goes so far as to dream "through" his mother in the same way that his model Augustine had appropriated the dreams of his mother, Monica. Furthermore, it is Guibert's mother, notwithstanding that she is a woman (although a semi-saint in the eyes of her son), who is at the center of the small "dream community" formed by Guibert, the attendant, the private tutor, and the pious neighbors: in the oral and imaginative world of dreams, this is the equivalent of the "textual communities" which Brian Stock has brought to our attention for this same period.[73] Guibert's mother plays this role because her gifts as a visionary and also as an interpreter of dreams are unanimously recognized and put to good use by her family and neighbors. Dreams thus play a role that is on the one hand social, permitting individuals to forge links of friendship and understanding between them, and on the other hand personal, helping young Guibert shape and define his personality in relation to his mother and to God, in whom he sees his real father.

Guibert was only eight months old when his earthly father, Evrard, a lord of Clermont-en-Beauvaisis, died. Guibert suspects that, had he lived longer, his father would most likely have recanted on the promise he made at the time of Guibert's difficult birth: to dedicate him to the Church. Once the danger had passed, would Evrard not have turned away from the Church toward a military career and the vain, worldly feats of knights? The long dream that reveals to Guibert's mother the tortures of her deceased husband, and which she immediately relates to her son, underscores better than anything else the necessity of dreams in such an autobiography of conversion. Here the conversion consists of tearing oneself away from the world of flesh and false appearances in order to enter into a universe of immaterial values, a universe into which dreams give visual and premonitory access. It is in this dream relation to the divine and to an eschatological future that Christian subjectivity—that of a Guibert of Nogent or an Otloh of Saint-Emmeran—is built.

By Christian subjectivity I mean that the subject so constructed through dreams is not absolute, atemporal, nor transhistorical. We can grasp this subjectivity only in its historical context—not only in the context of Christian culture, its beliefs and references (especially biblical), but also in the context of eleventh- and twelfth-century monastic culture and the reforming spirit it engenders. It is in this context, amidst and because of the social, personal, and ideological tensions that dominate the foreground, that men of faith and letters such as Otloh and Guibert, who are at pains to justify themselves before God and to edify their brethren, scrutinize their consciousness and take note of their dreams. One therefore has to be very cautious with all attempts at a retrospective *analysis* of these corpora of dreams, lest we cover them over with psychiatric categories, as has been suggested for Otloh, or attempt a psychoanalytical interpretation, as has been suggested for Guibert.[74] The analogies with situations that are familiar to us—such as the "oedipal" relation that Guibert enters into with his mother, whom he worships, and his relation with his biological father, at whose premature death he nearly rejoices—indeed seem to impose a move in this direction. This would be worth trying if the only objective were to learn how better to untangle the complicated web of social and symbolic relations that these texts present.[75] But it should not be forgotten that these "short works," "dialogues," and other monastic "monodies" have nothing in common historically speaking with our private confessions on the analytic couch: neither their situations of enunciation, nor the status of their speech, nor their horizon of beliefs, nor even their representation of the self can compare. Under these conditions, it is self-evident that their modes of interpretation are likewise different.

The place that autobiographies accord to both the accounts of dreams and their interpretation allows for a comparison, from past to present, of the different ways of understanding these dreams. For Guibert, the content of those dreams that he recounts (*tenor visionis*) has, by definition, a meaning, since he is telling "true" dreams, or dreams that have a divine origin. In order to understand their meaning, Guibert defers to his tutor and especially his mother, both veritable "professionals" in dreams and their interpretation. In the twelfth century such specialists are indeed recognized: in the *Life of Saint Thierry* (d. 1086), the abbot of Saint-Hubert in Ardenne recounts, following

one of the most typical hagiographical topoi, that the saint's birth was announced to his mother in a dream. But she only understands the meaning of
her dream after having gone to find "an old woman, living in saintly continence, to whom, because of her virtue, God had granted, among other faculties, the ability to announce the future. . . . [The mother of the future saint]
recounted her vision to this old woman . . . so that she might explain its
meaning."[76] In England during this same period, Christina of Markyate was
the beneficiary of many dream visions that she interpreted either on her own
or with a spiritual friend named Evisaudus. Her gifts earned her the ironic
name "the dream woman" (*somniatrix*)[77] among her enemies, a name given
apparently without regard to the dignity of this title in Genesis, where it is
applied to Joseph. But dreams in the twelfth century continue to arouse
suspicion, especially when women appear to take a more important part in
their interpretation.

Guibert, for his part, is quite pleased with the visionary gifts of his
mother. Here is what he says after his mother's attendant dreamt that she
would remarry: "My mother, who was most subtle in such matters (*in talibus
versutissima*), did not need an interpreter. Without speaking, she turned
toward my tutor and let him know that the steward's dream was a portent of
that love of God that they had spoken of together and that she desired to be
God's bride."[78] In this case, because the dream concerns her, she immediately
unlocks the meaning. When she herself dreams of her son, she hastens to
speak to him: "Whenever an unpleasant dream disturbed her most pious
mind—and she was an extraordinarily subtle and perceptive interpreter in
such cases—she would interpret the acute discomfort these dreams brought
her as a sign (*portentum*). Then she would summon me and talk with me in
private about my activities, what I was doing and how I was behaving."[79]
Guibert's tutor, who dreams of his student, acts no differently: "My tutor
related this scene to me, and we both had the same interpretation of the
dream."[80] The mother and the tutor always offer the dreamer a global interpretation that takes into account the totality of the account and discern the
meaning in a single try. Their mode of interpretation consists in confronting
dream images and the objective situation of the dreamer. Guibert explicitly
says that his mother interpreted her own dream "*ex convenientia visionis, veris
vera conferens*,"[81] by confronting the objective "truths," that is, the past or
present situation of her son, with the "truths" revealed by this "true" dream,
which treat of Guibert's future destiny.

This mode of global interpretation is quite different from the minutely analytic one that prevails in the *Keys of Dreams*, where a particular meaning of universal character is applied to each dream image. The same is true with regard to dreams for the Talmud and medieval rabbinic literature, even if the interpreter must take into account the particular situation of the dreamer: for although the content of the dream should be the same, its implications might vary from one person to the next.

In appearance, the structure of the interpretation of the dream in the final chapter of Herman's *Opusculum* is hardly different from that of the *Keys of Dreams* or the Talmud: each image (the emperor, the white horse, the baldric, the seven deniers, the plate of vegetables, etc.) is associated with a Christian signifier (God, the altar table, the words of the Gospel, the Eucharistic sacrifice, etc.). There are, nevertheless, some notable differences. The *Keys of Dreams* provides very simple interpretations that follow a binary logic opposing good predictions (long life, health, richness, happy marriage, etc.) to bad ones (premature death, illness, poverty, etc.), in a manner seemingly similar to that which old Isaac unsuccessfully tries with young Judas. But for the converted Herman in chapter 21 each signifier resounds with a multitude of echoes that come from the scriptural and Christian metaphorical traditions. Thus sharing in the emperor's meal is not only a good omen: the image also evokes all the Christian symbolism of the Eucharistic and salvific meal, at which one partakes not of real herbs and roots, but of the flesh of the mystical Lamb and the spiritual food of the Gospel.[82] And the whole supper becomes as well the image of the eschatological meal announced in the Apocalypse. Beginning with concrete and familiar images—the king, a horse, a table, vegetables, or the arms of a knight—the interpretation proceeds by a vertiginous descent into the depths of exegetical moralization and Christian preaching. We come to forget that it is a dream and not a sermon. Thus, the very mode of expression of the text poses the question of its function: was the *Opusculum* intended, as several scholars have suggested, to provide arguments with an eye to the conversion of Jews? Or, as I am tempted to believe, was the work instead aimed at offering the canons of Cappenberg in the form of a dream an illustration of their spiritual excellence?

The Visionary Exegesis of Rupert of Deutz

Dreams call for their decipherment. This likens them to other forms of medieval hermeneutics, the most important of which is biblical exegesis. No figure demonstrates this better than Abbot Rupert of Deutz, who lived in the same region and at the same time as Herman's *Opusculum*. That alone would be sufficient justification for turning our attention to the personage and work of this great theologian did another reason not draw us in that direction: not only is Rupert a great *somniator*, one of the most inspired and eloquent "men of dreams" in all of Christian writing, but he is also the author of an anti-Jewish treatise, the *Anulus*, that occupies a choice place in the apologetic and polemical literature of the early twelfth century. Given his celebrity, there is therefore nothing surprising about his being personally invoked on multiple grounds as the principal interlocutor of young Judas in the *Opusculum*.

If Rupert's life is particularly well known,[83] it is thanks to him: he never ceased to sprinkle autobiographical remarks throughout his many works and took great care in dating them exactly, something that is rather rare among authors of this period. Rupert was born near Liège around 1075. Like Otloh a generation before him and like his contemporary Guibert, Rupert was "offered" to a monastery in earliest childhood. The monastery was Saint-Lawrence at the gates of Liège, and he lived there from 1082 to 1091. Here, too, the introduction of religious reform, in this case from Cluny, provoked tensions. From 1092 to 1095 Rupert went in exile to France at Évergnicourt. His return to Saint-Lawrence coincided with the abbey's adoption of Cluniac customs (1100–1105). Rupert heard the call to reform as personal obligation: between the ages of twenty-five and thirty-three (1100–1108), he comes to have visionary experiences of unusual intensity, experiences that he will later describe. Humbly attached to his status as a simple monk, he refuses to be ordained a priest, but finally accedes in 1108 to the pressures of the bishop, Otbert of Liège. The priesthood is, by his own admission, his great mission in life.

The following years are devoted to writing theological treatises, including the *De divinis officiis* (1109–1112) and the *De sancta Trinitate et operibus suis* (1112–1116). At the same time, in Liège, he engages in public debates on the Eucharist with the Cluniac Alger de Liège (1113–1115) and on the subject of predestination (*De voluntate Dei*, 1116). But these debates do not go in his favor: in 1116–1117 he is exiled to the abbey of Siegburg under the protection of his friend, the reforming Abbot Cuno, who in 1126 becomes bishop of Regensburg. Upon returning to Liège, he pursues the writing of his *De omnipotentia Dei*, and leaves for Laon to debate William of Champeaux, the bishop of Châlons-sur-Marne and founder of the Parisian cathedral school of Saint-Victor, an important site for intellectual innovations of the early

twelfth century. In comparison to him, Rupert represented the more traditional monastic theology and exegesis. At Liège he begins a controversial
teaching on angels. In 1119 he leaves for Cologne at the request of the archbishop Frederick, a friend of Cuno and a firm defender of the monastic
reform that the latter had introduced at Siegburg.

In 1119–1120, Rupert agrees to the request of Abbot Markward of Deutz
that he rewrite the *Vita* of Heribert (999–1021), archbishop of Cologne.
There already existed a first *Vita* of this prelate Saint attributed to Lambert
of Deutz. But after the reform of the abbey, it became necessary to rethink
this text and add elements that underscored the exemplary character of Heribert's pastoral activities.[84] Almost simultaneously, in 1120, Rupert became
the new abbot of Deutz, even though these black monks were facing a new
danger: Norbert of Xanten had just created the Premonstratensian order of
canons regular which immediately began spreading in the region of Meuse
and the Rhineland. Controversy soon erupted between the black monks, who
plead for the sanctity of their way of life outside of the world, and the canons
regular, who also followed a Rule (as *monachi* do), but who additionally
prided themselves—a sign of their times—on their presence in the world as
clerici. Rupert opened hostilities by composing an *Altercatio monachi et clerici*
(1120–1121) directed against Norbert. Norbert responded by accusing Rupert,
in his *De divinis officiis* (1124), of holding heretical beliefs.

Upon returning from a trip to Rome, Rupert writes two treatises that
are of particular relevance to us: his commentary on Matthew's Gospel (*De
gloria et honore Filii Hominis super Matthaeum*) in 1125–1127 and, in 1126, his
treatise against the Jews (*Anulus*). It is also in 1128, following Gerlinde Niemeyer's chronology, that Rupert of Deutz would have publicly debated in
Munster the young Jew Judas of Cologne, the future Herman.

On 24 August 1128, the abbey of Deutz and the agglomeration that surrounds it fall prey to fire: Rupert immediately writes a remarkable first-hand
account (*De incendio oppidii tuitii*)[85] of this catastrophe that was fortunately
limited by divine protection. He eventually dies in Deutz, 4 March 1129.

The corpus of writings left by Rupert of Deutz is exceptionally large,
taking up no less than four volumes in the old edition of the *Patrologia Latina*
(the most for a single author).[86] His writings also touch on all the genres of
religious literature for the period: numerous exegetical commentaries (on the
twelve Prophets, on the Gospels of Matthew and John, on Apocalypse), a
commentary on the Rule of Saint Benedict, two Lives of saints, and apologetic and polemic works attacking adversaries of all kinds. Rupert did not

write an autobiography as such, but he does speak extensively about himself in the prologues to his works and even in his exegetical commentaries.[87] To characterize Rupert in a single word, we could say that he was an intellectual "conservative," both on the basis of his defense of traditional monastic theology against the ferment of early scholasticism in the urban schools, and on institutional grounds by his hostility to the novelty represented by the new order of canons regular. But he is no less attached to a certain evolution, and indeed reform, of the Church, and to the hope that a solution may be brought to the conflict between *regnum* and *sacerdotium*, between empire and papacy.

It is only Rupert's dreams that concern us for the moment. In the totality of his work, one can count more than fifteen accounts of visions and personal dreams, often cited in support of his exposition of this or that point of theology.[88] In some cases, his accounts have an explicitly autobiographical character. In others, as in his *Vita Heriberti*, where dreams are particularly numerous and important, the dreams told by Rupert are clearly those of other people, such as a saint, a bishop, the emperor, or a poor man. Finally, Rupert also on occasion mentions a dream, or some other supernatural event, that one of his brothers had witnessed and then related to him. In these cases one can wonder whether Rupert is not attributing to another person, whose names he hides, something that happened to him personally, unless, inversely, he is appropriating the experience of someone else to the point of no longer being able to make the difference, in the model of the dream and "textual community" of the monastery, between what happened to him and what happened to others. The whole of Rupert's work is thus marked with dreams that one suspects may concern him to the highest degree. They are never memories from long ago, as with Otloh, Guibert, or Herman: Rupert makes note of them and uses them along the way as his work progresses, thus giving it an autobiographical and dreamlike tonality of a very individual kind.

Before examining his more personal dreams, we must look more closely at the first chapter of the *Vita Heriberti*.[89] As is customary for works of hagiography, Rupert first describes the birth of the saint. And as is frequently the case in the Life of a saint, it all begins with a dream. However, contrary to what we might expect, this is not a dream of a "pregnant mother" (as is the case for Saint Bernard, Saint Dominic, and many others), but rather a dream of a father, count Hugo, and especially a Jew, who is his "familiar."[90] The night Heribert's mother gave birth, Rupert explains, "an immense celestial light" was seen "with the eyes of the heart" by certain sleeping people, and "with the eyes of the body" by those who were awake. "The father of the small baby slept and with him was one of his friends, a Jew no less, who had come to join them in order to follow, as was their wont, the conversations and business that they were familiar with." This passage forms part of the additions Rupert made to Lambert's *Vita*. It is a precious witness to the close relations that could exist between Christians, such as Hugo, and Jews in the region of Cologne and Worms. It testifies also to Rupert's keen personal interest in Jews and their situation in Christian society. As such, the passage can be compared to Rupert's *Dialogue Between a Jew and a Christian* (*Anulus*), and the role played by Rupert in the *Opusculum*, a "dream" work if there ever is one.[91] Most remarkable of all is the fact that Rupert is very precisely interested in the Jew's dream, which brings us yet closer to the *Opusculum*. We are forced to note that the Jew's dream is no different from the Christian's dream: according to Rupert's formulation, the Jew and the count not only had similar dreams, they actually shared the *same* dream. Better yet, Rupert gives priority to the Jewish dreamer: it is his dream that he narrates, content to say that the father's dream was identical. And it is the Jew who is charged with announcing (*nuntius*) to the father, on the faith of the wonder witnessed by those both sleeping and awake, what remarkable destiny awaits his son. Here is what follows in Rupert's account:

> Both were sleeping at the moment when this light announced the blessed birth, and both thus had the same dream; upon waking, they spoke to one another as if they each were telling their own dream, unaware that it was a single and shared dream. The first to tell his dream was the one who, as has been said, came as a friend. His dream was as follows: the room in which the woman was lying, and whom we knew was about to give birth, opened in the front to let in a light as radiant as the mid-day sun. At the same hour, according to custom, the women were awake surrounding the parturient, and with the eyes of their bodies, as has been said, they saw the miracle of the infusion of the celestial light.[92]

Next, we are brought closer to what some had seen but others dreamt, this so as to convince us that the omen was not an empty promise and that the miraculous light was the sign that the child would have a great destiny.

Distinct from this and other dreams that Rupert tells in his *Vita Heriberti*[93] are those that he attributes to himself and which take up a central place in his work. In a passage in his *De divinis officiis* from 1111–1112, Rupert relates a nocturnal *miraculum* which, if not really a dream, strongly resembles one. The interpretation he gives it resembles the interpretation of dreams practiced by Guibert of Nogent's mother during the same time. Rupert inserts this account into a passage where he refutes those who deny the resurrection of Christ and his apparition in front of his disciples in a house with closed doors. The monk, whose vision Rupert recounts and who preferred to remain anonymous, only told the event to two brothers, "of whom only one survives," but neither of whom are named. Is Rupert the one who witnessed the miracle or the surviving confidant? Whatever the case, the fact remains that he immediately takes part in the account: "While we were writing these things down, so then it happened that a miracle befell one of our brothers." The temporal coincidence is perfect: the miracle occurred in 1111 during the night of Easter Saturday, the same night that the Church celebrates Christ's rising. In the church-abbey of Saint-Lawrence, the monks proceeded according to the extinction of twelve candles, one for each of the twelve Psalms sung that night. It was at the moment that the last light went out and when Abbot Berangar began singing in darkness the hymn of saintly women who visit the tomb of Christ that his belt, although tightly strapped around his waist, falls to his feet. He tries several times to pick it up, but to no avail. He then hears a voice tell him: "Thus Christ was able to come out of the closed tomb." He understands on his own the meaning of the miracle centered on him: the tightly strapped belt became undone just as the Saint-Sepulcher miraculously opened on the day of Resurrection. Then a passage from Saint Augustine's *City of God* comes to his mind, the passage where Augustine recounts the adventure of Petronia, a sick matron who went on pilgrimage in the hopes of being cured. On the advice of a Jew, she carried with her as a talisman a ring firmly fastened to her belt by a lock of hair. When on the road her ring suddenly fell from her belt, she saw in this a favorable omen and threw the ring and her belt into a river.[94] The idea of closing—such as the tomb of Christ, the belt of Petronia, and the belt of the anonymous monk—begs an interpretation of the sort proposed by Rupert. Following the example of Guibert's mother, he examined "the true with the true" throughout the account in order to disclose the meaning of this idea and apply it in the service of doctrine.

In 1117, when in exile in Siegberg, Rupert dedicates the treatise on the Trinity he had finished the year before to his protector Abbot Cuno. He thanks Cuno for having taken him in when he was chased by the hatred of his enemies. And he recounts this dream of his: during the chorus's prayer, he sees himself amidst monks celebrating the feast of the martyr Saint Denis; he hears himself singing the *responsorium* of the feast day with them: "Now, Lord, give me to my brothers, your servants, and the martyr's crown." He hears his enemies' voices louder and louder, but he fears nothing, for Berangar, his former abbot from Saint-Lawrence, takes his hand and places it in his own, "like a stranger's hand enveloping mine in a manner too marvelous for me to express, and each of my fingers fell perfectly next to his, like in a glove (*chirothecam*)." This hand leads him out of his enemies' reach, while Rupert sings praises to God in an increasingly louder voice that draws the admiration of all those present. This stranger's hand, he writes to Cuno, "represented your hand, as is demonstrated by present reality" (*manu me deducente, quam dixi manum tuam figurante, ut nunc res ipsa probauit*). There, too, it is the relation between two levels of reality, assured by the common symbol of the hand, that permits understanding the meaning of the dream: sublimated here in the form of a dream ritual, the *manumissio* by the pontifical glove (denoted by the technical term *chirotheca*) is indeed a ritual of the Church that allows passing from one *patrocinium* to another; this is what is dreamt by Rupert, who replaces the protection of Abbot Berangar who died the year before (1116) with that of Abbot Cuno.[95]

In 1125 Rupert completes two works: a commentary on the Rule of Saint Benedict and a commentary on the Song of Songs, which he once again dedicates to Cuno of Siegburg.[96] But he no longer feels threatened, as he did when he dedicated his treatise on the Trinity in 1117. On the contrary, he is called to Cologne that same year to become the next abbot of Deutz. His commentary on the Rule, however, does carry the title *Liber de apologeticis suis*[97] because, once again, he sees the need to justify himself. This time he faces "teachers," several of whom are "bishops" attracting flocks of students "in France." They scoff disdainfully at his lowliness. *Quis est hic?* "Who is he?" they ask mockingly. Rupert responds as a disciple of Saint Benedict: *Ego sum pauper*, "I am poor." Indeed he does not have enough money to buy parchment for writing, so he thanks Cuno for having procured some at his own expense. But if he did not possess any material good, at least he could say: *Sed vidi sapientiam Dei*, "But I saw God's wisdom." His visionary talents are all his wealth. In weaving his apology for his life with his account, he affirms having seen the Word incarnated under the appearance of a body formed of gold from which water was flooding out through some sort of pipes. To explain this vision, he looks for parallels in the Bible, in Job (30,

10), Isaiah (45, 7), Proverbs (8:17–21), and Ecclesiastics (24:44). The interpretation of the vision conforms to the familiar mode of exegesis.

In fact, it resembles a type of interpretation found in chapter 21 of the *Opusculum*: a signifier is given for each image. Gold is the symbol for heaven and the divinity that resides there. The streams of water that spout out from Christ's body are the salutary waters of paradise. Water symbolizes the Holy Spirit. The live waters are the gifts of the Holy Spirit. They come from the interior of the body, the soul, where God resides. This vision and its interpretation may seem conventional, but they do not characterize all of Rupert's experience. Other accounts have a more personal tonality.

In the prologue to his commentary on the Song of Songs Rupert justifies the title he gives his work (*De incarnatione Domini*). It is in homage to the Virgin, an idea that came to him in a dream "several years ago, when I was young" (*ante annos aliquot cum essem junior*). His propensity for dreaming was already well known, to the point that he would be teased for it . . . Seeing him, a brother said one day: *Ecce somniator*, "Here is the dream-man!" He was sitting in the solitude of night when two verses (*versiculos*) extolling the miracle of the Annunciation and the virginity of Mary crossed his mind. "Having returned to me" (*reversus ad me*), Rupert felt again the urgency of writing a work that would carry the title: "the incarnation of the Lord." Several lines later, Rupert moves on to this other title, which goes back "to the same period": a young brother said to him that he saw in a dream Christ sitting on his altar surrounded by the college of saints with Rupert himself holding the Song of Songs in his hand. It is a clear sign of the will of the heavens, yet Rupert neglects it until Abbot Cuno prevents him from sleeping in order to force him to write this book, which he can now dedicate to Abbot Cuno.

This introduction is immediately followed by the commentary on the Song of Songs itself. Holding to standard practice, Rupert follows the order of the text, verse by verse. The tradition of exegesis has for a long time sublimated the carnal images of this love song to terms of spiritual contemplation. But the sensual language is there and the images exercise a profound influence on the monk's imagination. Indeed they awaken Rupert's memories of stunning nocturnal visions. When he arrives at Song of Songs 5:4, "My beloved put his hand through the hole of the door, and my bowels were moved," he begins by duly questioning the terms of the poem: what is this "hand," this "hole," this "touching," this "moved"?[98] But he does not answer point by point, as one might expect. Changing discursive modes completely, he recounts a vision, and immediately afterward, he tells another. Let us listen:

> In our time, a young girl (*adulescentula*) one night saw something like a hand (*similitudinem manum*) reach down from the top of her bed while she was barely awake, or not sleeping at all, and touch her breast. The touch of this hand, which seemed to be a right hand, was most soft. Grabbing it with her two hands, she caressed it by making the sign of the cross. She caressed it all over and the hand seemed to enjoy this (*delineamentis*). After having made the hand feel the delights of this saintly sign, the young girl reached for the arm, then the person (*personam*) whose hand she still held. But the hand began to move about and shake rapidly, smoother than oil, more lively than a bird's feather, and by its movement she understood that the hand did not want to be caught. This same adolescent, that is, the soul, remembered that she was destined for a wedding and for nuptial chants since the Beloved, making himself visible in a night vision, advanced his hand on her breast as if passing through the hole of a door, and captured her inner heart, restraining it for some time with a light squeeze, and the heart exulted with ineffable joy, leaping and dancing between the hands.[99]

Without transition, Rupert immediately adds this second account:

> Furthermore, on the subject of this trembling, this healthy and divine trembling, she [the adolescent] reported this event that happened to her: in a church, she stared (*aspiciebat per visum*) at an image of Christ fixed on the cross at a great height, where it is customarily placed for people to pray and adore it. Since she was looking at it more intensively, the image looked alive to her, like a royal image with radiant eyes and a noble appearance. Then the Beloved deigned to detach his right hand from the cross and, with a magnificent expression, he made the sign of the cross she was watching. This was not a purposeless vision; on the contrary, to she who was watching, she immediately understood the meaning of such a great miracle (*virtus*). For then, just as the leaf of a tree trembles in a strong wind, so for a while she was shaken in her little bed with a gentle trembling, a really pleasant and extremely smooth trembling.[100]

Here, Rupert, as if he had forgotten to be precise, reverts back for a moment to the time of the dream immediately preceding the waking of adolescence:

> In this dream (*in ipso visu*), before she awoke, the strength (*virtus*) of the aforementioned sign [of the cross] elevated the one who, faster and more ably than it is possible to say, saw her outreached hands toward His hands fixed on the cross, in such a way that her mouth also seemed to move toward his mouth, and her whole body toward his body. And when awakened from her sleep she trembled for some time with a divine trembling, as has already been said, and this gave her great pleasure. Here in a few words is what I had to say of the experience (*experimentum*) of the hand, the touching, and the divine trembling.[101]

Rupert concludes his commentary on verses 5:4 of the Song of Songs with a last paragraph directly addressing the "Beloved of the unique Beloved" (*O dilecta dilecti singularis*): this account, he says, concerns "your person" (*de tua persona*): the obvious agitations (*ex istorum similitudine*) of this hand seen in the dream do not suffice to make her understand the greatness of what God is doing for her, which far exceeds the letter, meaning, and faculties of understanding.

At the beginning of his dream account Rupert seems to cite the testimony of an actual young girl, but as the account progresses, this *persona* loses her concrete reality and becomes identified with the Beloved of the Song, and eventually Rupert's soul. Rupert is simultaneously divided in two: from witness and third-person narrator he becomes the subject of the dream and of the account, opening his heart so that we may feel the quivering of his soul. The dream alone allows for the blurring of limits between the levels of reality. And only the dream allows for using these most carnal images to paradoxically suggest the strength (*virtus*) of a contemplation that thinks itself above meanings and understanding. The place of this rapture, where the fantastical experience of meanings mixes with divine contemplation, is the "little bed" (*in lectulo*). This "little bed" comes straight from the love poetry of the Song of Songs (3:1) and it entered very early on into the tradition of Christian rhetoric, running from Boethius to the mystics of the high Middle Ages, to signify the place of solitary meditation.[102]

That same year, 1125, Rupert begins a third work: his commentary on the Gospel according to Matthew, entitled *De Gloria et honore Filii Hominis super Mattheum*, a work in which Walter Berschin saw "the autobiography of Rupert of Deutz."[103] Once again, Rupert will dedicate this oeuvre to his protector and friend Cuno of Siegburg, who has in the meantime become the bishop of Regensburg. The thirteen-book commentary follows the order in Matthew, but Rupert successively distinguishes four phases in the Gospel illustrating the four Christological mysteries of the *incarnatio* (books I–IX), the *passio* (books X–XI), the *resurrectio*, and the *ascensio* (books X–XI). At the heart of this treatise is book XII, which corresponds exactly to the moment when Jesus expired on the cross. But Rupert skips over Matthew 27:32–50, precisely those verses that relate to the crucifixion. These verses are a sort of blind spot in the commentary, a silence that Rupert fills by speaking of himself and his visions instead. He does this by evoking on the one hand his own inner sufferings, his doubts and hopes, and his indescribable love for Jesus on the cross, in whom he places all his hopes. It is by suspending his exegetical commentary and replacing it with his visionary experience that Rupert manages to accede to the transcendental truth of the sacrifice of the Savior. Book XII alone comprises no less than nine consecutive accounts[104] of personal visions written in the first person. These personal visions are, however, considerably different from the many visionary accounts that Rupert gives in his other works: here he does not hide behind the anonymity of another brother or the adolescent figure of his soul. Moreover, Rupert associates the interpretation of these dreams to their *narratio* in order to help Cuno.[105] Another remarkable characteristic is the avalanche of visions that follow immediately after one another: even more than in his commentary on the Song of Songs, the dreams tie in with one another at a rapid, almost panting, pace and Rupert indicates their stages and length ("in the same time," "at dawn the next morning," "the third day"). Barely awake, Rupert falls back asleep and experiences new dreams.

The dreams in question go back to 1117–1118, a period full of adversity for Rupert and before his return to Siegburg and his new departure for Cologne. One of these dreams predicted that he would die eight years later.[106] In 1125, seven years have already passed and Rupert now lives awaiting his imminent death.

The series of dream accounts seems to have been set off by Rupert's recollection of the prophet Ezekiel's vision of the Tetramorphe (I, 10) and by the commentary on it by Saint Jerome. Rupert explains that he remembers having groaned as he discovered this text when he was "a child or young adolescent" (*puer sive adolescentulus*).[107] Once more, a gradual shift takes place from the representation of childhood, an age of innocence, to the representation of the soul, the subject of divine revelation. He takes the words of the prophet and makes them his own: "I was sitting on the banks of the river Chobar," which signifies "despondency and distress."[108] So, Ezekiel says, "the heavens opened up and I saw the visions of God." "What is there similar to this?" Rupert asks. Immediately, he offers an assured answer: "My eyes opened up and I saw the Son of God."[109] He is a new Ezekiel, but his vision is fully Christian: it is Christ in person whom he saw when he seized a wooden crucifix:

Awake, I saw him, the Son of Man, alive and on the cross. I did not see him with my corporeal eyes for, at the moment of seeing, my eyes immediately fainted, but better eyes opened up; that is, my inner eyes opened while I was holding the wooden cross on my breast, kissing it and the image of the same Savior that was on it. I was secretly seated behind the holy altar in a church of Saint Mary forever Virgin, and in the clarity of dawn I fixated on the image, adored it and covered it with many kisses and stayed seated with frequent bowings of the head. I had the habit of doing this, but on this day, at dawn, I was all broken in the humility of the spirit. What aspect do we see in him? The human language cannot express it in words and I will only say that I briefly understood what he himself says in truth: "learn of me; for I am gentle and lowly in heart" [Matthew 11:29], which is what the apostle truly says of him: "he was heard for his godly fear" [Hebrews 5:7]. His face bowed down in a marvelous and ineffable fashion and the light in his eyes meant that he accepted the kisses and adoration of the one who was adoring and kissing him. This only lasted a moment. Returning to the common vision, I placed the cross back on the altar. An ineffable taste, the taste of his sweetness would stay in the mouth of my soul for some time, inducing me to remember this verse: "O taste and see that the Lord is good!" [Psalms 34:8].[110]

This is followed by other scriptural citations and an emotive eulogy on Saint Augustine's *Confessions* where Rupert believes to have found the consolation to which he aspires. He invokes the Trinity and the name of God against his "invisible enemies" whose threatening presence he feels around him. "At this same time" he has a "memorable vision." Full of sadness because of these demonic attacks, he falls asleep at the hour of prayer when, suddenly, "half awake" (*semivigilans*) in his "little bed," he sees a vivid light cast upon him and he hears coming from the church the sounds of the bell calling everyone to prayer. He sees himself (*visus sum*) leave his bed and run to prayer. He hears chants in the church, but a demon lying in wait at the door forbids him entry and throws himself on him, which awakens Rupert from his sleep . . .[111]

For the entire day he is steeped in a deep sadness. At dawn the next day he finally falls asleep, but at the usual hour of prayer:[112]

> Since I was sleeping lightly, I saw, as I did the night before, a sign pushing me toward prayer. I awoke and ran to the church, and there the church was filled with a crowd of many different orders, principally monks, and a hoary bishop conducting the mass as if a solemn festival were taking place. A great procession of venerable people of both sexes seemed to climb toward the offertory and after the Gospel in order to make an offering to the holy sacrifice. I ran, as if to ask for one of these offerings. And there standing at the right corner of the altar were three persons so venerable in their countenance and their dignity that no words can describe them. Two of these were very aged, their hair all white, and the third was young and beautiful and could be recognized by his habit as being of royal dignity. One of these people, as I have said, who was very pleasant by the venerable whiteness of his hair and the calmness of his face, took me by the hand and kissed my hand saying several words that I no longer recall but that concerned the office and the service of writing. The royal person, this handsome young man, said not a word, but looked at me with a very fraternal affection, with the respect and dignity of a brother, and with a calm and moderate face, a look that penetrated my heart. Only afterward, but not at the moment, did I recognize them to be the Holy Trinity, and the young man the Son of God.[113]

Indeed it was at this moment that the evil spirits pounce on Rupert from both sides, drag him before the altar, and begin shoving their pointed fingers in his sides. Listening to the advice of the other two persons, Rupert calls out to Jesus for help. Jesus then climbs the steps of the altar and comes to free Rupert. The three persons of the Trinity then open a great book on the altar, place Rupert upon it and raise him high above. The one who kissed his hand in the beginning of the vision tells him to fear nothing. He shows Rupert the golden reliquary of a saint on the altar and assures him that he is even "better" than the saint . . . The clarity of his vision reminds Rupert of Saint Paul's quote about being delighted in the third heaven: "His face was indescribably clear: 'whether in the body or out of the body I do not know, God knows' (2 Corinthians 12:2)." In his vision, he knows that he ran out of his "little bed" and into the church, for he sees himself naked and unclothed and hastens to return to his bed. And thus he awakens.

Rupert holds Cuno witness to the manifest meaning of his dream, which he need not explain in detail: the vision of the book of Holy Scriptures and of the relics of saints are the promise of divine consolation. Nevertheless, he laments his own fate, as does Job: "He" (God) laughed at his sufferings, but Rupert does not hold it against him, he forgives him (*non imputo illi, jamduadum enim condonavi*), even if, in the following days, his face carries the mask of affliction.[114] Once again Rupert has a vision (*visus quippe mihi*): the Ancient One appears to him seated behind the altar; he holds a cross, the sign of a great pain, and, like a father full of goodness, he extends to him his right hand: " 'Friend, he says to Rupert, do to me as I have done to you.' And right then I slapped his hand to confirm my pardon so violently and so suddenly that he, in turn, squeezing me with force, pulled me completely toward him in order to hug and kiss me. Without delay, the extreme intensity of this holy and divine pleasure pulled me out of my sleep."[115]

These things are not "childish," Rupert assures us. One has to forgive the wrong that is done to us because we ourselves have sinned. Then Rupert begins longing to leave this valley of tears, as Christ did, so as to attain the joy of the vision of God.

"Father, he says to Cuno, I will recount as you have implored me to do how 'he' [God] scoffed at my sorrow and consoled me." Reminding us that he is commenting on the Gospel of Saint Matthew, Rupert describes how, on the night of Saint Matthew's feast day, a venerable man appeared before him looking at him in a familiar way, but refusing to let his hand be kissed. "You will die in eight years," he said twice. Hearing this, Rupert awakens.[116] He calculates that seven years have gone by since this dream and that the eighth has begun . . . Rupert, "converted in himself" (*converses in me*),[117] meditates every day more intensely on death. He reads Saint Augustine's *City of God* and prays to the Trinity that he be enlightened and visited. He has already spoken of his vision of the three persons of the Trinity and, more specifically, of the Son. He must also recount the vision he had of the third person, the Holy Spirit.[118] He was lying down half asleep in his "little bed" when he saw himself descend the stairs of the brothers' dormitory. A multitude of evil spirits with cruel faces stood up against him like a fortress. A single word came to his mind: "Holy Spirit." As soon as the word was uttered, the demons, who cannot stand hearing this word, fled in chaos. But they come back charging and Rupert flees to a meadow closed off by columns (might this be a dream image of the cloister?). An old man holding a cane in his hand awaits him and calls to him: "'godson, godson,' in the name given by godfathers to the children they hold at the baptismal font." Rupert recognizes the Holy Spirit who takes him under his protection and, with great wings, makes him some shade in front of an immense fire, the fire that the Lord lit on earth.

During "the same days," Rupert's faith in the Holy Spirit is reinforced by numerous other visions.[119] While sleeping lightly at the beginning of a period of fasting, Rupert gets the feeling that he is talking to a friend. Rupert confesses to this friend that he is preparing for death. He sees the sky open up before him and there, at a phenomenal speed, "an apparition of luminous talent, heavier than gold and sweeter than honey," and of an enormous weight, comes down and penetrates his chest. And it begins to move within him, and circulate, becoming bigger and heavier and flooding Rupert's soul and heart in abundant waves. After this, it calms down little by little and Rupert's chest empties out. In the end, Rupert makes out the substance of the talent, which is gold. The only explanation he takes from all of this is that he will die within the year.[120]

In the following pages, Rupert turns from visionary discourse to spiritual considerations on his doubts and hopes. He speaks of his soul, which he again calls "my adolescent" (*adolescentula mea*).[121] Then, for Cuno's sake, he returns to the conditions under which, following a dream, he long ago accepted to become a priest. This dream is therefore much older than the ones he has just recounted. It goes back to 1108. For Rupert it is the crucial dream, one that is equivalent to the "dream of conversion" of most monastic authors, the dream that decided the meaning of his life. He was sleeping lightly in his "little bed" when he saw himself standing before the altar. On the altar stood the Lord's cross bearing the image of the Savior.

> As I watched it attentively, I recognized the crucified and living Lord who watched me with opened eyes. When I realized this, I bowed my face toward Him and said: "Blessed is he who comes in the name of the Lord." He received this salutation with such humility and by bowing

His head so nobly that I could say nothing other than that which the inner man can understand, but by seeing it and what He truly said about Himself: "Learn of me, for I am gentle and humble in heart." But this was not enough for me, I had to grab it by the hand and hold it in order to kiss it. But how would I do this? The altar was too high for me to reach it. When He saw what were my thoughts and my wishes, He desired it too. I understood that He wished it when, as a sign of His will, the altar split open in the middle and allowed me to run in. I entered in haste and I grabbed the one "whom my soul loves" [Song of Songs 1:7]. I held Him, hugged Him, and kissed Him for a long time. I felt the joy He received from this gesture of love when, during my kiss, He opened His mouth so that I might kiss Him even more deeply.[122]

In support of his dream, Rupert cites the Song of Songs (8:1–2). He gives the meaning of his dream as he interpreted it after awaking in the night: the opening of the altar and the mouth of the Lord signifies the depth of the sacraments and the diffusion of priestly love within his spirit. Immediately, he gets up and goes to tell his spiritual father that he can no longer wait and that he accepts ordination as a priest.[123]

Thirty days later, however, another divine sign comes to him.[124] At the end of the day, Rupert is once again resting in his "little bed." His eyes barely closed, he sees bending over him "the appearance of a man" hiding his face. This appearance enters inside of him and quickly fills his whole interior being, much faster even than a seal pressed with the greatest strength would penetrate the softest wax. Rupert awakens and feels a very light weight giving him great pleasure. "What can I say? 'My soul was liquefied' [Song of Songs 5:6]." And Rupert carries on with a sort of hymn on the pleasures of the soul. And again he addresses Cuno to thank him for his spiritual direction.

Contrary to what he thought he understood in his dream, Rupert did not die that year, in 1125, but only four years later, several months after describing the fire he witnessed in the abbey and town of Deutz. Such an event is a sign of God, an omen whose eschatological dimension can leave no doubt. It is thus no surprise that Rupert is stricken with a new, and final, vision, one for which he again finds the time to tell his brothers[125]: he sees himself filled with hope and fear appearing before the throne of the supreme Judge. Behind him, he feels the greedy presence of a pack of demons. He climbs the steps that lead up to the throne, where Christ is seated and surrounded by "senators" and "princes" of the kingdom of God. Rupert prostrates himself on the ground and awaits the verdict. But he awakens without knowing whether he will be saved or not . . .

One could say that Rupert of Deutz dreamt his life as much as he lived it. Through dreams, his conscious existence finds a means to expand in all sorts of directions. They also allow him to sound the depths of his soul—his "young adolescent"—by putting him in direct contact with the divine persons who hold his destiny in their hands: the Holy Spirit (whose elderly looks could also suggest the Father), and especially the Son the Savior. Rupert's dream experience follows the course of time: throughout his life it accompanies the development of his writings. It also commands a return to past memories, "eight years ago," or even eighteen, recalling the dream of his ordination as a priest in 1108 when Rupert was approximately thirty-three years old, the same age that Christ was when he suffered the Passion . . . But the dream experience also projects him into the future: that of his death foretold and of last things.

The appearances seen in the dream are "ineffable," Rupert says, for they raise the "eyes of the soul," and not the "eyes of the body." Nevertheless, the perceptible impressions mingle strangely with the "spiritual vision." And whether they concern the specifics on the "little bed" of the dreamer, his "semi-awake" state, the feeling of being transplanted in a dream to familiar places in the monastery, or the substitution of a wooden crucifix that he took from the altar for an immaterial crucifix that he hugs and kisses avidly, all of these accounts of dreams unfurl in a total ambiguity between body and soul, between spiritual joy and the pleasures of the senses. And the happiness of the celestial vision that excites the soul lasts some time after he awakens: "As soon as I was awakened from my light sleep I felt the same soft weight that I had enjoyed the night before, but what could I say?" Then the interpretation of the dream can begin: "since I came back to myself and I recalled this very soft vision during the night vigils, I gave it this interpretation."[126] But the interpretation is often shortened: Rupert does not have a didactic plan to develop, he confides in his protector and friend Cuno of Siegburg, who understand Rupert's thoughts without needing them spelled out. In any case, it is the "global" mode of interpretation that is sketched out here, not the analytical commentary treating each dream motif one by one.

In many ways, the personal dreams that Rupert of Deutz describes resemble those of other contemporary monks, including Guibert of Nogent and, before him, Otloh of Saint-Emmeran: they all share a fantastical imagination that appears to be marked by the stamp of a strong and singular personality, a personality that must confront both a surrounding hostility and the drama of an inner crisis. The theme of a spiritual "conversion" linked to some of the most important choices in life—adhering to monastic reform, accepting priestly ordination—is at the center of this dream-filled exuberance as well as the need to confide in writing.

The Confession of the Dream

The number of dreams that Rupert recounts greatly exceeds the confessions of the dreamers mentioned earlier. This surge in confessionary dreams fore-shadows the "dream autobiography" of Gerald of Barri (or of Wales) (1146–1223). This archdeacon of Saint-David dreamed until the end of his life of becoming a bishop, but this never happened. In his heavily autobiographical works, the *De invectionibus* (1200–1216) and the *De rebus a se gestis* (1208–1216), written at the age of sixty or seventy, he lists in almost continuous succession more than thirty dreams—his own as well as those of others that concern him—which he interprets as omens favorable to his Episcopal election. He also finds in them motifs for consolation in the adversity he feels victim to, as well as promises of future rewards for his great merits, if not in this world at least in the next.[127]

In order to stay in a period and region closer to Rupert of Deutz and Herman's *Opusculum*, it is more befitting to establish a comparison with the visionary writings of the Rhineland nuns Hildegard of Bingen (1098–1179) and Elizabeth of Schönau (c. 1129–1164). In three of Hildegard's works, the *Liber Scivias* (*Know the Ways*) (1141–1151), the *Liber operum divinorum* (1163–1170), and the *Liber vitae meritorum* (1165–1174), she analyzes her own visions as prophetic texts that call for an exegetical interpretation. This close relation between vision and exegesis connects her to Rupert. But in contrast to Rupert, Hildegard does not have dreams for she even defends herself to the last against any such notion in the prologues to all her works. She says she experienced her "spiritual visions" while in a state of consciousness and in full possession of her reason. The miniatures that represent her receiving the divine inspiration show her not in a position of dreamer, but wide awake, seated and writing down dictations from heaven.[128]

In 1175 and 1176, Abbot Guibert of Gembloux and the Cistercian monks of Villiers ask her about the nature of her visions: "Did you contemplate these visions in dreams while sleeping, or while awake in a full state of consciousness?"[129] Hildegard replies by saying once again that her spiritual visions have nothing in common with the dreams experienced in sleep and the dark of the night.[130] She mistrusts dreams that are inspired by the devil, *fantasmata*, diabolical illusions that enter into the mind during sleep when the vigilance of reason lets down its guard. And she also insists on the fact that she received her visions in "open" places, not secret ones: she has witnesses, like her faithful secretary Volmar. Rupert of Deutz also notes the "incommensurable distance" between "dreams of man" and the "prophetic words of God."[131]

Hildegard introduces a clear distinction, not only between dreams and spiritual visions, but also between visions and the "ecstasies of the mind," the latter of which she did not have. These ecstasies do, however, characterize her contemporary and correspondent Elizabeth of Schönau. Elizabeth and her brother Eckbert were, through their mother, the grand-niece and grand-nephew of the bishop Eckbert of Munster, whom the *Opusculum* accords an important role in Herman's conversion. Like Hildegard's visionary works, Elizabeth's *Liber visionum*[132] is rich in biographical specifics: Elizabeth says she was "visited" for the first time by God at the age of twenty-three, 31 May 1152 (and not at the age of five like Hildegard); according to the testimony of her brother, her visions only came to an end with her death on 18 June 1165. They would have thus lasted in total "13 years and 18 days." Whereas Hildegard imposes a logical order on her visions and commentaries, thus constructing veritable theological treatises out of them, Elizabeth recounts hers in simple chronological order and to the rhythm of the liturgical feasts that occasioned them. She gives particular attention to the concrete conditions of her visions, the vicissitudes of their unfolding, and to the spatial-temporal facts of the encounter with the supernatural. The subjective experience, restored in a concrete and lived reality, is more important for her than making theological statements. In this sense, Elizabeth provides a better comparison than Hildegard does to monks such as Otloh, Guibert, and Rupert.

Nevertheless, like Hildegard, Elizabeth defends herself against the notion of telling dreams: she does, however, evoke ecstasies, or "abductions of the mind" that Hildegard excludes. She is not ignorant of diabolic fantasies either, fantasies that Hildegard sets aside by definition since she only has experiences of divine inspiration that are "true." For example, on the feast of Saint-Maximin, at complines, and again at matins, *fantasmata* assail her first under the appearance of a little monk, then a monstrous man, then a terrifying dog, and finally, right before mass, a "big and terrible bull."[133] According to her account, Elizabeth did not dream this: it is during a wakeful state that she withstood the assault of these "illusory spirits."[134] But immediately after, she indicates that she was "happy in ecstasy" and received the refreshing vision of the Virgin accompanied by two angels, Saint Benedict, and a celestial "young man."[135] The ecstasy thus comes while Elizabeth is awake. She comes out of it, however, with a feeling of awakening, as if she was leaving a sort of sleep at the moment when her mind reunited with her body, from which it had seemed to be momentarily separated.[136] But Elizabeth insists that the ecstasy is associated neither with sleep nor with dreams.

Hildegard of Bingen, Elizabeth of Schönau, and Rupert of Deutz represent three essential and contrasting modalities of the "spiritual vision" in twelfth-century visionary literature: Hildegard, perfectly awake and master of all her intellectual faculties, receives a visual and auditory revelation of divine mysteries and final ends; this revelation is unfurled in the form of vast symbolic, theological, and prophetic expositions that relegate the account of the circumstances of the vision to the background. With Elizabeth, on the contrary, even if the symbolic interpretation remains important, the attention she gives to the subjective experience is stressed more; it culminates in the description of the momentary separation of mind and body, something Hildegard explicitly excludes. Neither Hildegard nor even Elizabeth (who nonetheless has visions of the Devil) admit to having dreamt. This is not the case with Rupert, who for the most part speaks only about visions dreamt or perceived in the uncertain and deceiving in-between of a half sleep. I think that if Rupert, like Gerald of Barri after him, does not exclude the dream, but on the contrary gives it a quasi-exclusive place in his accounts, it is not only because he hopes to speak most faithfully about himself and what he has felt, it is because he is able to do so. Because of their rank in the Church and their gender, Otloh of Saint-Emmeran, Rupert of Deutz, and Guibert of Nogent each wield the authority necessary to tell their dreams without attracting suspicions of having given into diabolical illusions. Dreams and autobiography go together in the discovery of a Christian subject, one who can only think under the active watch of God. A Hildegard or an Elizabeth does not escape from the contemporary conjuncture of the "discovery of the subject"—an expression that seems to me more precise than "discovery of the individual."[137] But contrary to Abbots Guibert of Nogent or Rupert of Deutz, these nuns insist on not speaking about their dreams (though they must surely have dreamt as well!) out of fear of being accused of falling prey to *fantasmata*.

In speaking of visions or ecstasies (and it is not impossible that their experiences were different from those of men), they can confront the truth of their revelations. Everything reminds these women of their subordinate situation, even when they claim to benefit directly from the prophetic or ecstatic revelations of God. Hildegard does not stop professing her humility and lack of education—"wretched am I and I am more than wretched in my womanly role," she writes to Bernard of Clairvaux—while at the same time impressing us with her tremendous knowledge. This speaks less of herself than of the divine Wisdom that holds her fully in its power and which supposedly speaks through her. As with Elizabeth of Schönau, does the rhetoric of ecstasy not consist of a momentary loss of personality when the spirit becomes separated from the body? Ecstasy also opposes the full discovery of the self. Only Rupert shows himself as he is, a man who dreams in his "little bed" and, thanks to dreams, discovers that he is the stake in the battle between good and evil, between God and the Devil.

If we have just explored the multiple uses, and even refusals, of dreams in Christian literature of the Middle Ages, it is for the purpose of finally returning to Herman. The fact that the *Opusculum* accords such an important place to the child's dream, a first step toward an eventual conversion, should not come as a surprise to us: we have sufficiently seen how profound the link was between autobiographical writing, conversion, and dreams. It is true that the initial—if not initializing—role of the dream at the start of the *Opusculum* gives it a particular setting. And this is just as true as the fact that the investiture ritual that is the object of the dream is inscribed in a hierarchic system of rites and values that underlie the entire *Opusculum*. I see in it the sign of a particularly careful construction of an account that is also confirmed by the placement in final position of the interpretation and the analytic character that it possesses. Nevertheless, without necessarily doubting that an authentic lived experience might be the origin of this account, the rhetorical elaboration of the dream-interpretation pair, distributed between the beginning and the end of the work, disguises the more direct expression of a singular personality that is attested during the same period by Otloh of Saint-Emmeran, Guibert of Nogent, and Rupert of Deutz, but with completely different dramatic intensity. Herman offers a first-person *account* of the story of a dream. Otloh and Rupert tell *their dreams* and share with us fantastical experiences, shifting and confusing images, strange voices, the confusion of time, and the frustration of an awakening that comes and interrupts it all.

Chapter 4

Conversion to Images

The Critique of Christian "Idols"

When Herman takes up the account of his conversion in chapter 2 of the *Opusculum*, seven years have passed since his boyhood dream. Now about twenty years old, he is sent by his father to get from Bishop Eckbert of Munster (1127–1132) repayment of a loan that the young man had thoughtlessly made to the prelate without security. The bishop had needed the money in order to cover expenses for a stay in Mainz where Emperor Lothar's court was temporarily residing. This motive appears to be entirely made up for the purpose of the account, since neither Lothar nor Eckbert seem to have stayed in Mainz during 1127 or 1128. On the other hand, it fits well in the narrative plan of the work: beyond the control of his parents living in Cologne, Judas would have arrived in Mainz on the occasion of a fair and shown excessive generosity toward the bishop, an obvious sign of a favorable disposition toward a future conversion. Historians have doubted the historical likelihood of this loan, for although it was normal for a bishop to call upon Jewish moneylenders, it was unlikely that a loan be made without security and without interest. As is said in the *Opusculum*, this act is contrary to the custom (*mos*) that the security represents double the value of the loan.[1] But in the logic of conversion, which is the logic of the *Opusculum*, this generous loan to a bishop appears as a positive sign that helps presage the favorable events that follow. It shows Judas's predisposition to Christian charity. As for the security that satisfies him, this is to be found in the bishop's reputation for *fides*, for "good faith" in business, in anticipation of the recognition of his Christian "faith." The ambiguity of the text is clear and allows one to predict the destiny of the future convert.

For "twenty weeks" Judas waits to be reimbursed under the watchful eye of his aged relative Baruch who is charged with looking after him. Already, he is attracted by the sermons of the bishop, all the more since he recognizes in the passages of the Old Testament the Jewish books of the Bible that he remembers well. What is completely new to the young man, on the other hand, are the typological commentaries that allow the New Testament to illuminate the Old, and the Old the New. Discussions with the bishop and his clerical entourage begin to teach him about the Christian religion and stir his desire to go further. It is with these inclinations, and pushed by his own "curiosity," that Herman one day enters the cathedral of Munster.

Until that point, the cathedral of Saint Paul was for him but a "pagan temple" (*delubrum*). He had painstakingly examined the interior appearance, the "sculpted devices" and the "variety of paintings," but these only reinforced his prejudices. Things turned scandalous when he finally saw a "monstrous idol" (*monstruosum quoddam ydolum*): the crucifix, though it is not named and is merely described as an unknown and unnamed object. The precision that Judas gives in his description is quite rare for a text of this period:

> Examining all things with great care, I saw among the sculptured devices and variety of paintings a monstrous idol. I discerned one and the same man humiliated and exalted, abased and lifted up, ignominious and noble. He was hanging wretchedly from high to low [or: underneath] on a cross, and from low to high [or: above] by the deceiving effects of the painting, he was sitting enthroned and as if deified. I admit I was stupefied, suspecting that effigies of this sort were likenesses of the kind common among the pagans. The doctrines of the Pharisees had, in the past, easily persuaded me that it was truly thus.

The deceptive "devices" of the Christian image confirm the young Jew in his judgment: the idol that faces him is among these "effigies" that are mere "likenesses" (*simulacra*), another name for idols. Herman employs the exact same words that the cleric Bernard of Angers, writing in the early twelfth century and with the same feeling of scandal, had used to describe the statue-reliquary of Sainte-Foy of Conques; Bernard had placed its legitimacy in doubt until the evidence of miracles accomplished by the saint through her reliquaries and her statue succeeded in convincing him otherwise. Bernard of Angers finally "converted to the image," just as young Judas will too.

Yet the translation of this passage in the *Opusculum* is not without difficulties. In two places, an alternative is possible, which I have signaled in brackets. In seeing in the adverbs *deorsum* and *sursum* only the two contrasting *states* ("underneath" and "above")—which medieval Latin permits—and not the two opposing movements ("from high to low" and "from low to high")—which would be closer to classical Latin—Karl F. Morrison deprives his English translation of a dynamic tension which I believe should be maintained. This option leads Morrison to distinguish two images: a sculpted crucifix on which Christ seems humbled, and a painting of Christ in majesty (*pictura*), where he is glorified.[2] This translation is perfectly legitimate. But we might prefer another, one that better takes into account the contradictory movement referred to by the text: thus a single "idol" would be replaced by "a one and the same man" (*unum eudemque hominem*) who is both humbled "from high to low" and exalted "from low to high."

Morrison's translation has several virtues. Archaeologically, it is perfectly plausible: it is the rule during this period to erect a crucifix in the axe of an apse covered with the mural painting of the *Majestas Domini* or the *Pantocrator*.[3] Additionally, the text does indeed seem to mention two distinct objects, the "idol" and the "painting." Better yet, the next phrase speaks of "effigies" (*effigies*) in the plural as being "likenesses" (*simulacra*), terms that could apply to a sculpture and a separate painting. And in fact, in the texts of this period, the word *effigies* can refer indiscriminately to paintings or sculptures, while the word *imago* instead designates, though not exclusively, sculptures.

In any event, the judgment passed here on these "sorts of likenesses" is general and not specific to the images Judas has before his eyes. It should also be pointed out that, traditionally, it is the sculpted images devoted to a cult that give rise to accusations of idolatry.[4] One might, then, consider the possibility that a single "idol," the crucifix, is under discussion here, held between two opposing movements. This proposed translation conforms to the clerical conceptions of the religious image in the beginning of the twelfth century.

Without claiming that this is a description of a crucifix that would really have existed in the Munster cathedral in the beginning of the twelfth century, we can connect it without difficulty to the great crucifixes of the period that have come down to us. There is, for example, the case of the famous *Gerokreuz* in the Cologne cathedral, one of the oldest monumental crucifixes still preserved. The date of around 970 for this large wooden sculpture is attested to by a passage in the early eleventh-century chronicle of Thietmar of Merseburg: having had it sculpted, the archbishop Gero of Cologne noticed that there was a crack in the head of Christ; he placed a consecrated host in the crack and it immediately closed up. This miracle clearly illustrates the innovative character and still uncertain legitimacy of such a three-dimensional sculpture: it demonstrates that its image is pleasing to Christ; better yet, the introduction of the consecrated host into the wood assures the real presence of Christ in the image and thus transforms it into a miraculous image, one none other than the "true" *Corpus Christi*. Just as the relics contained in the *majestas* of Sainte Foy help the statue benefit from the devotions traditionally offered to the relics, so too was the crucifix of Cologne, thanks to the archbishop's deed, able to benefit from the Eucharistic cult.

I would especially like to focus on the crucifix of Benninghausen (near Soest, in proximity to Munster), which was sculpted in Cologne around 1070–1080.[5] Although a century later than the Cologne *Gerokreuz*, the two share many formal characteristics. We can indeed recognize in this sculpture the tension between these two contradictory movements of exaltation and humiliation spoken of by the *Opusculum* (fig. 1). Is this tension between opposing forces, "from high to low" and "from low to high," not more generally characteristic of what Meyer Schapiro has called the "esthetic attitudes" of the Romanesque period?[6] Jean-Claude Bonne has called attention to the strong presence of these "esthetic attitudes" in the sculpted tympanum of Autun, and more specifically in the central figure of Christ of the Parousia, who seems to be seated on his throne (*deorsum*, we might say) while at the same time standing up and already climbing (*sursum*) toward the eternal Father.[7] Written texts of this period are not unaware, moreover, of what seems to be a fundamental paradigm, one not only of plastic figuration, but of moral and ideological representation as well. In his *Institutio novitiorum* of the same period, Hugh of Saint Victor specifies what the ideal gestures of novices in the abbey should be[8]: their *modus*, or positive aspect, consists of the perfect balance produced by two negative, but contrary, movements that cancel each other out. The virtuous gesture must be both gracious, but not too soft, and severe, but without agitation; calm, but without laxity, and mature, but not too forward; grave, but not slow, and quick, but not rash. The movements of the body, like the apparent movements of the sculpture going "from high to low" and "from low to high," exist in a tension between opposing forces that in effect characterize all moral life, for it is out of the contradiction of vices that virtue is born.

In the *Opusculum*, Judas describes the so-called idol of Christ as "monstrous." This seems to echo the famous description of Bernard of Clairvaux, who called the sculptures of the Cluniac cloisters "monstrous hybrids." Just as the crucifix of Munster was stretched in two directions at the same time, so too did the "monstrosity" of the Cluniac sculptures exist in the unnatural association, in the body of a single animal, of body parts belonging to different beasts—for example the paws of a quadruped and the tail of a snake. Worse yet, this monstrosity exists in a logical contradiction—"several bodies for one head or several heads for one body"—most splendidly expressed by Bernard's use of rhetorical balancing and the sound of Latin words (for which there is no equivalent in English): *"quid facit illa ridicula monstruositas, mira quaedam deformis formositas ac formosa deformitas?"* ("what is this ridiculous monstrosity, this astonishingly beautiful ugliness, this astonishingly ugly beauty?").[9] Under the pretext of denouncing the sculptures of the cloisters that present vain and worldly "distractions" to the monks, this language of contradictions in fact pays homage, almost in spite of itself, to the audacious beauty of the monstrous forms. And prior to being swept away by the spirit of Bernard of Clairvaux's austere reform, these hybrids made from the confrontation between animals and humans could be found in the illuminations of the first Cistercian manuscripts, the Bible of Stephen Harding, and the *Moralia in Job*. For what the miniatures of Citeaux at the turn of the eleventh-twelfth centuries expressed is what Conrad Rudolph has called a "spiritual struggle," one that went through the souls of the monks, the busy hands and eyes of copyists, and even the wide-open cloister. The turn of the century is placed under the sign of battle, between knights, between clergy and warriors, against infidels, heretics, and Jews, but mainly against sin. The most vivid tension is inherent to contemporary representations, in the admirable writings of Saint Bernard of Clairvaux as in the manuscripts of Citeaux. We encounter this tension again in the *Opusculum*, which exposes in a parallel fashion the apparent scandal of a so-called idol for the purpose, in the conclusion, of better proving its legitimacy.

The theme of the scandal of the crucifixion is, for that matter, far from new: the first and true scandal is that Jesus accepted the sacrifice of the cross, the most ignominious death, one that was reserved for slaves in the Roman Empire. Yet it is by this vile death that he proclaimed his kingdom, for what is scandalous in the eyes of humans is glorious in the eyes of God. But only

Christians can understand it: "blind" Jews keep to the appearances of the world. If Judas confesses his "stupefaction" (*Fateor, obstupui . . .*), it is because he still holds the crucifix as a representation of a criminal's punishment. He is still far from being able to understand what a general inversion of signs the coming of the Messiah called forth.

From the start, this Christian image stands between Jews and Christians as the first *palpable* hurdle that the future convert must overcome. In his confrontation with Christians, Judas is still advanced only up to the deceptive experience of the senses; He is deprived of all judgment, fit only for the "carnal" understanding of which a Jew would be capable. It is not yet the time for him to give into the "reasons" of his Christian mentors. But the path toward the anticipated conversion is well indicated by the *Opusculum*: starting at the end of chapter 2, Judas begins to engage in discussion with clerics. After having entered into the cathedral in order to *see*, he enters their school in order to *read* its books. Has his Jewish education prepared him for the reading, facilitating his learning of the Latin characters? Once again, the simple explanation is unconvincing. It is more necessary to understand the logic of the conversion narrative than to find the trace of a real experience (the possibility of which I do not deny) underlying the text.

Chapters 3 and 4 follow immediately and tell of the debate between Judas and the Abbot Rupert of Deutz. Anna Sapir Abulafia, however, believes that chapter 9, which describes the debate between Judas and the clergy of Cologne, fits better between chapters 2 and 3 and must have been moved at a later date. It therefore follows that the debate with Rupert would not have taken place at Munster, but at Cologne, which accords better with what we know about Judas's whereabouts.[10] In chapter 9 (or 2a if one prefers), Judas discusses with the clerics "in order to achieve knowledge of the [Catholic] truth." The discussion deals essentially with the Christian explanation of the Old Testament authorities. It is logical that the instruction of the young Jew begins there. The beginning of chapter 3 seems the logical follow-up to this debate. At Cologne (and not Munster), Judas calls upon Rupert of Deutz, who is reputed for his knowledge of "divine and humane letters," to answer his questions "with reason and authority."

Speaking first, Judas expresses his complaints about Christians to Rupert: they hate the Jews, despite the fact that the latter are God's chosen people. An avalanche of citations from the Old Testament (always cited from the Vulgate) proves Judaism's sound foundation. Christians, on the contrary, are unfaithful to the letter of Scripture: in order to break away from his pact with the latter, they claim to give these texts a "mystical" meaning; they correct them when they are inconvenient, or, worse yet, they see in them the "old wives' tales." This "foolish audacity" makes of the Christians the "cursed" ones. Judas takes up only "one fact among others": their "idolatry." And he describes his experience anew: he saw "with his own eyes" how "in your temples you place large images in the open, painted or sculpted with elaborate art," and how "you bring about your own downfall by [venerating] the image of a crucified man." Since Scripture curses "anyone hung on a tree" (Deuteronomy 21:23) as well as those who "make mere flesh their strength" (Jeremiah 17:5), it will be even more the case for those who place their hopes in a crucified man. Even worse, Judas adds, you Christians pride yourselves in this "superstition." Rupert is cornered: he must prove to Judas the "authority" of such a cult or else "shamefully confess that this error is contrary to sacred law and therefore should be condemned."

The arguments put forth by Judas are not those that could surprise a cleric involved in the Jewish-Christian debate of the period. They are common in contemporary texts and are equally present in Christian iconography of Jews and the Synagogue. In the Missal of Stammheim (written at Hildesheim around 1170),[11] the full-page images of Christ in Majesty and the crucifixion face one another (figs. 3, 4). This diptych recalls Judas's description of the "idols" he saw in the cathedral of Munster, particularly if one accepts that Judas distinguishes between two different images of Christ, and not just one. The presence of the Evangelists and the Prophets and the banderoles that provide an exegetical commentary within the image itself characterize their miniatures. Let us only focus on one figure: that of the Synagogue, which is recognizable by the pointed hat of the Jew. She stands above the cross and to the left of Christ, on the same side as the Moon (*Luna*), Death (*Mors*), and Night (*Nox*). Opposite is the crowned figure of the Church on the same side as the Sun (*Sol*), Life (*Vita*), and Day (*Dies*). The figure of the Church holds a phylactery inscribed with a quotation from the epistle to the Galatians (3:13): "Christ redeemed us from the curse of the law." It is precisely with a quotation from the Law, that is, the Old Testament, that synagogue replies: "anyone hung on a tree is under God's curse" (Deuteronomy 21:23), which is the exact biblical verse used by Judas in his debate with Rupert.

Let us not conclude too hastily that Judas's arguments only take up those that Christian polemicists have a habit of placing in the mouths of Jews. This is true, but one finds them too in the rabbinic writings against Christians.[12]

In the late twelfth century, Joseph Kimhi of Narbonne cites Exodus 20:4 in recalling the prohibition of images, and he draws from Deuteronomy 4:15 in order to insist on the fact that Yahweh spoke to Moses at Horeb without showing his face. One should therefore not represent God in an image. He also says that those who worship idols will "become like them" (Psalms 115 [113B] 8 and 135 [134]:18).[13]

Similarly, the anonymous *Nizzahon Vetus*,[14] dating to the late thirteenth century, develops the arguments of Jews from Exodus 20:4 (the second commandment), Numbers 21:9 (the bronze serpent), and Exodus 25:18–22 (the cherubim of the Temple). He asks why God allowed Moses to make the serpent out of bronze when He had forbidden all images. It concludes that God's intentions are unfathomable and that even when they seem contradictory one should not look for the reason why. One has to obey all divine orders without removing or adding anything. Yet the prohibition on the making of images "for oneself" had not been violated by the making of cherubim since they were intended for the Temple and not for personal use. He adds that Moses did not make the bronze serpent in order to worship it, but to edify the people. The accusation of idolatry brought against Christians is particularly harsh regarding Isaiah 42:8 ("I am the Lord, that is my name; my glory I give to no other, nor my praise to idols") and 46:7 ("If one cries out to it, it does not answer or save anyone from trouble").[15]

Some Jewish polemicists, though still denying that Christ is God, recognize that Christians do not really worship the wood of the cross. Christian authors ignore this concession on the part of their adversaries. This does seem, it is true, to be fairly isolated within a polemical literature where mutual incomprehension prevails. For example, at the time of the Paris controversy in 1240, between the apostate Nicholas Donin and four rabbis (Yehel of Paris, Vivo of Meaux, Judas of Melun, and Samuel ben Solomon or Moses of Coucy), these latter would have assured "that it is permissible to curse and scorn Christian idols."[16] It is on a similar radical position that Judas, in the third chapter of the *Opusculum*, confronts Rupert of Deutz. In the logic of the account, this is not surprising: the more Judas shows himself to be obstinate and hostile to the Christians and deaf to their arguments, the greater both his own merit will be in converting, as well as that of the Christians who will have known how to convince him. Among these, Rupert of Deutz, who responds to him throughout chapter 4, occupies a place of primary importance.

The "Reasons" for Christian Images

In his "response," Rupert is sure of himself and of the effectiveness of his demonstrations. The *Opusculum* has him too speaking in a direct style. The tone is sarcastic: he will have no difficulty in demonstrating to his adversary that what he calls "idolatry" is in fact "full of piety and religion." Rupert shows Judas that the Christian position is fully justified by the "authorities" of the Old Testament, which alone is recognized by Jews. He shows how well founded this is through "clear reasoning." His argumentation successively unfolds at two levels.

He first explains what he calls the "general reason of images" (*imaginum generalis ratio*). "We do not venerate as a divinity the image of the crucifix or any other thing; but under the form of the cross we represent with pious devotion the Passion of the Christ." Thus, "when in the likeness of the cross we give an exterior image of his death, we are inwardly burning with love for him and we continuously remember that he who was immune from all sin endured an ignoble death for us." Rupert thus takes great care in distinguishing the material form of the image from what it signifies, which alone is worthy of worship. But he insists even more on the fact that the crucifix inwardly enflames the one who looks at it and prays to it, awakening his "love" for Christ.

To these reasons, Rupert adds "particular" (*specialiter*) reasons for the "simple-minded," the "illiterate," the "people": images, notably the one of the crucifix, *represent* for them what clerics read in books.

Heretofore, Rupert's arguments are quite traditional. In his famous letter to the Bishop Serenus of Marseille, Gregory the Great had mainly justified the making and veneration of images in Christian worship in terms of their didactic function for the illiterate.[17] He added that it also allowed for the *recollection* of events in sacred history. Finally, he did not exclude more emotional purposes, since religious images, according to him, were conducive to feelings of *contrition*. In his letter to the Sardinian hermit Secundinus, which, since the eighth century, has been interpolated into the letter addressed to Serenus, giving the two the appearance of a single text, Gregory insists even more on the feelings of love that these images conjure up: the hermit having impatiently asked him for an icon, Gregory compares Secundinus to a lover who tries to hide himself in order to see the woman he loves pass by . . .[18]

The arguments with which Rupert opposes the Jew's critiques are therefore not original, but because they come from him, the evocation of the "fire of love" that burns "inwardly" within a cleric who looks at the crucifix does carry a decidedly personal flavor. If it is not Rupert who is really speaking in the *Opusculum*, it certainly seems so, for his reply to Judas appears to echo his own commentary of the Gospel of Matthew: we shall recall that Rupert had described himself behind the altar holding the crucifix in his arms, that he dreamed that Christ placed it on his body and lifted him up while he covered the Savior in kisses, retaining in his mouth the sweet taste . . .

Let us return to the ideas Rupert expresses in the *Opusculum*. He promised Judas that he would prove by the authorities of the Old Testament that the worship of images was already authorized therein. Jews are wrong not to recognize this. The authority chosen is Joshua 22: having succeeded Moses, whom Yahweh had forbidden from entering the promised Land, Joshua endeavors to have the twelve tribes of Israel cross the Jordan River. All the tribes will relocate to the other side of the Jordan, with the exception of "two and a half tribes" that were chosen at random. These are the tribes of Ruben and Gad and half the tribe of Menasseh, who live on the left bank of the Jordan (in Transjordan). Separated by the river from the other tribes, these two and a half tribes amass stones in an effort to build an altar. But it is not for a sacrificial altar, for there can only be one for all of Israel, and it is in Zion (where Jericho lies). The altar of the "two and a half tribes" only holds value as a "witness" (*testimonium*) to their belonging to the twelve tribes of Israel. It is thus that future generations will remember the random separation of the tribes. Using the rhetorical figure of the *similitudo*, Rupert gives the typological meaning of the biblical account: for just as this altar was to remind the separated tribes of their original unity with the twelve tribes of Israel, so too do we Christians have great respect for the image of Christ hanging on the cross because it reminds us of the sacrifice of the Passion. But we do not profess worship of the cross, for it is a material object. Worship is reserved for God. What the altar erected in Transjordan was for the "two and a half tribes," the cross is for Christians: a "witness," a pledge of redemption, a promise of the heavenly Jerusalem. Herman esteems that in this debate Rupert had countered the young Jew who he was at this time with the "most beautiful reasoning" and the "most solid authorities." For now, nothing changes: both "blind" and "deaf," Judas persists in his error.

The direct but improbable debate staged by the *Opusculum*, in which the young Jewish moneylender confronts the great Abbot Rupert of Deutz, who was near the end of his life and at the height of his fame as an exegete and monastic theologian, conforms to the now classic genre of a *Dialogue*

Between a Jew and a Christian. This genre flourished especially at the turn of the century. But it belongs to a much older tradition of intellectual polemics between Jews and Christians, one that can be traced back to Saint Paul's Epistle to the Galatians and to the Fathers of the Church.[19] For a long time, however, the question of images had only a small place in these debates. Even when, starting in the late eleventh century, it becomes more present, it never becomes a major question: the more important issues that are always debated are the Jewish refusal to recognize Christ as the Messiah or to accept belief in the Trinity, the cult of the Virgin, and the power of the Church.

The Council of Elvira (305–306) mentions the question of images only discretely among other more important points of disagreement between the two confessions. In the ninth century, the Archbishop Agobard of Lyons, who inveighs against the "Jewish superstition," notes that Jews reproach Christians for their idolatry. Agobard is personally interested in images, but his position on them is more reserved than most other Carolingian prelates. Against the iconoclasm of Bishop Claude of Turin, three prelates of importance—Bishop Jonas of Orleans, Abbot Dungal of Saint-Denis, and Walafrid Strabo, the abbot of Reichenau—take more "iconophile" positions than the theologians of the preceding generation (Theodolphus of Orleans and Alcuin) at the time of Charlemagne and the *Libri carolini*. Agobard remains rather loyal to the suspicion this earlier generation had regarding images; to justify this, he must distance himself from the Jews and their radical hostility toward all forms of representations of God and living beings. But for Agobard and others after him, the "Jews" who figure in these debates are less real beings than rhetorical figures in the service of a polemic internal to elite Christian intellectuals.[20]

From Gilbert Crispin to Petrus Alfonsi

At the end of the eleventh century, the polemic between Jews and Christians witnesses a shift in tonality and in certain cases acquires more reality, though it is difficult to be sure that a written *Dialogue* was the result of an actual debate. This question first appears in the *Disputatio Iudei et Christiani* written by Gilbert Crispin (d. 1117), abbot of Westminster. If Gilbert is to be believed, he would have indeed been involved in a discussion with a Jew from Mainz. In his dedicatory letter to the Archbishop Anselm of Canterbury, the abbot of Westminster explains that he had business relations with this Jewish merchant, whose knowledge he also esteemed. Afterward, Gilbert's monks asked him to put their debate into writing. The Rhineland origins and merchant activities of this interlocutor call to mind the dialogue between Judas of Cologne and Rupert of Deutz as it is staged in the *Opusculum*.

Of all the authors of anti-Jewish works between the end of the eleventh century and the beginning of the thirteenth (I count at least seventeen), only four in the early twelfth century mention a debate regarding images.

Gilbert Crispin's *Disputatio* most likely dates to before the First Crusade, around the years 1090–1095.[21] In comparison to later dialogues, this work is rather peaceful in tone. Dedicating the work to his teacher Anselm of Canterbury,[22] Gilbert Crispin asks of him authorization to issue the text more widely, for he has already been able to verify its beneficial effects. One Jew converted following one of the "disputes" that Gilbert had with his interlocutor. The debate between *Christianus* and *Iudaeus* deals with Christian observance of the Law, Christ, the Incarnation, the Virgin Mary, and whether Scripture predicted Jewish non-recognition of the Messiah in the person of Christ. *Christianus*'s quotation of Psalm 97 (96):7, "Let all worshipers of sculpted images be put to shame, those who glory in worthless idols," is turned against him by *Iudaeus*: the idolaters are Christians who "sculpt, make, and paint" images and "worship and profess a cult" in the crucifix. Christians, he adds, do not respect the explicit prohibition of Exodus 20:4: "You shall not make for yourself an idol." The exchange is pursued along Old Testament lines: the Book of Kings, the visions of Ezekiel and Isaiah allow *Christianus* to demonstrate that there were already images in the Temple and the Tabernacle, despite the prohibitions of the Pentateuch. How does one explain the apparent contradiction that "God forbade the making of sculptures, and yet, as we read it, sculptures were made by God's order"? It is that the Hebrews, like the Christians of today, offered to God paintings and sculptures, but without "worshiping" them as divine. To be sure, the verb *adorare* is ambiguous and Gilbert Crispin proposes a clear distinction between the "worshiping" of God alone and the "veneration," "cult," and "honor" addressed to images and paintings. Finally, he recommends to the Jew that he reread Scripture in order to grasp the true meaning and so that he may recognize that the Messiah, in accordance with the prediction of the Prophets, has already come in the person of Christ.

Guibert of Nogent, whose *monodiae* and dreams we have already examined, is also the author of a *Tractatus de Incarnatione contra Iudaeos*,[23] written around 1110. In contrast to Gilbert Crispin's work, this treatise only occasionally takes the form of a dialogue. On the other hand, the Christian argument is much more lively and even willfully injurious. Guibert's feelings toward Jews are fairly well known from what he says in his *Memoirs*, where he never misses the occasion to denounce a Jewish doctor for giving himself over to evil spells, another for serving as a go-between, or yet another for putting his poisonous gifts in the service of an evil Lord, the count of Soissons. He relates without any particular emotion the massacres of Jews at Rouen at the time of the First Crusade, lending his attention to just one child who was spared in order to be baptized. He also mentions that Jewish converts entered the monastery.[24] In his *Tractatus contra Iudaeos*, Guibert, like Gilbert Crispin before him, reproaches the Jews for accusing Christians of idolatry.[25] He too retorts that Christians do not worship the wood of the cross, but rather the invisible "substance" of God.

In another departure from Gilbert Crispin, Guibert introduces into the debate other Old Testament authorities for the purpose of showing that the Hebrews already knew forms of devotion prefiguring the Christian worship of images: in Joshua 7:6, Joshua prostrates before the Ark; in Daniel 6:11, Daniel turns toward Jerusalem three times a day, something that is also a form of veneration in front of a material object. Guibert does not fail to mention the most traditional arguments of the polemic: how to deny that the bronze serpent (Numbers 21:9) and the gold cherubim placed on the Ark (Exodus 25:18–22) are images?[26] Or let the Jews, then, stop "laughing" at the so-called idolatry of Christians: they are just as poorly placed to do this as their "relatives," who worshipped Belphegor, "that is Priapus." The issue of idolatry changes sides: Guibert doubles the accusation back against the others before explaining and justifying the Christian position. For this, he abandons the "authorities" in favor of "reason" (*qua ratione*). His argument contains three points:

- Images are only "visible signs"; they are not what we Christians worship, but rather the divine and invisible "signifieds." This theme is well known: Christians raise themselves from the *visibilia* to the *invisibilia*.
- The second argument is formulated in a more original way: the paintings that one often looks at allow one to "fix the wandering mind" and enjoin it to return to "inner things" (*ad interna*). Guibert tries to define rationally the dynamic relation between the perception of meaning and interiorized piety. What Rupert describes in his exegetical

commentaries as a personal and intense spiritual experience, Guibert attempts to express in the language of reason.

• Yet Guibert does not forget the inescapable lesson of Gregory the Great: images are aimed at different "publics": "we," that is monks, who have direct knowledge of Scripture, can bypass the world of images (*remota imaginatione*). On the other hand, images teach the illiterate what clerics read in books.

The *Dialogue Between Peter and Moses* written around 1110 by the convert Petrus Alfonsi is of an entirely different significance.[27] For the first time, an author speaks with a real knowledge of the issue: a Jew from Huesca, but originally from al-Andalus, converted to Christianity in 1106 at the age of forty-four, Petrus Alfonsi had lengthy inside knowledge of Judaism and also of the dominant Muslim culture in which he lived before emigrating to Aragon. The Judaism he contests is not seen exclusively through the prism of the Old Testament: Petrus Alfonsi knows the Talmud, the Haggadah, and the religion of contemporary Jews. His *Dialogue* quickly benefited from a renown and dissemination comparable to that of Gilbert Crispin's *Disputatio*, and infinitely greater than those of the other twelfth-century treatises: 79 manuscripts survive—21 from the twelfth century alone—compared to 22 for Gilbert Crispin, only 5 for the Cluny Abbot Peter the Venerable's *Adversus Iudeorum inveteratam duritiem* (1143), only 5 too for Joachim of Fiore's *Adversus Iudeos*, and just 3 for Peter Abelard's *Dialogus inter Philosophum, Iudaeum et Christianum*.[28] In later debates between Jews and Christians, Petrus Alfonsi's work is cited as an authority along with the Bible and the Church Fathers. It is also used for exegesis of the Old Testament.

The work is in fact composed of twelve "dialogues": the first four are devoted to the refutation of Judaism, the fifth consists of an attack on Islam, and the last seven offer a defense of Christian truth. Jews are accused of having put Christ to death through *invidia*, all while *knowing* that he was in fact the Messiah.[29] "Moses" says that Jesus was only a magician; "Petrus" replies that he performed real miracles. The destruction of the Temple is punishment for the Jews; this deprived them of attending their rituals of purification, and this is why, since then, Jews are "impure." The Haggadah is nothing more than a deviation from the Law. Jews give a narrowly literal interpretation of the Bible: when God says, "Let us make humankind in our image, according to our likeness" (Genesis 1:26), or when he says to the prophet Moses, "you shall see my back" (Exodus 33:23), they interpret this

word for word as if God did have a "back" and a "body," for which they
then claim to give measurements. Finally, Petrus makes fun of several Jewish
legends and Jewish millenarianism for they too rest on an erroneous understanding of certain passages in the Old Testament (Deuteronomy 32:39;
Isaiah 26:19; Daniel 12:2; Ezekiel 37:3–14): the church's correct understanding
of these passages shows that they refer either to the last Judgment, or to the
return of the Hebrews from captivity, and what is meant by the "spirituality"
of this "return" is in fact the conversion of Jews.

Jews, on the other hand, represented by the voice of "Moses," reproach
Christians for having abandoned the Law. "Petrus" sets out to refute this
reproach and defend Christianity. He cites "authorities" one after the other,
and even more the "reasons" to justify the Trinity, the Incarnation, the Resurrection, and the Ascension. In his search for rational proofs, Alfonsi goes
further than Gilbert Crispin, even though the latter was a disciple of Saint
Anselm. The reason for this is that Petrus Alfonsi relies on another strand of
"rationalist" thought, one that has nothing to do with the schools of Northern Europe: that of the neo-Aristotelian circles in Judeo-Arab Spain.

Finally, he tackles the Jewish reproach of idolatry among Christians.[30]
"Moses" begins by insinuating that Christians choose a tree that they cut
down in order to sculpt the wood, give it the appearance of a man, polish it
and paint it, after which they worship it, while Isaiah 44 had already condemned this. Let us listen to the dialogue that ensues:

> *Petrus*: It is not what you think. We neither make nor worship idols, but
> rather we make a cross on which we place (*superponimus*) the image
> of a man. The cross stands for the altar and the image stands for
> the sacrifice that takes place on the altar. Just as they [the Hebrew]
> sacrificed on the altar, so too was the Lamb of God sacrificed on
> the cross. And just as they didn't make anything of the stones with
> which they built an altar, so do we not make anything of the re-
> mainder [of the wood] of the cross or of the image that we place
> on it. Just as Solomon and the others prostrated in front of the
> altar, but without worshipping it, since they worshipped only God,
> so too do we kneel before the cross, but it is neither the cross nor
> the image placed upon it that we worship, it is God the Father, and
> his Son Jesus Christ.
>
> *Moyses*: What you say would be reasonable (*ratio esset*) if you possessed
> the cross on which the Lamb of God was sacrificed. But today, it is

another cross that you adore, one on which no Lamb of God was ever sacrificed.

Petrus: Indeed, we do not possess this cross, but this is neither good nor bad, so long as we make other crosses that resemble it and so long as they are of the sort that those who did not see Christ's cross can at least see the other crosses made to resemble it and remember (*recordentur*) the sacrifice that took place upon it and understand it as sons. Indeed, the sons of Ruben had built on the other side of the Jordan an altar resembling the one in Jericho. They built it in such a way that their sons and wives, who were unable to climb up themselves, were able to see it and know it as a witness (*in testimonium*) to the other altar, just as you can find in the book of Joshua [22].[31]

Petrus Alfonsi poses real questions, not all of which he answers: most notably the one regarding the relation between the *real* cross and the crosses made to resemble it. The multiplicity of all these "copies" is the assurance that not one of them can become an idol. Without seeking to feed his argumentation with earlier speculations on the virtue of the cross (one thinks for example of the *Praise of the Holy Cross* by the Carolingian Rabanus Maurus, the success of which persisted into the twelfth century), Peter Alfonsi uses resemblance alone to justify the respect that Christians must pay to these many imitations. His principle goal is to insist on the recalling function of the crucifix, on its nature as a "witness" to the Passion. For this, he cites the same authority the *Opusculum* accords Rupert of Deutz in his dialogue with the young Jew Judas: Joshua 22. He even specifies the lessons, inflecting them with a slightly different meaning in order to give an accurate understanding of Christian images:

- The altar built on the left bank of the river Jordan is not a sacrificial altar, such as the main altar built by the tribes on the right bank; it only bears "witness" to the other altar of Zion. In and of themselves, the innumerable crosses made by Christians cannot rival the dignity of the Real Cross, for they are only witnesses to it.
- The stones that make up the altar are not the object of worship. For that matter, the Hebrews made nothing of the stones that were left once the altar was built. Similarly, it is not the material of the cross

that matters: once sculpted, no one cares about the offcuts and shavings of the wood.[32]

Rupert of Deutz, Jews and Images

Rupert of Deutz is himself the author of the important treatise entitled *Anulus sive Dialogus inter Christianum et Iudaeum*, written in 1126 at the request
of Rudolph of Saint-Trond, Abbot of Saint-Pantaleon in Cologne.[33] Rudolph
follows the Jewish-Christian polemic closely. In his own book, the *Deeds of
the Abbots of Saint-Trond*, he mentions the discussions that he had with the
Jews of Cologne in 1121–1123. He and Rupert are well acquainted with one
another: a letter from Rudolph addressed to Rupert is preserved acknowledg-
ing receipt of the *Anulus*, which was dedicated to him, and he praises it as an
admirable contribution to the *monomachia*—the singular struggle—between
Jew and Christian. Rudolph takes the opportunity to request that Rupert
include additional proofs of the existence of the Trinity and of the necessity
of the Incarnation of God's Son.[34] Rupert does not take up this suggestion,
since he esteems that Jews cannot understand the mystery of the Trinity so
long as the "blindfold" that prevents them from correctly interpreting the
Bible has not been lifted from their eyes. Regarding Jews, the primary task is
to teach them the principles of Christian exegesis. Theology only comes afterward. But Rudolph's suggestion does not fall on deaf ears either. In response
to his letter, Rupert immediately writes a theological treatise on "the glorification of the Trinity and the procession of the Holy Spirit" (March–August
1128).[35]

Rupert and Rudolph also both know Eckbert, the Bishop of Munster
who is Judas's debtor in the beginning of the *Opusculum*. In his *Deeds of the
Abbots of Saint-Trond*, Rudolph notes the dual presence of Eckbert and Rupert of Deutz at Saint-Pantaleon in Cologne on the occasion of the election
of a new abbot.[36] If we add to these three men Rupert's best friend Cuno,
Abbot of Siegburg (1105–1126) and later bishop of Regensburg, or even Rupert's other "patron," the Archbishop Frederick of Cologne (1099–1130), we
can clearly see how a close circle of high-minded literati that shared the
highest ecclesiastical offices were able to prepare and develop all these anti-
Jewish exegetical and polemical argumentations.

If Rudolph calls upon Rupert, it is because the letter is known for the
force of his arguments against the Jews. It is his reputation as "expert" in this

matter that makes him worthy of being solicited.[37] It is probable that this same reason explains his presence opposite Judas in the *Opusculum*. In his commentary on the Minor Prophets (*In XII Prophetas minores*), Rupert mentions the debates that he had with Jews, and in his commentary on Matthew he deplores the fact that Jews refuse to recognize Jesus as the Messiah.[38] The *Anulus* is thus the product of this intellectual ferment and these debates, some of which may have actually taken place, others perhaps not, but which were carefully structured for publication.

In the Prologue to the *Anulus*, Rupert explains his reasons for choosing the dialogue form. This form reproduces in writing a sort of duel; it thus suits very well the singular struggle (*monomachia*) that the Christian must wage against the Jews. Rupert adds that his work will be particularly useful to the *tirunculi*, the "young gladiators" that surround him—young monks who are quicker to do battle with the adversary through words and writing than the *veterani*. The purpose of the work is to supply them with weapons of debate, in this case all the "authorities" and "reasons" that prevail. In addition to *Dialogus*, Rupert also gives the name *Disputatio* to his work, thereby connecting it to the long line of theological and exegetical "disputes." As for the "ring" (*Anulus*) that serves as title, it signifies the ring of the New Covenant promised to those who accept to receive the light.

The work of Maria Ludovica Arduini, John Van Engen, David Timmer, and Anna Sapir Abulafia has done justice to Rupert of Deutz's *Anulus*, recognizing its important place in the history of exegesis in the early twelfth century. By means of the Jewish-Christian controversy, Rupert wrote a veritable theoretical treatise on Christian exegesis. To his "meaning of Scripture," he opposes all the limits of Jewish interpretation of the Old Testament. The "blindfold" that Jews keep over their eyes when they read the Bible—the emblematic figure of the Synagogue—marks their obstinacy in refusing to recognize Jesus as the Messiah. Their "blindness" justifies the malediction that God places upon them as well the fact he has entered into the New Covenant with the church. Jews concentrate in themselves all the vices of "this world" (*hoc saeculum*), in particular envy (*invidia*), but also avarice, pride, and lust.[39] These vices all proceed from the same principle of *carnalitas*.[40] Their attachment to the "carnal" is evident on the moral level because it is first and foremost intellectual: unable to rise above the exclusively literal, "carnal" meaning of Scripture, Jews are incapable of grasping its "spiritual" meaning. This spiritual meaning is reserved for the church, which offers a typological reading of the Old Testament: behind the letter of the Bible, it shows how, "spiritually," Christ is indeed the Messiah announced by the Prophets.

The *Anulus* contains a veritable avalanche of Old Testament quotations that first the Jew and then the Christian each explain in their own way, reversing to their own advantage the opposing interpretation. This is notably the case in book III regarding images.[41] Once again, the accusation of idolatry brought against Christians serves as a point of departure. Rupert responds in terms we have already met: Christians do not worship the material object of a *simulacrum*, but rather the cross that, as such, is the *signum veritatis*. He enjoins the Jew to take as he does the "middle road" (*sic medium tene*) between two equally detestable attitudes: pagan idolatry and the categorical denial of all images. Jews refuse images, but the Bible whose teachings they claim to follow shows that they are wrong. The golden cherubim that Yahweh commanded Moses to place on the Ark (Exodus 25, 18–22) and the bronze serpent which, endowed with miraculous qualities, prefigures the redemptive Passion of Christ on the cross (Numbers 21:9), demonstrate that the Hebrews did not spurn images. Contemporary Jews would be well advised to do the same.

Rupert, however, is conscious of the changes that have taken place in sacred history since the times of the Old Testament: the Incarnation of Jesus has transformed things completely. "Before" (*tunc*), when the Son of God had not yet appeared on earth, God could not be present in human form. This is why Moses, on Horeb, saw no form in the middle of the fire. Only the *humaniformii*, who "claim that man is made in God's image according to the workmanship of the body" and not of the soul, had violated this prohibition. But "now" (*nunc autem*) that God has become man, and now that he has been "seen on earth" following the prophecy in Baruch 3:38, it is permissible to represent him in human form. The Incarnation is the main justification for Christian imagery, most especially for the image of the crucifixion.

Two of Rupert's arguments in this passage may come as a surprise. The first is the evocation of the *humaniformii*, which is a completely literary allusion to the ancient heresy of the "Four Big Brothers" which Theophilus of Alexandria combated at the end of the fourth century. There was no necessity to speak of it here, other than the fact that Rupert had a personal interest in the little-known heresy, which he discusses in other works as well.[42] The second surprising argument is the quotation from Baruch 3:38. The passage is frequently cited in anti-Jewish polemical treatises, but Jews considered this prophetic book to be apocryphal and the argument must therefore have carried little weight for them. Christian exegetes, on the other hand, paid close attention to it. Like Rupert and many others, Gilbert Crispin used this authority,[43] but attributed it to Jeremiah, eliciting an abrupt reply from his Jewish interlocutor: "Jeremiah did not write or say that!" Peter the Venerable takes the precaution of citing "Baruch or his colleague Jeremiah."[44] The association of these two prophets is also found in the Missal of Stammheim (c. 1170) (figs. 3, 4). The Majesty of Christ is flanked by the Tetramorphe (the symbolic representations of the four Evangelists) and the four prophets of the Old Testament: Moses and Daniel at the bottom, Baruch and Jeremiah at the top, each holding a phylactery with a quotation from his prophecy.[45]

Responding to Rupert's arguments, the Jew cites Psalm 115 (113B):8, which states that the idolaters become "similar to their idols." In their devotion to the crucifix, Christians worship a *simulacrum* made by human hands: they will therefore become like the substance of their idol. Rupert disagrees: it is not the human body that can become similar to the substance of the idol, but the human mind which, in its contemplation of the crucifix, becomes assimilated with Christ "by the grace of adoption" (*per gratiam adoptionis*). The "worship of the cross" is thus given a quasi-sacramental character described in terms of the Christian *adoptio*, in other words baptism. But there is one pre-requisite: the recognition that Jesus is the Messiah. Rupert wrote the *Anulus* in 1126, at the same time that he was working on his commentary on the Gospel of Matthew, where he relates his ecstasies in front of the crucifix (1125–1127). He speaks, then, from experience. For him, the idea of "adoption" expresses first the force of spiritual lineage that links him to Christ and which he feels intimately and passionately in the contemplation of the crucifix. Because it has to do with convincing a Jew and, if possible, converting him, the baptismal meaning that the word *adoptio* acquired in Christian Latin during the early Middle Ages is fully justified.[46]

Apparently convinced on the issue of the crucifix, the Jew remarks that the Christian churches are full "of countless other male and female images that are not Gods." Can Rupert justify their existence? Once again, the abbot finds his arguments in the Old Testament. In the Temple, both Moses and later Solomon multiplied the cherubs, palm leaves, and paintings without contervening God's command (1 Kings 6:23). "Much later, many more *memorabilia* of much greater size were made by the ministry of Holy angels," such as the palm leaves which, following Psalm 92 (91):13, decorated "the House of the Lord." Christian imagery follows this tradition, says Rupert, who does not refrain from speaking of them in the first person: "It is why I legitimately carve the wood on all the walls of the church, multiplying not only the cherubs and the palm leaves, but also the different paintings that call to mind for me the deeds of the saints, the faith of the patriarchs, the truth of the prophets, the glory of the kings, the beatitude of the apostles, and the victories of the martyrs, while between the sacred images of them all, the lovely cross of the Lord dazzles me with its refulgence."

The essential aspects of Rupert's conception of Christian images, then, are as follows:

- Images belong to a long tradition going back to the Hebrews of the Old Testament, that is, to the decoration of the Temple in praise of Yahweh.
- There is continuity in the history of images, just as there is continuity in the history of the servants of God, from the patriarchs of the Old Testament through the Holy martyrs of the history of the church.

Furthermore, the modes of figuration that he describes are of three types:

- Rupert evokes the whole field of the decoration of the sanctuary, which aspires to the visual praise of God and is common to the Temple of the ancient Hebrews and the churches of today, with their angelic and plant motifs (the cherubim and the palm leaves), and the "multiplicity" and "diversity" of sculptures, paintings, carvings, and worked wood. Rupert evokes in a striking manner the decorative and nonfigurative background of images that introduce into the church a sort of music for the eyes and a visual counterpoint to the choir of angels.
- Against this ornamental background, the *memorabilia* emerge in the form of narrative images that recall the *gesta* of those who have played significant roles in sacred History. These are specific to Christian churches for they serve a commemorative function by calling to the minds of the faithful all of sacred History, from the time of the prophets to the saints. This was a function already assigned to images by Gregory the Great, especially for the instruction of the illiterate.
- Finally, the image of the crucified Christ stands out from the ornamentation and narrative images: by its brilliance, by its mode of justification—the Incarnation legitimizes the representation of God—and by its redemptive function for those who "worship" it and find themselves

"adopted" by Christ while contemplating the image of the Passion, the crucifix is more than an "aide-memoire." It is an object of worship, and, just as Rupert experienced it, an object of visionary contemplation.

When Rupert speaks of the decoration of churches, of images and of the crucifix, one can make out an astute observer of the visual forms offered to the faithful for veneration. A chapter in Rupert's *Vita Heriberti* presents a striking example.[47] Having finished the foundations of the church abbey of Deutz, the Archbishop of Cologne Heribert decides to have a wooden crucifix sculpted for the church. He calls upon "artists" (*artifices*) and they put in their best effort, but to no avail: they must throw away one after the other each piece of wood that they are attempting to carve without ever completing their work (*artis officium*). Discouraged by these repeated failures, they quit. At that time, the archbishop goes to have lunch in an orchard, where he is struck by the shape of the branches of a pear tree that "imitate" the extended arms of Christ on the cross. Upon seeing this Heribert is seized by a "divine terror" as if the sudden appearance of the crucified lord invaded him. But, having made the sign of the cross, he understands what divine sign he has been given. He has the tree cut down and out of it is sculpted "without difficulty and with elegance," "the cross of the Lord, and on it the image of the Savior." Rupert concludes his account, saying that God does not care much about the quality of any particular wood for the making of images. What matters to him is "the sign or the image of the cross which the Christian worships in memory of the Savior" (*in recordationem Salvatoris*) when it is raised before his eyes.

All the important themes that are generously commented upon by Rupert of Deutz in his other works can be found in this small text: a new image to be worshipped, the crucifix especially, must be legitimated by a divine intervention;[48] the material image takes the *forma* from the divine prototype which ordinarily appears in a vision though here it makes an exceptional appearance in the "human" form of a tree; the *recordatio* of the Passion is the most important function of the crucifix; the Old Testament supplies ample justifications for the making and worshipping of images, and the account of the bronze serpent, often used in debates between Jews and Christians, is one of the most frequently cited arguments.

In many respects, Rupert of Deutz, the quintessential man of letters, is just as much a man of images. Hrabanus Haacke, the chief editor of Rupert's works, has gone so far as to question whether his thought did not serve as a "program" for many artists in the region of the Meuse and the Rhine in the twelfth century,[49] citing the typological iconography of the altar of Klosterneuburg, made by the goldsmith Nicholas of Verdun, the reliquary of the Three Kings, the reliquary of Anno in Cologne, the wall paintings of the Romanesque cathedral of Cologne, and the sculpture of the Madonna of Siegburg. Haacke even believes to have detected Rupert's influence in much later works such as the altarpiece of the mystical Lamb of the brothers of Van Eyck in Ghent. But this is going too far. These works relate to Christian themes that are far too general to be able to tie them down to a particular author, whatever his influence may have been. Moreover, one should not overestimate Rupert's intellectual influence: he is more representative of the tail end of a tradition, right before the arrival of scholasticism pushes artists in new directions.

Much more convincing is the approach taken by John Van Engen, which establishes a close parallel between the thought of Rupert and that of Theophilus Presbyter, a Benedictine monk and priest who lived in the same region around 1120 and who wrote a sort of practical manual for "artists," the *De diversis artibus*. Beneath the name of Theophilus may be hidden the monk and goldsmith Roger of Helmarshausen, named after a monastery close to Paderborn, where Rupert's works were well known.[50] Comprising three books, the manual successively considers materials and painting (pigments, gold, manuscript illuminations, wall paintings, pictures), the work of stained-glass windows, and finally the metal work, the ivory work, and the stonework. But each part is preceded by a prologue in which the author avoids exclusively technical considerations in order to evoke the theological background of Christian art. On a number of points, however, Theophilus's positions are shared only by a limited number of ecclesiastical authors of his period. Van Engen was even able to demonstrate that they only fully reflect the position of a single theologian, Rupert of Deutz. Rupert and Theophilus each propose an original interpretation of Genesis 1:27, "So God created humankind in his image (*imaginem*), in the image of God (*similitudinem*) he created them," a passage that forms the basis of both Judeo-Christian anthropology and Christian reflection on the *imago*. Rupert and Theophilus each insist on the necessity of distinguishing, more than traditional exegesis did, between the terms *imago* and *similitudo*: for them, the divine *imago* continues to characterize the rational soul of *all humankind* after original sin.

On the other hand, original sin caused the *similitudo* of God to be lost.

It is through reason (*ratio*), the appropriate "instrument" for those who wish to use it, and through God's grace that Christians can hope once again to find their divine "semblance."[51] Better yet, Theophilus expands his conception of the *rationalitas* as an "instrument" allowing the soul to find its *similitudo* with God, from the spiritual activities of clerics or monks to those of the Christian artist-artisan like himself, or like, too, the *artifex* of the *Vita Heriberti*. "Art" is thus raised to a level of spiritual and technical exercise proper to advancement on the path to Salvation. Not only, as Gilbert Crispin writes, does the contemplation of saintly images allow one "to hold down a wandering soul," but the work of hands that give shape to images is an antidote to the *vagatio animi*.[52] Like Rupert who expresses himself in similar terms, Theophilus is faithful to the Benedictine tradition of valorizing manual work, but it is not a matter here of working in the fields: it has to do with the work of the goldsmith or the window maker, or even the sculptor, as we have just seen. Such occupations assume apprenticeship and mastery of difficult technical skills: Theophilus and Rupert propose for the first time seeing in the parable of the talents that traditionally symbolizes the "gifts" of the Holy Spirit, an illustration of the "talents" of the human spirit including the practical knowledge necessary for manual arts.

The promotion of "mechanical arts" is certainly not reserved, in the early twelfth century, to these two authors: as it happens, the role played by Hugh of Saint-Victor's *Didascalicon* in the 1120s and also by Honorius Augustodunensis's *Elucidarium* (both authors of Germanic origin) is well known. But according to John Van Engen, Rupert of Deutz would have had a slight advance on them, proposing as early as 1117 in his *De Trinitate*, that the *scientia illiteralis* of the sculptor or the goldsmith[53] should be included among the *scientia litteralis* (clerical knowledge from books), their "savoir-faire" not learned from books but through visual and oral apprenticeship. Finally, Rupert and Theophilus both insist on the continuity between the decorations of the Temple in the Old Testament and those of Christian churches: on this point Van Engen cites the *De divinis officiis*, but we have seen that the *Anulus* says the same. Rupert is here again in perfect agreement with the *De diversis artibus* of Theophilus Presbyter, who also insists on the utility for Christians of meditating on the decorations of the Temple described in the Old Testament in order to grasp its "spiritual" meaning.[54]

We are now in a position to characterize two important and inseparable aspects of Rupert of Deutz's work: the Abbot is both an exegete famed for his polemics with Jews and a theologian attuned to the spiritual merits of decorations and images, and to the dignity and knowledge of those who make them. These two aspects can provide ample justification for the *Opusculum* making Rupert of Deutz, astonishing as it may be at first, the interlocutor of the young and obscure Jew Judas. But do they really allow one to assert, along with Gerlinde Niemeyer and other historians, that this debate on images between Rupert of Deutz and Judas actually took place "in January or February 1128"?

While Rupert of Deutz invokes a litany of scriptural arguments in the *Anulus*,[55] never does he cite Joshua 22, the episode of the construction of the altar on the left bank of the Jordan by the "two and a half tribes." This "authority" is no more used by other authors of polemical treatises. Gilbert Crispin and Guibert of Nogent both omit reference to it. The same is true in the thirteenth century of Christian polemicists such as Inghetto Contardo, who does however repeat several of the arguments found in the *Anulus*.[56] The only author who follows the example of Herman's *Opusculum* and cites the passage is, as we have seen, the convert Petrus Alfonsi. One could well ask if, in both cases, the status of being a convert helps explain the recourse to such an exceptional argument. But this hypothesis hardly holds water since another convert, William of Bourges, ignores the passage as much as other Christian authors do. In his polemically entitled treatise *The Book of the Lord's Wars Against the Jews* (*Bellum Domini adversus Judaeos*, c. 1235), William of Bourges uses the Old Testament passage concerning the cherubs of the Ark of the Covenant in order to elaborate on the famous letter by Gregory the Great concerning the utility of images for the illiterate.[57]

The rarity of the argument concerning the crossing of the Jordan is all the more remarkable for the fact that it was possible to see in this image a metaphor for conversion and baptism. Certain exegeses on the origin of the name of the Hebrews went in the same direction. Genesis (10:22–25 and 11:14–16) indeed enumerates the descendants of Shem, Noah's eldest son. In the fourth generation was born Eber, who "lived four hundred and thirty years and begat sons and daughters." Hebrew exegeses see in this only one name, or else they consider that *eber* is an adverb of place, an adverbial preposition signifying "beyond" or "across." In other words, the ancients understood this passage (Genesis 10:21) in at least two ways. Namely: "Children were also born to Shem, who is the father of all of Eber's children"; or: "Children were also born to Shem, who is the father of all the sons (who have come) from beyond (the river)." The allusion to the crossing of the

Jordan is explicit. For their part, the Church Fathers, especially Augustine (*City of God*, XVI, iii, 2) and Isidore of Seville (*Etymologies*, VII, 6, 16 and 23) were able to understand this "arrival from beyond the river" as a "mystical crossing," but they "generally chose to make Eber a biblical hero rather than an adverbial locution."[58] According to Saint Augustine, however, Eber had escaped the confusion of Babel and had therefore transmitted the purity of the Adamic language up until the time of Christ. Thus the real descendants of Eber, and through him the descendants of Abraham, are the Christians. This amounted to refusing to the Hebrews (or Jews) the benefit of the "mystical crossing" of the "river" and the "spiritual" intelligence of this image. The evocation of the crossing of the Jordan by Joshua and the "sons of Israel," which is attributed to Rupert of Deutz in the *Opusculum* and also cited by Petrus Alfonsi, made numerous symbolic developments possible. But this possibility was not grasped, both because at stake in the debate was only the legitimacy of images (it was therefore not necessary to gloss the multiple connotations of the name "Eber," who is not even mentioned), and because the polemic with Jews ended up placing emphasis on their "carnal" understanding of Scripture (the literal and historical significance of the crossing of the Jordan being the only thing under discussion).

In addition to the observation about the argument's rarity and its limited use in the texts that interest us, one must add the following: Christian iconography often represents the crossing of the Jordan under Joshua's leadership, and in particular on baptismal fonts, where artists make full use of its baptismal symbolism; but the more specific scene of the construction of the altar by the "two and a half tribes" is practically never represented. The bronze baptismal cistern of Hildesheim, around 1220–1225,[59] shows an armed Joshua followed by Hebrews in pointed hats, some carrying stones. The inscription insists on the baptismal symbolism: "The Hebrew people (*Hebreus*) cross the river to enter their homeland. In the baptismal fonts we are led by you, God our leader, in our homeland."[60] Let us note that the Hebrew people are here designated by the sole name Eber, *Hebreus*, the eponymous ancestor of the "crossing" whose name came to designate the entire people. But here the episode represented is Joshua 4, not Joshua 22. In other places as well, for example on a mosaic of the Roman basilica of Santa Maria Maggiore and in the Byzantine iconography,[61] the scene usually represented corresponds to Joshua 4: on Joshua's orders, the twelve tribes of Israel cross the Jordan whose waters are momentarily drawn back; a representative of each tribe places a stone in the middle of the river bed in memory of his crossing. This is what one finds in a number of illuminated manuscripts from the eleventh century onward.[62] One should not confuse these twelve stones with the building of the altar after the conquest of Jericho and the return into Transjordan by the two and a half tribes who must live there. I have found only one representation of Joshua 22, though chronologically too late for us, in the *Historic Bible of Padua* written in Italian in the fourteenth century.[63] There is no doubt in identifying the scene, as the manuscript contains both a representation of the twelve stones in the river bed of the Jordan, according to Joshua 4,[64] and, further on, a representation of the construction of the altar on the bank of the river, following Joshua 22.[65]

Our analysis of these texts and images leaves us with a whole series of questions regarding Herman's *Opusculum*:

- Did the person (or persons) who wrote this short work, be he Herman/ Judas or an entirely different Premonstratensian canon, describe a real debate with Rupert of Deutz, or did this author (or authors) stage the debate by placing in the mouth of "Rupert of Deutz" an argument that the real Rupert of Deutz had not used in his own work?
- Was the argument regarding Joshua 22 not more likely borrowed from Petrus Alfonsi's *Dialogue Between Peter and Moses*, which dates to 1110 and enjoyed an immediate and exceptional success?
- Was this argument not placed here because it lent itself particularly well to a story of conversion, especially given the baptismal symbolism that clerics usually gave to the biblical episode of the crossing of the Jordan? Even if the *Opusculum* says nothing about this baptismal interpretation (and says even less about the metaphoric meaning of the Hebrews), but rather only seeks to justify through this authority the commemorative function of Christian images, we cannot exclude that its citation at this moment of the account implicitly announces the baptism of Judas/Herman.
- Above and beyond this particular argument, how does one explain the fact that the *Opusculum* gives such an important place to the Benedictine Abbot Rupert of Deutz when the work comes from an abbey of Premonstratensian canons?

Why Rupert?

Even though Rupert of Deutz was more famous than others in his time for his involvement in the Jewish-Christian polemic as well as the debate about images, one cannot help but wonder why the *Opusculum* gives him such an important role opposite Judas. His relations with the Premonstratensian canons, beginning with their founder Norbert of Xanten, were miserable. Abbot Rupert is representative of the old *ordo monasticus* that looks scornfully at the emergence at the turn of the eleventh-twelfth centuries of canons regular, most notably the Premonstratensians, who claim superiority over monks. The canons adopt the Rule of Saint Augustine, which compels them neither to a life of prayer and study nor to monastic steadfastness. They think of themselves as open to the world and present themselves as the "clerics" par excellence, dedicated to preaching, an activity they see as superior to meditation and asceticism.

Starting in 1120 the conflict intensifies between these two key figures: Rupert of Deutz, on the side of the monks, and Norbert of Xanten, on the side of the canons. It is Rupert who takes the initiative during the years 1120–1122, the very moment at which Norbert founds Prémontré. He writes an *Altercatio monachi et clerici*, a short dialogue that claims to have taken place between a *monachus* (himself) and a *clericus* (by all evidence Norbert). (The dialogue form for polemical writings is already familiar to us.) Their dispute bears on the comparative status of the monk and the cleric, from which it emerges—according to Rupert—that the former is superior to the latter: indeed the cleric distinguishes himself neither through knowledge (*scientia litterarum*), nor by his tonsure nor habit, but by the "office of the altar" (*altaris officium*). But the monk, and this is true of Rupert, as of a growing number of monks in this period, had also acceded to the priesthood. Since he is also under the venerable Rule of Saint Benedict, he obviously wins out over the cleric: "You are only a cleric, I am a monk and a cleric" (*Nam tu clericus tantum, ego et monachus et clericus sum*). As a result, Rupert even asserts his right to preach, as clerics do.[66]

The conflict is revived in 1124 after Rupert sent to Norbert, upon his request, his recent treatise *De divinis officiis*. In a letter that dates to the summer of 1128, Rupert complains to his old friend Cuno of Siegburg about the calumnies heaped upon him by Norbert. Norbert claims that the *De divinis officiis* contains heresies about Mary's virginity. Rupert is not kind about his adversary: "You know him well," he writes to Cuno, "this man who is well connected, but whose conversion is very new and whose reputation is questionable"; he is already a "prelate and preacher, even though he was never subject [to a hierarchic superior]" . . . The mood is set, and Rupert reproaches Norbert specifically for his too rapid rise in the canonical orders. He recalls the whole polemic: Rupert sent his treatise to Norbert as he had requested, but Norbert "received it, put it aside, read it when and as he wished," and then gave Rupert no feedback at all. "And thus after a number of days" a rumor began to make its way to Rupert and everyone was asking him if he really did hold the positions attributed to him concerning the Virgin Mary. "I admit that I am appalled," says Rupert, who wonders how he can be charged with saying that the incarnated Word would have entered the uterus of the Virgin Mary! Norbert, he explains, "proclaimed that my book was heretical and worthy of being burnt," but he is ignorant (*inscius*), envious (*invidus*), and hungry for glory (*gloriae cupidas*). The rest of the text is a solidly argued—and, it might be added, perfectly orthodox—exposition of the doctrine of Incarnation.[67]

The Premonstratensians did not see themselves as defeated. Anselm of Havelberg is an immediate disciple of the order's founder, Norbert of Xanten. In 1129, Norbert, upon being appointed archbishop of Magdeburg, is succeeded as bishop of Havelberg according to his wishes by his close disciple, Anselm. Anselm launches a counterattack in an apology for canons regular that he addresses to one of their declared adversaries, Abbot Eckbert of Huysberg.[68] Anselm had the opportunity to read a piece of writing by Abbot Eckbert on the privileges of monks, and it seemed to him full of errors. Under the pretext of defending the "seamless tunic" of the Church, the monks oppose the canons whom they accuse of "tearing" it. At Hammersleben, a canon named Peter left his position in order to enter a monastery, but he later returned to his order, thus proving its superiority. Anselm takes up the Gospel episode of Martha, who symbolizes the active life with which clerics identify, and the story of Mary, who symbolizes the contemplative life of monks. Did Christ not answer Mary that Martha, too, had her share of virtues? Anselm of Havelberg pursues the debate in another far lengthier work, the *Liber de ordine canonicorum*, an all-out defense of the life of canons. He first highlights their great antiquity by associating them with the Levites, the servants of the Ark of the Covenant during the Exodus whose responsibilities are described in the book of Numbers. The argument is thus current among the Premonstratensians, and it can be found in another work coming most likely from the same order, the *Libellus de diversis ordinibus*.[69] The canons even find holy ancestors for themselves in the book of Genesis, first in the person of Abel, murdered by his brother Cain, then in Joseph, who was also persecuted by his brothers. But Joseph's father, Jacob, raised him above them and named him his successor. And Joseph's dream, in which he saw the stars that symbolized his brothers grow dim before his own, and their sheaves of grain bow respectfully before his own—divine signs of his preeminence—is echoed in the numerous visions of the Premonstratensian brothers which Anselm meticulously retells and uses as justification for the superiority of his order.[70]

Shortly thereafter, another Premonstratensian named Philip of Harvengt (d. 1183) takes up the torch of criticizing the monks. He is one of the great ecclesiastical writers of his time. Several of his letters, which develop the ancient precept of "know thyself," render him, along with Bernard of Clairvaux, one of the witnesses to the internalization of spiritual life that characterizes the twelfth century.[71] His treaty *De institutione clericorum* represents "one of the greatest efforts in the Middle Ages at trying to establish a clerical spirituality that is markedly different from monastic theology."[72] The lengthy work comprises six parts, each one illustrating the canon's way of cultivating virtues with dignity, science, justice, continence, obedience, and silence.

The section on continence (*De continentia clericorum*) is for Philip an occasion to cite Joshua 22, not regarding images but in the context of a discussion of the precedence of priests over secular rulers.[73] Let us at least note the use of this biblical authority among arguments familiar to the Premonstratensians. In that same section, Philip recalls the conflict a generation earlier between Norbert of Xanten and Rupert of Deutz, but without explicitly mentioning their names.[74] He has the upper hand in refuting Rupert's arguments: even when they are priests, the monks are not mainly clerics. Philip makes use of an eloquent comparison: "being a horseman does not make one a knight." The duty of monks is to fast, to keep vigil, to work with their hands, to devote themselves to contrition, and to maintain silence. The duty of clerics is to serve others and maintain contact with the outside world. A sign that the Benedictine monks are different (and inferior) is that they dress in black. It is them alone whom Philip opposes, for reformed monks, such as the Cistercians—who are contemporary with the order of Prémontré and also participate in the great reform movements of the eleventh and twelfth centuries—dress in white as a sign of their conversion and their authentic humility. The Premonstratensian canons also dress in white. They are *candidissimi*, a color symbolizing the eternal light to which they have been promised. How can one not dream, as Judas did, of the white-colored horse?

If we do not know how the *Opusculum* was made, we do at least know that it comes from the Prémontré abbey of Cappenberg. It is therefore surprising to see Rupert of Deutz play a primary role in refuting Judas's critique of

Christian images. This paradox has hardly been seized upon by the commentators of this text, perhaps because of the lack of an explanation. But if Rupert, upon closer examination, does indeed play an important role, it is not a decisive role in Judas's conversion. It is not "signs"—ordeals (chapter 5) or an unanswered call for a vision (chapter 7)—that can influence his decision. More effective are the "examples" of Christian charity (the attendant Richmar in chapter 5) and of piety (the canons of Cappenberg in chapter 6). But ultimately it is the prayers of two obscure women from Cologne (chapter 12) that succeed in putting Judas on the right path. These women are named—Berta and Glismut (the latter name signifying the virtue of temperance, *Gleichmut*)—although we know nothing about them. In this sequence of useful means to conversion, the "reasons" given by Rupert of Deutz have very little effect, and they only place second immediately after the useless "signs." It is not that the Premonstratensians scorn *a priori* reason, which cripples the intellectual work of their greatest writers. But it is divine grace, the obtaining of which is facilitated by humble and sincere prayers of the heart, which is the real and only engine for conversion.

The entire skill of the Premonstratensian text thus consists in using the figure of Rupert of Deutz, who is the major expert in questions regarding the Jewish-Christian polemic and the matter over images. At the same time, because he is the sworn enemy of the Prémontré order, the *Opusculum* confines him to a secondary, non-determinant role in the conversion of the account's hero. As to the *Vita* of Godfried of Cappenberg, it does not speak of Rupert. If it were necessary, one could find here new proof of the carefully constructed character of the *Opusculum*. It is by no means the simple testimony of a convert spontaneously describing his lived experience. It is possible that a real conversion was the occasion for this text. But the composition of this account and the role clearly given, though severely limited, to Rupert of Deutz bear the marks of a deep familiarity with polemical debates and great skill in the matter of using an opponent's arguments. The text incorporates the arguments Rupert made to Judas because they stand for the arguments of the entire church against the Jews. Even if no negative judgments are brought to bear upon the effectiveness of his reasoning, and in fact the opposite is true, Rupert nevertheless comes across as a weak "convertor" of the Jew in the *Opusculum*.

Figure 1. Wooden crucifix of Benninghausen, Cologne, 1070–1080. Parish church of Saint Martin, Benninghausen (district of Soest). Oakwood. Height: 66 inches. Foto Marburg/ Art Resource, NY.

Figure 2. The "Binity" of Psalm 109. Bodleian Library, University of Oxford, MS Douce 293, fol. 100v.

Figure 3. The majesty of Christ with the figure of the prophet Baruch (upper left). Missal of Stammheim, Hildesheim, around 1170. J. Paul Getty Museum, Los Angeles, ms. 97 MG 21, fol. 85v.

Figure 4. The Crucifixion, Church, and Synagogue. Missal of Stammheim, Hildesheim, around 1170. J. Paul Getty Museum, Los Angeles, ms. 97 MG 21, fol. 86.

Figure 5. Baptismal font of
Freckenhorst, Westphalia,
1129. Detail: Christ's baptism.
Author photo.

Figure 6. Effigy of Frederick
Barbarossa transformed into a
reliquary of Saint John, around
1155. Church of Cappenberg.
Gilded bronze. Height: 12
inches. Bildarchiv Preussischer
Kulturbesitz/ Art Resource,
NY.

Figure 7. Baptismal basin (Taufschale) given by Frederick Barbarossa to his godfather Otto of Cappenberg, 1156. Berlin, Kunstgewerbe Museum. Bildarchiv Preussischer Kulturbesitz/ Art Resource, NY.

Figure 8. Monument to the founders Godfried and Otto of Cappenberg, around 1320–1330. Cappenberg church. Foto Marburg/ Art Resource, NY.

Figure 9. Tombstone of Godfried of Cappenberg, early fourteenth century. Cappenberg church. Foto Marburg/ Art Resource, NY.

Chapter 5

Baptism and Name

The baptism of young Judas in chapter 19 marks the culminating moment in the account of his conversion. It is also the most dramatic event. In this respect, the *Opusculum* is no different from the many other accounts from late antiquity onward that deal principally, but not exclusively, with Jewish converts. Baptism is the public act of renouncing "Jewish superstition," or, for pagans, of renouncing "idolatry." Later, it concerns more generally the children of Christians who are thereby integrated into the community of those who are baptized and cleansed of original sin. If the meaning of the rite is that the souls be flooded by divine grace, then the immersion of adults into the baptismal water, or, increasingly, the pouring of water over the child's head, serves principally as a physical proof for those who are witnesses. Today, the cries of the child, anticipated and commented upon, still mark the turning point of the ritual, releasing the tension of the congregation and introducing a touch of humanity into the administration of the sacrament.

Forced Baptisms

The circumstances in which, according to the *Opusculum*, Judas receives his baptism are inscribed in, and offer a Christian echo to, a very long narrative tradition relating to the conversion and baptism of Jews. For their part, Jews deplore the treason of the renegades who have broken with their community. If certain Jews were baptized by force, others accepted it voluntarily. These themes are present from the commentaries of the Talmud and the Halacha to the Jewish chronicles contemporary with the First Crusade and the *responsa* of the rabbis. The moment that the *Opusculum* seems to refer to, between the First and the Second Crusades, is characterized on either side by the intensification of antagonisms. One can observe on one hand a stronger will to evangelize that will stop at nothing to achieve its ends, and on the other a greater intolerance toward the renegades whom tradition, until the beginning of the twelfth century, persisted in considering as "brothers," even if they were temporarily lead astray.[1]

The several witnesses that have come down to us for the early Middle Ages generally portray a confrontation between a bishop and a suddenly worried community of Jews who had until then enjoyed relative peace. Jews are pressed to convert when an irruption of new factors threaten the cohesion of the social body and the power that the bishop exercises over it. What is at stake in these confrontations, or at least in these given accounts, is not only a religious matter. Christians, and especially priests and bishops, are all the more willing to tolerate the "superstition" of Jews to the degree that it offers further proof, *a contrario* of the truth of Christianity. The stakes are primarily political, then, in the sense that the power of the bishop in the city is always complicated by the coexistence of the different communities living within it. The hagiographic and miraculous tone of these accounts gives the scale of these stakes, which ultimately leave the Jews with only one alternative: to accept collective baptism or to leave the city.[2]

A passage in Gregory of Tours's *Historia Francorum* (c. 540–594) describes the long-time efforts of Avitus, the bishop of Clermont, to get the Jews of the city to recognize the Christian faith.[3] He goes on to succeed in the weeks between Easter, the feast of the Assumption, and Pentecost, following an event unexpected in the way of miracles.[4] On the day of Easter, a Jew disappears into the procession of catechumens dressed in white. The hostile and sacrilegious reaction of one of his coreligionists provokes the anger of the Christians who, on the day of the Assumption, raze the synagogue to the ground. The bishop confirms to the Jews that he does not intend to force them to convert, but that he wishes to maintain the peace in the *civitas* under his sole crozier. Those who are obstinate will have to be exiled. On the day of Pentecost—under the sign that marks the arrival of the Holy Spirit—five hundred Jews accept baptism while the remaining others (whose numbers are not given) leave the city for Marseille.

The case of Minorca is at least as explicit. In the seventh century there circulated a "Letter on the miraculous conversion of the Jews of Minorca" attributed to bishop Severus of Minorca, the principle witness of the event that took place two centuries earlier. The arrival on the island, in 418, of the reliquaries of the proto-martyr Stephen prompted a shift in the relations between the Christians and the large and powerful community of Jews, whose leader Theodorus was the de facto ruler of the entire island's society. Strengthened by the many miracles of Saint Stephen, Bishop Severus succeeds through baptism in bringing Theodorus and his people into submission.[5] The turnover of power is not without violence, and there, too, the Christian crowd burns and razes the synagogue to the ground. Also in Minorca, the baptism of a single individual, Reuben, opens the path to the conversion of all the others. This incident was announced to Theodorus in a premonitory dream, but, like Herman, he only understands its true meaning later on.[6] Following a *topos* of hagiography, his first reaction is to resist to such an extent that a miracle is needed to end his blindness: while the Christians enjoin him to convert by crying out "Theodorus, believe in Christ!" (*Theodorus, credas in Christum!*), God causes the Jews to hear a very different call: "Theodorus believes in Christ!" (*Theodorus in Christum credit!*). They are stupefied to learn too of the conversion of their leader, and Theodorus, understanding finally that the will of God has been expressed, accepts baptism.[7] Following Theodorus's example, the other Jews of Minorca, numbering "five hundred and forty" (approximately the same number as at Clermont), also submit to the Christian rite.

A later poem of twenty-three hexameters written before the First Crusade (no doubt before 1074) and referring to events of the seventh century can be compared to the two texts cited above. It describes the "dialogue of a Jew and a blind Christian who regains his sight."[8] Here too a miracle is the engine for conversion. The hagiographical fiction, this time placed in the service of the Marian cult, is all the more evident because it partakes of the legendary Roman Pantheon, itself converted into a Christian church—Santa Maria Rotunda—under the pontificate of Boniface IV (608–615). The Roman Jews had become upset by the new appointment of the site and had begun doubting publicly the divinity of Christ and the virginity of Mary. But the miraculous healing of a blind Christian on the feast of the Purification of Mary forces them to recognize their error as "five hundred" among them accept baptism while the others leave the town. Through either their baptism or their flight, the Jews make the admission that the blindness of their eyes is nothing compared to the blindness of their soul, which is the symbol of the synagogue. As in other texts, it is the collective and even mass character of the conversion that is emphasized: it is confirmed that "five hundred" is a good number. An individual baptism can intervene at the beginning of the story, but it is not the most important part of the account.

The individual conversions spoken of by the documents of the period are more concerned with Christians who passed over to Judaism. These are exceptional cases. The most famous is that of Bodo the deacon in 839, a regular at the court of Louis the Pious. While undertaking a pilgrimage to Rome, he left for Muslim Spain. There he had himself circumcised, let his beard grow, assumed the Jewish name Eleazar, and married a Jewess. Bodo's conversion is known only indirectly through four letters of Paul Alvarus of Cordoba (himself a Jewish convert to Christianity). Alvarus tries through his writings to lead Bodo/Eleazar back to the Christian faith. The arguments and the tone of his letters anticipate the eleventh- and twelfth-century dialogue genre between a Jew and Christian.[9]

Another famous conversion of a Christian to Judaism is that of the Calabrian priest John of Oppido Mamertina (later known under his Jewish name, Obadiah) sometime between 1070 and 1121. It is to him we owe the account of his conversion, which followed the conversion of Andrea, who then became archbishop of Bari. Shocked by the persecutions inflicted by the Christians on the Jews during the First Crusade, John of Oppido came to doubt the authenticity of the Messiah, as he explains in his "autobiography of conversion," a portion of which was found in the archives of the Cairo Geniza. Much like Herman, John of Oppido describes his hesitant progression, but in the opposite direction. This text may have been used by the Jewish communities in their anti-Christian polemic.[10]

The persecutions associated with the first two crusades (1096 and 1146–1147) inaugurate a new era in Jewish-Christian relations, we have already noted. The choice Jews were presented with was no longer between baptism and exile, but more often between baptism and death.[11] Evidence for this is provided by the Christian chronicles and, on the Jewish side, by the "books of memory" that commemorate the "martyrs" who preferred to die and even to sacrifice the lives of their children (*Kiddush ha-Shem*) rather than renounce their faith.[12] A particularly dramatic case is the story of the Cologne Jew Schamarja as recounted in Jewish sources: in July 1096, he takes his family and flees his town for Dortmund, where he hopes to find the support of his relatives. But there, too, the Christians wish to baptize him by force. He refuses, preferring death for himself and all of his family. And so he is executed.[13] Following Ephraim bar Jacob of Bonn (1132–1197), it is this choice between death and baptism that the monk Raoul (Radulfus) imposes upon the Rhenish Jews in 1146. Bernard of Clairvaux protests, but too late.[14] The constraints placed upon the Jews, especially those in the imperial cities,[15] flouts the canonical tradition that requires both the consent of baptized adults and a long preparation of the catechumen for the sacrament.[16] It also scoffs at the protection given by the emperor to the Jewish communities in many of the towns in play: beginning in 1090, Henry IV grants protection to the Jews of Worms and Speyer and, in 1097, against the Pope's wishes, he allows Jews who were baptized by force to return to Judaism. In 1112, Henry V renews the privileges granted to the Jews of Speyer. In 1157, Frederick Barbarossa extends these privileges to all the Jews of the empire and it is at this time that there appears for the first time the notion of *Kammerknechtschaft*, as we have already seen.[17] All the emperors impose a delay of three days of reflection on Jews wishing to convert so as to prevent hasty or forced baptisms. The Jews address themselves to the emperor so that the children of massacred parents are protected from the evangelical zeal of Christians.[18] In the early thirteenth century, Pope Innocent III declares baptisms committed by force to be invalid. When they can, Jews who have been forcibly baptized rush to "judaize," that is, to revive more or less overtly their earlier religious practices. It is noteworthy that the "letter to brother Henry," which Herman uses to introduce the *Opusculum*, evokes hasty conversions that are too "easy" for his taste; he contrasts them with his own long, well-considered, and voluntary path to conversion: "I did not convert with the ease with which we see many infidels, Jews, and pagans convert to the Catholic faith through a sudden and unanticipated change, of the sort experienced by those whom yesterday we deplored for the error of their faith, but whom we celebrate now as having become coinheritors with us in Christ." Perhaps it is fitting to see in this passage an allusion to the forced baptisms administered during the First Crusade, though this is not said explicitly.

Voluntary Conversions

The circumstances of Herman's conversion have nothing in common with the forced baptisms of Jews terrorized by massacres. The experience that he describes does, however, relate to other cases of voluntary conversion and free acceptance of baptism in a more peaceful atmosphere. Indeed the *Opusculum* may be compared to several contemporary works. Most often, these conversions, like Herman's in the *Opusculum*, are of children or youths, boys and girls. Alfred Haverkamp has compiled for the *regnum teutonicum* an exhaustive inventory of these conversions. This study is made even more valuable because of the close attention paid to the nature of the sources—either "documentary" or "narrative" according to his terminology—and to the individual treatment given to each of them.[19]

With regard to young baptized Jewish girls, Haverkamp notes that they had no option beyond marriage or entering a convent, and from which they could dream only with difficulty of returning to Judaism.[20] In Cologne especially, where the communities were more mixed than elsewhere, the encounters between young Jewish girls and young Christian men, including clerics, could set the scene for the turn toward Christianity. In 1190, a charter from the Cistercian abbey of Neuberg in Alsace, near Haguenau, mentions a *domina Anna* who had converted some time before and in unknown circumstances (*pervenit . . . de iudaismo ad fidem catholicam*) under the influence of a prominent canon named Burchardus, the *vicedominus* of the church in Strasbourg. Burchardus bequeathed lands to the monastery while retaining a considerable portion of the revenues for himself during his life and for *domina Anna* should she outlive him; he further stipulates that they should both be entered into the *liber memorialis* of the monastery. The archives of the parish of Saint Laurence of Cologne (which included the quarter in which Jews represented the majority) offer another analogous case. Toward the middle of the twelfth century, the client of a lawyer and his wife Sophia, herself the daughter of a Jew named Vivus (*Theodoricus de B. homo advocati et uxor eius Sophia filia Vivi Iudei*), renounce their and their descendants' inheritance from Vivus.[21] Sophia was no doubt baptized, but this is not explicitly stated. The marriage cannot be a new one, as the couple have descendants who are already of a sufficient age that they are not named in their relatives' act of renunciation. Other documents allow one to believe that Theodoricus is the vassal of Gerhard Unmaze, a very high-ranking lawyer in the good society of the city. Haverkamp notes that Anna and Sophia both had stable, domestic, or even marital relationships with Christians of an elevated social position. "Their relationship could have existed before the [woman's] conversion and may even have been the reason for her receiving baptism."[22]

The cases of young Jewish girls entering into a convent after baptism are different, and first of all for reasons of documentation: if the archives are silent or at best vague on this issue, the miracle accounts and the *exempla* are, on the contrary, copious and repetitive. In the region of Cologne the principle witness is the Cistercian Caesarius of Heisterbach (c. 1180–1240), author of the *Dialogus Miraculorum*, one of the most influential anthologies of miracles and *exempla* of the Middle Ages. The accounts that concern the conversion of Jews are not found in the first "distinction" of the anthology, entitled *De conversione* (which concerns the inner "conversion" of Christian sinners), but in the second, entitled *De contritione*. What Caesarius is concerned with above all is Christian penitence, for which Jews can occasionally and despite themselves be the instrument. Thus Caesarius kills two birds with one stone: by denouncing in passing the "perfidy" of Jews, he catches Christians, particularly young clerics who are moved to seduce young Jewish girls out of carnal desire or the lure of gain. The confession of the seducer and also the baptism and monastic confinement of the young seduced girl restore a temporarily disturbed order.[23] This string of accounts ends with a good example by demonstrating the attitude a virtuous Christian ought to have toward a young Jewish girl.

There once was a young Jewish girl in Linze (between Bonn and Koblenz) who had long yearned for baptism. She confided in a Christian woman who introduced her to a "poor young knight." In contrast to the corrupt clerics, this knight—the real hero of the account—takes care of her "as though she were his daughter." He offers her "advice, help, and material support" (*consilium, auxilium et temporale* are the words of feudal vocabulary) and hopes to marry her to a Christian or enter her into a monastery.[24]

Another *exemplum* is particularly deserving of our attention: it concerns the conversion of the "blessed" Catherine of Louvain, *alias* Rachel.[25] Caesarius of Heisterbach does not cite his source, but another Cistercian of the thirteenth century, Thomas of Cantimpré, tells the same story and asserts that he saw with his own eyes the convert in question in the monastery of Moniales du Parc-des-Dames in Brabant where she was admitted following her baptism.[26] Luckier than our Herman, this Jewish convert turned nun was admitted to the calendar of saints and blessed persons, her feast day being 4 May.[27] From the age of five, Rachel, who lives with her parents in Cologne, asks herself "why there is a difference in name between Jews and Christians, while the peoples of both lines have the same faces and the same ability to speak."[28] Instinctively pushed toward Christianity, she secretly carries bread to the little mendicants in order to hear them rapturously pronounce in their thanksgivings the sweet name of the Virgin Mary. Then her parents leave for Louvain in Brabant. Now aged ten and a half, the little girl makes frequent visits to a priest, master Rénier, in the company of other Christian children. For six months, and at her request, the priest explains the Scriptures to her and the meaning of the Christian faith. Her parents suspect nothing, and one day they decide to send their daughter beyond the Rhine to marry. With the complicity of the priest and the aid of the Virgin Mary who appears to her in a dream, she runs away and takes refuge in the monastery of Parc-des-Dames where she is baptized under the name Catherine. Her father registers a complaint with the duke of Brabant, the bishop of Liège, and Pope Honorius III. In return for a large sum of money, he succeeds in having his daughter returned to her family until she is twelve and can freely choose her faith. Two years later, the father is defeated by the obstinacy of his daughter who is finally able to enter the monastery. Her father lays a rude trap for her by scrambling to find a young Jewish man who had been fraudulently baptized and having him solicit the young novice for spiritual guidance. Catherine has no trouble seeing through the plot. Thomas of Cantimpré praises her admirable devotion. She particularly loves praying in front of the image of the Virgin Mary, complaining that the other novices "receive consolation and joy from their mothers and their friends," while she is an "orphan" (*paupercula pupilla*), having only Mary to help and protect her.

Even if this account does not offer the same autobiographical form as the *Opusculum*, it does contain several traits characteristic of conversion accounts of young Jews: the spontaneous movement—which is already the call of grace—that pushes these children toward visiting the church, mixing with young Christians, sometimes participating clandestinely in communion, and following the teaching of priests;[29] the resistance of Jewish parents and the obstacles they place in front of their defiant children, particularly by trying to marry them off; the solitude of the convert who is deprived of his/her original parentage and has to remake a Christian "family" composed of brothers and sisters of the religious orders, and also of Christ and the Virgin. Thus a powerful narrative matrix is revealed, capable of influencing many accounts, including perhaps those of "authentic" conversion cases. It matters little whether Rachel/Catherine of Louvain really lived or not, her *legenda* also passed through a similar filter. The comparison between her story and Herman's autobiographical account sheds light on the fecundity of a narrative matrix, without allowing us to affirm definitively that Judas/Herman ever actually lived, nor that he is a pure "fiction." This, I repeat, is unverifiable, but whatever the case may be, the principal question is to what extent narratives are constructed.

The conversion accounts of Jewish boys given in chronicles, miracle accounts, or *exempla* reproduce and adapt the same schemas. The anonymous monk who wrote the *Annals of Egmond* in Holland around 1170–1180 mentions for the year 1137 a story that he claims to have heard from the mouth of a young Jewish convert (*Iudeus christianus*) originally from Regensberg on the Danube. There lived in this town a rich Jewish moneylender named Isaac, the father of a boy named Jacob who from a very young age secretly adored the Christian faith. Clandestinely, the child steals and accumulates money from his father in order to realize his desires and help Jewish converts who, in accepting baptism, were deprived by imperial law of their possessions. One day, profiting from the absence of his father, Jacob asked the archdeacon of the city for baptism, giving his treasure over to the archdeacon. But the moneygrubbing archdeacon goes to find the father and, being granted the right to keep the money for himself, he returns the child. Since the child remains obstinate in wanting to become Christian, his father in the end ties his feet together and throws him into the Danube, where he drowns. The crime is discovered by a blind widow who, following a vision, is miraculously healed by moistening her eyes with the water of the Danube. As soon as she opens her eyes, she sees in the river the corpse of the young martyr. Once alerted, the bishop has the body fished out and orders that an inquiry be made. The father is questioned, but denies his crime by explaining that he was not worried by his son's absence since he had sent him to study in Spain "in accordance with Jewish custom." He is accused by other Jews and finally admits his crime, but not without denouncing the indelicate archdeacon, who is promptly executed. The Jew, his wife, and many other Jews convert. The body of the young martyr is given a fitting burial and miracles begin to take place on his tomb.

Several of the historians who have taken up the *Opusculum* of Herman the Jew have commented upon this text. Avrom Saltman insisted on the "numerous similarities" between the Egmont monk's account and Herman's account.[30] In both cases the father is rich, the son conceals money from him for a good cause, there is the issue of leaving to study far away (in France for Judas/Herman, in Spain for Jacob's son), and an unworthy cleric plays an evil role: in the *Opusculum* chaplain Wolkwin agrees to bring to the Jews of Mainz the letter denouncing Judas (chapters 14 and 15); in the *Annals of Egmont*, the greedy archdeacon betrays the confidence of young Jacob despite his wishes to become Christian. Saltman also notes that the motif of the miraculous discovery of the body of a crime victim can also be found in the *Motiv-Index* of oral traditions.[31] Aviad Kleinberg, who takes the opposing position that the *Opusculum* is "authentic," sees "fictive history" only in the

Egmont account. It is true that the healing of the blind woman in the Egmont account introduces a miraculous touch absent in the *Opusculum*. The only extraordinary detail recounted in the *Opusculum* is the speed—five years—with which Herman succeeds in learning Latin. One could just as well account for this feat by an exceptional gift for foreign languages.

Alfred Haverkamp has introduced a more interesting element into the discussion.[32] He reminds us that the Egmont monk was writing many years after the events and that he could not in Holland—"*in extremo margine mundi*"[33]—have direct knowledge of the most important Jewish communities of the time, those of the Rhineland (Cologne, Worms, Speyer, Mainz). As for Regensberg, where the events are said to have taken place, the town did not have a Jewish community at this time. The elaboration of the account, aided by its geographic and temporal distance, only augmented the legendary character of the narrative. Nevertheless, the legend does make reference to some established practices within the Jewish communities, such as the custom of sending educated youths to study "in Spain," or more especially the practice of the *Kidddush ha-Shem*, a father's sacrifice of his children in order to avoid their forced baptism, as occurred during the persecutions of 1096. In its Christian reinterpretation the motif of Jewish sacrifice could be transformed into a brutal crime, without however concealing that the motive of the crime was to prevent the child from being baptized. This motif is less visible in the *Opusculum*, particularly since the hero of the account is not a child but a young man of around twenty years old. Nevertheless, he too is threatened with death by his community of origin. The nature of the text and the storyline differ in the case of Judas/Herman, but it is not impossible to think that this account also effects a compromise between the strong imprint of Christian ideology and the traces of contemporary Jewish culture. Once again, rather than locking ourselves into the "fiction or truth" alternative, it is better to multiply the comparisons between the two related but distinct texts and show that there is no historical "reality" that is not transmitted in a constructed form, that is, reconstructed for precise purposes.

One could speak similarly about another case of conversion, one that Alfred Haverkamp has also compared to that of Judas/Herman. Here the convert is a certain Joshua/Bruno, the Jewish doctor of the archbishop of Trier who is mentioned (rather summarily) in one of the "continuations" of the *Gesta Treverorum*.[34] This is not an autobiographical account, nor is the conversion that of a young man, but rather of a mature adult who enjoys a high social position. What is more, Haverkamp does not doubt the veracity of the event, even if the construction of the account inevitably conforms to some very clear ideological purposes. The two stories offer more than mere analogy. In both cases, the Jew asking for baptism has long been in attendance at an ecclesiastical court, that of the bishop of Munster in the case of Judas/Herman, that of the archbishop of Trier in the case of Joshua/Bruno. In these Episcopal courts, each has long discussions with clerics, and slowly his obstinacy melts. For both individuals, baptism is the result of a long and winding evolution, not a sudden and miraculous change. Both converts then persevere and prosper in the Christian faith. Finally, neither of the two accounts place hatred of Jews and Judaism in the foreground. But if anti-Judaism, which does on the other hand characterize the bloody *Annals of Egmond*, is not the object of these accounts, what then is their purpose?

One finds further confirmation of the necessity to always consider the purpose of these testimonies in order to understand their form and inflexions by examining the conversion account of another Jew, this time a foreigner in Germanic lands. In the second part of his *Memoirs*, the monk Guibert of Nogent recounts various anecdotes about the monks of his former monastery of Fly. One of them was "of Jewish lineage" (*genere hebraeus*).[35] When very young, he escaped the massacre of Jews at Rouen during the First Crusade thanks to the pity of a knight named William, who entrusted the young boy to his own mother, the countess of Hélissende and widow of count William I of Eu. Guibert of Nogent is related by marriage to the countess, who calls him "my son." On the insistence of the pious woman and out of fear of dying the very death he had miraculously escaped, the Jewish child accepts baptism. His savior gives him the name William. A marvelous omen marks the progression of the rite: at the closing of the ceremony, a drop of the Easter candle falls into the water of the baptismal font and immediately takes the form of a tiny cross, so perfect that it would have been impossible for a human hand "to make anything like it with so little material." The countess reports these admirable deeds to Guibert of Nogent, and they are confirmed by a priest who witnessed them. This "sign" announces the exceptional fate of the child: in order to thwart his family's attempts at finding him, he is brought into the monastery of Fly where he immediately displays a great love of the Christian faith. As soon as he is a little older, "he is made to go from the Hebrew alphabet, in which he had begun his education, to the Latin alphabet," in which (as might be expected) he makes rapid progress. His reputation for intelligence and virtue grows steadily and Guibert gives him the short work he had written against the "Judaizing" Count John of Soissons, a vicious and thieving lord whose smallest crime was not protecting the Jews.[36] On the main issues, the story Guibert tells about William seems to be truthful. Sermons have been preserved that are explicitly attributed to the convert who became a monk under the name William of Fly (or Flay): *Wuillelmi Flaviacensiis monachi ex Judaeo conversi.*

The circumstances in which William and Herman became Christian and entered the religious life are noticeably different. Yet their destiny as converts presents more than one analogy: each voluntarily accepted baptism, and in each case their baptism is accompanied by wondrous signs; their original families each attempt to bring them back to Judaism; they are both distinguished in their rapid acquisition of the Latin language and Christian customs. But we cannot doubt that William, whose sermons have been preserved, really existed, and Guibert of Nogent takes great care to authenticate his account: he himself lived at Fly and knew the countess Hélissende. He even corresponded with William. Nevertheless, his relation of the events, with, for example, the appeal to the Christian supernatural in regard to baptism, is in no way different from the standard outline of other conversion accounts of a Jewish child in the twelfth century. The stories of Catherine of Louvain and, even more, William of Fly are seemingly or at least in part "true," but, like Herman the Jew's *Opusculum,* they are still *narratives.*

It is true that one could classify these accounts according to their degree of plausibility and call, for example, the account of William of Fly authentic, that of Herman doubtful, and that of Jacob of Regensberg frankly legendary. These judgments are based in the first place on the role played by the miraculous in these accounts, since we are no longer prepared today to believe in miracles. The mention, for example, of a corpse who comes back to life makes us perhaps overly suspect that the account can only be a legend. On the other hand, we crave objective elements of proof external to the account itself. It is because we still have extant manuscript versions of the sermons of William of Fly that we take Guibert of Nogent at his word. Herman the Jew, on the other hand, is known only from his own account. This is why Gerlinde Niemeyer moved beyond the account and went searching through the archives for some objective proof of his existence. But archives are only as good as what one does with them! Niemeyer went too far in assimilating the author of the *Opusculum* with the provost of Scheda (*Hermannus Israelita*) mentioned in 1170, and especially in insisting on reconstructing the whole supposed biography of Herman well after the point at which his account ends.

To focus on the narrative structures in order then to better understand their function constitutes in my eyes the only legitimate approach. It is by placing contemporary texts in the same field of vision that one can start to understand the specificity of each. Let us offer one last example, this one taken from the *Chronica Slavorum* of Arnold of Lübeck.

Living in the far north of Germany, this chronicler claims knowledge of a "miracle" that happened in the distant Rhineland town of Cologne. A young Jewish boy enters into a church on Easter Sunday and, moved by his genuine *curiositas*, he has a vision: he sees himself receiving baptism while the dove of the Holy Spirit hovers over his head. This revelation is not enough for him to abandon the *perfidia judaica*. One year later, while visiting the synagogue on Good Friday, he sees Jews crucifying a wax effigy of Christ. Immediately, he professes his belief in Christ and is baptized the following Easter Sunday. Alfred Haverkamp points out that this story was told in Lübeck and not in Cologne where the mutual acquaintance of Jews and Christians was too strong for the stereotype of Jews re-crucifying Christ in the form of an effigy to have any impact.[37] In this regard, Haverkamp writes, this story offers "no sure guide to the history of Jewish-Christian relations in Cologne."[38] However, the visit of the Jewish child to the church and the vision of the Holy Spirit in the form of a dove, a first step toward baptism, cannot help but appear as more widely diffused narrative themes, traces of which can be found, among others, in Herman's *Opusculum*. Assuredly, such a story forms part of the multifaceted background that illuminates the conversion account of Judas/Herman by allowing one to place the uniqueness of his case in perspective.

Herman's Baptism

A change of name during baptism is characteristic of Jewish, pagan, and Muslim converts.[39] The children of Christian parents receive their Christian name at birth and this name is confirmed upon baptism. In principle, this used to take place on the first feast of Easter following the birth of the child. But starting in the twelfth century the practice of *quamprimum* baptism, which takes place as soon as possible after birth, became more widespread; this out of the fear that a child might die without having received the sacrament necessary for salvation in the hereafter.[40] We have seen that several miracle accounts on the subject of the baptism of a Jewish child take place on Easter Sunday in accordance with tradition. But while the account of Herman's baptism conforms to tradition in regard to the time spent from the preparation of the catechumen to the sacrament[41]—four weeks—it makes no mention of Easter. If one believes Gerlinde Niemeyer, the baptism could even have taken place in late November.[42]

During baptism, the child officially receives his or her name. It can happen that the godfather(s) or godmother(s) name the child,[43] but this prerogative belongs rather to the father, with the godfathers or godmothers and the priest confirming the choice at the time of the rite.[44]

Herman likens himself to a child receiving baptism, for with this sacrament, he explains, "the church, virgin and mother, [. . .] placed me in the world like a newborn child" (*me per lavarum . . . in novam peperit ecclesia virgo mater infantiam*).[45] He thinks of himself as "the child of the church" which, along with the substitution of his name, again reinforces the notion of a complete identity change. The solitude of the Jewish convert is mitigated by a new spiritual lineage with his "mother" the Virgin-Church, as was shown by the case of Catherine of Louvain.

Baptism is for every Christian a new birth, but in the case of the conversion of an adult it appears as a dramatic rupture, as is shown by Guibert of Nogent and more especially by Herman. The devil would have tried until the last moment to prevent the sacrament from being administered. Through his stratagems, he would have pushed the catechumen out of the baptismal font in order to prevent the triple immersion in the name of the Trinity. His face streaming with cold water, the soon-to-be-renamed Judas neither sees nor hears the clerics who use voice and gesture to enjoin him to stay in the water. The scene borders on the comical, and one can ask what the effects were on Herman's listeners: did they see the humor, or did they see further cause for worrying about the devil's traps? This account is also astonishing in a period during which baptism was administered to children in a baptismal font. In describing the baptism of an adult, the *Opusculum* seems to speak of immersion. Medieval iconography continued for some time to represent the rite of baptism by the immersion into a large stone font, not only in the case of adults, but also in the case of children.[46] Among early examples one thinks especially of the prototype for all later baptisms of converted Jews—the baptism of the Levite Judas in the legend of Saint Helena. Thanks to his testimony, Constantine's mother was able to discover the hidden location of the Holy Cross. Once a Christian, the former Levite later succeeded to the bishopric of Jerusalem under the name Cyriac.[47] This legend, which appeared in the fifth century and was taken up in the thirteenth century by Jacobus de Voragine in the *Golden Legend*, was the subject of a rich and ancient iconography.[48] Regarding the baptism of children, the story of Cappenberg provides extraordinary testimony.

The abbey indeed possessed a baptismal basin (*Taufschale*) that may have served for pouring baptismal water on the head of the child (or adult) admitted to baptism. It is especially precious, both for the quality of its silver work and because of its origin. It is at once a "monument" to the glory of Cappenberg and its founders and a visual exaltation of the central importance of Christian baptism. The iconography of this basin, now preserved in Berlin,[49] has never been connected to the baptism of Herman the Jew. In 1122, immediately after the foundation of Cappenberg, the son of Frederick II of Swabia is baptized, the future Frederick Barbarossa. His godfather is none other than Otto of Cappenberg, brother of Godfried of Cappenberg and cofounder (with his brother) of the abbey of which he will be provost from 1156 to 1171. The same year that Otto becomes provost, his godson Frederick Barbarossa is crowned emperor. It is on this occasion that the emperor offers to his godfather the gilded silver basin featuring the celebration of his own baptism in 1222 in the presence of Otto, his *patrinus*.

Let us examine this basin closely (fig. 5). The exterior rim is decorated in a finely etched pattern of notched leaves. The interior of the basin shows the baptism of the young Frederick. At the very center is the naked child, with either a full head of hair or wearing some kind of hood. The cylindrical font in which he is immersed is richly decorated with three horizontal and circular bands and placed on a paved surface. The ecclesiastic building is not represented. An inscription in the form of a cross placed right above the child's head identifies him by his name and his future title:

FRI

DE

RI

C[US]

I[M]P[ERA]T[OR]

The child is plunged into the font but supported below the arms by two people: On his left is a bishop wearing the mitre and attended by a tonsured cleric. In keeping with the traditional iconography of baptism, the bishop places his hand on the child's head, a gesture also illustrated, for example, in the Carolingian image of the baptism of Judas the Levite.[50] On his right the child is supported by his godfather who simultaneously places his left hand on Frederick's shoulder. Otto is also identified by his name, which can be read in one direction as in the other:[51]

OT
TO

Encircling the central image are two bands of two inscriptions, the outer one in larger capital letters. The inner inscription explains the symbolism of the baptismal water:

+ QUEM . LAVAT . UNDA . FORIS . HOMINIS . MEMOR .
INTERIORIS . UT . SIS . Q[U]OD . N[ON] . ES . ABLUE . T[ER]GE .
Q[U]OD . ES +

[You whom the water washes exteriorly, remember the inner man;
to become what you are not, wash and clean that which you are.]

The baptismal water should therefore "wash" the soul of original sin the same way that ordinary water washes the outer body of man. The inscription also invokes "memory," for that too is a function of the basin, piously pre-served throughout one's life in order to remind the baptized of the force of the rite that he underwent in childhood.

The outer circle carries a second inscription that refers explicitly to the gift given by the emperor to his godfather:

+ CESAR . ET . AUGUSTUS . HEC . OTTONI . FRIDERICUS . MUN-
ERA . PATRINO . CONTULIT . ILLE . D[E]O +

[Frederick, emperor and augmenter of the Empire, gave these gifts
to his godfather Otto, whom God blesses.]

The plural noun *munera* seems to indicate that the basin was not Freder-ick Barberossa's only gift to Otto of Cappenberg. No doubt one has to count among them the reliquary head that we shall consider later on.[52] For now, let us simply remember the close connection between the ideology of baptism and the prestige of the new foundation of Cappenberg. In this connection, the gift of the baptismal font cannot be separated from the attention given to the baptism of the "Hebrew brother" in the *Vita of Godfried of Cappenberg*, a veritable miracle proclaiming that the new abbey is truly blessed by God. Neither can the gift of the basin be separated from the centrality that this same baptism occupies in the *Opusculum*.

The baptismal font of the Westphalian church of Freckenhorst, close to Cappenberg, should also be placed in relation to the baptism of Herman/Judas in the *Opusculum* (fig. 5). It dates to 1129, the year of the consecration of the church.[53] Its decoration precisely evokes the bands that encircle the image of the baptismal font on the silver basin of Cappenberg: above an imposing base are the figures of the prophet Daniel and four recumbent lions symbolizing the forces of evil against which man can only be delivered through baptism and divine mercy (Psalms 23 [22] and 7:2–3). Immediately above, seven arcades going from right to left contain scenes from the life of Christ: the Annunciation to Mary, the Nativity, the Baptism of Christ, the Crucifixion, the Descent into Hell and the Resurrection, the Ascension, and Christ in glory surrounded by the symbols of the Evangelists. The head of Daniel in the lions' den is directly underneath the scene of Christ's baptism. It is also from this spot that one reads, from left to right, the extraordinary inscription that separates the two iconographic registers:[54]

+ ANNO . AB .INCARNAT[IONE] . D[OMI]NI . M . C . XX . VIII . EPACT[IS] . XXVIII . CONCURR[ENTIBUS] . I . P[OST] . B[ISSEXTILEM] . INDICT[IONE] . VII . II . NONAS . IUN[II] . A VENERAB[ILI] EP[ISCOP]O . MIMIGARDEVORDENSI . EGEB-ERTO . ORDINAT[IONIS] . SUE . ANNO . II . CONSECRATU[M] . E[ST] . HOC . TEMPLUM .

[In the year 1129 of the Incarnation of our Lord, epactis 28, concurrent 1, after a bissextile year, indication 7, the second none of June [4 June], by the venerable bishop Eckbert of Münster, the second year of his ordination, this church was consecrated.]

The bishop Eckbert of Münster was thus the author of the dedication of the church of Freckenhorst, situated in his diocese. The same bishop, according to the *Opusculum*, places the young Judas during these years on the path toward baptism. In every respect, then, the theme of baptism appears central not only for this prelate, but for the entire ecclesiastical milieu of the early twelfth century in which he exercises his authority: Münster, Cappenberg, Freckenhorst, and Cologne. What is more, the relation between the *Opusculum* and the font of Freckenhorst allows us to highlight the connection between the foundation of a church and baptismal ideology. It is on the font itself, and not elsewhere in the building, that one finds the inscription commemorating the foundation. Finally, the lions that threaten Daniel in the pit recall the symbolic meaning of baptism by echoing the description of the rite that Herman underwent. Baptism is largely understood as an exorcism intended to chase the demonic forces away from the body and soul of the baptized. In the eleventh century, the canonist Burchard of Worms (d. 1025) strongly noted the connection between baptism and exorcism. In the early thirteenth century, Marie of Oignies (d. 1213) had in the doorway of a church a vision of the devil furious at having to drop his prey, after he had just caught a young catechumen; no sooner was this youth baptized than the saint saw angels encircling and elevating his soul. Synodical statutes of the time also prescribe that the baptismal font must remain covered between two ceremonies in order to protect the holy water from "impurities and spells." For these reasons one must also keep under lock and key the chrism and holy oil.[55] Concern over the harassment and evil spells of the devil are all the greater as the child brought to the font is not yet cleansed of original sin: the child is therefore easy prey for the devil. Finally, the attention given to evil doings is only equaled by the attention given to the beneficial deeds and words of the priest, while the formalism of the baptismal ritual is a self-enforcing process.[56]

The purifying water and its infusion by the priest should, according to Christians, repulse all the forces of evil. But the horror of spells and impurity is no less strong for contemporary Jews; it is simply transposed onto the baptismal water itself, which is judged loathsome and something from which a pious Jew must turn away. Similarly, the interpretations of the Old Testament offered by Christian theologians for the defense of baptism are systematically contested by the rabbis: neither Moses' crossing of the Red Sea with the Hebrews, nor the crossing of the Jordan by the tribes of Israel under the guidance of Joshua (an episode that for Christians prefigures the baptism of Christ in the same river)[57] is in any way justification for baptism.[58]

The Change of Name

With one exception, none of the historians who have studied the *Opusculum* have asked why the alleged author of the work elected to take the name

Herman upon conversion rather than some other.[59] Several scholars have
noted that that this name is not reserved for converts and that it is even fairly
common: within the Premonstratensian order, for example, we find not only
the blessed Herman Joseph of Steinfeld (died in 1241 or 1252), but Abbot
Herman of Cappenberg (1171–1210) and the first superior of Scheda to be
appointed abbot, Herman of Scheda, mentioned in 1197 and again in 1217.[60]
The name Herman gains frequency in German-speaking lands in the twelfth
and thirteenth centuries, a fact confirmed for example by the obituary frag-
ment preserved from Cappenberg where it appears at least once every two
pages.[61] In the *Opusculum* Herman is named four times: in the incipit written
after his death we read of "brother Herman formerly a Jew, of good memory"
(*bone memorie fratris Hermanni quondam Iudei*). More interesting is that in
the other three instances, it is Herman who names himself: in his introductory letter to his "very dear son Henry" he gives his name, *Hermannus* or
Herimannus depending on the manuscript. At the beginning of chapter 1, he
presents himself as "I, Herman, unworthy priest, formerly named Judas, of
the line of Israel, of the tribe of Levi, having as my father David and my
mother Sephora."[62] Finally, in chapter 19 where he describes the vicissitudes
of his baptism, he indicates that it was at this moment that he took the
Christian name Herman: "Having changed in this basin of water the order
of my inner life as well as my previous name, which was formerly Judas, I
took the name Herman."[63] In the course of his account, Herman insists on
the fact that he changed his Jewish name (Judas) for this Christian name and
that this substitution took place during the rite of baptism. The text also
evokes two different modes of identity: the young Jew is identified not only
by his name, but by those of his parents, David and Sephora, and by his
tribe, the tribe of Levi. According to Genesis 46, Levi was the son of Jacob
and Leah, thus the half-brother of Judas, who in turn was born to Rachel.
Contrary to what Avrom Saltman affirmed, these biblical names are perfectly
plausible in the Jewish communities of the period. In citing both his Jewish
name and the names of his parents, Herman is also following a form of
designation attested to among contemporary Jews.[64] This is in sharp contrast
to the manner in which Herman cites his Christian name: here no parentage
is given, as Herman is alone and without a family. All that counts is the
personal name he received at baptism.

What can we say about this name? It is Germanic in origin, linking the
old High German prefix *Heri-* or *Hari-* with the suffix *Mann*, man. The
prefix of the root *Harja* (which can also be used as a suffix) signifies etymologically "the people" and, by extension, "the army" (*Heer*). The proper name

Harriman, Heriman, or Herman (or any other form) is well attested to by the eighth century and becomes widespread in Germany in the Middle Ages.[65] Etymologically, Herman has the most general meaning imaginable, of "man," man in the sense of belonging to his people, "man in arms," the "warrior." In the sixteenth century, Luther is still very well aware of its meaning "warrior," indeed even "knight."[66]

In imagining that the "warrior" meaning was understood in the twelfth century, the choice of this name by (or for) a young Jewish convert devoted to the priesthood may seem paradoxical. But one has to bear in mind the child's initial dream of the emperor bestowing upon him the arms and charger of a dead lord: would his conversion and entry into the order of Prémontré not make him a *miles Christi*, or "soldier of Christ"? One should perhaps also consider a "popular etymology" of the name that would understand "Herman" as meaning "the man of the Lord" (*Mann des Herren: Herrenmann*). But this is pure conjecture.

Whatever its meaning, real or imagined, was Herman a name of choice among Jewish converts? Documents of the period and the region mention several other instances of Herman the Jew (or Herman the Israelite, or Herman the Hebrew). Ludger Horstkötter has, with good reason, argued against the assimilation of these with the author of the *Opusculum*. But neither this name, nor any other, seems to have been slated for converts. There existed in Cologne a well-established Christian family by the name of Jude (or "Jew"), for whom no possible links to an earlier convert have ever been shown with any certainty.[67]

These questions send us back to the long and complicated history of individual appellations in medieval society. This history is marked in the West by two great turning points: the first, which Michael Mitterauer has called the "Constantian turning point," took place in late antiquity when the Roman system of *tria nomina* (*praenomen*, *nomen gentilice*, and *cognomen*, such as Gaius Julius Caesar) slowly disappeared. By the Middle Ages all that remained was the *cognomen* (which was henceforth called the *nomen*), a single name used for designating the individual. At the same time, the number of names used greatly diminished, something Mitterauer called "the great anthroponomic depression" (*der grosse Namenschwund*). The single name that remained often referenced saints or the local prince (in the latter category one finds, for example, William, Robert, or Richard in Normandy and in Anglo-Norman England; Heinrich and Konrad—"Heinz und Kunz"—in the German Empire). These two functions could sometimes come together in a single personage, such as Edward the Confessor in England, Henry II in Germany, or Saint Louis in France.[68] Their reputation of saintliness and their royal prestige simultaneously explain the success of their names in countries brought under their dominion. In the high Middle Ages, the concentration of names is considerable: in the region of Toulouse, for example, the nine most common names are borne by 80 to 90 percent of the men (and the same is true for women).

The second turning point started during the thirteenth century, beginning in aristocratic milieus:[69] to the single name (*nomen*) was added a second name (which reused the title *cognomen*). The cognomen referred to a land, a fief, a locality, or a profession, a social status, or even a physical particularity of an individual. In time, this evolution gave birth to the modern system of a "family name" that follows the "first name." Was it the extreme reduction of the stock of single names that necessitated the adding of a second name in order to distinguish individuals? Or rather, as Mitterauer suggests, was it the appearance of the "family name" that accelerated a reduction in the number of *nomina*?[70]

The choice of a new Christian name made by or for converts was subjected to the same rules governing the naming of Christians. Petrus Alfonsi (formerly Moses) explains in his *Dialogus* (1110) why he chose this double name: he received his baptism in Huesca on 29 June 1106, "the day of the feast of saints Peter and Paul." This is why, he continues, "out of veneration for the apostle Peter and in memory of him I took the name Peter. My godfather was Alfonso [I of Aragon] who held me at the baptismal font; this is why I added his name to my aforementioned glorious name, giving myself the name Petrus Alfonsi."[71] The contemporary account of Guibert of Nogent concerning William of Fly likewise illustrates the role of the godfather in the naming of a young Jewish convert at the time of his baptism: William carries the name of the knight William of Eu who saved him during the massacre at Rouen.[72] In the early thirteenth century, the Jewish convert William of Bourges, author of the *Book of the Lords' Wars Against the Jews* (c. 1235), takes his name from William of Dongeon, archbishop of Bourges (d. 1210).[73]

We do not know precisely under what circumstances another Jewish convert, Pablo Christiani, was led to change his name.[74] Most likely born in Montpellier, Pablo was raised by Rabbi Eliezer ben Emmanuel of Tarascon and Rabbi Jacob ben Elijah Lattès of Venice, was married, and had a family. He converted as an adult in 1209 and became a preacher at the instigation of Raymond of Peñafort. In this latter capacity he served as the principal protagonist on the Christian side in the Barcelona Disputation of 1263 in which he confronted Rabbi Moses ben Nahman (Nahmanides) in the presence of King James I of Aragon. His Jewish name had been Saul, which he changed, as one might expect, to Paul: by all evidence, he was looking to imitate the apostle in every respect including his change of name.

Returning to Herman, no emperor, king, or saint had previously carried the name Herman. (The blessed Premonstratensian Herman-Joseph was born around 1150 and so his name could not have exercised any influence.)[75] Nor was the name suggested to the young Jew in either the dream or the vision he had before baptism: the emperor whom he dreamt about is not called Herman, whereas in the case of Catherine of Louvain (formerly Rachel) it is the Virgin who, when she appears before the young Jewess, gives her the Christian name.

In the absence of princely patronage or an eponymous saint, or, as in the case of miracle accounts, the intervention of the Virgin, another practice is employed in the Middle Ages, which is that children are given names that are already popular in the family (what Mitterauer calls *Nachbenennung*). This was first done in aristocratic families, the function of a heightened awareness of their lineage and the memory of their ancestors (*memoria*): the name is seen as a patrimonial asset among others (castles, domains, crests, etc.) and is frequently passed on by "skipping a generation," for example from grandfather to grandson.[76] This skipping normally has as a condition that the ancestor be deceased at the time of the new birth. As Christiane Klapisch-Zuber has shown in the case of Florentine patricians between 1360 and 1530, the parents gain by this practice the possibility of "remaking the name" of the deceased ancestor, almost allowing him to be "reincarnated" in the grandson. But in the case of Herman the Jew, any strategy that involves his "carnal" parents is excluded, for in accepting baptism Herman has lost his Jewish family.

Through baptism, however, he enters a new family, a "spiritual" family that includes all the Christians of the church, and more especially the clergy of Cologne who are delighted to see him undergo baptism. At the first level of a "spiritual" family is the godfather or godfathers of a baptized male, and the godmother or godmothers of a female. In the high Middle Ages baptismal parentage, a role well established since the sixth century, acquires unprecedented importance. Take for example the exclusion of blood relatives from the rite of baptism and the prohibition against any matrimonial alliance, and by consequence the exclusion of all relations that would lead to a crossing between spiritual and biological parentage.[77] Or consider the rather frequent practice of a godfather or godmother giving their name to the child. We have already seen that King Alfonso of Aragon gave his name to his godson, the Jewish convert Petrus Alfonsi. This practice was no less common for Christian children. An excellent early thirteenth-century instance of this is the Franciscan chronicler Salimbene of Adam. In an autobiographical passage of his chronicle, he indicates that "in the world" he carried the name Baliano "because of a lord by the same name [Baliano of Sagitta] who held me at the baptismal font." But this name was not the name he took upon ordination, nor the one he eventually took upon entrance into the Minors.[78]

In the case of Herman, it must surely be the case—if we hold to the thesis of the authenticity of the account—that one of the persons in attendance served as his godfather, no doubt one of the clerics who influenced him. Curiously enough, chapter 19, which describes his baptism in detail, makes no mention of any such presence. This silence deprives us of knowing whether Judas/Herman had a *patrinus* by the name of Herman. Another explanation is possible, but it requires that we once again leave Cologne (and its Cathedral of Saint Peter where Herman was baptized) in favor of the abbey of Cappenberg, founded in 1121 by Counts Godfried and Otto. Let us listen to the account of this founding from the anonymous *Life of Godfried of Cappenberg,* written at Cappenberg in the middle of the twelfth century. Following the rules for this hagiographical genre, the text begins by evoking the *stirps,* the noble lineage to which the local "saint" belongs:

> In the time of the glorious Henry, the fifth of that name to rule the Roman Empire [Henry V, 1106–1125], in the province of Westphalia Godfried was chosen and loved by God; born to very noble parents with royal lineage, he took charge of his country out of fear of God. His father was named Godfried, his mother Beatrice. But this man who was very venerable and worthy of being counted among the friends of God had a grandfather (*avum*) by the name of Herman who, we have learned about through the very frequent recounting of elderly persons, was distinguished above all by his charity, which he devoted to the work of forgiveness. He was the greatest defender of peace against the troubles of insolent knights, and when still alive he performed the following miracle: a blind man who lived off of charity affirmed that one day God revealed to him that he would regain his sight if he ran over his eyes the water

with which the count had washed his hands. He took this water, applied it to his eyes and immediately was able to see. His tomb now bears the proof of the miracles that he accomplished (*indicia ostensarum virtutum*); I saw them with my own eyes: those who, having recovered their health, returned healthy and left on the tomb evidence of their miracle. The grandson (*nepos*) of such a great lord, our Godfried, began to dedicate himself to God in his early adolescence.[79]

The old castle of Cappenberg, transformed into an abbey, houses the sepulcher of a man, the grandfather of the founder, venerated for his holiness and his miracles. The name of this glorious Herman passed neither to his son, nor his grandson, each of whom was named Godfried. We can, however, ask ourselves whether by entering into the "spiritual family" of Cappenberg, the person whom the *Vita* proudly calls the "Hebrew brother" was not in fact appointed to receive a name that had been skipped by several generations, that of the holy spiritual ancestor of the canons. The silence maintained by the *Opusculum* on the question of Herman's godfather is perhaps not accidental: it permitted a "remaking of the name" of this "saint Herman" in the person of the Jewish convert, the youngest of the "sons" of the abbey. Is the quasi-miracle that is this conversion according to the *Vita*, even more so than the ex-votos ever visible on the tomb, not the best evidence of the inexhaustible *virtus* of the old "saint Herman"?

Only the convergence of the factors examined above allows one to conclude this hypothesis with some degree of likelihood. Even if impossible to verify, one has to measure its implications for the debate over the "truth" or "fiction" of the *Opusculum*. For it is not the clerics of Cologne, witnesses to Herman's baptism, but the canons of Cappenberg who could have given Herman his name in memory of the highly venerated grandfather of their holy founder. This hypothesis should not for that matter lead us completely to reject the thesis of Herman's "reality" and the "authenticity" of his autobiography. But it does point in the direction indicated by Avrom Saltman: if the brothers of Cappenberg wrote the *Opusculum* all the while using the first person and attributing the work to the "Hebrew brother," whose coming into the abbey filled them with pride, then they had good reasons for giving such a name to their hero.

Mind you we have not yet said the final word about Herman's name. At the beginning of the *Opusculum*, we recall, the Christian name under which the work is presented is *Hermannus quondam Iudeus*. Should his *quondam* ("formerly")[80] not stay with us as much as his original Jewish name, Judas ben David ha-Levi, and the Christian name, Herman, which came to replace it?

Chapter 6

"A New Era of Conversion"

The moment of baptism marks not only the pinnacle of Herman's conversion account; during the course of the twelfth century it is situated more generally at the heart of liturgical practice, imagination, and imagery, all of which emphasize its importance. Herman's account echoes a number of other conversion accounts that share the same framework and many recurrent themes. Conversion is no more of a purely individual experience than is a dream. It signifies adherence to a broader paradigm that, during this period of *reformatio* and *renovatio* of the church and Christian society, commands people's destiny and indeed the destiny of the world that surrounds them. The call to "conversion" concerns not only Jews and "pagans," but Christians too. The entire society and culture of the times are impelled to "convert," that is, in the literal sense of the term, to turn around and face in the right direction.

Norbert of Xanten

If we do not know who wrote the *Opusculum*, we do at least know that the work was composed at Cappenberg, the first Premonstratensian establishment in Germanic lands. For this community of "clerics" the founder Norbert of Xanten (c. 1080/1085–1134) incarnated the conversionary model par excellence, that of Saint Paul. The two versions of his *Vita* (a short version A written by a cleric of Magdeburg, and a long version B written by a Premonstratensian canon) continually return to the dramatic and exemplary conversion of the founder of the order. The same is true of the *Miracles of Saint Mary of Laon* written after 1136 by Herman of Laon (in close proximity to

Prémontré), the *Additamenta* or additions to the *Miracles* of Norbert compiled at Cappenberg after his visit to the abbey (*Additamenta fratrum Cappenbergensium ad Vitam Norberti posteriorem*), and the *Vita of Godfried of Cappenberg* that describes the same visit.[1] The story of the conversion is a classic one: Norbert's father Héribert, the lord of Gennep in Limbourg, and his mother Hadiwigis gave him up at childhood to the clergy following a dream. Norbert becomes a "worldly" cleric active in the imperial court (he attends the coronation of Henry V in Rome, an occasion that nearly had him named bishop of Cambrai) as well as in the service of the archbishop of Cologne, Frederick of Schwarzenberg, the faithful prelate to the emperor in the Investiture controversy (*Investiturstreit*). He belongs, then, in his beginnings, to the imperial faction that opposes the party of the pontifical "Gregorian" reformers. The *Vita* begins in 1115 when, under the reign of Pope Paschal II and Emperor Henry V, the cleric Norbert turned subdeacon goes from one success to another.

> And so, one day, he appeared at a place called Wreden [in Westphalia] in a habit of rare silk (*in cultu vestis sericae*) accompanied by a single boy (*puer*). The dark clouds, the lightning bolts, and the rumbling of thunder were all the more disturbing since there was no village close by to provide refuge. He and his companion were at an emotional extreme when, in the terrifying peal of the thunder, he saw lightning strike the ground in front of him, opening up a hole roughly the size of a man. Out of the hole came a terrible stench that clung to him and his clothing. Having fallen from his horse, he heard a voice that seemed to chastise him. This voice brought him to his senses (*ad se reversus*) and immediately set him on the path to penitence while he contemplated (*revolvebat*) the words of the Psalms: "*Depart from evil, and do good*" [Psalm 37 (36):27]. It was in this spirit that he retraced his path (*reversus est*). Once back at home, pushed into the spirit of salvation out of the fear of God, he donned a hair shirt under his outer clothing and substituted for his prior life one devoted to the care [of his soul] and to penitence. He entered the monastery of Siegburg in the edifying vicinity of Abbot Cuno from whom he took instruction and lessons in the fear and love of God.[2]

The long version (version B) of the *Vita* expands every passage of the account:[3] the storm is more intense, and more importantly, the companion takes over the narrative in order to offer a commentary explaining the ideo-

logical references within the text: "Now what? The illiterate does not abandon the learned, the servant does not leave his master, the boy calls out to
his elder: 'Norbert, where are you going' (*Norberte, quo vadis?*) 'Lord, what
are you doing?' (*Domine, quid agis?*) 'Come back, father, come back (*revertere*), the powerful hand of the Lord is against you.'"

This is followed by a comparison between Norbert's fallen horse and
Balaam's ass that is terror-stricken at the sight of the Lord's angel standing in
the road with a drawn sword in his hand (Num 22: 22–30). And the hagiogra-
pher continues: "The Lord seemed to want to remind him rather than convert him (*plus ad revocandum, nec tardus ad convertendum*), as if he said:
'Norbert, Norbert, why do you persecute me?'" The divine admonishments
give way to the crash of the lightning. The child is stupefied and Norbert is
on the ground half-dead, as is his horse. After an hour, Norbert seems to
awaken. Coming to his senses (*reverses ad se*), he addresses God: "Lord, what
do you want me to do?" The divine voice answers him: "*Depart from evil
and do good.*" He immediately turns himself around. This is followed, with
much greater detail than in the A version, by the account of the transformation of his life and his retreat to the side of Abbot Cuno of Siegburg.

It is not difficult to see in this account, and especially in its long version,
a "true replication of the scene of the road to Damascus," a slavish imitation
of the passage in the Acts of the Apostles (9:3–9) describing the "conversion"
of the Jew Saul, alias Saint Paul:[4]

> He was going along and approaching Damascus when suddenly a light
> from the sky flashed around him. Falling to the ground, he heard a voice
> that said to him: "Saul, Saul, why do you persecute me?"—"Who are
> you, lord?" he said. And he: "I am Jesus that you persecute. But get up
> and enter the city, and you will be told what you are to do." His travel
> companions were stopped, speechless in their wonder as they heard the
> voice but saw no one. Saul stood up, but though his eyes were open, he
> saw nothing. So they led him by the hand to Damascus. For three days
> he was without sight, and neither ate nor drank.

The differences between the two accounts are not negligible, but the
general framework, the details of the lightning and the fall from the horse,
the words exchanged with God, and the consequences of the event are in fact
the same. Norbert's "turning around" is conceived of, following the model
of Saint Paul, as an abrupt and decisive moment. Thus it is not quite of the

same nature as the hesitation-filled progression that leads Herman the Jew on the path to baptism. Herman never even received the awaited "sign" that would immediately indicate the path to follow. The process of conversion can therefore submit to different rhythms. Sometimes, it is longer and more torturous, as for Augustine in his *Confessions*. In other instances conversion can appear as sudden as lightning, as with Saint Paul, and following him, Norbert of Xanten.

We would do well, however, not to oppose two distinct models of conversion: when Norbert turns himself around, not all is won and, in the "familiarity" and "saintly conversation" of Cuno of Siegburg, he will still have to do a long penance. By contrast, for Saint Augustine, the episode of the orchard where he receives the divine order to read Scripture (*Tolle, lege!*) marks a sharp turn in the story of his conversion, whatever were the ups and downs along the way. For Herman, for whom conversion was long and fraught with difficulties, there was also an initial shock, that which provoked in his spirit the sight of the crucifix. Moreover, the *Opusculum* refers twice, and at length, to the conversion of Saint Paul, "miraculously transformed from Saul to Paul, from fox to lamb," and it describes in detail the episode of the "path to Damascus."[5] For this Premonstratensian text, Saint Paul is even more of a model than is his emulator Norbert (who, in contrast to the Apostle, is not named in the *Opusculum*). The Jewish convert Judas/Herman is a true carbon copy of the Jewish convert Saul/Paul.

What distinguishes Norbert's conversion above all from those of Herman and Paul is that he is not, at the outset, a Jew. It is not the purpose of his conversion to arrive at baptism. Norbert had been baptized at birth just like all Christians. For him, conversion consists of performing penitence, abandoning his life of sin (symbolized by the silk habit), and, in the literal as well as figurative sense, of "turning around" (*se revertere*). Two levels of symbolic opposition combine in this account, as in many others, to express Norbert's *mutatio*: on one hand there is the opposition between outer and inner (*foris/intus, exterius/interius*), between the care of the body and the care of the soul, and between the sumptuous clothing of a worldly life (symbolic of the sinful soul) and the religious habit (symbolic of the purified soul). On the other hand there is the spatial opposition between going and returning, which is symbolic of the moral turnaround that replaces the search for worldly vanities (the goal of the excursion to Wreden in the company of a boy is not even specified) with the "inner voyage," the interiority and introspection under the spiritual guidance of the wise Cuno of Siegburg.

Once instructed, Norbert goes to perform penance at the feet of the archbishop of Cologne from whom he receives a special dispensation to be consecrated deacon and priest on the same day. However, it is not in conformity to canonical law to skip stages and Norbert's enemies, beginning with Rupert of Deutz, are quick to attack him for it. Norbert's haste seems to be explained by his desire to preach to the people. The irritation that he provokes and the derision that he draws are, in his mind, proof that there is urgency in spreading the word of God. Indeed the ideal of the *vita apostolica* exerts an attraction that becomes increasingly clear: he spends a long time with the hermit Liudolf, gives his possessions to the poor, and makes a barefoot pilgrimage to Saint-Gilles, where Pope Gelasius II grants him a license to preach. Upon his return in the north, he receives the support of Bishop Burchard of Cambrai, who places at his disposal a cleric named Hugh of Fosse (who will later succeed him as head of Prémontré). The striking "novelty" of their lifestyle (*novum genus vitae*) and their capacity to reestablish public peace, everywhere that it is threatened, leads to some considerable success. Two years go by in which Norbert continues to live hermetically (*quasi solitarius*), wearing "goat and sheep skins." His behavior begins to disturb church authorities and in July 1118 he has to justify himself in front of the papal legate: he affirms having followed the example of Saint John the Baptist and Saint Cecilia.

In 1119, at the council of Reims, Pope Calixtus II confirms the authorization to preach that was granted by his predecessor. Norbert follows him to Laon, where Bishop Bartholomew decides to station him. For Norbert, as for many other "new apostles" of the day, this is a decisive moment. The itinerant and dangerous life that rouses the emotions of the crowds, but which also disturbs the ecclesiastical hierarchy, comes to be replaced by the stability of the church-controlled cenobitic life. Norbert refuses the first two places that he is offered, but does not hesitate to accept the third: in the forest of Coucy "he chooses a completely deserted and solitary location which the inhabitants have since time immemorial called Prémontré." *Prae-monstratum*: was this location not "pré-montré" (i.e., previously shown), that is, predestined? Once again, the belief in supernatural signs and the rhetoric of signs that bring it into focus (for example, the triple designation of the predestined location) are made vivid in the representations. This is true whether it be the souls thirsting for a miraculous revelation (as is the case for Judas/Herman) or the choice of a place where man's project goes hand in hand with God's plan (as in the case of the foundation of Prémontré and many other abbeys).

By dint of miracles, visions, and exorcisms, Norbert quickly surrounds himself with a small group of loyal men and women. By 1121, thirty novices are living around him. Bishops and abbots look to counsel him on the religious form that his new community should take. Each gives their advice, "some advise a hermetic way of life, others an anchoritic lifestyle, and others still advise him to adopt the Cistercian order." These words seem to echo the *Libellus de diversis ordinibus et professionibus qui sunt in aecclesia*, a contemporary work by an anonymous regular canon—perhaps a Premonstratensian— who, like Norbert, seems to be from the diocese of Liège. The *Libellus* describes and justifies the "diverse orders that are in the Church" and especially the more or less strict modes of life that are somewhat distanced from the people and the world and possible under each rule. It begins by considering hermits, then monks, then canons, and then (though the second volume is lost) the community of women.

In conformity to the intellectual techniques in vogue during the twelfth century, the author uses the models present in the Old Testament to justify the diverse orders of monks and canons that have appeared "in our time."[6] Thus the different types of Levites enumerated in the book of Numbers correspond presently to the diverse sorts of canons: those who live furthest from the world, like the Premonstratensians, those who live closer, and finally those who lead a worldly life and are for that reason called secular canons. Canons can ascend to the priesthood, since certain Levites were priests.[7] In such a comparison between biblical times and the present, it is, once more, the paradigm of conversion that one sees at work, a major characteristic of the clerical culture of the time. Just as the Old Testament "type" is "converted" by biblical gloss into a Christian "prototype," the biblical model of the Levite is "converted" into the Christian and actual figure of the "cleric," canon, and priest. This is why the biblical figure of the Levite is so dear to the Premonstratensians, which is also demonstrated by the above-mentioned works of Anselm of Havelberg and Philip of Harvengt. The same idea underlies the exposition of Judas/Herman's development in the *Opusculum*: born of the tribe of Levi—*tribu Levita*, reads the text—after his baptism and his entry into the Premonstratensian canons of Cappenberg, Judas ascends all the minor and major orders up until the priesthood, which makes of him, so to speak, a "Christian Levite." In the chapter devoted to the canons of Prémontré, the *Libellus* enumerates with precision the entire ladder of the orders that Herman had to climb, but notes that not all the canons are called to the priesthood: "though, like the Levites, they are taken from God's people, they do not receive the sacred commandments; some are devoted to priestly ministry, some are promoted to the office of the deacon, a few are admitted to the rank of sub-deacon, a few are appointed to the order acolytes,[8] exorcists, porters, readers, and in a pinch, those who are the least apt for these functions are admitted into the church as clerics, and this is why they call themselves converts (*conversi*)."[9]

The last category, which most likely assumes the defining tonsure of the cleric, shows even in its name what is meant at its most profound level by conversion: to renounce the world, choose the path of God, and merge into the Christian community. Following this, the modalities of the choice are countless. But Judas/Herman, "our Hebrew brother," could do no less than achieve the priesthood, the summit of the hierarchy of the orders, where he becomes the perfect and most accomplished Premonstratensian figure.

Urged to choose a Rule under which to live with his brothers, Norbert relies on his conscience and on God and sets his heart on the Rule of Augustine, which traditionally governs the canonical life. Godfried of Cappenberg then confides in Norbert his own plan to voluntarily embrace poverty and to "convert" (*commutaret*) his castle into an abbey (1121). It is needless here to go into the third and last phase of Norbert of Xanten's life, when in 1125 he accepts the metropolitan seat of Magdeburg, sowing turmoil in his earliest disciples, among them Godfried of Cappenberg. We know that, in contrast, Bernard of Clairvaux never accepted the Episcopal responsibilities that were offered him.[10] But Norbert, trained in the territory of the empire and in the Ottonian tradition of the church, knows the power conferred upon the holder of the seat of Magdeburg. From Magdeburg, and until his death in 1134, he will assure the new order a remarkable expansion in the regions of the east, toward Brandenburg, Prussia, Saxony, and Bohemia.[11]

In a few intense years, between 1115 and 1119, Norbert would have lived like a Wanderprediger "dressed in goat and sheep skins," arousing the enthusiasm of the poor, but also arousing the worries of certain members of the clergy, who end up fixing him to the ground and enclosing him in the bosom of the ecclesiastical hierarchy. His situation at the threshold of orthodoxy and heresy is far from unique at the turn of the eleventh century, particularly in the south of France where Norbert made a pilgrimage and where he was able to learn of new forms of the "apostolic life." Examples of these are the hermit Stephen of Muret (c. 1040/1050–1124), who is at the origin of the congregation of Grandmont in the Limousin, or Bernard of Tiron (c. 1046–1117), who was first a hermit in Maine and then founded the monastery of Tiron, or his friend Robert of Arbrissel (c. 1045–1116), the founder of the double monastery of Fontevraud (which is in many ways comparable to Prémontré).[12] But other "paupers of Christ," starting from smaller places, were rejected as heretical, often for having usurped the right of preaching, which, as we have already seen, occupied Norbert in his early years. Among those pursued and condemned were Henry of Lausanne in western France (around 1145) and, in the region of Utrecht, Tanchelm (c. 1115), whose principal adversary was Norbert.[13]

A double tension governs the destiny of all these persons, and Norbert of Xanten was no exception: on one hand it consists in a spirit of "conversion" that invites a "turning back" in order to "avert" the attractions of the world and a "turn toward" the love of the Lord. On the other, it consists in the occasionally contradictory necessity of choosing a way of life, a *habitus* and a *regula*, that escapes the perils of the itinerant life through founding a stable religious community. More than anything else, this tension and these contradictions characterize the most innovative and most exalted figures of the time, including Norbert of Xanten. But even the Black monks themselves, all these visionaries of whom we have spoken—an Otloh of Saint-Emmeran, a Rupert of Deutz, a Guibert of Nogent, who all express in their dreams the desire and pains of their "turning around"—do not escape this same paradigm of generalized conversion. Let us return to one of our examples, Guibert of Nogent, who was witness to his own "conversion" as well as other "conversions" characteristic of a society in full transformation.

The Conversion of the World

The monk Guibert of Nogent (as rabid in his anti-Judaism as he is interested in dreams) was well attuned to both the evolutions of society—witness his description of the community of Laon in 1111—and the movements of his soul. He was fully aware of all these tensions in the portrait he offers of the "religious lives and conversions," of which he was a witness. The three portraits of "converts" that he paints in chapters 8 to 11 of the first book of his *Memoirs* are inserted into the long description of the life and moral qualities of his mother and occur before he returns to his own spiritual evolution, his "conversion" and his "confession," an act of penance and an admission of his love of God at the heart of the monastic community.[14] Here I follow

Dominique Iogna-Prat, who has provided a fine analysis of Guibert of Nogent's concepts and words in this part of the text.[15]

Guibert presents the destinies of three contemporaries, each of whom belonged to the aristocracy of the north of France to which he was himself connected by his family origins. He has his information first-hand from these persons. For them, conversion consisted in leaving the noble and worldly life they lived. But what sort of religious life should one choose? Guibert reminds us that the time when an older monasticism flourished, at Luxeuil for example, has now passed. For reasons especially having to do with the practice of oblation, monasteries have stooped into spiritual and material decadence. But then came the ambiguous signs of renewal: Count Evrard of Breteuil suddenly left his castle situated in the borders of the Amiennois and Soissonnais in order to take up a life of wandering and anonymity in "I do not know what foreign country." With several companions, he started to make and sell charcoal, as did before him another noble named Thibaud, "whom everyone today recognizes as a saint." But Evrard's wanderings come to a sudden stop when he is confronted by a spirit (*simulacrum*) who is none other than his own double under the guise of the lover (*amasium*) that he once was. The spirit's clothing are sumptuous and—like Norbert of Xanten before his conversion—he wears "silk leggings," a sign of his dissolute morals. The spirit makes it clear to Evrard that the path of exile (*exsul*) that he has chosen would not please God. Moved by this revelation, Evrard and his companions "headed for Marmoutier where, taking the monastic habit, they observed that way of life forever."[16]

Immediately following this, Guibert moves on to the case of another convert, whom he describes as a "new Saint Paul." Simon of Crépy was an adolescent who belonged to the highest aristocracy and his deeds in battle were well known. When his father died, he was so distraught at the sight of the putrefying corpse that he immediately left his way of life, renounced his plans for marriage, traversed France and Burgundy, and took refuge in the Jura where he donned the monastic habit. A great many men and women followed his example.[17]

After having discussed lay nobles who were tempted by the wandering life of "poor voluntaries," but then thankfully joined the monastic life, Guibert adds: "it was to be predicted that one of the learned should, in the very same spirit, draw behind him a crowd of those in holy orders."[18] Indeed Bruno, the "rector of schools" of the church of Reims, revolted by the simony of the archbishop Manasses, departed from the city with a troupe of clerics who, like him, were in favor of the idea of reform. Fleeing Champagne, Bruno arrived at the diocese of Grenoble where, with the aid of the bishop Hugh of Grenoble, he founded the Grande Chartreuse whose customs and moral and religious elevation Guibert described with enthusiasm. Bruno then left to found a new house in Calabria, at Squillace, and—like Bernard of Clairvaux, but unlike Norbert of Xanten—obstinately refused the Episcopal dignity that the pope offered him.[19]

"These, I say, were the people who ushered in a *new era of religious conversion*," Guibert concluded.[20] Men and women, children and aged seem to revive the faith of ancient martyrs, causing the construction or enlargement of monasteries and the "conversion" of the most uninhabited places into sites devoted to God: "even places that in former times had been the lairs of wild beasts or the dens of robbers were now devoted to the name of God and the worship of the saints." As for the nobles who retained their worldly possessions, they showered the new religious communities with gifts drawn from their own fortune. But according to Guibert, this flourishing age has passed and the descendants of these benefactors only think of taking back the goods bequeathed by their parents.[21]

The three or four firsthand examples given by Guibert of Nogent invite a comparison with the more northern but analogous case of Norbert of Xanten. He too was of aristocratic origin, he had the same sudden conversion as Simon of Crépy, the same attempt to live a poor and wandering life, the same arrival at last at a cenobitic life or (as in the case of Bruno) of founding a new order. They each removed themselves from their secular condition and especially from their family origin in order to experience a period of wandering (or even real "savagery" in the case of the colliers Evrard and Thibaud), before reintegrating themselves in a new community, that of the monastery and the church. This well-known narrative schema is none other than the "rites of passage" that Arnold Van Gennep has already described as three successive stages of "separation," "marginality," and "aggregation."[22] At this level of generalization, it is clear that the autobiographical account of Herman's conversion follows the same principal. From his separation from his family of Jewish origin in Cologne (chapter 1) there follows a period of wandering (between Munster, Cappenberg, Mainz, and Worms) where the idea of conversion slowly develops (chapters 2 to 18), the baptism in Cologne (chapter 19), and finally the aggregation of the "orphan" to his new *familia* which is at Cappenberg, Prémontré, and the church all at once (chapters 20 and 21).

Godfried of Cappenberg

Even more than the Pauline model of conversion that was revived by Norbert of Xanten, the example of his emulator Godfried of Cappenberg would immediately have struck the mind of the *Opusculum*'s author. The destiny of Cappenberg's founder, who was born around 1097 and died 13 January 1127, in many ways resembles that of several noblemen from northern France. The context of the call to reform the church is the same. In Rhine-Westphalia, however, the bitterness of the investiture controversy between the emperor and the pope leaves a certain mark on Godfried's *Vita*.

The conflict in the empire for domination of the church, especially for control of the naming of bishops, is most intense between the last quarter of the eleventh century, when the reforming popes Leo IX and Gregory VII (1073–1085) rise up against the emperor Henry IV (1050–1106), and the Concordat of Worms in 1122. The humiliation of the emperor at Canossa in 1077 marks a first victory for the papacy, but without ending the conflict. Indeed the conflict reaches its heights in the early twelfth century and extends from Westphalia to Saxony. In the eastern portion (*Ostphalen*) of this vast region the great figures are traditionally hostile to Henry IV and his successor, Henry V (1106–1125), be they laymen (such as the count of Meissen) or religious (such as the bishop of Halbertstadt). The partisans of the emperor are found in the western areas (*Westphalen*): the bishops Benno of Osnabruck (d. 1088) and Burchard of Munster (d. 1118), the counts of Werl and especially the powerful Count Frederick of Arnsberg, who is none other than the godfather of Godfried of Cappenberg. But Godfried is the ally of Lothar of Saxony, another pretender to the empire, and a rival of Henry V. Lothar is also supported by the new bishop of Munster, Dietrich II of Winzenburg (1118–1127) who was regularly elected by the canonical chapter, but against the wishes of the bourgeois, the *ministerales*,[23] and the emperor, the latter coming in person to Munster in 1119 to try to impose his own candidate. Lothar's party is continually scoring points: in 1115 at Welfesholze he defeats the imperial faction led by Frederick of Arnsberg. Then in early 1121, once the burghers of Munster have expelled their bishop with the help of Henry V, Lothar of Saxony seizes the town with the support of Count Herman of Winzenburg (the brother of the deposed bishop) and Counts Godfried and Otto of Cappenberg, reinstating Bishop Dietrich on the throne. Present at this last victory, in 1121, is Bishop Eckbert, whom we have met in the *Opusculum* and in the dedicatory inscription of the baptismal font of Freckenhorst. But the majority of the city and the cathedral of Saint Paul (*templum nobiliter constructum*) are engulfed in flames. The next year, in 1122, the concordat of Worms is concluded, provisionally putting an end to the conflict between pope and emperor.[24]

The fire in the cathedral of Munster, which had been consecrated in 1090,[25] seems to have played a decisive role in Godfried of Cappenberg's "conversion" and in the relinquishment of his castle to Norbert of Xanten.[26] The *Royal Chronicle of Cologne*—an obviously partisan work—blames the fire on Counts Godfried and Otto of Cappenberg by labeling them *huius facti auctores*. Another document speaks of *offensa regia*, which could practically be understood as a crime of lèse-majesté directed against both Emperor Henry V and God. The gift of the castle is a penitential deed aimed at repairing the sacrilege that was committed. In addition, the counts give themselves to the church and to God.

Norbert of Xanten's merit is to have known how to profit from the deep divisions of local aristocracy and from Godfried's favorable arrangements. In the autumn of 1121 Norbert was in Cologne searching for relics for the foundation of Prémontré. His discovery of some bones allegedly belonging to Saint Gereon and Saint Ursula arouses much enthusiasm. It is on this occasion, according to the long version of the *Vita Norberti*, that Godfried must have heard of Norbert for the first time. He comes to find Norbert in Cologne, and there reveals his plan for the founding of a monastery, handing over to Norbert his possessions and himself as an offering to God.[27] Cappenberg thus becomes, in 1122, the third house of the burgeoning order and the first to be founded in the territory of the empire.[28]

It is remarkable that Godfried's *Vita* does not itself speak of his misdeed—the burning of the cathedral—which nonetheless seems to have played an important role in his decision. On the other hand, in conformity with the hagiographical genre, it reserves considerable space for the marvelous in its relation of events.[29] "Divine revelations through visions extremely worthy of faith" (*diversis fidelissimarum visionum ostentionibus revelatum est a Domino*) would have announced in advance Godfried's conversion and the transformation of his castle into an abbey. In a dream (*in visu noctis*) the priest Wicamannus sees a column of gold rising out of Cappenberg toward the sky. A certain Eckbert, a friend of the count, goes to see Godfried and there dreams of Cappenberg as a "town" as white as snow, rising straight up to the sky. It is also in a dream that Godfried's cousin, the abbess Gerbege, sees a "young man" (*juvenem*) with a celestial face who repeatedly says to her: "What a perfect place Cappenberg would be to assemble a spiritual congregation!" Once informed of this dream, which coincides so well with "the idea that he held for a long time" (*iam enim diu id ipsum concupierat*), Godfried says to his cousin that he will submit himself to the will of God. That is when Norbert appears, arriving as an instrument of a well-ordered divine will.

Godfried and his brother are immediately conquered by Norbert's holy words and, shortly thereafter, "both having discarded their secular clothes, they take the religious tonsure and the habit of the monastic life."[30] They each place themselves under the authority of the Rule of Saint Augustine and take a vow of obedience to Norbert. As Godfried is married, but is childless, he convinces his wife Iutta, daughter of Frederick of Arnsberg, to take the veil. With the consent of his unmarried younger brother, he gives to Norbert not only the establishment at Cappenberg, but also those of Varlar and Ilbernstadt along with their dependencies so that two more *coenobia* may be erected.

After having spoken of Norbert's very special affection for Cappenberg, and of the earliest successes of the new foundation—illustrated by the presence of a "Hebrew brother" within its wall—the anonymous author of the *Vita* returns to Godfried. His decision aroused the fury of his father-in-law, Frederick of Arnsberg, who asserts that Cappenberg constituted his daughter's dowry (*dos*). He intends to reclaim possession by force and decides to besiege the abbey. In a premonitory vision, a brother sees a lion swallow the aggressor. Despite the sarcastic remarks that take aim at him, Godfried confronts his father-in-law without looking to resist him, and the miracle comes true: Frederick backs down. He continues to search for a peaceful resolution with his son-in-law, but without success, since he dies in 1124, struck by the fire of heaven.[31]

On 15 August 1122, the feast of the Assumption, Bishop Dietrich of Munster dedicates the new church of Cappenberg. Godfried is as generous to him as he is to Norbert of Xanten: he makes a gift of one hundred and five *ministeriales* from Cappenberg to the church of Munster and does the same to the metropolitan church of Cologne.

The author of the *Vita* again quotes the testimony of an aged brother (*senior*), whose trustworthy accounts the author himself collected. These concerned Godfried's virtues, his hatred of lies, his fasts, his mercy for sinners and his compassion for lepers and the poor, and his humility in refusing to be called "count" by his brothers.[32]

Godfried is the *fundator* of Cappenberg, but he does not take charge of the community that he has founded. He leaves the role of *provisor* to Norbert. He no doubt participates in the life of the new community, but does so while remaining on its margins. In fact he has a *hospitalis per se* built (which the anonymous author was again able to see with his own eyes) where he has the habit of washing the feet of the poor. He contents himself with the title *acolyte* that, along with his brother, he obtained at Prémontré: out of humility he does not wish to elevate himself above the orders of minors. When, on the contrary, Norbert of Xanten accepts the seat of the archbishopric of Magdeburg in 1126, Godfried is among those who regret seeing him "succumb to the pomp and turmoil of worldly affairs."[33] He dies in the odor of sanctity—like his grandfather Herman—in 1127 at Ilbenstadt, from where his remains will be translated to Cappenberg on 13 January 1149.

Godfried's younger brother Otto, who at first was reluctant but then became associated with the foundation, meets a quite different fate. Contrary to Godfried, he accepts material management of the abbey, becoming the provost from 1156 until his death in 1171. But he will never be considered a saint like Godfried. Nevertheless, monastic tradition will ensure that the two brothers are closely associated, even representing them as twins: they are portrayed this way at the foot of a monument commemorating the foundation of the abbey, sculpted around 1315 and still preserved in Cappenberg (fig. 8).

If in 1121 Godfried's destiny partakes in the "new era of conversion" of which Guibert of Nogent speaks, it also presents some original traits. One of these consists in the semi-marginality of the founder, who nevertheless avoids the instability that accompanies the refusal, out of humility, of any hierarchical position. Unlike his brother, Godfried will never be provost of Cappenberg. The most distinct trait consists of the association of the "conversion" of the castle with that of the count. Corresponding to the *mutatio* of the heart and the habit is the *mutatio* of the walls of Cappenberg within which a monastic church is quickly erected.

Castles Converted into Monasteries

The paradigm of conversion is infinite. It extends to space, to edifices like castles that dot the landscape, and to material objects, particularly the more precious among them. Nor is the phenomenon new. It was even of considerable importance during the first millennium, the period of the expansion of Christianity and the eradication of paganism. For if idols were effectively destroyed, the buildings that housed them could be preserved and "converted" to new religious uses, and indeed to the new faith. In his famous letter to the monk Augustine, deployed to evangelize the Anglo-Saxons, Pope Gregory the Great recommends that the pagan "temples" not be destroyed, but rather transformed into churches, so that the force of the habit might draw barbarians toward them, who might thereby accept baptism more easily.[34] Continental Europe led comparable campaigns of generalized conversion (of both people and places, the one through the other) that lasted a very long time. The dating of place names, when possible, testifies to the slowness of the process of Christianizing space, which had barely begun by the Carolingian era, and which was only really completed with the establishment of the network of villages and parishes in the eleventh and twelfth centuries.[35]

One part of this phenomenon is the transformation of castles into monasteries or abbeys. The castle is a structure and a location (usually elevated) that is highly symbolic. It is the expression of values of the world, of the warrior function and also of physical violence often exercised against the church and those whom she protects (clerics and the poor). One symbol can transmute into another. The castle can be "converted" into a monastery, a symbol of the spiritual life, of the first *ordo* of Christian society, of continuous prayer, and of the service of God. The model of such a *conversio* (the word is used conjointly with *mutatio*) is persistent to the point that it is found even in oral and folkloric literature. In "tale-type-470" of the Aarne and Thompson classification, a tale that is well attested to starting in the twelfth century, a young nobleman having completed a wondrous voyage in the hereafter under the aegis of an angel returns to his country after three or four hundred years believing he has been absent for only a few moments. He realizes his error when he discovers, according to several versions of the story, that the family castle, which was dedicated to secular activities, has in the intervening years been transformed into a monastery where the monks are now singing God's praises.[36] It is not impossible that such legendary accounts influenced real practices. In any case they echo known foundations. Medieval chronicles indeed relate a number of "conversions of castles" comparable to that of Cappenberg, and not only in Germany. In England, the twelfth-century chronicle of Waltham speaks of a hunting lodge that belonged to an Anglo-Saxon nobleman, Tovi the Proud, who in the eleventh century transformed it into a monastic church in order to house a stone cross that was miraculously discovered following a dream. Waltham's church then became a canonical chapter placed under the protection of the Anglo-Saxon and later Norman kings.[37] According to a late twelfth-century legend, the monks of Charroux, fleeing before the incursion of the Normans, find refuge in the castle of Saint-Yvoine (*castrum de Petra-Incisa*), which they turn into a monastery. Later, freeing themselves of their mother abbey, they destroy the *castrum* and set off to construct the venerable abbey of Issoire. Amy Remensnyder, who has carefully examined this tradition, mentions other comparable abbeys, such as Mozac and Maillezais.[38] Closer to Cappenberg, the monastery of Deutz is especially deserving of mention. It was, in the words of Rupert himself in his *Vita Heriberti*, none other than an old castle "purged" (*mundatus*) of all worldly possessions by the will of the saintly bishop.[39] Bishop Heribert ardently wished "to build" (*construere*) a monastery, but he could not find an appropriate location. "Turning to God and his mother" (*convertens sese ad Dominum sanctamque eius genitricem*), he sinks into fasting and praying in the quest for the revelation of divine will. One night, exhausted by his sleeplessness, he falls asleep and sees in a dream "the queen of angels and of all things," a vision that Rupert describes in terms of the office of the Assumption. The Virgin introduces herself to the Bishop (*ego enim sum Maria, mater Domini*) and assures him that his wish is granted; he must "purge" the castle of Deutz (*castrum Tuitiense*) and erect (*constituere*) in her honor a monastery, "so that there where sins and the cult of demons are abandoned, justice reigns in the multitude of saints." This castle possessed a "court belonging to the bishop" (*curtis pertinens ad servitium episcopii*), from which Heribert removes everything that recalled its earlier purpose. The place is completely "cleansed" (*emundatus*) and, immediately afterward, the bishop rushes to build new and magnificent buildings (*structura speciosa*). It is from this monastery and its adjacent "town" that Rupert describes the terrible fire of 1128 as well as the dream that he had on that occasion.[40]

Frederick Barbarossa's Head

The conversion of people leads to the conversion of places and objects that they possess. One could cite, for example, well before Godfried of Cappenberg but in some sense similar to him, the case of Saint Gerald of Aurillac (c. 855–909). To justify the comparison of these two saints, who are two centuries apart, we might say that Gerald of Aurillac is to the *monastic* reform of the tenth century, in other words Cluny, what Godfried of Cappenberg is to the *clerical* reform of the twelfth, in other words Prémontré.[41] But unlike Godfried later on, Gerald does not completely abandon the secular life, which makes him, for his period, a highly unusual person with no saintly precedent. He continues to exercise his responsibilities as count, meting out justice and maintaining peace. He does not turn his castle into an abbey, but constructs below his castle the monastery of Saint Peter of Aurillac, which he gives to the pope. Meanwhile, he burns with the desire to become a monk, and this is why he shaves his beard, adopts the tonsure, and refuses to touch his sword, which a servant carries in front of him when he is on horse. As for his baldric—in the *Opusculum*, young Judas's dream has shown us heavy symbolism of this portion of the military costume—"he orders that a golden cross be made from it."[42] The symbolic inversion (or, to put it better, the conversion) is complete: the symbol of strength and war, characteristic of the "second function," that of the *bellatores*, changes into the actual sign of Christ, a reminder of the blood spilled for the salvation of man, a symbol of the "first function," that of the *oratores*.

Even more remarkable is the "conversion of objects" for which the abbey of Cappenberg itself was witness roughly two centuries later. To celebrate his accession to the imperial throne in 1156, Frederick Barbarossa offers his godfather Otto, who is the brother of Godfried and who becomes provost of Cappenberg that same year, a gilded bronze effigy of his own head. This head must have been among the "gifts" (*munera*) that the emperor gave Otto and which are mentioned in the inscription that runs along the silver baptismal basin discussed earlier. The head is mounted on a base that is also made of gilded bronze (fig. 6). The total height of the object is twelve and a half inches. One should not a priori take this head as a "portrait" of Frederick Barbarossa in the modern sense of the term. Even if the arrangement of the hair and the beard gives the impression that the silversmith wished to portray the individual features of a particular person, the full face and the hieratic quality of the effigy no doubt aim at expressing Barbarossa's imperial dignity. The influence of late antique models is evident, especially in the presence of the band along his forehead. It is possible that the intent was to render three-dimensionally the type of imperial effigy present on seals or coins.[43] At any rate, this genre of arrangement was not uncommon during the Middle Ages. One can think for example of the reuse of the emperor's golden head, probably dating from the fifth century, mounted in the tenth century, covered in

gilded silver, on the wooden body of the "majesty" of Sainte-Foy of Conques.[44] But in the case of the Cappenberg bust, the head and the base were
roughly contemporary.

In a document of the third quarter of the twelfth century, the provost
Otto of Cappenberg lists the gifts he has made to his church: "For the perpet-
ual honor of the aforementioned church I made the irrevocable gift of a
golden cross said to belong to Saint John, a silver head in effigy of the emperor with his basin (*sua pelvi*) entirely in silver, as well as a chalice that was
sent to me by the bishop of Troyes."[45] The cross of Saint John is lost. The
"basin" is perhaps the baptismal bowl mentioned earlier; it seems here to be
inseparable from the head (though it is not in silver), which had no doubt
already become a reliquary but which the testator continues to call "the effigy
of the emperor." One can well imagine that the head reliquary was placed in
the basin and that, following a common practice of the Middle Ages, water
was poured onto it that was then collected in order to serve in the ritual
healing of sick people. A chalice received from a bishop also figures among
the gifts made by Otto to his abbey.

Like the chalice, the head was thus twice a gift: from the emperor to his
godfather Otto and from Otto to his church. Over time it was transformed
and its original function was changed. From a personal gift intended to commemorate a ceremony it became a reliquary of Saint John the Evangelist. No
document speaks about the "conversion" of this secular object into a cult
object. But the inscription that runs along the neck allows one to be sure of
the result:

+ HIC. QUOD. SERVETUR. DE. CRINE. IOANNIS. HABETUR /
+ TE. PRECE. PULSANTES. EXAUDI. SANCTI. IOANNES
[What is kept here is a hair of Saint John / Listen, Saint John, to those
who are praying to you.]

Immediately below, on the crenellated base that three angels support,
one can read the following on two superimposed lines:

APOCALIPSA. DATUM. TIBI. MU[NUS]. SUS[CIPE.GR] ATUM /
[E]T. P[I]US. OTTONI. SUCCURE. PRECANDO. DATORI
[Lord of Revelation, take with good grace the present that is given to
you / and come with goodness to the aid of the giver Otto who beseeches
you.]

Otto is indeed the *donator* who transformed the bust in order for it to conform to the liturgical uses of his religious community. It is possible that the bust reliquary seated in the basin was, for certain feasts, put in the open hand of the stone effigy of Godfried of Cappenberg that was sculpted around 1155, and which can still be seen today in the old church abbey (fig. 8).

Herman of Scheda

The history of the Prémontré priory of Scheda, mentioned for the first time in 1146[46] as a dependency of Cappenberg, also supports the conversion paradigm of people and places within close proximity to the mother abbey.[47] The loss of the library of Scheda unfortunately deprives us of much information regarding the origins of its foundation. We depend largely on a relatively late compilation, the *History of the Church of Westphalia* by the learned Gerhard von Kleinsorgen (d. 1591),[48] who describes among many other things the origin of the Premonstratensian "abbey" of Scheda. The account conforms perfectly to the framework of foundation legends. A local nobleman, Volandus de Ardeya, would have built in his castle a chapel dedicated to Saint Severin. After his death, the preacher Echardus would have convinced Volandus's widow, Wiltrudis, and his two sons, to turn their entire castle into an abbey. The Jewish convert Herman would have become the first "abbot" of Scheda.[49] On this point at least, we know that this was not so, since in the twelfth century a simple priory was not governed by an abbot. What is more, the provost of Scheda mentioned in 1170 in the archives under the names *Herimannus Israhelita prepositus* or *Herimannus Schedensis prepositus*, assimilated by Niemeyer to the author of the *Opusculum*,[50] seems to have been confused by Kleinsorgen and then Johannes Caesar with the similarly named Herman II (1197–1217). This later Herman is the first to carry the title of abbot, at the time when the priory obtained its true independence from Cappenberg.[51]

The account of the founding of Scheda, collected by Kleinsorgen, must have relied on a locally written document, such as the necrology (*Totenbuch*), which unfortunately disappeared at the time of the Thirty Years War. One surmises that the rivalry between Cappenberg and Scheda (for which certain clues from the late twelfth century show vague desires for autonomy)[52] must have helped in the development of the tradition. The fact remains that there is a striking parallel with the account describing the origins of Cappenberg:

in a situation of rupture (here the sacrilege committed at Munster by the counts of Cappenberg, there the death of the lord of the land, Volandus of Ardeya), the hero (here Godfried, there Wiltrudus), with the consent of his family (here Otto and Gerberge, there the sons of Volandus) and at the instigation of a saintly man (here Norbert of Xanten, there the priest Echardus), decides to transform his castle into a religious establishment.

But was it not the essential purpose for Scheda to provide itself with a "founding saint"? Prémontré had Norbert. Cappenberg had Godfried. Scheda could thus claim Herman the Jew, glorified as he was by the circumstances of his conversion and by his autobiographical account and also because he was easily identifiable as one of the first provosts. To have a tutelary saint whose remains could still be unearthed in the seventeenth century is a guaranty of independence and proof of great collective merit. This presupposed only that the reputation of the Jewish convert redounded to the glory of the new foundation. It had already allowed the mother abbey of Cappenberg to proclaim the excellence of its spiritual influence and to establish its prestige.

"Quondam Judaeus"

At the time of his baptism, Herman changes his name. He remains, however, the "former Jew" (*quondam Judaeus*). As with those who are born Christian, the single name Herman is not enough to identify him. Though baptized, made a cleric, canon, priest, and an accomplished Premonstratensian "cleric," he is not quite a Christian like the others. Beneath his Christian identity there remains inscribed, audible, if not visible, his Jewish identity.[53] Thus in the seventeenth century his tombstone was deemed found, decorated with an effigy. It was recognizable by the habit of the Premonstratensian canons, but especially by the pointed hat of the Jews placed at his feet. This hat, a veritable attribute, would have followed him into the hereafter.

This is not an isolated case. It is precisely this same *quondam*, or some other equivalent expression, which allows one to recognize in written sources the mention quite frequent in this period of Jewish converts and even of their descendants. All while being Christian, the convert retains something of his/her Jewish self. This does not make their insertion into a new community easy. As far as I know, it is never a question of a physical trait that reveals their origins. Even the iconographic documents do not, before the fourteenth century, depict Jews with particular physical characteristics; and when this becomes the case it has less often to do with contemporary Jews than with players in the Passion of Christ, who are depicted in profile with crude and grimacing features, an accentuated nose and bulging eyes—similar to the way in which many other people who are viewed negatively are represented.[54]

What distinguishes Jews, on the other hand, is what Sander L. Gilman has called their "stigmata":[55] it is nothing more than the fact that they *were* Jews and, in a certain sense, still are, while no longer being so.

A good number of twelfth- and thirteenth-century accounts bear witness to this inextricable situation, and not only in Germany. King Henry III of England supported two converts who bore the names Roger *the Convert* and John *the Convert*.[56] On the other hand, such a qualification in name did not apply to the baptized Jew Henry of Winchester, who was knighted (like Judas in the dream). But when this same Henry was appointed witness to the canonization process of Thomas of Cantiloupe, he was challenged by the clerics because he was only a convert and not born a Christian. Earlier, in 1170, at Tournai, a convert named Milo was refused a prebend by the canons of the cathedral under the pretext that he was a convert; Pope Alexander III had to exercise his full authority with the bishop in order to sway the decision of the chapter. Sometimes this "smear" can even extend to the child of a convert even though the child is baptized at birth like other Christian children: in 1197 the *Royal Chronicle of Cologne* (*Chronica regia coloniensis*) mentions "a certain Jew born of a Jewish father, but converted," which leads one to think that the original "Jewishness" had made a strong comeback in the second generation . . .[57]

The suspicion that the conversion is not completely sincere, that the new Christian is guilty of "Judaizing" (*judaisare*), may partly explain these prejudices among other Christians.[58] We have seen that the theme of hypocrisy is taken on by Judas/Herman in chapter 16 of the *Opusculum* against the Jews of Worms who treat him as a "half-Christian" (*semichristianus*). Seen the other way, he was also a "half-Jew." But such a worry does not suffice to explain so many testimonies. There seems to me to be a deeper, anthropological, reason: namely that conversion does not erase everything, beginning with the religious sign of one's belonging to Judaism, the *signum* of circumcision, inscribed forever in the flesh of the convert. It is a carnal sign that, for other Christians, characterizes the intrinsic "carnality" that they assign to Jews. We recall, among other things, that when Judas is still a "half-Jew" he searches in vain for material "signs" (a vision, a miracle) that can convince him of the truth of Christianity.

In his Epistle to the Romans (Romans 4) Saint Paul explains that the baptism of grace—a spiritual sign imposed by the soul—has for Christians replaced the carnal sign of circumcision. Christian theologians since the Church Fathers have commented at length on the *signum* of the Jews and have compared it to baptism. Some have likened circumcision to the "sign" that God imposed on Cain after the death of his brother: it marks Cain for fratricide while at the same time protects him from those who wish to kill him. Similarly, the Jews, duly "marked," must be protected in all the kingdoms they inhabit so that they may continue to bear witness to the crime they committed against Christ. The mark imposed upon them by the Fourth Lateran Council in 1215 (a garment distinct in form or color, or the wearing of a badge) is itself likened to the "sign" of circumcision and the "mark of Cain."[59]

In his *Sermon on the Circumcision of the Lord*, Abelard characteristically avoids using a polemical tone toward Jews.[60] He reminds us that in the time of the Patriarchs circumcision was the "sign of justice and faith" symbolizing exteriorly for Abraham the "cut" of vices that threaten the soul. At the end of Exodus Joshua himself circumcised the male children of the tribes of Israel who had crossed the river Jordan with him. Abelard says that he wishes "to convert his style into allegory" in order to understand the lesson of the Old Testament: the water of the Jordan River symbolizes the sacrament of baptism and the circumcision performed by Joshua with a stone announces the "second circumcision," that of the soul, in other words baptism in the faith of Christ. Joshua—even in his name—is none other than the prefiguring of Jesus. One recalls that the crossing of the river Jordan is evoked in the *Opusculum* while the sacrament of baptism appears in the final explication of the dream as the ultimate reward for the convert's efforts.

The fact remains that the Jewish convert, though baptized, remains circumcised in the flesh. Conversion is in no situation an erasing of the first situation, for something of the prior state always remains. Like a *trace*, the process of conversion remains visible in the person or thing that was converted. This model is omnipresent and central in the Christian culture of the high Middle Ages. From the first controversies on the Eucharist in the tenth century (between Ratherius of Verona and Ratramnus of Corbie), and their sudden revival in the eleventh century (along with Berengar of Tours), to the scholastic debates of the twelfth century and the first doctrinal decisions taken by the Fourth Lateran Council, clerics were constantly thinking about the crucial question of the transformation of the sacramental "substance" under the seeming permanence of "accident," in other words the "sacred species" of the bread and the wine.[61] Beyond doctrinal discussions, the Eucharist occupied a substantial place in the practice of communion (though rather restrained for this period) as well as, if not more so, in the imagination of the time.[62] In its own way, the *Opusculum* bears witness to this, for not only does it give a central place to the episode of the crossing of the Jordan, which might evoke the "mystical crossing" of baptism, but it also ends with the image of the "sacred feast" which *in fine* gives the "key" to the earlier dream of the meal taken at the emperor's table. This time the *conversio* is hermeneutic: it follows the example of all Christian exegesis of the Old Testament and allows for the spiritual and Christian meaning of a "carnal" allegory, in this case taken from the royal ceremony seen in the dream.

Let us, however, beware of running all the levels of representation together. They are structurally homologous precisely because they are not of an identical nature. Differences between the interpretations of dreams and Biblical exegesis have to be observed, as must the differences between the transformation of Eucharistic species into the Body and Blood of Christ and the "conversion" of a castle into an abbey or of an emperor's head into a reliquary. The nature of objects, like the significance of their mutation, is different. Nevertheless, they are joined by some main themes, beginning with the general use of the same words (*conversio, mutatio*) and the central idea that the "convert" retains material traces of his/her earlier state. The castle of Cappenberg has become an abbey all the while keeping (or rediscovering) the appearance of the castle that it once was; in fact it has done this so well that it retains the name today Schloss Cappenberg. Similarly, one speaks of the *Barbarossakopf*, the "head of emperor Frederick Barbarossa," in order to describe the relic of Saint John the Evangelist. In the final state of the object or person "converted" there remains written and visible the traces of the process of conversion. It was no different for Judas/Herman, *quondam Judaeus*, "the former Jew," or for many other Jewish converts of the twelfth century who continued to be called "the convert" or even "the Jew."

Conclusion

The point of departure for this book was a question starkly put in 1988 by an excellent historian of Judaism regarding the supposed autobiography of a medieval Jew who converted to Christianity: "Truth or Fiction?" Is this text, the *Opusculum de conversione sua* by a certain *Hermannus quondam Judaeus*, the autobiography of a conversion to Christianity by a person who really existed, or is it a pure "romance" devoid of any real basis, written in the twelfth century by Premonstratensian canons in Westphalia?

Throughout this book I have tried to show that this question is, in my mind, badly put. Such an alternative does not take into account either the complex genesis of such a historical document or the interpretation of the historian. For both of these lines of inquiries, "truth" and "fiction" are not, if one agrees on meaning, mutually exclusive, and in any case they are not diametrically opposed.

Reflection on the medieval notion of "truth" must take into full account its dimension of "faith" (in the sense of religious belief as well as witness to "good faith"), and also its dimension of "authority": the medieval "author" is in the first instance one who cites "authorities" in his quotations and who possesses the "authority" required in order to affirm something. A medieval author's work can never be strictly individual: by the appearance therein of texts of the Bible or Fathers of the Church that give it its legitimacy and, by the voices of a "textual community" in which the person or persons composing the text participate, the work is profoundly collective in both its genesis and nature. This is for that matter what is suggested in the dedicatory letter to "brother Henry" that introduces the conversion account of Judas/Herman in the *Opusculum*: it is the men and women living religiously at Cappenberg who urged Herman to put into writing an account that they had often heard him tell. We must not imagine an old man writing his memoirs alone at his desk, but rather a circle of listeners hanging on his words, asking questions and taking an active role in the creation of the account.

Medieval "fiction" is not necessarily pure invention. It consists of the shaping, construction, and development of a plot based on many different preexisting materials. This is obviously the case for such a medieval "life story," where even the use of first person evokes a conventional setting or piece of writing.

Historians today are themselves forced to come up with a plot, to imagine ways to fill in the documentary gaps, and to formulate hypotheses relative to what they know and who they are at the moment of writing. In this sense, and without the slightest intent of undermining the historian's discourse, we might equally have spoken of the historian's "fiction." Obviously this does not mean that the work of a historian and the work of medieval clerics should be labeled by one word, even if some medieval clerics boasted of having written a *historia*. Notions of truth, proof, and causalities, like the work methods and aims of this intellectual enterprise, all forbid it. And yet historians today know very well that what they describe is not "reality as it actually happened." That doesn't prevent them from trying to uncover a certain "truth" that is intelligible and acceptable by them and their contemporaries. So it is a delicate task to contrast "truth" with "fiction." All historical texts (the products of the past, *Geschichte*) and all texts of history (the history of historians: *Histoire*) are both "truth *and* fiction."

These observations go contrary to the overly stark (though healthily provocative) article by Avrom Saltman. They likewise steer clear of the statements of Gerlinde Niemeyer and all those who, reacting to Saltman, have wished to show that Judas/Herman "really" existed, that he was the "author" of his "autobiography," in short, that things did happen the way the *Opusculum* says they did. Too often historians have isolated a particular passage, a particular word, a possible evocation of a Jewish custom, or a particular quotation that supposedly refers to the Torah or the Talmud rather than the Vulgate or the Church Fathers in order to demonstrate the "authenticity" of the whole *Opusculum* and, in so doing, the "reality" of Herman's existence. I do not question either the possibility that such a conversion took place (many conversions of Jews are known for this period) or that a convert turned canon could have contributed to the elaboration of this Latin account with his "brothers and sisters" at Cappenberg. But the confirmation, or denial, of this is impossible. One can multiply at length the arguments in one direction or another, especially if they are removed from their context. The only certitude is the existence of a Latin text dating no later than the late twelfth century (and which in fact in its definitive form presents itself as a posthumous text).

The text of the *Opusculum* is an exceptionally rich document relating to the culture of the twelfth century, and one has to approach it on the condition that it be both considered in its context and studied in connection with the vast problems that it poses: the subject of autobiography, the dream, images, the process, and indeed the very notion of conversion. It is at this level that the text is clearly, for us, a *document* of history, and this history cannot easily be settled by assigning it to either Jews or Christians. Whatever were their suspicions of one another, their hatreds and sometimes even their tragedies, both Jews and Christians lived along the Rhine valley during the twelfth century. They inhabited the same towns (Cologne, Mainz, Worms), often even in the same quarters, and their exchanges, both material and intellectual, were frequent. There were doubtless fewer differences between a Jew from Cologne and a Christian from Cologne than between a Jew from Cologne and a Jew from Cairo.[1] The matter of dreams has shown for example the profound analogies that exist in the conception and content of dreams of Jews and Christians as well as in the manner of interpreting them. Once again, I do not exclude the possibility that one or several Jewish converts to Christianity could have served as a point of departure for the composition of the text, but it seems to me impossible and, on the whole, of little interest, to attribute the authorship to that person or persons.

Even if there are no surviving manuscripts of the *Opusculum* that come directly from Cappenberg, there is no doubting that this text originated at Cappenberg. For me, that is where the essence and the purpose of the work is to be found. I do not believe that this was primarily a proselytizing text designed either to attract other Jews toward the Christian faith or to complete the job of convincing Jews who were already "half-Christian."[2] Rather, this text seems to me to have had an internal function in the Prémontré abbey of Cappenberg. Being crafted by the canons, or several among them, it was likewise aimed at them. The fact that they claim to have drawn in a Jew without pressuring him, that he was integrated after his conversion, and that he was led to the priesthood (which was the clerical ideal and not a priori the monastic ideal claimed by the canons), allowed this very young community of canons to proclaim their spiritual excellence and to assert their legitimacy. The force of seduction exerted by this convert was so great for that matter that Scheda, a priory of Cappenberg that did not delay in claiming its independence, soon claimed him for their own benefit.

A number of converging clues have been gathered together during this investigation, all of which confirm that the *Opusculum* is, as a text, a perfectly coherent ideological construction of the Premonstratensians of Cappenberg. I present them as hypotheses that have until now never been formulated, but all of which point in the same direction. Certain clues concern the figure of Herman, such as his name, which may relate to "Saint Herman," the grandfather of the founder of the abbey. The same goes for Judas/Herman's claim to be of the "Levite tribe," the tribe that the Premonstratensians saw as the biblical source of their "clerical" elite. The apparently well-placed presence in this text of the Benedictine Abbot Rupert of Deutz is paradoxical. To be sure, he was in this region and was during this period the great expert on the "Jewish question." But we also know that the Benedictine monks, and particularly Rupert of Deutz himself, were violently opposed to the Premonstratensians as well as their founder, Norbert of Xanten, who was Godfried of Cappenberg's mentor. On closer inspection, then, the place of Rupert in the text is not as enviable as it might seem at first. It is not his reasoning (*rationes*) that sways Judas's decision, but rather the humble prayers of the two saintly women from Cologne, Berta and Glismut. Some have endeavored to learn where and when the great monastic theologian could have encountered Judas, the son of an obscure Jewish moneylender (not even a rabbi), and taken up the challenge to debate with him. In this form, the episode seems unlikely. Yet it is no less central in the economy of the account or in the ideological background. The supreme skillfulness of the Premonstratensians would thus have been to enlist their adversary in order to have him play a secondary role. In any case, the *Opusculum* does not refer to contemporary debates between Jews and Christians. Implicitly or not, it also concerns the great ecclesiological debate that, through Norbert of Xanten and Rupert of Deutz, opposes "clerics" against "monks."

All the questions asked of this text overlie an even greater question regarding the subject of "conversion." In the first place this has to do with the conversion of individuals, beginning with Judas/Herman himself. But along the way I have been led to see in the notion of conversion a more general paradigm of Christian culture for this period. The conversion of this Jew to Christianity becomes a metaphor for all the other types of *conversio* which an examination of this text and the other documents allows one to recognize: the conversion of the castle at Cappenberg into a Premonstratensian abbey and the conversion of Lord Godfried into a canon and saint; or even the conversion of the effigy of Emperor Frederick Barbarossa into a reliquary of

Saint John. Conversion is an ideal that concerns all Christians, Christian society itself, as well as places and things. To the eyes of the clerics, the goal of conversion is to "spiritualize" society, to convert the *flesh*—represented by carnal Jews—into *spirit*, the spirit claimed by the new orders of the *vita apostolica*. The story of Judas/Herman is the story of each new member of the new order of Prémontré, but in an ideal form where the use of the first person lends even more reality and effectiveness. Each person is called to convert and to contemplate the surrounding world that is in full conversion. For them the *Opusculum* endlessly repeats the message that "flesh" must be converted into "spirit." This is after all the central principle of Christian ideology that clerics have always wished to disseminate. This principle is the key to an exegesis that calls for the conversion of the "word" of the Old Testament into the "spirit" of the New Testament. Such a model experiences a renewal at all levels during the twelfth century with the emergence of new orders and new currents of thought in the church. It is this that gives an unparalleled meaning to the *Opusculum*.

Indeed this is exactly what Judas/Herman says: the *carnal* in him has been converted into the *spiritual*, he has gone from Jew to Christian, to being baptized (*conversus*), a canon, and finally a priest. And yet he remains a "convert." Such is the final law for the conversion of beings, words, places, and things. "Substance" is transformed, but "species"—such as the bread and the wine—maintain their appearance and the mark of what they once were. If "Herman," the "Hebrew brother" of Cappenberg, is only the mask (*persona*) of the entire canonical community, if he invites his brothers to follow his example, he also enjoins them to remember where they came from and who they are. He has created, on their behalf, a work of memory. From his present state as a Christian, he "turns around," or performs a conversionary reversal we might say, on his past in order to examine the traces that from their Jewish origins—a metaphor for error and sin—lead him to his present state. He changes his name, just as Saul became Paul, but he remains *quondam Judaeus*: "former Jew." Conversion transforms, but it does not erase.

Extract from the Vita of Godfried, Count of Cappenberg
(c. 1150–1155)

[Ed. P. Jaffé, MGH, *Scriptores*, XII, ¶ 3, p. 517,
line 12 to p. 518, line 23]

[. . .] The aforementioned father Norbert [of Xanten] loved the monastery
of Cappenberg tenderly and more than any other place. I shall not leave
unmentioned what he said regarding this place when he was staying with the
brothers: "Dearest brothers," he said, "once when I was near here I saw
for certain the Holy Spirit descend upon this place. Another time I was
contemplating a great and luminous light that was emanating from this place
and shining all around. This is why, dearly beloved, you must glorify our
God, for this place is truly 'the mount of his sanctification' [cf. Psalms 78:54],
the mount, I say, which his right hand acquired." I heard these things when
I was living in the same monastery of brothers so as to prevent anybody with
the spirit clouded by perfidy from daring to contradict the radiant truth. I
also heard in the communal chapter this same champion of orthodox truth
add the following: "I know one of the brothers of our order who applied
himself to studying our rule. He had, not by his own merits, but thanks to
the prayers of his brothers a vision of Saint Augustine who pulled out from
along his right side the golden rule and held it out to him saying these
splendid words: 'I am Saint Augustine, whom you see, the bishop of Hippo.
Take my rule, which I wrote; if your brothers, my sons, will militate well
under it, then Christ will protect them from the terror of the last judgment.'"
And [Norbert] followed with similar humility, and we have no doubt about
the brother to whom this was revealed.

I also do not think that the two great marvels he accomplished in that
place ought to be passed over in silence. One day he foretold that there would

be a famine in Westphalia that would be a spiritual punishment for the brothers themselves. It ravaged the land, just as the man of God had foretold, and this calamitous food shortage killed many people. It happened one day when the brothers went to dine that, since they handed out to their guests and to the poor everything that they had abstained from themselves, there was no bread to eat and there was not even any way of finding any. But because the man of God had several times proclaimed these words from Scripture: "The Lord does not let the righteous go hungry" [Proverbs 10:3], so suddenly the Lord sent through his faithful such an abundance of bread that the brothers ate plentifully and offered heartily to those who came. And from that day onward never again did the brothers lack sustenance. Another time, when the saint wished to entrust a mission for the monastery to one of the brothers, but found him overcome by a strong fever, he reminded him of the duty of obedience by giving him this one command in the name of Christ: "go," he said, "and return, and be not feverish" [cf. Matthew 9:6; Mark 2:11; Luke 5:24]. The brother immediately regained his strength and accomplished what the Holy Father had ordered of him. Thus the word of the man of God achieved its purpose and made the enduring fever instantly disappear.

In this same place a brother had led a praiseworthy life. One night that deceased brother appeared before a very faithful friend who had stayed awake praying many times for his soul, and he addressed him in a familiar tone: "My brother, I give you thanks for having not yet forgotten me when other friends and even my parents no longer remember me. I now exhort you to preserve this attitude, to persevere in it, and to not turn your soul away from this order in the event that you would find a more powerful one, for I cannot show you an order that is more beneficial to your soul or more useful to you. I have come to announce for your charity that the prayers of your brothers are being recited every day on a golden altar placed under the eyes of God. I exhort you also never to shirk from the duty of obedience. No other virtue will give you a higher and more fruitful merit before God."

The prophet says: "so that the tongues of your dogs may have their share from the foe" [Psalms 68:23]. Many are the Jewish enemies who have become and still become converts, barking with the tongues of dogs in order to keep the house of the Lord from the enemies. Should you ask: "wherefore comes such good?" he would have answered: "from this same good," which means from his grace, not from their efforts. We say this because of the grace that God showed in our time to the Hebrew brother. Graced by the gift of God, after a long detour in error, he began to search for answers regarding an ardent desire about the Christian faith. Thus he disputed with Christians the subject of the law and the prophets. And since, following the words of the Apostle, they said to him that he kept a "veil over the heart" [2 Corinthians 3:15], he thought that there was no better way to lift this veil than by the sign of the cross. He therefore began crossing himself, but did so in secrecy because he was afraid of the other Jews. And because Jews "require signs" [1 Corinthians 1:22] he devoted himself to fasting and prayer and began to solicit from God a sign that would allow him to know if he was worthy of divine grace. Persevering in this attitude, he suddenly saw himself placed before the throne of Christ where he also saw a golden cross shining on the shoulder of the Lord.

Seeing several of the Jews close by, he said: "Do you not recognize that it is about Him that Isaiah says: 'authority rests upon his shoulders' [Isaiah 9:6]?" Already converted by such a sign, he tried to free several of his own people from the false faith of Judaism, and at the house of his parents in Mainz he cleverly tried to take his brother by the hand from his Jewish surroundings and lead him out of the city. But through the work of the Devil he lost his way with the child, he circled the street and failed to find a door through which he might depart. After he became terribly distressed from turning around, he finally understood that the Devil was the cause of his error; he thus armed his forehead with the standard of the cross and immediately found the exit with open eyes and fled the city in great joy. Having in this way taken the child with him, they both received the grace of baptism. And with the divine gift continuing its effects, they joined our army together a short time afterward.

Herman the Former Jew
Short Work on the Subject of His Conversion

[Ed: Hermannus Quondam Judaeus, *Opusculum de conversione sua*, PL, vol. 170, cols. 803–836]

Herman's Letter

To his dearest son Henry, Herman, who by the grace of God, sends his heartfelt love in Christ. Many religious men and women persist in trying to find out from me how I converted from Judaism to the grace of Christ and whether, in the early stages of my conversion, I endured temptations from the clever Enemy. Indeed, it was in your presence recently that I was made by some devout women, in the course of a holy conversation, to recount the whole sequence of events. For I did not convert with the ease with which we see many infidels, Jews, and pagans convert to the Catholic faith through a sudden and unanticipated change, of the sort experienced by those whom yesterday we deplored for the error of their faith, but whom we celebrate now as having become coinheritors with us in Christ. By contrast, my conversion was faced with powerful and increasing waves of temptations at the beginning, with many treacheries by the ancient Enemy, with the longest fluctuations, and with the greatest toil. For these reasons, it ought to be all the more delightful for pious ears to hear of what admirably came to pass amid such difficulties. Thus, dearest brother, aroused by the devotion of many, and, most of all, encouraged by your pious urgings, I have thought it worthy to commit this [conversion] to writing and, through it, faithfully to proclaim to believers of the coming age, as of the present, the inestimable grace of he who has called me "out of darkness into his marvelous light" [1 Peter 2:9], and thus to serve his everlasting praise and glory.

End of the letter

In the name of the Lord, here begins the short account of brother Herman's conversion who, of good memory, was formerly a Jew.

Chapter 1: *Concerning the vision that he saw while still a boy.*

Now then, I, Herman, who was once called Judah, am a sinner and an unworthy priest. I am of the Israelite people and the tribe of Levi and I was born of David, my father, and Sephora, my mother, in the city of Cologne. While I was still caught in the grip of Jewish unbelief, God showed me by a most joyful premonition the future blessings of his grace. In my thirteenth year, I saw in a dream how the Roman Emperor Henry [Henry V, 1106–1125], who was ruling at this time as predecessor of the glorious King Lothar, had taken possession of all the holdings of a certain mighty prince who had suddenly died. That king, so it seemed, came to me and gave me a great horse, white as snow, and a belt woven of gold with consummate craftsmanship, and hanging from it a silk purse that held seven very heavy coins. All of this he handed over to me, saying: "know that my dukes and princes take great offense at the benefice I have conferred upon you. Nonetheless, I shall add to these even greater gifts and I will give you the entire inheritance of this deceased prince so that you may legally possess them in perpetuity." Then, returning due thanks for his royal munificence, I buckled the noble belt, climbed on the horse and accompanied the king all the way to his palace. There, while he feasted with his friends, I sat down to the table beside him, as if his dearest friend, and from the same platter as he I ate a dish composed of all sorts of herbs and roots.

When I awakened, joyful of the vision, I did not judge with the levity of a child—even though I was a child—the most extraordinary things that I had seen to be devoid of meaning, but saw them as announcing something great for me in the form of a premonition. I went to see a certain relative of mine named Isaac, a man of great authority among the Jews, and I told him my dream in the order that it occurred so that he could interpret it for me in the manner that he knew how. But knowing only those things that "are of the flesh" [Romans 8:5], he set forth for me a conjecture that explained the dream in terms of carnal rewards, saying that the great white horse signified that a noble and beautiful wife would come my way, that the coins in my purse signified that I would possess great riches, and that sharing the feast of the emperor meant that I would in the future be highly honored among the

Jews. But divine grace later fulfilled the spiritual benefices of this vision for me more clearly, as the interpretation of this very vision that follows will indicate and the outcome of the matter will prove. For the moment, however, I shall explain sequentially by what circumstances my conversion began.

Chapter 2. *On what occasion he first joined the Christians and how much he profited from their company.*

In the seventh year following these events I arrived in Mainz with various merchants for the purpose of conducting business. Indeed all Jews are the slaves of commerce. The glorious king Lothar [1125–1128] was there at that time along with the venerable bishop Eckbert of Munster [1127–1132], who was in all things a "man of council." Because the king kept him there, occupied with the affairs of the kingdom, the bishop had been detained longer than he planned and the money in his coffers had been spent. He was therefore forced by necessity to borrow money from me. Contrary to the practice of Jews, I took no security from him since I thought that the good faith of so great a man was itself a worthy guarantee. When my parents and friends found out, they scolded me harshly saying that I was overly negligent for having lent money without a guarantee to anyone, especially to a man frequently away tending to his many duties. According to the custom of the Jews, which I knew well, I ought to have asked for a pledge of twice the amount of the loan. As a result they said that I should accompany the aforesaid bishop and remain with him until he repaid me the entire debt. However, they feared that in going about with Christians I might be tempted by them to turn away from following the tradition of my forefathers (something that does happen), and so they arranged for a certain Jew named Baruch, who was advanced in age, to look after me with care and resourcefulness. Following the advice of my parents and friends, I went to Munster, which was the see of his bishopric. When I found the bishop there I raised the matter of the debt with him, saying that I did not dare enter my parents' sight again until I was reimbursed. Not having the money to repay me, the bishop kept me with him for nearly twenty weeks.

During this time, since it was this good Shepherd's habit to administer the fodder of God's word to the sheep entrusted to him, I mingled with this flock of sheep and was led on by an adolescent curiosity, or rather by a certain thoughtless presumption, since, on account of the stench of error, I deserved to be counted among the goats instead of the sheep. There I heard a "scribe who has been trained for the kingdom of heaven" to bring forth "what is new and what is old" [Matthew 13:52], linking the Old Testament to the New and vindicating the New with sound reasoning from the Old. He also taught that some precepts of the Law, such as "You shall not commit adultery; You shall not steal; You shall not bear false witness; Honor you father and your mother" [Exodus 20:14–16, 12], were to be kept only according to the surface of the letter. But others, such as "You shall not plow with an ox and a donkey yoked together" [Deuteronomy 22:10]; "You shall not boil a kid in its mother's milk" [Exodus 23:19; 34:26; Deuteronomy 14:21], which were completely vacuous according to their literal meaning, he translated through a most beautiful way of reasoning into an allegorical explanation. With this sort of distinction, he gave the example of the Jews who, content with the letter of the precepts, are like beasts of burden, while the Christians, steeped in reason, refresh themselves with spiritual understanding as with the sweetest pith of the straw. As I listened with great eagerness and delight to the bishop address the people on these and like matters, I retained in my own memory those things that he was recalling from the histories of the Old Testament and which I had often read in Hebrew manuscripts. Knowing also that those animals that do not chew the cud are unclean according to Law, I transferred whatever things I had heard in his preaching that pleased me to the stomach of my memory for frequent rumination.

When the Christians, dumbfounded with amazement, saw that I listened most attentively to the things that were being said, they asked me whether I was pleased by the bishop's sermon. I answered that some parts pleased me more than others. They congratulated me on my curiosity and, while at the same time pitying my error with pious affection, they urged me most devoutly to join myself to the catholic union. They explained that their Jesus was most merciful and would send away none who turned to him, according to the testimony that he himself gave in the gospel, saying: "And anyone who comes to me I will never drive away" [John 6:37].

To give credence to the magnitude of his grace, they also offered me the example of their Apostle Paul, in whose honor the smaller basilica of that city had been built and dedicated. They said that he had first been a Pharisee and so great a follower of the Law that having received authority from the chief priests, he persecuted Christ's faithful and with an insatiable cruelty. But in the midst of his attempt to accomplish his crime, he was thrown to the ground by a bolt of heavenly light, and when from on high Christ forbade him from continuing such savagery, he was miraculously changed through God's clemency from Saul into Paul, from wolf into lamb, from persecutor into preacher. With these sermons and, if I dare say, with the enchantments of certain Christians, I was urged to shed the burdensome yoke of the Mosaic Law and to shoulder the easy one of Christ [Matthew 11:30].

As time went on, their intense conversations made me increasingly eager to inquire quite diligently into the sacraments of the Church. I entered the basilica that I had once denigrated as a pagan temple not so much out of devotion as out of curiosity.

Examining all things with great care, I saw among the sculptured devices and variety of paintings a monstrous idol. I discerned one and the same man humiliated and exalted, abased and lifted up, ignominious and noble. He was hanging wretchedly from high to low on a cross, and from low to high, by the deceiving effects of the painting, he was sitting enthroned and as if deified. I admit I was stupefied, suspecting that effigies of this sort were likenesses of the kind common among the pagans. The doctrines of the Pharisees had, in the past, easily persuaded me that it was truly thus.

Moreover, my above-mentioned tutor, who was cleverly looking into what I was doing, caught me attending Christian gatherings as often as I could and crossing into the precincts of churches. He sharply rebuked me, as one given over to his custody, and he affirmed that he was going to report to my parents' ears all the instances of my illicit curiosity. As though deaf and not hearing his threats and arguments at all, I gave every day over to my new curiosity, so much so that, living under the care of the bishop, I was entirely free from all business. In addition, I frequently entered the schools of the clergy and received books from them, with which I considered the properties of individual grammatical elements and studied the words in detail. I began at once, without a teacher and to the immense astonishment of those who listened, to join letters to syllables and syllables to expressions so that, in brief, I came to know how to read Scripture. If this seems incredible, it should be ascribed not to me but to God, for whom nothing is impossible.

Chapter 3. *Concerning the disputation held by him with Rupert, Abbot of Deutz.*

At that time a man named Rupert, the abbot of the monastery of Deutz, was staying [in Cologne].[1] He was subtle in temperament, learned in eloquence, and most accomplished in sacred as well as human letters. I saw him and invited him to engage in a disputational conflict. To use the Apostle's words, he was "ready to make a defense to anyone who asked about the faith and the hope that is in Christ" [cf. 1 Peter 3:15]. He promised that at the agreed place and time he would, with God's help, give me satisfaction on whatever matter I wished, both by reason and by the authority of Scripture.

Then, I addressed him in the following way: "You Christians bear a great prejudice against the Jews. You spit upon them and loath them with curses as though they were dead dogs, even though you read that in antiquity God chose them for himself, as his own people, from among all the nations in the world. He considered them alone worthy to know his holy name [cf. Deuteronomy 7:6]. For them alone did he deign to give the most perfect rule of his justice and, in observation of it, that they live and become holy, as he is holy [cf. Leviticus 11:44, 45 and 19:2; 1 Peter 1:16]. He not only commanded that rule by proclaiming it, but he even wrote it with his own hand on tablets of stone. He gave the Law to them alone, I say, for this Scripture itself, which you chew over in your mouth every day says: 'He declares his word to Jacob, his statutes and ordinances to Israel. He has not dealt thus with any other nation; they do not know his ordinances' [Psalms 147:19–20].

"But you, blinded by overwhelming envy of the divine benefits toward us, you loathe above all mortals the very ones whom you know, from what you read, to be more honorable and beloved to God than all other human beings. So be it.

"Indeed we bear patiently and with equanimity the invectives and mockery of men, and still we faithfully persevere in God's law and ceremonies. Certainly, it is better for us to fall into the hands of men than to abandon the Law of our God [Daniel 13:23]. For what is more fearful: to endure the wrath of men or to endure the wrath of God? To be spat upon by men or cursed by God? In the divine Law it reads: 'Cursed is everyone who does not observe and obey all the things written' in that book [Galatians 3:10; Deuteronomy 27:26]. In these words are found our just cause, based on the Law, defended by insuperable authority against all your mutterings. Likewise, your pride, by which you vainly boast of observing the Law, is manifestly condemned, although you derogate us for keeping the Law with a straightforward observance that we received from our fathers. For there is no distinction and no exception to the universal rule: 'Cursed is he who does not observe and obey all the things that are written' in the book. You are not doers of the Law, as you claim, just plain judges of the Law [James 4:11]. Laughable as it is, you correct the Law as it pleases you. You accept some things but reject others. Either you reject things as superstitious, or you accept them as mystical, though not in the way in which they were actually said, but according to whatever stupidities, old wives' tales, and depraved fictions anyone pleases. It is plain stupid temerity and folly worthy of derision for human beings to wish to correct what God established and commanded them to observe under penalty of a terrible curse.

"You Christians are especially liable to the curse, since while you presume to be judges of the Law, you are also condemned as its prevaricators. For the moment, let one thing from among the many suffice to illustrate your total damnation. Why is it that you who vaunt yourselves on the observance of the Law defy it with the impiety of manifest idolatry? Behold what I have seen with my own eyes. In your temples you have erected for yourselves as objects of adoration large images skillfully adorned with the arts of painters and sculptors. If only, to consummate your perdition, you worshipped the likeness of something besides that of a crucified man! For since, according to the Law, 'cursed is everyone who hangs on a tree' [Galatians 3:13; Deuteronomy 21:23], how much more are you accursed for worshipping one who hangs on wood? Moreover, since, as another passage in Scripture attests, 'cursed are those who trust in mere mortals and make mere flesh their strength' [Jeremiah 17:5], how much heavier is the sentence you incur since you place your hope in a crucified man?

"Not only do you not conceal the folly of your superstition, but you even glory in it, which is a far greater crime, for you preach your sin as Sodom did. Choose whichever of these two options you prefer: Either offer me the authority for this abominable worship of yours, if you in fact happen to know it, or else, if you cannot do that, consequently confess openly instead that you cannot, bearing the shame of this damnable error, which is in every respect contrary to sacred Law."

Chapter 4. *Rupert's Response*

To these remarks Rupert answered: "In these circumstances, I am undaunted by any of the arguments that you have set up for me to oppose. For in order to defend and confirm the truth of our religion there is in your very own books an abundant supply of authorities from which to draw. Armed with these authorities, as with an invisible shield, we may be able both to dodge and to return the shots of your objections. From them I shall now demonstrate by conclusive reasoning, if you accord me your patient attention, that what you call our idolatry is full of piety and religion and radiates the light of all truth.

"We therefore abhor and execrate in every way the crime of idolatry that you are attempting to impose upon us. We faithfully embrace the cult of the one and true God. Nor do we worship as a divinity the image of a crucified man or of anything else, as your slander maintains. Rather, with pious devotion, we represent to ourselves through the adorable form of the cross the Passion of Christ, who 'redeemed us from the curse of the law by becoming a curse for us' [Galatians 3:13]. We do this so that while externally we project the image of his death through the likeness of the cross, internally we are inspired with love for him so that we may continually remember that he, entirely untainted by any sin, endured so ignominious a death for us and that we, enveloped in as many and great sins as we are, may always consider with pious reflection what a great obligation we owe to him. This is the general explanation for the images that you observe among us.

"There is also a specific explanation. Images were devised for the benefit of the simple and unlettered so that those who could not learn about the Passion of their Redeemer by reading books could see the very price of their redemption through the visual appearance of the cross. What codices represent to us, images represent to the uneducated masses.

"But to keep the ritual of our religion from appearing to be constructed by human reason alone, allow me to demonstrate its support in the authority of the Old Testament, for ancient history provides us with a very similar account. When the children of Israel were led into the promised land, 'the Reubenites and the Gadites and the half-tribe of Manasseh' [Joshua 22:9–10], they went into that land of theirs and came to the hills along the Jordan where they built an altar of immense size. But the Lord had commanded by law that all the children of Israel should have one altar in common for celebrating the rite of sacrifices and that it should stand in the place that God choose for invoking the power of his majesty. That place, as everyone knew, was located in Shiloh.

"And so, when this deed done by the Reubenites and the Gadites was reported to the children of Israel, they rose up against those prevaricators of the law and seized weapons to punish the audacity in those responsible for this heinous act.

"And yet, acting on provident council, they temporarily withheld their hands from spilling the blood of brothers until, from the inquiries of the envoys from each tribe that were sent to them, they could learn what had been the reason for such a great effrontery. When the envoys arrived and admonished them for having presumed to erect an altar in violation of the law and to the scandal and ruin of all Israel, they received a response from them of the following kind:

> The All-Powerful Lord God, He knows! If it was in a spirit of prevarica-
> tion toward the Lord that we built this altar, or if we did so to offer
> burnt offerings or cereal offerings or peace offerings on it, may the Lord
> himself judge us and take vengeance. But we did it from fear that in time
> to come your children might say to our children: "What have you to do
> with the Lord God of Israel? For the Lord has made the river Jordan a
> border between us and you, you Reubenites and Gadites; you do not
> partake in the Lord." And through these words your children might
> make our children cease to worship the Lord. Thus we said, "Let us now
> build an altar, not for burnt offerings, nor for sacrifice, but to be a
> witness between us and you, and between the generations after us, that
> we do perform the service of the Lord." [Joshua 22:22–27]

"And so they constructed the altar, not to sacrifice victims and burnt offer-
ings upon it, but to demonstrate by such a testimony that they and their
posterity belonged to God's people. Thus we, too, and for a similar reason,
hold the cross of Christ in great reverence because of who hangs on it, but in
no way do we worship it as divine. Just as the altar was made for them in the
form of a testimony, so also the cross is for us a witness, so that while we
may consider that the price of our redemption hangs upon it, we may also
rejoice that through that price we belong to the company of saints and to the
eternal heritage of the Heavenly Jerusalem."

In this way Rupert met all my objections, both with the most elegant
arguments and with the most valid authorities of Scripture. Through the
brilliant rays of his answers, he deflected my objections as though they were
shadows of the darkest night. However, wretched as I was, "like the deaf
adder that stops its ear" [Psalms 58:4], I did not perceive the words of Rupert's sweet speech with the ears of my heart, and I was not able to see the
light of truth with the eyes of reason, darkened as they were by the cloud of
Jewish blindness.

Since it would take a very long time to unfold the entirety of our debate, let it suffice to have touched on it here in part. Now let us turn to the task of historical description.

Chapter 5. *That the charity and faith of a certain man was for him a great motivation.*

Now a memory comes back to me of something that I think should be inserted here, notably because by its sweetness it served for me as a great stimulus for conversion and also because it may give the reader an outstanding example of perfect charity and sincere faith, one that is to be imitated.

The aforementioned pontiff Eckbert had as the purveyor of his household a certain man called Richmar who was deeply religious in his whole manner of life, as was well proven to me. One day in the middle of dinner, the bishop sent his butler to deliver to him half a loaf of white bread and a portion of roast, as lords do. But because Richmar was so completely filled with the emotions of piety, he, with prompt and loving kindness, set before me (for I was sitting beside him) what had been sent to him, contenting himself instead only with bread and water following the religious practice to which he was accustomed. Not only was I overjoyed on account of this deed, but I was also stricken with wondrous admiration that a man whom thus far I had thought godless and beyond the Law could possess such a measure of virtuous charity, especially toward me. For indeed he could just as easily have detested me as the enemy of his sect, rather than show me love, especially considering the just sentence in which the Old Law states, "love your neighbor and hate your enemy" [Matthew 5:43; cf. Leviticus 19:18].

This man acted as a disciple of the true law of the gospel, in which it is said, "love your enemies, do good to them who hate you"; that is, do good not only "to those who belong to the family of his faith" but also "to all" human beings [cf. Matthew 5:43–44; Galatians 6:10]. Although I was unworthy of his good deed, he meticulously showed his love toward me and labored assiduously through conversations that were both exhorting and beseeching to draw me away from the error of my fathers and to win me for Christ. He knew indeed, as the Apostle James said, that "whoever brings back a sinner from wandering will save the sinner's soul from death and will cover a multitude of sins" [James 5:20].

But when he saw that these acts of piety could not soften the adamant hardness of my heart and bring me to the true faith, he saw to my needs, saying that, as the Apostle testifies in a certain place, "the Jews demand signs" [1 Corinthians 1:22]. With a resolute determination, he proposed the following bargain: if, as a trial of his faith, he sensed no burning while carrying a hot iron in his bare hand (as one normally would), I would faithfully submit to the cure of holy baptism and the dark cover of all unbelief would be washed over my heart. If, on the other hand, his hand were branded, it would still be up to my judgment what I wished to do or choose, but he would no longer attempt to persuade me in the matter. I heartedly accepted this resolute proposal and he, as though already sure of my conversion, could not have been more pleased. He eagerly made haste to ask the bishop if he would graciously exorcise the iron to be used in this spectacle of faith. But because my time for mercy had not yet arrived, the outcome of his pious request was just the opposite of what he had hoped for.

The bishop did admire and praise the great constancy of faith in him, but, evaluating it on the higher scale of his discernment, censured his request as being more inordinate than pious and offered him a mild rebuke. He said that he had, in this matter, "the zeal of God, but it is not enlightened" [Romans 10:2]. God was in no way to be tested by examinations of this sort. Instead, the bishop continued, God was to be beseeched so that he "who desires everyone to be saved and to come to the knowledge of the truth" [1 Timothy 2:4] would see fit to untie the knots of unbelief by his own most merciful piety when and as he wished and turn a master of error into a disciple of truth. Furthermore, he continued, you are never to ask or, above all, yearn for some sign from God to bring about this change, for nothing would be easier than for his omnipotence to convert whomever he wished without any miracle and only by the secret visitation of his grace. A sign that is displayed visibly to the external sight would be useless if he did not work invisibly through grace in the heart of a human being. And, indeed, we read that many have been converted without signs, but also that countless others have persisted in their infidelity even after witnessing miracles. It must further be known that faith which is undertaken not on account of any miracles, but because of simple piety and pious simplicity, has the greatest merit before God and the highest praise. Our Lord himself, author of this faith, bore witness to this in the Gospel when he set forth the rule of unbelief, saying "unless you see signs and wonders you will not believe" [John 4:48]; and that the faith practiced by the centurion before he saw a sign, or rather the faith through which he became worthy to receive a sign, was so extolled by Christ with the glorification of his praise that he said "not even in Israel have I found such faith" [Luke 7:9]. This is also why [Christ], after his resurrection, looked distrustfully at the unbelief that kept Thomas from being able to believe unless he touched the scars of his [Lord's] wounds: "You have believed because you have seen me" [John 20:29]. By adding, "Blessed are they who have not seen and yet have come to believe," he commended the faith of those who he foresaw would be believers in him only through the preaching that they heard. Thus the eminent teacher invalidated the pact of our agreement, the outcome of which we were both bound to with equal eagerness. He did this not through his episcopal authority to forbid, but by dissuading us with the manifest truth of his reasoning.

May those reading this brief treatise with pious intentions gain something fruitful and useful and also imitate the example of great discernment in the bishop and the example of wonderful faith and, above all, of perfect charity that he set forth. For [Richmar] did not curse me as perfidious and unworthy of Christian companionship. Instead, he most devotedly communicated to me works of charity and piety as though I were his fellow Christian.[2] May those stirred with the zeal of piety be horrified at spitting upon the Jewish (or any other human) error, as some customarily do. Rather, as true Christians (that is, imitators of Christ who prayed for his crucifiers), may they in goodness extend to adherents of error the embrace of fraternal charity. For "since," as the Savior himself says, "salvation is from the Jews" [John 4:22], and which is likewise attested by the Apostle Paul who says that "through their stumbling salvation has come to the Gentiles" [Romans 11:11], there is a reciprocity entirely worthy and pleasing to God that consists of Christians who strive with all their might for the salvation of those from among whom they have justly received the author of eternal salvation, Jesus Christ.

If they are commanded to extend their love to those who do them ill, how much more ought they to extend that love to those through whom came the general good? Let them confirm their love of them, therefore, as much as they can, sharing necessities and being for them a model for all piety in order that those who cannot be won by word may be won by example. For truly, as someone said, people are taught better through example than through words. Let them pour out earnest and suppliant prayers for them to the "Fathers of mercies" [2 Corinthians 1:3], as the Apostle says, should it happen that "God may perhaps grant that they will repent and come to know the truth, and that they may escape from the snares of the devil, having been held captive by him to do his will" [2 Timothy 2:25–26]. But having said all this by way of a digression, I hope that it is neither vain nor useless. Let us now return to the sequence of events I had undertaken.

Chapter 6. *How, when he came with Bishop Eckbert to the monastery of Cappenberg, he was stricken with compunction upon seeing the lifestyle of the brothers.*

Because I was still joined to the same venerable bishop in expectation of repayment of the debt, I accompanied him in his frequent visitations of different places in his diocese and one time it happened that I arrived with him at the monastery of Cappenberg. This distinguished place was situated on the summit of a mountain in what had once been the most celebrated castle in all of Westphalia. Its counts, Godfried and Otto, were men of magnificence and regal generosity. They were brothers, flourishing in the rosy blossom of their youth and abounding in riches and the delights of all worldly pomp when, inflamed by the fire of divine love, they abandoned with a sudden devotion for Christ whatever pleasures they had or could have had in this world. Gladly making the oblation to God with the "upright simplicity of their heart" [cf. 1 Chronicles 29:17], they turned the castle along with the most ample lands of their patrimony into that monastery of clerics observing the rule of St. Augustine. Knowing, however, that the perfect renounce not only their possessions but also themselves, these most fervent emulators of gospel perfection relinquished themselves as well as all that was theirs. Having donned the habit of that very perfection, they submitted their tender necks to the yoke of foreign moderation, striving to outperform the other brethren in their surrender to total humility as they had outperformed them in worldly dignity.

Coming to that place, as I had begun to say, in that society of Christ's faithful assembled from persons of varied conditions and diverse nations, I saw the prophecy of Isaiah concerning the times of Christ spiritually fulfilled. However, in reinforcement of my error, I carnally thought that the prophecy was to be accomplished in the coming of the Christ: "The calf, the lion, and the lamb will feed together and a little child will lead them" [Isaiah 11:6]. The Jews defend their perfidy on the basis of this prophecy. They do not see that this carnal prediction has been fulfilled. They deny that he whose advent was predicted in these words has already come.

But how did it happen that in that place the wise and uneducated, the strong and the weak, the noble and the lowborn alike were nourished by the sustenance of the divine Word, except that "the calf, the lion, and the lamb were feeding together"? It is they whom the little boy looked after as a spiritual father, a small child in malice but perfect in understanding, and governed them in the name of Christ.

From observing the religious way of life followed by these counts and monks, it thus seemed to me ignoble: I saw the removal of hair by razors or shears, the manifold renunciation of their lifestyle, macerations of the flesh, and continual prayers and vigils. Wretched and pitiable as I was, I deemed the cenobites most unhappy because I judged that they persevered in their toil in empty hope and without receiving any fruit in return. To take an example: If I saw a man who did not know the road running quickly off the beaten path, I would judge him the more pitiful the further I saw the speed of his running carry him away from the path. They were powerful runners through their strenuous labors and, accordingly, I thought these men were to be pitied rather than despised. But because they had departed, or so I thought, from the royal path of observances prescribed by the Law, I thought them more pitiable men than any other because they seemed to be afflicting themselves with empty labor in this life. Not only would they be unable to find any consolation before God, the Judge, after this life for their past afflictions, but they would instead incur from him a sentence of eternal damnation as skeptics and unbelievers.

From my inner human feelings I felt sorry for them, miserable wretch that I was, and drawing deep sighs from the depths of my heart I began to argue within myself about these questions, as though arguing against God, as if they were the wretched.

"Lord, of what sort is the abyss of your judgment, so deep and difficult to comprehend that you repel from your commandments your most devout servants, who search for you with all their heart, and from whom your path of truth is hidden, who are in error but should they follow it could be saved? Rejecting all delights of the world in order to follow you alone, they have chosen you as the object of their love and have placed with faith all their 'trust in you' [Psalms 55:23] for the love of whom they endlessly persist in the martyrdoms of a labor so immense it is greater even than death. It is not your way, you who 'judge the world in equity' [cf. Psalms 96:13], and for whom all your ways are mercy and truth. It is not your way, I say, to obstruct the advancement of your servants, to abominate those who love you, and to hide yourself from those seeking you and striving to know you. Your voice is indeed the one that says, 'I love those who love me, and those who seek me will find me' [Proverbs 8:17]. You have also, through the words of the prophet, declared that word full of mercy: 'I wish not the death of a sinner, but rather that he convert and live' [cf. Ezekiel 33:11].

"Therefore, showing that you desire the life of sinners, you invite them to conversion so that they may live, and it is altogether worthy and fitting for your goodness, 'of whose mercy there is no reckoning,'[3] that by your most kind mercy you turn again to these brethren who have already turned to you in strict penitence. Elsewhere through the prophet you deigned to promise: 'Return to me, and I will return to you' [Zechariah 1:3]. According to the words of your promise, you once accepted the three-day penitence of the Ninevites and, by mercifully sparing them the sword of your vengeance, you warned them with mercy [cf. John 3:10]. By this example, you clearly demonstrated with what fatherly feelings you desire the penitence and salvation of sinners. 'For you, Lord, are sweet and mild and of much mercy to all who call on you' [cf. Psalms 86:5]. And if you are for all, then how much more are you for these your servants who perform, not a penance of three days as the Ninevites once did, but continual penance, and who, out of love for you, despise not only 'the world and the things in the world' [1 John 2:15], but, with complete humility and abasement, themselves as well, which is much harder."

As I groaned within myself I considered these things and in a certain fashion wrestled with God (if it is right to put it this way) for judgment in favor of these monks, when abruptly a heavy scruple of doubtfulness arose in my heart concerning the diverse and contrary laws established by Jews and Christians. For since God's nature is goodness and his judgment mercy, I saw that it would be most appropriate for him to show the way of truth to his servants who truly "are being killed all day long" for him, according to the word of the psalm [Psalms 44:23]. I began to waver within myself and to wonder if perhaps the Jews had lost their way while Christians might be running in the "path of the Lord's commandments" [Psalms 119:32]. For if observance of the legal rites still pleased him, he would not have deprived the Jews, who observed those rites, of the aid of his grace and scattered them far and wide through all the nations of the earth, depriving them from all goods and a homeland. Conversely, if he in fact cursed the sect of the Christian religion, he would not have allowed it to spread and prosper so greatly throughout the earth.

Facing this two-pronged doubt, I was unsure where to turn or which path to trust, as I had absolutely no idea what might result from these uncertainties. Stuck as I was, I endured in my heart the greatest battles of thoughts fighting among themselves. I remembered things about the conversion of St. Paul that I had once heard from both Christian clergy as well as laity [cf. Acts 9:1]: namely, how, when called to the catholic faith by God's wonderful clemency, he became a preacher and protagonist of the Church that he had earlier persecuted with a tyrant's cruelty. I immediately converted to God with all contrition, and I prayed to him in tears that if he were the author of the Christian religion he would reveal this to me through secret inspiration, or through the vision of a dream, or, surely, through some visible sign. I also prayed that he who drew the Apostle Paul to the flock of his Church, even as his pride resisted the instigation, would also draw me, a man most humble and obedient to his commands, to that very flock. But God, who always piously hears a righteous request, long deferred but did not reject my desire. Later he not only fulfilled my desire but deigned to lavish even more plentiful gifts of his grace upon it, as the sequel to this narrative will demonstrate.

Chapter 7. *How he was accused by his Jewish guardian when he returned home to his parents.*

Following these events Easter came and went. The bishop repaid his debt to me and along with my Jewish guardian I returned to the city of Cologne where I lived. Delivering on the threats he had been making for some time, he greatly weakened the affection of my parents and friends toward me by the accusation that, contrary to what I was allowed, I had attached myself to Christians in such an earnest and familiar way that I should now be considered a Christian rather than a Jew. It was only out of a kind of fake piety that I had feigned, purely out of habit, to follow my ancestral religion.

But the Lord, "God of vengeance" [Psalms 94:1], soon paid him back for this malignant accusation, for, in accordance with the words of the prophet, he struck him down "with double destruction" [Jeremiah 17:18]. Suddenly stricken with a severe and painful fever, he died within fifteen days and passed from the suffering of this world into the eternal torments of hell. Thus, the "righteous Judge" [Psalms 7:11; 2 Timothy 4:8] in one and the same act showed mercy and truth: truth by repaying him with the punishments justly merited, and mercy by liberating me from his attacks and accusations.

Chapter 8. *How he self-imposed a three-day fast for the sake of enlightenment.*

I was now even more trusting in God's piety having experienced it through the vengeance inflicted upon my accuser. I again began to implore him, as I had earlier done with continual prayers, to deign to reveal to me "the way of the truth" by a night vision as he once revealed to holy Daniel the mysteries of dreams [Daniel 7:1]. Following the example of Daniel [cf. Daniel 9:3], I devoted myself to a three-day fast to God in order to obtain that which was my most ardent desire.

I knew that Jews and Christians did not keep to the same rules of fasting, since Christians eat on fast days at the ninth hour, while abstaining from meat, whereas Jews, maintaining the fast until evening, are allowed to eat meat and all other foods. Not knowing which of the two pleased God more, I decided to observe both equally. And so, according to the Christian custom, I abstained from meat, while I also extended the fast until evening in accordance with Jewish custom, contenting myself with just a little bread and water. Because of the excessive impatience of my desire, I went to sleep earlier than usual, hoping that I would be granted divine consolation according to the order with which I had sought it. But in vain. For such was the measure of my sins that night passed without result. I mourned deeply but did not let my impatience get the better of me. On the contrary, my desire increased because of this delay. Thinking that my self-denial of the previous day was insufficient given the magnitude of what I was asking, I decided to eat nothing at all that day. Going to sleep earlier, as before, I awaited with unspeakable desire the aid of a divine visitation. That night too passed away in vain, and while it took its shadows with it, it left me miserable and consumed in darkness and unbelief. Yet I did not despair of God's consolation. Again shedding tearful prayers before his pious eyes, I begged him to realize my wish and to end the suspense of my ardent desire.

Later on, exhausted by extreme abstinence from food in this summer weather, my whole body languished and I was unable to keep the vow of fasting until evening. About midday, an intolerable weakness of the flesh forced me to drink a little water. The third night arrived, the one on which the supreme expectation of my visitation depended. But it, too, passed by without the least result. The next morning, awakening and seeing the darkness of night reddened by the sun, I groaned deeply and grieved more than can be said or believed, because I had not been worthy, following the example of Daniel, of being enlightened by Christ, the true "sun of righteousness" [Malachi 4:2].

The Jews saw me in a state contrary to usual practice: tortured by abstinence. They duly suspected that I had committed some crime among Christians, the accusation of the aforementioned Jew [Baruch] lending credence to their condemnation. When I learned of their suspicion, it caused me further distress and thus increased the burden of grief in my heart. Having always lived among the Jews in a good harmony and without strife, I could not stand this ill repute among them without unease. However, I considered that God is merciful and more disposed to give humans great things after testing their perseverance in prayer and their patience under delay. Amid this weakness I regained my constancy of mind and began again to knock relentlessly with tears and prayers at the door of divine goodness, seeking to obtain the outcome of my desires. With the prophet, I said to him, "make me to know your ways, O Lord, teach me your paths; lead me in your truth" [Psalms 25:4–5].

Chapter 9. *That he spent time in disputation with clerics in order to inquire into the Catholic truth.*

Once again, reflecting on the studies to which I was applying myself in search of the knowledge of truth, it seemed good to me to look for men of the Church who were most skilled in the Old Testament and to confer with them about the contrary religious ways of Christians and Jews. If they could show me the authority of [their] sect from the manifest testimonies of the Law and Prophets and affirm in a probable fashion that entrance into the Kingdom of Heaven was open to their sect alone, as they state, I would yield to reason and take counsel for my salvation. I would reject the ancestral tradition that I followed and freely embrace what had been approved to me as truth. And so, moving forward opportunely or inopportunely, I did not cease day in and day out to harass the religious teachers of the Church with my questions, and especially those, as I have said, who were skilled in the Old Testament. Seeing that I did this not in order to stir up conflict but out of concern for knowing the truth, they labored by means of disputations and admonitions to separate me from "the Synagogue of Satan" and to incorporate me into the bowels of the holy church.

They presented me with many testimonies from the Law and the Prophets concerning Christ's advent. But I either contended that the passages in question had nothing to do with Christ, stubbornly supporting myself by the letter alone, or if I could not deny the connection, I perverted them with some sinister interpretation. If, trapped by clear reasoning, I could do neither, I did at least employ my craftiness and verbal ambiguities in order to evasively move onto another question.

Indeed, since I was judged by my people a "scribe learned" in the Law [cf. Matthew 13:52], I was shocked to be won over and trapped by the assertions of the Christians which the Jews contemptuously regarded as old wives' tales. Wretched as I was, I did not consider that this confusion, which was caused by my own error, pleased God and that it brought me, not shame, but glory. Therefore, in an appetite for vainglory, I closed and locked the door of truth to myself so that I would not believe, just as in the gospel the Lord says to the Jews: "How can you believe when you accept glory from one another and do not seek the glory that comes from the one who alone is God?" [John 5:44]. But even if I seemed to be disputing the assertions of the clerics with words, still whatever things they had proven to me by plain reason and manifest authority I received with a grateful mind, and the very beautiful allegories that they elicited from the Old Testament I most diligently placed in the treasure chest of my heart.

Chapter 10. *How he was forced to marry a woman against his will and purpose and, through his love for her, remained entangled in his old error.*

But the Devil, author of envy, still held me in the grips of unbelief. He saw me daily scurrying to church to eagerly hear the word of God, which itself fortified me against all his tyrannical assaults. Consumed in great envy of the progress that I made in these ways, he attacked me with the weapons of his ancient fraud. He who administered the taste of death to the first parent through a woman and reserved for most holy Job his only wife, among all his goods, not for consolation, but subversion, thus also, to my ruin, hitched me to a woman in marriage.

Now a certain Jew named Alexander came to me so that I might become betrothed to his virgin daughter. He began to strongly insist that I set a date for the wedding, admonishing, exhorting, and urging me to do so. Yet I was still uncertain whether I should persist in Judaism or turn to Christianity. I decided for the time being to put the marriage off as long as possible until I was worthy, through God's grace, to know by some sure sign what I had to do to heal my soul, for I prudently judged that, if bound to a wife, I would have to devote my time to household affairs rather than engage in disputations, as I had become accustomed to doing.

Thus, with a plan in mind, I answered that I received his advice with a grateful mind, as though it descended from charity itself, but that I would not be able to heed it because I had decided first to go to France for my studies. He often tried to persuade me to assent to his wishes. But seeing that he was not having any success, he turned from prayers and blandishments to threats and terrors, like a scorpion brandishing its tail. In the presence of a council of Jews, he pleaded that I had been so depraved by the pestilential tales of the Christians that neither the pious council of my parents and friends nor, more seriously, the legal authority could ever make me inclined to consent to marriage.

Interrogated by the Jews as to whether this was true, I responded that I did not entirely decline marriage but wished to put it off for the moment on grounds of expense. I presented the same reason for delay to them as to my father-in-law. Hearing that I wanted to go to France, and suspecting that this reason was not sincere (as indeed it was not), they all opposed me with one accord, shouting with raucous voices that this was a sign of apostasy. They said that it had nothing to do with my intent to study, as I maintained, but rather that it was motivated by an impulsive love of inquiring into Christian superstition.

And what else? When they saw the constancy and resolve of my mind, they proposed that I choose one of two alternatives: either I agree to consummate the marriage without any excuse and in accordance with the precepts of the Law, or, if some other course of action pleased me, to leave their synagogue.

Lest anyone perhaps deem this a light matter, they should know that for a Jew to be outside the synagogue is the same as for a Christian to be excommunicated from the Church. For, as Scripture says, "Where there is no fence, possession will be plundered" [cf. Ecclesiastes 36:27]. Wretched man that I was, since on account of my unbelief, I was not fenced in by divine protection and I had lost to the Devil's theft what little possession that I had gained through my early devotion to seeking out the "way of truth."

At the first warning of the Jews, I was frozen with immense fear, as if all options for any further remedy were closed to me once I was excluded from their synagogue. But if there were some approach to salvation outside the synagogue, I did not know it, nor, as I had proven, was I able by any efforts to achieve it. Nevertheless, I thought it would be safer for me to persevere to the end in that tradition which I had suckled from my mother's breasts, as it were, than to aspire ill-advisedly to some new religion for which I was unconvinced by the lack of signs or reasons, especially since through the error of my unavoidable ignorance I might perhaps secure an easy forgiveness from a pious judge.

I wasted time in this demented manner of thinking, "and my senseless heart was darkened" [cf. Romans 1:21]. My every earlier purpose was pushed aside and the most fervent desire that had burned within me in pursuit of truth was abandoned. I gave great joy to the Devil who was raging against me and gave myself over to destruction, conforming to the words with which the Lord reproaches some through the prophet: "A covenant with death and a pact with hell" [Isaiah 28:15] of false security. Obeying the unanimous will of the Jews, and without any further reevaluation, I fixed for them a date when the nuptial bed would be occupied. My marriage gave them great joy. The gratitude shown by all toward me was so great that the general excitement they demonstrated attracted me to them as much as the earlier terror had repelled me.

When the day of the wedding feast was at hand, many came together, not only Jews but also my Christian friends: the former delighting in my false happiness, the latter grieving with Christian affection over my deadly misfortunes, praying for some pious relief from above.

"Miserable Judas," they said, "how did you fall so easily from your good intention into such an abyss of perdition? Why, 'having your hand on the plow' did you 'turn back' so quickly [cf. Luke 9:62]? We were always giving you admonitions of salvation with the hope that you would eventually assent and believe in Christ, the author of our salvation. And yet, against our hope, you have chosen instead to follow your lusts. Having despaired of salvation, you have given yourself over entirely to perdition. Oh unhappy wretch, how you have deceived us and were yourself deceived. 'If only you knew and understood and foresaw the end of days!' [cf. Deuteronomy 32:29]. Then could you know what torments await you, what fires of blazing hell will greet you if you remain in this superstition.

"Wherefore, may the saving counsel of our charity please you now, and while the entrance of penitence is still open to you, take urgent care of your salvation. For if you are unwilling to do this while you can, it will be too late when you begin to have the will to change, but are then unable. But if you embrace the Christian faith with all your heart, and if you are revived by his saving bath, you will obtain from him full forgiveness of all your errors and a perfect knowledge of the whole truth into which you have begun to inquire. For indeed, as he says, he 'will drive away no one who comes to him' [cf. John 6:37], he bestows grace more abundantly upon those who revert to him by faith. He says that he was sent by God the father solely for those who reject their error, saying, 'I was sent only to the lost sheep of Israel' [Matthew 15:24]. He who first came searching for you will easily allow himself to be found if you search for him with a straight faith and a pure heart."

By this exhortation of theirs, the Christians strove to break through the iron hardness of my heart and to soften it to the grace of compunction. As if deaf, however, I did not hear their healthy warnings. I did not have ears of the heart, the ears of understanding, which the Lord in his gospel requires: "Let anyone with ears listen" [Matthew 13:9, 43]. Because I lacked spiritual hearing, I despised these things that I heard with corporeal ears alone. And thus I fulfilled what Scripture says: "When the sinner comes into the depth of evil, he despises" [cf. Proverbs 18:3].

Immediately, I experienced the corruption of the flesh. Deceitful pleasure and emotions for the woman I married so blinded my mind that I could not feel the very heavy languor of my soul, the lack of which is ordinarily a sign of extreme despair. I had overcome none of the harassments of temptations that had tested me earlier. Instead I was completely defeated and rendered powerless by them. I considered myself blessed in this false peace of vices. I started to pride myself of the supreme pleasure of the flesh, by which I had earlier feared to be cast down.

As the Apostle wrote concerning husbands and wives: "The married man is anxious about the affairs of the world, how to please his wife, and his interests are divided" [1 Corinthians 7:33]. I began to stray through the various cares of this world and to seek none of those things that belong to God. I attended only to those things that would make me pleasing in the eyes of my wife.

Chapter 11. *How, after being bonded to his wife, his devotion to truth was rekindled.*

After three months had passed, during which time I had started to toil under this lethargic sickness of my soul, I returned to my heart, by the mercy of

God, as though waking from the slumber of earlier ignorance. I began to ponder from what point I had descended through negligence and into what a pit of wretched delight I had fallen. I began to suffer terrible pain as I considered my miserable condition, for, as we read, "He" who knows "wisdom" also knows "grief" [cf. Isaiah 53:3].[4] I beat my breast with my fist, and shed streams of tears amid continual groans. I pronounced myself wretched and unhappy because, for the modest pleasure of the flesh, I had cast myself down into a vat of perdition.

Through the renewed grace of this compunction I slowly began, with confidence in God's great piety, to cut out from my mind the superfluous cares of this world. "Just as I had exposed" my "body parts" to be weapons of "iniquity" for sin, so I also worked to present them to God as weapons of righteousness [cf. Romans 6:19]. And yet, still retaining the earlier doubt about the mutually opposed beliefs of Jews and Christians, and knowing that "without faith it is impossible to please God" [Hebrews 11:6], and that "whatever does not proceed from faith is sin" [Romans 14:23], I began to search once more for some way in which, with God's help, I could expel the dark cloud of this ambiguity from my heart and find the light of true belief.

As I had done before, I diligently sought out the most learned teachers of the Church and demanded from them a rationale for their faith and their religion. They supplied me with an abundance of witnesses from Scripture and various figures of the Old Testament. But I, pursuing these things in reverse order and wishing to precede faith with reason, was therefore never able to attain that understanding which is correctly paired with faith according to the words of the prophet who said, "Unless you believe, you will not understand" [cf. Isaiah 7:9].

And so one day I happened to enter into a disputation with a certain master, whom I have already mentioned. When, after a prolonged discourse, no acceptance could be extracted from me concerning the things that he was rightly saying, one of the clerics assisting him, discerning the hardness of my heart, said, "why, O master, are you striving in vain? Why 'are you speaking into the air' [1 Corinthians 14:9]? Why are you casting seeds into the sand? Surely you know, as the Apostle says, that 'to this very day whenever Moses is read to the Jews, a veil lies over their heart'" [cf. 2 Corinthians 3:15].

Hearing this, and understanding the context that elicited this remark (for I was extremely well trained in the Old Testament), I was seized with fear. I recognized that just as the children of Israel were not able to look upon the face of Moses without a veil, when it shone brilliantly on the mountain, so neither would I, at the pinnacle of my intellect, be capable of attaining the mystical understanding of the Law of Moses without the interfering shadows of some kind of carnal figures.

I began to foam with anxiety once more. I did not know what to do or how to remove this veil from my heart so that I might grasp the bright light of truth with the uncovered eye of the mind. I fled to the "Father of lights" with a contrite and humbled heart, shedding tearful prayers in the sight of his goodness and exclaiming with the psalmist, "open my eyes, so that I may behold wondrous things out of your law. Give me understanding, that I may keep your law and observe it with my whole heart" [Psalms 119:18, 34]. Because I recognized that through the teachings of Christians the power of the holy cross was great, I frequently crossed my heart, hoping that its aid would be most effective in removing from me the veil of perfidy.

But what could that ferocious Enemy, with his thousand arts, do when he saw me armed against him in such defense—I under whose tyranny he held "captive" in the "snares" of disbelief [2 Timothy 2:26]? Or when would he endure to see his servant, whom he held by just laws, take leave when he never ceased with impious and illicit cruelty to chase down and capture even the very servants of his own Lord, that is, some of the faithful? This is why, in an effort to seduce me more easily while I was off guard, "he disguised himself as an angel of light" [2 Corinthians 11:14], assailing me, not with an open frontal assault, but also with subtle fraud. He thus began to stir my memory with the mandates of the Law, among which was the precept of the Jews that in no regard whatever were the impure rites of the Gentiles, execrable to God, to be imitated, lest those whom God had elected as "out of all the peoples on earth to be his people" [Deuteronomy 7:6] be seen to partake of those superstitions in some way or to be like them.

I believe that the craftiest Enemy did this in order to deflect more easily my intention from its purpose, for his actions showed me to be a prevaricator of the Law. The following occurred: By a diabolic inspiration, my own conscience began to admonish itself harshly as a transgressor of the divine law on this topic. And to ensure the pardon for my enormous error, as I thought, it chastised me with a strict penance of tears and fasts.

Later, after this mental breakdown, I came to my senses and perceived that this penance was one of offense, rather than of appeasement. Again I began to deplore the error of my ignorance. With heartfelt devotion, and with the same frequency as before, I defended myself by making the sign of the cross. But alas! I was unworthy to feel its healing remedy, for I did not yet perceive that I had been redeemed by its living cost from the curse of the Law.

What could I do? Hope for all counsel and assistance fled from my mind. Once again, tears streamed down and wrenching sobs began to erupt from the depths of my heart. I said to myself: "Oh miserable wretch that I am! What am I to do? Where am I to flee? What hope of salvation can there be for me anymore, since I am neither perfectly Jew nor Christian? If my end of days, 'coming swiftly like a thief in the night' [1 Thessalonians 5:2, 4], finds me such as I am now, where then shall I go? I shall surely perish."

So great indeed was the bitterness of my heart that even when the tongue fell silent, the thinness and desolation of my face conveyed it better. For all those who had known that I was born of great lineage and that I abounded in knowledge of the Law, as well as in possessions, were all the more astonished to see me so suddenly and unusually emaciated, for they had never seen me beset by any need.

Chapter 12. *How he was enlightened by the prayers of religious women.*

In full confidence I fled to God, who alone "regards toil and sorrow" as a "tower of strength." I "poured out my prayer in his sight" and "declared the tribulation of my heart before him." I beseeched him with tearful prayers that, on account of the great quantity of grief in my heart, his consolations might gladden my soul and he might deign to extend the right hand of his majesty to lead me out of "the darkness and shadows of death" [Luke 1:79], seeing that I was utterly dying of my own weakness.

What I faithfully asked of him, I therefore merited to receive effectually. From his inward inspiration I prudently began to consider how, if a servant has lost his lord's favor, he cannot regain it unless friends of the same lord intercede on his behalf. Therefore, unless intercessions of the holy Church came to my aid, I could not obtain the grace of Christ.

And as I thought about whose prayers I could commend myself to in order to obtain a greater merit before God, I recalled two sisters who led the celibate life together in Cologne, cloistered for God next to the monastery of St. Maurice.[5] One was named Bertha, the other Glismut. Their holy way of life had spread the sweet scent of good repute throughout the entire city. Hoping that their patronage could be of great assistance for me before God, I made haste to see them. I disclosed to them with many tears the many temptations that were inciting me, and I humbly beseeched them to direct their worthy prayers to God for my enlightenment.

With deep inner piety and compassion, they spilled profuse tears over my great miseries, and they promised that they would put forth unwavering supplications to God on my behalf until I was worthy to receive the hoped-for consolation of heavenly grace.

O how true are the words of the Apostle James: "The constant prayer of the righteous yields much" [cf. James 5:16]. Shortly thereafter, through their merits and prayers, so great a brightness of Christian faith shone suddenly in my heart that it entirely chased away the shadows of all former doubt and ignorance; an appropriate turn of events for women to raise up, by their prayers, a man who had fallen because of a woman. O you devout and holy women, therefore, whoever may read these words or hear them read, receive from these women the outstanding and imitable example or prayer, know that the quieter and more sincere your prayers are, the more effective they are before God for achieving whatever you seek.

Behold me. Neither the arguments given by many concerning the faith of Christ nor the disputation of great clerics could convert me to the faith of Christ. The devout prayers of simple women did.

Chapter 13. *How he progressed in the faith.*

Having found, by God's grace, "a precious pearl" [Matthew 13:46], I began out of love for it, following the example of that merchant in the gospel, to despise all temporal things, so that I might be worthy of being enriched by such joyous and salubrious a possession. Liberating myself of all cares, as much as I could, I became impatient of every delay. I hardly took food at home and began to visit the basilicas and saints with great devotion. Listening to the word of God, I joyfully incorporated what I heard with the hearing of the heart as much as with that of the body.

I acted secretly, since, still weak and tender in faith, like Nicodemus who "came to Jesus by night" [John 3:2], I feared persecution by the Jews. I heard the Lord thundering terribly in his gospel toward that same Nicodemus, "no one can enter the kingdom of God without being born of water and spirit" [John 3:5]. I began to desire ever more passionately the cleansing of this regeneration, since, in the absence of its remedial power, I should never according to this statement of the Lord be able to enter the kingdom of heaven.

Chapter 14. *How he exacted his brother from Judaism and how the Jews conspired against him.*

Knowing that the Lord had commanded the children of Israel not to go out of Egypt empty-handed, but to despoil it as they left [Exodus 11:2; 12:35], I (instructed by such an example) did not want to leave empty-handed and in the darkness of Jewish disbelief. But nor did I plunder gold and silver, or any precious raiment. I took away a rational being which would not only adorn the temple of the supreme King, but would also be worthy of his temple, for as the Apostle Paul says, "for God's temple is holy, and you are that temple" [1 Corinthians 3:17].

In Mainz I had a seven-year-old brother, not from my mother's side but from my father's side. I most passionately wished for him to become with me a coinheritor of divine grace through the regenerative cleansing [of baptism]. So while we did not have the same carnal mother by birth, we would similarly have the Church as our mother through rebirth in the spirit.

The Jews, however, saw that I no longer frequented their synagogue with regularity, even though, as can be learned above, I greatly feared being absent from their congregation. They realized that the circumstances of this very unwelcome change were not to be taken lightly. Therefore, laying traps for me, they began to scrutinize with curiosity my every ways and acts. When they caught me doing nothing during the day except devoting time to the routines of the Church, they so zealously flared up against me that, should it have occurred to their faculties to commit the crime, they would not have shrunk from stoning me with their own hands. Blinded by the darkness of their perfidy and malignity, they strove, to add to their damnation, to involve others in the crime of parricide that they were not able to perpetrate themselves. But they committed no crime other than casting themselves into the guilt of wishing it.

When it was discovered that I had decided to go to Mainz, "they met together against me," as it is written [cf. Psalms 2:2], taking up "plans that could not be made firm." For, without my knowing, they dispatched letters written in Hebrew to the Jews of Mainz, transported by Wolkwin, a chaplain to Queen Richenza. The contents of those letters were that they had discovered me to be an unbeliever and an apostate, and that they had imposed a suitable punishment upon me in accordance with the rigor of legal censure,.

But, as the Apostle says, "If God is for us, who is against us?" [Romans

8:31]. He who "frustrates the plans of the Gentiles and condemns the plans of princes" [cf. Psalms 33:10] frustrates *their* own plan in a wink. Not only did he powerfully free me from their clutches, but he also fulfilled the pious wish I had envisioned of freeing my brother.

Chapter 15. *In what marvelous way he intercepted the letters written against him by the Jews.*

By a disposition of God I happened to fall into the company of the above-mentioned cleric as he was heading to Mainz to deliver his mission. Neither of us were aware of the business of the other, and so we chatted about many things along the way. He began to mention by name some of my relatives who lived in Mainz, not knowing that they were related to me, stating that he had some secret message to deliver to them. When I heard this, still fully ignorant of the Jewish trap against me, I nevertheless began to suspect, as was the case, that through his mission the Jews had devised a great evil against me. And so, when I spoke to the cleric about this, I said that he carried the letters of the Jews with the greatest concern for his own soul.

He denied that he was carrying any letters, since he had been asked to conceal the matter. But I gave little credence to his denial. I continued to insist that the matter was as I had said, adding that a heavy weight of divine vengeance loomed if, against my advice, he presumed to deliver to the Jews of Mainz the letters he had accepted, for in them lay the seeds of great evil.

Employing urgent prayers and threats, I at last extorted from him a confession of the truth. He confessed to me that everything was as I had said, and he asked that I disclose to him the affairs of those letters. Then— miraculously, but most true, as God is witness—I announced to him the contents and meaning of those letters, solely from the conjecture of my heart, as though I had read them or learned about them from another source.

This happened, not by chance, but by the inspiration and providence of God, who engineered events so as to "snatch me" out from the most malign "expectations of the people of the Jews" [cf. Acts 12:11] and to resolve to a glorious outcome the holy business I had undertaken. Receiving the letters that he extended to me, I unfolded them and read them over, wherein I found, as I had suspected, the most malign accusations against me by the Jews. And with the greatest exultation I gave thanks to God for my deliverance and burned those pestiferous writings in the fire.

Chapter 16. *How, arriving in Worms, he faithfully preached Christ in the synagogue of the Jews.*

I then celebrated with indescribable joy the dance of the psalmist: "Our soul has been snatched as a sparrow from the snare of the hunters. The snare is broken, and we have escaped" [cf. Psalms 124:7]. I began to burn so powerfully out of love for the catholic faith and religion that, freed from fear, charity chased away my every trepidation [1 John 4:8]. I not only dared to believe that "Christ was the power of God and the wisdom of God" [1 Corinthians 1:24] for justification, and to confess the same "with my mouth for salvation" [Romans 10:10], but indeed I also dared to preach constantly and freely to his enemies, the Jews.

Arriving at Worms, where I had a brother named Samuel, I entered the synagogue of the Jews on the day when they usually gather there. I heard them reading the superstitious commentaries of their Gamaliel on the Old Testament. Soon, ignited by divine fervor and animated with great confidence and grace of speech, I entered into a disputation with them over prophecy in which I opportunely demonstrated to them to which faith I belonged and how much I had profited from the many disputations with Christians I had had concerning the orthodox faith. Against the stupid old wives' tales that that same Gamaliel had assembled from written texts, I produced for them honey-sweet spiritual allegories. With many and valid authorities of divine sayings, I shut their mouth up, for in their blind pride and proud blindness they had presumed to blaspheme Christ and to rise "against heaven" [Psalms 73:9] by denigrating his holy church.

Can you imagine how great a stupor of amazement then seized all the Jews who were present when they saw me so strongly assail the traditions of my fathers, when they had hoped that I, a Jew of the Jews, would be their faithful defender? Taking on the head of the synagogue (David was his name) and the aforementioned brother through the singular combat of debate, I lengthily reviewed the pages of the Law and the Prophets against them. Defending and proving the Christian faith through the most sufficient testimonies of these pages, I closed off every avenue they had to calumny against Christ and his holy Church.

When they saw that I favored Christians with such stubbornness, they began to call me "semi-Christian." They reproached me with this name so as to suggest that I had been badly circumvented by their crafty persuasions.

Finally, however, they argued whether my mind and tongue agreed in all the things that I had set forth against them for the defense of the Christian faith. I feared that if I confessed the bare truth to them, their traps should somehow prevent me from abducting my brother, and so I mitigated my response. I neither denied that I was a Christian, nor did I openly declare it: "Since I frequently dispute with Christians, I have learned in great measure their subtle arguments against the Jews. I wanted to disguise myself with their persona so that, instructed by this preview of my assertions, you would seem the better informed to them if you should find yourselves in a situation that called for it." They gratefully accepted this response.

Chapter 17: *How, arriving at Mainz, he secretly kidnapped his brother.*

Afterward, I came to Mainz where I furtively kidnapped the boy from his mother. Out of "fear of the Jews" [John 19:38], I wished to take him in secret out of the city to a certain place where I had ordered a servant to wait for us with horses. But the most odious Enemy of human salvation, understanding that this flight had been perpetrated not by his own instigation, but by God's, and that it belonged, not to his, but to God's lot, tried by the malignant art of his fraud to prevent me. For although the route across the city was well known to me, my eyes were so blinded with diabolic illusion—amazing it is to say—that from the first to the sixth hour of the day I wandered in the all the city streets without being able to find the exit. The boy was weary and sobbing from his weariness. Taking pity on him, I hoisted him onto my shoulders. Seeing this, many Christians mocked me as a fool.

In a state of unbelievable anguish of heart and with a look of great confusion, I humbly beseeched the only refuge available to me, divine assistance, and secretly marked the sign of the cross on my forehead. Then, an astonishing thing! No sooner had I armed myself with the sign of the cross when, suddenly, the diabolic illusion that had blinded me foundered: I found and joyously recognized the gate to the city, which earlier I had been unable to locate circling round and round. When I exited the city, I found the servant with horses where I had ordered him to be.

A short while after we left the city, the Jews of Cologne arrived by boat and divulged to the Jews of that city [i.e., Mainz] those things about me which they had perceived as hostile to their religion; namely, how at Cologne

I had concealed books and money with Christians, inasmuch as I had obstinately decided to cross over into their sect. Hearing of this, the mother of the boy, deeply troubled and frightened, had me carefully searched for. When I was nowhere to be found, the excesses of her grief made her mad. She ran to the leading men of the city wailing bitterly, and with a sorrowful voice proclaimed that her son had been furtively abducted. At once they sent messengers to apprehend me. But just as one can never "resist what God has ordered" [Romans 13:2], so they could not catch me, for I was serving that order.

Therefore, proceeding with the boy on the journey I had begun, I arrived in the evening at the monastery called Welanheim [Flonheim]. When the brothers realized the pious desires of my heart, they received me with great joy and charity. While we were still eating, lo, a messenger who was sent looking for us stood at the gate and asked the porter whether a Jew escorting a boy had entered. The porter, a simple man, suspected no danger in the messenger and gave him the simple truth. To keep the brothers from sustaining any harm on my account, I commended the boy to them so that they might instruct him in the sacred letters. Then, I secretly fled to the monastery called Ravengiersburg. There I was kept in great exultation by the brothers and catechized on the third of the Calends of November.

Chapter 18. *Concerning the vision that he saw before baptism.*

After about three weeks passed by, and after I was made a catechumen, on the fourth day before the Sunday when I was to be baptized, I saw a dream that was as sweet to see as to recount. Toward the east, I saw the "heavens opened" [Acts 7:55]. The imaginary structure that appeared before my eyes was adorned throughout with the purest gold. There, I saw the Lord Jesus seated on an elevated throne with all power and honor and in the majesty of the Father, holding in the place of a scepter the triumphal sign of the cross upon his right shoulder.

He seemed to me to be accompanied by his most excellent friends, and I was basking incalculably in the indescribable sweetness of contemplating him when, lo, I saw the two sons of my aunt, Nathan and Isaac were their names, passing nimbly behind my back. So swift was their pace that it was easy to understand, for those paying attention, that this blessed scene had been shown to them, not for solace, but for torment, so that they might be interiorly tormented in the mind by the fact that they were not worthy of experiencing the glory of the saints which they were seeing.

I turned to them and said: "O wretched and unhappy men, does the sign of that cross which you see upon Christ's shoulder not recall to your mind Isaiah's prophecy, 'whose empire is upon his shoulder' [cf. Isaiah 9:6]? You once scorned the belief, despite my admonishments, that this prophecy referred to Christ. Now you find yourselves perpetually confounded by its fulfillment."

Trembling with great fear, they were barely able to answer me with low and halting voices, saying: "O cousin, the things that you remind us of have been proven true, but alas, it is all too late for us, for having missed the opportunity for salvation through penitence, we have been consigned to eternal hell." No sooner had they spoken these words than they were suddenly removed from the scene, fulfilling what is said in Scripture: "Let the impious be removed, that he may not see the glory of God" [cf. Isaiah 26:10].

Awakening, I recalled the amount of prayers and tears and frequency of fasts I had exercised in order to obtain such a vision from heaven for my enlightenment. From these things that I saw I began to overflow with spiritual joy and to repay God my debt of gratitude for so sweet a vision, through which I was worthy to be confirmed in his faith.

Chapter 19. *How he was baptized, and what tricks of the Devil he had to endure up until that baptism.*

The Sunday came on which I was to put off "the old man with his practices" and "put on the new" [cf. Colossians 3:9] through the cleansing of rebirth. And so all of the clergy of the city of Cologne gathered in festive exultation at the basilica of St. Peter, prince of Apostles, where the font had been prepared to celebrate the saving mystery. At about the third hour, when the font had been consecrated and made fecund for the regeneration of souls through invocation of the Holy Spirit, I confessed with my whole heart the faith of the holy Trinity and stepped into it with great devotion and contrition of heart.

But alas! Hard as it is to say, the Enemy's deception did not desist from its assaults against me even at the moment of baptism. For just as, according to the Evangelist's witness, the epileptic boy who was about to be freed from possession of demons by the mercy of the Lord fell down in a graver seizure when the evil spirit was compelled to come out [Mark 9:16; Luke 9:39], so also the ancient Enemy assaulted me even more when he saw that I had been snatched from his tyranny by the divinely instituted sacrament of salvation.

If indeed I had been sufficiently steeped, in accordance with my capacity, in other matters concerning orthodox faith, the one thing I had not been taught is that baptism involves a triple immersion in the name of the holy Trinity. This ignorance was due either to negligence on the part of the ministers, or by the trickery of the Enemy who was laying traps for me.

I entered into the streams of the life-giving font. Immersed for the first time, toward the east, I believed that one immersion would be sufficient for the renewal of the ancient state. But the clerics standing around the baptistery clamored that I ought to be immersed more than once. Having just emerged from the font, I could not hear their voices distinctly, nor could I see clearly the gestures that they were making at me, since water was streaming down the hairs of my head. Therefore, wiping the water from my face with my hands, I heard what they wanted, although at first I did not willingly accede to their wishes, because I was stiff from the bitter cold of the font. But, swayed by the gentle admonitions of my baptizer, I did what had to be done for salvation. And so, having reckoned that by a second dipping I had satisfied the divine mysteries, I began to want to get out of the font. I was almost stiff as a board by the extreme cold. But once again the clergy shouted vociferously that to complete the sacrament I humbly had to submit to be immersed to the south in the saving waters.

Beset by diabolical traps, I therefore suspected that they were making fun of me. Consequently, just as Naaman the Syrian once indignantly began to depart when he received the prophet Elisha's command to dip himself seven times in the Jordan [2 Kings 5:10–12], so I too, inflamed with a great fury of mind and impatient of all delay, wanted to jump out of the baptistery with equal madness. But thank God that, while the Enemy "rose up against" me [cf. Psalms 12:5], he did not prevail. For in the same way that Naaman, swayed by the admonition of his companions, yielded to the prophet's salutary counsel, so, too, the sweet exhortations of religious clerics who were present strengthened my faintheartedness in the faith so that the contagion of suspecting evil which the Enemy had stirred up in my mind was cast out.

So, then, to compare new things in detail with the old: Naaman, washed in the streams of the Jordan seven times, was visibly cured of leprosy of the flesh, and I, in baptism, was invisibly cured of the leprosy of the soul by the seven-form grace of Holy Spirit. His flesh, cleansed of the stains of leprosy, recovered the purity of an infant. As for me, my skin was stripped of the old existence through the cleansing effect of regeneration, and the Church, a virgin mother, gave birth to me in a new infancy. Having changed in this basin of water the order of my inner life as well as my previous name, which was formerly Judas, I took the name Herman.

With what great applause and with what great joys in common did not only the clergy but also the whole faithful people celebrate this glorious change by the right hand of the Most High, this return to the holy Church's flock of the lost sheep carried on the shoulder of the pious Shepherd [Luke 15:4]! And not without reason. For how should the Christian people not rejoice over the penitence of a converted sinner for whom, as the Lord bears witness, the hosts of angels rejoice more than ninety-nine just persons? But the Jews, who have zeal for the law, "but not according to knowledge" [Romans 10:2], grieved for me inconsolably and with the bitterest sorrow as one both perfidious and lost.

Chapter 20. *How, after baptism, he renounced the world and devoted himself to divine service under the order or canons.*

And so, the "impure spirit" [Matthew 12:43] was expelled from the house of my heart by the cleansing of regeneration. I was afraid, indeed trembling with fear, lest that spirit should return to find the same "house" to be "empty" of the practice of spiritual exercise, even if purified by the saving bath and "adorned" with the sacraments of Christ [Luke 1:24], and that it would then enter and occupy it with a plague seven times worse than previously, rendering my new state "worse than before."

I worked with sleepless care to make my habitation shut to the malign intruder and worthy of the kind Christ. And so, hearing the gospel precepts, "if you wish to be perfect, go, sell your possessions, and give the money to the poor, and follow me" [Matthew 19:21], and also, unless a man "renounce all that he possesses, he cannot be my disciple" [Luke 14:33], I cheerfully began to despise all the goods that I seemed to have temporally, in the hope and desire for eternal ones, so that once delivered from the laborious troubles of this world, I might walk expeditiously and freely along the narrow way "that leads to life" [Matthew 7:14].

Learning also, as the psalmist says, that "it is good and pleasant when kindred live together in unity" [Psalms 133:1], I escaped to the famous and

religiously filled canonry of Cappenberg, which I recalled above, as if to some
safe harbor from a shipwreck on this world's sea where I went to fight naked
with the naked Enemy. There, I changed my life and garb, according to the
rule of St. Augustine, to await the end of the present life and the promise of
next one.

I also took up the yoke of learning the Latin language and became, with
God's assistance, so proficient within five years that the charity of the brethren judged me fit to take holy orders and kindly drew me to them. I humbly
and justly felt that I was unworthy and protested that I was hardly suited for
this. I modestly refused as much as I dared and as much as was proper. But
"God, who always gives grace to the humble" [1 Peter 5:5], seeing me choose
the lowest place among his followers, saw it fitting to say to me, "Friend,
move up higher" [Luke 14:10]. Exalting in his call, not with prideful swelling
but "in trembling," as it is written [Psalms 2:11], I climbed the canonical
orders until I reached the office of priestly excellence.

Then, for the first time, I understood the dream that I had seen before
my conversion and that I inserted at the beginning of this short work prefiguring my future. As I promised above, I shall explain the interpretation of it.

Chapter 21. *That he then understood the first dream that he saw in childhood concerning the grace of Christ that was going to be in him, and how he interpreted it.*

Here, then, is the interpretation of the vision: the worldly emperor who
appeared to me signifies the heavenly king, of whom the psalmist says, "Lord
of virtues, he is the King of glory" [Psalms 23:10]. He had a certain great
prince, and he signifies that angel whom, at the beginning of creation, God
made more noble than all other angelic spirits and placed above all other
orders or angels. That angel is truly dead now, since, rising up against God
in his pride, he was stripped of the glory of his dignity as archangel and made
devil.

The King of kings deigned to visit me though his grace, giving me a
white horse when he granted me the grace of holy baptism, through which I
became "whiter than snow." He also gave me a belt, bestowing virtue on me
in order to restrain the flowing desires of the flesh. In the seven pennies of
heavy coinage are rightly understood the gifts of the seven-form Spirit;
whomever is completed by them is adorned with moral gravity. When,

through the gifts of the Holy Spirit, the purity of life begins to glitter like assayed silver, the person who receives them also begins to sparkle sweetly to others with the love of God and eternal life, which the sound of silver well signifies.

Lest they easily be lost, however, the seven pennies were contained in a purse. I hope that this signifies that the spiritual gifts of the Holy Spirit that were mercifully conferred upon me would not be neglected, but that they would remain with me to the end, to overcome all the aggressions of temptations and to attain the heavenly kingdom.

Furthermore, that the princes were indignant of my achieving so happy a success shows them to be malign spirits, whom the Apostle calls "rulers of the world" [cf. Ephesians 6:12]; and Jews, who, on account of the Law they received from God, usurped for themselves first place among all other nations, envied me for having been worthy to receive the grace of Christ which they themselves were unworthy to receive.

But I, fastened with that shining belt—i.e., the strength of continence— sat upon the royal horse because the grace of baptism "was not vain in me" [1 Corinthians 15:10]. The use of the horse indicates that grace is always to be perfected by spiritual exercise with God's help, and I labored to put it to good use. I also followed Christ the King, despising the world and "the things that are in this world" [John 2:15]. I rejected not only all things that were mine but also myself for love of him, doing the work that he claimed for himself when he said, "I have come not to do my own will, but the will of him [the Father] who sent me." [John 6:38]. And, well-seated on the horse as white as snow, I accompanied the King, since no one will be fit to follow Christ's footsteps without receiving the grace of baptism, which, as we said earlier, is figuratively represented by the white horse.

Further, I think that the palace into which I followed him designates the place of my conversion. Indeed, what is implied by the monastic houses of clerics and other religious persons living according to a rule throughout the world, if not the palace of the supreme King? In them, on account of their chaste and a religious way of life Christ is believed to dwell, by grace, as a king in his palace, at home in his fashion and among his own.

Moreover, I then approached the table of the King to be in his company where I undertook the sacrosanct mystery of the altar, even though unworthy. Truly, to sit at the table is humbly to approach the altar of Christ. But words cannot worthily describe how sweet are the delights of this heavenly banquet. It is known only to those who by the grace of God are worthy to experience it. Such, I say, is the banquet of the faithful soul that no one can understand it unless he approaches the reverend table of the altar with complete faith, with true humility and contrition of heart, and with sincere devotion of mind. Thus, as I said, may one be fattened at that table on the meats of the immaculate Lamb, Jesus Christ, and be inebriated with the cup of his sacrosanct blood.

Furthermore, the salad that I seemingly ate at the royal table I think designates the gospel of Christ. For just as that salad was prepared out of various kinds of herbs, so the gospel of Christ is composed of various precepts relating to eternal life. To eat a salad at the royal banquet, therefore, is for the priest assisting at the Lord's altar to consider carefully and subtly the precepts of the gospel, as though chewing the cud in the mouth of the heart. It is for him to weigh how humble, devout, radiant with chastity, and fervid with clarity he should be who wishes to celebrate the mystery of so great a sacrament in a manner that is acceptable to God.

Christ the King feasts with us because he is fed by the sweetness of our spiritual progress. Indeed, in the Apocalypse he himself attests that there is sweet refreshment for him in the heart that is pious and given over to divine services: "Lo, I am standing at the door and knocking; if anyone open the door to me, I shall go in and dine with him, and he with me" [Revelation 3:20]. I think that it was not off topic that I seemed to see myself eating from the same platter with the King. The one platter signifies the unity of the catholic faith. He who eats salad from the platter with Christ, therefore, keeps with the help of grace the precepts of the holy gospel in the unity of the catholic faith.

Now, therefore, it is in that unity, as was once shown to me by the presentiment of this most happy vision, that, by God's grace I serve him, as has been written, "with fear, and I exult with trembling" [cf. Psalms 2:11]. I exult, I say, with trembling, because I owe it to his grace, through which I am now faithful, to rejoice [Romans 11:33]; and I fear, for in the abyss of his most profound and unsearchable judgments that stay open before me I know not, according to them, "whether I am worthy of love or hatred" [Ecclesiastes 9:11].

What mortal, however just and however holy, does not fear that terrible sentence of our Savior, which says, "many are called, but few are chosen" [Matthew 20:16]? I have faith, however, in the Lord Jesus that "the one who began a good in me will bring it to completion" [Philippians 1:6]. Indeed, the magnitude of former benefits promises me the greatest hope of future ones. For behold, the merciful Lord has mercifully raised up "the poor from the dung heap and seated him with the princes of his people" [cf. Psalms 113:7–8]. Having mercifully snatched me from the most filthy and impious sect of Jewish superstition, he piously and mercifully deigned not only to join me to his faithful through the unity of the catholic faith, but also to gather me to the glorious banquet of his table, through the grace of the priestly office.

Who, O Lord, can worthily weigh these inner realms of your piety toward me, unworthy as I am? Who can worthily measure the immense riches of your goodness? I hope, Lord, and I believe, faithfully presuming from such great kindness, that "your mercy shall follow me all the days of my life" [Psalms 23:6], for you have already deigned to give me in advance such great pledges of grace, for which, as is worthy, I do not cease immolating praises and sacrifices of jubilation to you, my most pious illuminator.

And you, whoever may read or hear this account, "rejoice with me" and congratulate me, for I was dead and I live again. I was lost and I am found [cf. Luke 15:6, 9]. Therefore, "magnify the Lord with me" [Psalms 34:3], who lives and reigns unto the ages of ages. Amen.

Notes

INTRODUCTION

1. I found myself faced with an analogous situation leaning toward the no less re-markable case of Saint Guinefort. Cf. Schmitt, *The Holy Greyhound* (Cambridge, 1983). The scale of the object analyzed here and the nature of the questions asked about it may evoke certain questions regarding "microhistory." Cf. Revel, ed., *Jeux d'échelles* (Paris, 1996).

2. While focusing on the place of the text in the debate between Jews and Christians in the twelfth century, Jeremy Cohen, *Living Letters of the Law* (Berkeley, 1999), p. 291, recognizes the text's interest with respect to even more general problems: the story of Herman, he writes, "relates to some of the chief religious and social concerns of the day: the importance of the individual and his impulses, the nature of religious community, biblical hermeneutics, the use of *ratio* and *auctoritas* in theological argument, religious disputation, and the dynamics of the conversion process itself. The literary artifice of the *Opusculum* similarly testifies to the cultural climate in which it appeared." Of all the recent authors who have studied the *Opusculum*, it is Sabine Gäbe ("*Me peperit ecclesia mater*," 2000) who, it seems to me, has best underscored the necessity to examine first the "literary" construction of the text. Her article (which is dated 2000, but only appeared in 2002) was only brought to my attention after the completion of this book and I was delighted to see that our lines of investigation converge on multiple points.

3. Niemeyer, "Die Vitae," 1967. This reproach is addressed more to English-speak-ing historians than to German-speaking historians, who are generally more sensitive to the local realities of the vast region from where the *Opusculum* comes (i.e., Cologne, Munster, Cappenberg, Scheda).

4. *Vita Godefridi comitis Capenbergensis*, p. 521.

5. One can accept here the suggestion made by Anna Sapir Abulafia that chapter 9 is not in its rightful place and ought to be inserted between chapters 2 and 3. For indeed, this chapter mentions in logical order the development of young Judas's discussions with the clerics who were in the entourage of the bishop.

6. Niemeyer, "Die Vitae."

7. Ibid., p. 517: "*etiam cum ceteri amici mei vel affines immemores essent mei, tu nostri memoriam nullatenus omisisti.*"

8. Ibid., p. 518: "*conversi enim ex inimicis Iudaeis multi facti sunt et hodie fiunt, lingua canum pro domo domini contra inimicos latrantes.*"

CHAPTER 1. FICTION AND TRUTH

1. Robert Chazan, *Daggers of Faith: Thirteenth-Century Christian Missionizing and Jewish Response* (Berkeley, 1989); and Jeremy Cohen, *The Friars and the Jews: The Evolution of Medieval Anti-Judaism* (Ithaca, N.Y., 1982), p. 128.

2. By contrast to the other figures cited, Joachim Feller does not seem to have had an interest in Hebrew literature or anti-Jewish polemic. As librarian of the academy and a member of the college of the prince elector of Saxony, he seems to have been most interested by birds and especially swans. A poet with insomniac tendencies, he eventually killed himself falling out of his bedroom window.

3. Cologne, Stadtarchiv, Auswärtiges 324: J. Gelenius, *Farraginis diplomatum*, f. 64 v. Cf. Hermannus (Niemeyer), p. 15.

4. Ibid., f. 59 v: "Hic jacet in tumba non vulpes immo columba / Vir simplex totus et ab omni fraude remotus" ("Here lies in the tomb not a fox, but a dove / A simple man ignorant or all deceit").

5. Niemeyer, "Das Prämonstratenserstift Scheda im 12. Jahrhundert," *Westfälische Zeitschrift* 112 (1962): 320.

6. Léon Goovaerts, *Écrivains, artistes, et savants de l'Ordre de Prémontré: Dictionnaire bio-bibliographique* (Geneva, 1971), p. 378 and 380; and François Petit, *La Spiritualité de Prémontrés aux XIIe et XIIIe siècles* (Paris, 1947), pp. 102–115.

7. Van der Sterre, *Lilium inter spinas* (1627), p. 281.

8. This manuscript transcription is preserved in the city archives of Cologne, in the form of an eighteenth-century copy of the *Farraginis* of J. Gelenius, later A. Gelenius. Cologne, Stadtarchiiv, Auswärtiges 324 (saec. XVIII); see *Hermannus* (Niemeyer), p. 67.

9. *Hermannus* (Niemeyer), p. 15.

10. Ibid., p. 48.

11. Gilman, *Jewish Self-Hatred: Anti-Semitism and the Hidden Language of the Jews* (Baltimore, 1986), pp. 28–31.

12. Since his 1987 article entitled "The Mentality of a Medieval Jewish Apostate," Jeremy Cohen has returned to the case of Herman, most recently in his *Living Letters of the Law.*

13. To tell the truth, the *Opusculum* is not as categorical as Saltman says it is regarding Godfried and his brother Otto's presence at Cappenberg in order to welcome bishop Eckbert. They are mostly mentioned in chapter 6 as the founding saints of the community of canons.

14. Lotter, "Ist Herman von Scheda's *Opusculum de conversione sua* eine Fälschung?" *Aschkenas* 2 (1992): 217; Gilbert Dahan, *Les Intellectuels chrétiens et les Juifs au Moyen Âge* (Paris, 1990), p. 235 n. 29.

15. Following the example of Kleinberg, William Chester Jordan, in "Adolescence

and Conversion," in *Jews and Christians in Twelfth-Century Europe*, ed. Michael A. Signer and John Van Engen (Notre Dame, 2001), p. 84, adopts the opposing position of Saltman.

16. Kleinberg, "Haermannus Judaeus's *Opusculum*: In Defense of Its Authenticity," *Revue des études juives* 151 (1992): 353.

17. Karl Morrison, *Conversion and Text: The Cases of Augustine of Hippo, Herman-Judah, and Constantine Tsatsos* (Charlottesville, 1992). That same year, Morrison published *Understanding Conversion*, which had an even broader scope. See also his *History as a Visual Art*.

18. Jeremy Cohen, *Living Letters of the Law*, especially pp. 289–305.

19. Michael Signer and John Van Engen, eds., *Jews and Christians in Twelfth-Century Europe*, which can be seen together with James Muldoon, ed., *Varieties of Religious Conversion in the Middle Ages* (Gainesville, 1997), particularly for the contribution of Jonathan Elukin, "From Jews to Christians?" pp. 171–189, which is partly reproduced in *Jews and Christians in Twelfth-Century Europe*.

20. This is the case for several contributions to the volume edited by Michael Signer and John Van Engen, *Jews and Christians in Twelfth-Century Europe*: Ivan G. Marcus, "The Dynamics of Jewish Renaissance and Renewal in the Twelfth Century," pp. 27–45 (esp. 33); Jonathan M. Elukin, "The Discovery of the Self," pp. 63–76 (esp. 70–72); Jan M. Ziolowski, "Put in No-Man's-Land: Guibert of Nogent's Accusations Against a Judaizing and Jew-Supporting-Christian," pp. 110–122 (esp. 110); Michael A. Signer, "God's Love for Israel: Apologetic and Hermeneutical Strategies in Twelfth-Century Biblical Exegesis," pp. 123–149 (140, n. 2). Appearing almost simultaneously in another volume of essays is Fidel Rädle's study "Wie ein Kölner Jude im 12. Jahrhundert zum Christen wurde: Hermanus quondam Iudaeus De conversione sua," in *Konversionen im Mittelalter und in der Frühneuzeit*, ed. Friedrich Niewöhner and Fidel Rädle (Hildesheim, 1999), pp. 9–24, which returns to the thesis of its "authenticity." This does not prevent the author from comparing (p. 21) the episode of Judas's interception of the letter written by the Jews of Cologne to the Jews of Mainz (chap. 18) to a "*Kriminal Roman*," an expression Saltman did not reprove. . . A good example of the impasses that are reached by classical interpretations of this text, this article barely surpasses the level of a mere paraphrase, embellished in the final sentences by an analysis of pairs of oppositions which—as it should—structure this conversion account: light vs. blindness or obscurity, grace vs. sin, etc.

21. Jordan, "Adolescence and Conversion," p. 84. It is precisely this notion of "authenticity" from which I wish to escape.

22. Ibid., p. 87. "The text reveals under close scrutiny some of the ways in which male Jewish adolescence in the twelfth century constructed (or how Christians supposed that they constructed) new identities as converts in the emotional struggles they endured."

23. Alfred Haverkamp, "Baptised Jews," ibid., p. 278.

24. Here I follow as an example the remarks of Roger Chartier, *On the Edge of the Cliff: History, Languages, and Practices* (Baltimore, 1997) regarding "history between certitude and anxiety."

25. I thank Pierre Monnet for bringing to my attention the items of this polemical exchange.

26. Richard J. Evans, *In Defense of History* (New York, 2000), p. 217.

27. Hayden White, *Metahistory: The Historical Imagination in Nineteenth-Century Europe* (Baltimore, 1973), p. 430.

28. On this theme see also the comments of Gérard Noiriel, *Sur la "crise" de l'histoire* (Paris, 1996), p. 123, who insists on the sociological stakes of different critical "turns" or "revisions" which today crowd the historian's panorama.

29. Otto G. Oexle, "Marc Bloch et la critique de la raison historique," in *Histoire comparée et sciences sociales*, ed. Hartmut Atsma and André Burguière (Paris, 1990), pp. 419–433.

30. Paul Veyne, *Writing History: Essays in Epistemology*, trans. Mina Moore-Rinvolucri (Middletown, Conn., 1984), pp. 11–12, 32.

31. Anne Reboul, *Rhetorique et stylistique de la fiction* (Nancy, 1992), p. 15.

32. Michel de Certeau, *The Writing of History*, trans. Tom Conley (New York, 1992), pp. 35–36.

33. Augustine, *Soliloquia*, II, 16, ed. Gerard Watson, p. 93, cited by Roger Dragonetti, *Le Mirage des sources: L'art du faux dans le roman médiéval* (Paris, 1987), p. 19. See also Augustine's treatises *De Mendicio* and *Contra Mendacium*, ed. G. Combles, vol. II.

34. Horst Fuhrmann, ed., *Fälschungen im Mittelalter*, MGH (Munich, 1986), p. 88; Bernard Guenée, *Histoire et culture historique dans l'occidant medieval* (Paris, 1980), p. 140.

35. For the polemic regarding the relics of Saint Denis between the abbey of Saint Denis and the chapter of the cathedral of Notre Dame, see Guenée, ibid., p. 135 and 137.

36. Ibid., p. 144.

37. Dragonetti, *Le Mirage des sources*, p. 32.

38. Richard Firth Green, *The Crisis of Truth: Literature in Ricardian England* (Philadelphia, 1999), p. xiv and p. 1, regarding *trowthe*: "a word of enormous importance for understanding the culture of late-fourteenth-century England."

39. See Michael Clanchy, *From Memory to Written Record: England, 1066–1307* (Cambridge, 1979), obviously cited by Green.

40. Thus Richard Firth Green says what he owes to his knowledge of the indigenous cultures of Nigeria.

41. Jack Goody, *Representations and Contradictions. Ambivalence Towards Images, Theatre, Fiction, Relics and Sexuality* (Oxford, 1997), p. 156.

42. G. W. Bowersock, *Fiction as History: Nero to Julian* (Berkeley, 1994), p. 121.

43. Le Goff, "Naissance du roman historique au XIIe siècle," *Nouvelle revue française* 238 (1972): 163–173.

44. Suzanne Fleichman, "On the Representation of History as Fiction in the Middle Ages," *History and Theory* 22, no. 3 (1983): p. 299. On Jean Bodel, see the *Dictionnaire des Lettres françaises*, p. 748–751.

45. On the mid-twelfth-century *Chronique du Pseudo-Turpin*, see the *Dictionnaire des Lettres françaises*, p. 292. Gabrielle Spiegel (*Romancing the Past*, p. 68) sees in the

French prose translations that were commissioned for the great aristocratic families of northern France a reclaiming of their Carolingian ancestry (either real or imagined) directed against Philip Augustus's growing pretensions over their domains. Bernard Guenée, on the other hand, sees in these translations an illustration of the growing prestige of the Capetian monarchy.

46. On Jean Renart, see the *Dictionnaire des Lettres françaises*, pp. 838–841, and for a recent literary analysis of his works see Dragonetti, *Le Mirage des sources*, p. 59, and Zink, *Roman rose et rose rouge*. For the historiographical reminder and a critique of Dragonetti, see John W. Baldwin, "Jean Renart et le tounoi de Saint-Toul: une conjonction de l'histoire et de la litérature," *Annales ESC* (1990): 582.

47. Baldwin, ibid.

48. Baldwin, *Aristocratic Life in Medieval France: The Romances of Jean Renart and Gerbert de Montreuil, 1190–1230* (Baltimore, 2000), p. 31.

49. Natalie Zemon Davis, *Fiction in the Archives: Pardon Tales and Their Tellers in Sixteenth-Century France* (Stanford, 1987). For letters of remission in the late Middle Ages, see the study by Claude Gauvard, *"De grace especial": Crime État et société à la fin du Moyen Âge* (Paris, 1991).

50. Davis, *Fictions in the Archives*, p. 3.

51. Yann Thomas, *"Fictio legis:* L'empire de la fiction romaine et ses limites médiévales," *Droits* 21 (1995): 17–64.

52. *Hermannus* (Niemeyer), chap. 16, p. 113, lines 8–10.

53. Ibid., p. 114, lines 11–12.

54. See the elegant study by Nigel F. Palmer, "Der Auctor und seine Geschichte: Literarische Fiktion und Autobiographie im 'Ackermann aus Böhmen' des Johannes von Tempel," in *Autor und Autorschaft im Mittelalter*, ed. Elizabeth Andersen et al. (Tubingen, 1998), pp. 299–322.

CHAPTER 2. MEDIEVAL AUTOBIOGRAPHY

1. Michel Foucault, "What Is an Author?" trans. Josué V. Harari, in *Textual Strategies: Perspectives in Post-Structuralist Criticism*, ed. Josué V. Harari (Ithaca, N.Y., 1979 [1969]), pp. 141–160.

2. Chenu, "Auctor, actor, autor," *Archivium Latinitatis Medii Aevi* (Bulletin du Cange), 3 (1927): pp. 81–86. More recently, see the collective reflections in Ernst Jünger, *Autor und Autorschaft* (Stuttgart, 1984); and *Auctor et auctoritas: Invention et conformisme dans l'écriture médiévale*, ed. Michel Zimmermann (Paris, 2001).

3. Béatrice Fraenkel, *La Signature: Genèse d'un signe* (Paris, 1992).

4. A good example is provided in the *Liber de spiritu et anima*, a twelfth-century work most likely written by Alcher of Clairvaux, though it is has long been attributed, including by Migne, to Saint Augustine.

5. Roger Dragonetti, *Le Mirage des sources: L'art du faux dans le roman médiéval* (Paris, 1987), p. 9.

6. For the *Opusculum* see Misch, *Geschichte der Autobiographie*, III, *Das Mittelalter*, 2, *Das Hochmittelaltern im Anfang*, 1. Hälfte, pp. 505–522.

7. Dilthey is the author of a famous *Einleitung in die Geisteswissenschaften* in 1883.

8. Michael Jaeger, *Autobiographie und Geschichte: Wilhelm Dilthey, Georg Misch, Karl Löwith, Gottfried Benn, Alfred Döblin* (Stuttgart, 1995), p. 76.

9. Martin Heinzelmann (*Gregor von Tours* [1994], p. 32) underscores to what extent Gregory's "autobiographical" considerations are intelligible only if they are relocated in the eschatology that inspired the entire work.

10. See also the list of "spiritual autobiographies" from the third century until modern mysticism given by F. Vernet, "Autobiographies spirituelles," in *Dictionnaire de spiritualité* (Rome, 1981).

11. See the reservations of Walter Berschin in the introduction to the volume *L'Autobiografia nel Medioevo* (Spoletto, 1998), p. 3. The author does not explain the absence of the eighth-century Anglo-Saxon author Willibald or the twelfth-century Rupert of Deutz.

12. Jean-Jacques Rousseau, *The Confessions*, ed. P. N. Furbank (New York, 1992), p. 1.

13. Philippe Lejeune, *Le Pacte autobiographique* (Paris, 1975), pp. 14–15.

14. Ibid., p. 48.

15. Paul Zumthor, *Langue, texte, énigme* (Paris, 1972), pp. 165–180 (p. 168).

16. Ibid., "Le *je* du poète," p. 169.

17. Michel Zink, *The Invention of Literary Subjectivity*, trans. David Sices (Baltimore, 1999), p. 4.

18. Ibid., p. 5.

19. Ibid., p. 184. For this period it is Joinville and his *History of Saint Louis* that Michel Zink places at the center of his study.

20. Jean-Yves Tilliette, "Autobiographie en vers? Lyriques et élégiaques du XIIIe siècle," in *L'Autobiografia nel Medioevo*, pp. 131–154 (p. 145). The question mark in the title of the article is explained by the fact that Philippe Lejeune was hesitant to include poetry within autobiography, which he had first defined as a "prose account." In 1986 he adopted a more flexible position.

21. Ibid., p. 154.

22. For this critical point of view, see my own "La 'naissance de l'individu': une fiction historique," reprinted in *Le Corps, les Rites, les Rêves, le Temps: Essais d'anthropologie médiévale* (Paris, 2001). Let us also recall the scholarship of Walter Ullman, *The Individual and Society in the Middle Ages* (Baltimore, 1966); Colin Morris, *The Discovery of the Individual, 1050–1200* (London, 1972); Caroline Walker Bynum, "Did the Twelfth Century Discover the Individual?" reprinted in *Jesus as Mother: Studies in the Spirituality of the High Middle Ages* (Berkeley, 1982); as well as Chenu, *L'Éveil de la conscience dans la civilisation médiévale* (Paris, 1969); and Aron Gourevitch, *La Naissance de l'Individu dans l'Europe médiévale* (Paris, 1997). More specifically, see Jonathan Elukin, "The Discovery of the Self: Jews and Conversion in the Twelfth Century," in *Jews and Christians in Twelfth-Century Europe*, pp. 63–76.

23. Pierre Courcelle, *Les "Confessions" de saint Augustin dans la tradition littéraire: Antécédents et postérité* (Paris, 1963), p. 265. Jean-Yves Tilliette, in his already cited contribution to *L'Autobiografia nel Medioevo* (p. 153), speaks of "the rediscovery of Augustine as autobiography" in the twelfth century. See also Brian Stock, "Lecture, intériorité et modèles de comportement dans l'Europe des XI–XII s.," *Cahiers de civilisation médiévale* 33 (1990): 103–112. In the "Dream of the Rule" (Augustine, *Confessions*, III, xi, 19), Monica sees herself climb up onto a rule and cry for her son's sins. A *juvenis* appears to her and consoles her in an indirect style, though she was direct with him, telling her "wherever she is" her son "will be with her." And indeed, she sees Augustine on the rule. Monica then tells the dream to her son with the certainty that it announces his conversion. The assurance that drives Monica regarding the ineluctable nature of her son's conversion makes a strong impression on the young libertine.

24. See Patrice Cambronne's note regarding the most recent French translation of the *Confessions* (Paris, 1998), pp. 1364–1373.

25. Peter Brown, *Augustine of Hippo*, new ed. (London, 2000), p. 163. See also the remarks by Jean-Yves Tilliette, "Saint Augustin entre Moïse et Jean-Jacques: L'aveu dans les *Confessions*," in *L'Aveu, Antiquité et Moyen Âge*, pp. 147–168.

26. Brian Stock (*Augustine the Reader*, p. 210) warns against exaggerating the opposition between the groups of books, I–IX and X–XIII: "the disunity between the two major segments is more apparent than real . . . a mixture of discussion and reminiscence is characteristic of many works written between 386 and 401." Moreover, if in the autobiographical part Augustine plays both the role of the subject of his history and the role of narrator, this double role playing ends in Book X where Augustine, now Bishop, "becomes one."

27. According to the expression of Peter Brown, *Augustine of Hippo*, p. 157. The Montanist heresy, so-called because of its promoter Montanus who lived in Phrygia in the second century, professed the superiority of prophecy over ecclesiastical hierarchy. Tertullian, who like Augustine after him was originally from Africa, also adhered to this heresy for a time in the second century. It is the messianic aspects of the movement that would worry the Church and earn its condemnation.

28. Ibid., p. 171.

29. Augustine, *Confessions*, trans. Henry Chadwick, World's Classics (Oxford, 1991), VIII, vi, 14.

30. Psalms 36:35 (3).

31. Augustine, *Confessions*, VIII, vii, 16, p. 144–145.

32. Misch, *Geschichte der Autobiographie*, vol. II; *Das Mittelalter*, vol. I, pp. 317–355 (p. 317). Cf. Valerius, *Narrationes*, col. 439 s.

33. On this see Zink, *The Invention of Literary Subjectivity*, pp. 158–161.

34. Misch, *Geschichte der Autobiographie*, II, 1, 2, pp. 347–348.

35. According to Paul Edward Dutton and Herbert L. Kessler (*The Poetry*, 1997), Audradus even had himself represented, coterminous with Viven, in the dedicatory full-page image of the First Bible of Charles the Bald, or Vivien's Bible, Paris, BNF, ms. Lat.

1, f. 423. This bible contains poems that are generally agreed to be by Audradus, though this has been questioned by Francesco Stella, "Le spazio della soggetività nella letteratura carolingia," in *L'Autobiografia nel Medioevo*, pp. 75–77.

36. Dutton, *The Politics of Dreaming in the Carolingian Empire* (Lincoln, Neb., 1994), pp. 128–156. On the traditional role of prelates with regard to kings, and particularly Gregory of Tours and Chilperic, see Philippe Buc, *The Danger of Ritual: Between Early Medieval Texts and Social Scientific Theory* (Princeton, 2001).

37. Peter Dinzelbacher, *Vision und Visionliteratur im Miittelalter* (Stuttgart, 1981), p. 14 and passim.

38. This personal conflict between regular clergy and secular clergy, which fueled the entire twelfth-century reform movement, is very nicely analyzed by Misch, *Geschichte der Autobiographie*, II, 1, 2, pp. 586–623 (p. 603).

39. Ibid., p. 624.

40. Ibid., p. 627.

41. Ibid., III, 2, 1.

42. Richard W. Southern, *Saint Anselm: A Portrait in a Landscape* (Cambridge, 1990).

43. Michael T. Clanchy, *Abelard: A Medieval Life* (Oxford, 1997); and Peter von Moos, "*Occulta cordis*: Contrôle de soi et confession au Moyen Âge. 1. Formes du silence," *Médiévales* 29 (1995): 131–140.

44. Misch, *Geschichte der Autobiograpphie*, III, 2, 1, pp. 463–504.

45. Ibid., p. 463: "ein Sinnbild der in jener Zeit im Gang begriffenen geschichtlichen Bewegung, die von der Unruhre des geistigen Aufschwungs zu der Stabilität des vollendeten Mittelalters führte."

46. Walter David, *The Life of Ailred of Rievaulx*, ed. and trans. P. W. Powicke (London, 1950), pp. 9–16.

47. Guibert of Nogent, *A Monk's Confession*, ed. and trans. Paul J. Archambault (University Park, Pa., 1996), pp. 10–11. Guibert was baptized immediately after his birth because his parents thought he would die. He does not explain why his parent's chose Guibert as a first name, but he does humorously evoke the names of saints that were in vogue among children's first names at the time, such as Peter, Nicholas, or Remigius (p. 12).

48. Ibid., pp. 109–110.

49. Ibid., pp. 210–212.

50. The Latin title *De vita sua*, which Guibert himself did not use, was once proposed by Dachery and Migne and taken up by G. Bourgin in 1907. "Autobiographie" was preferred by Edmond-René Labande for the 1981 French translation, and "Memoirs" for the edition by John Benton (*Self and Society in Medieval France*, 1984), for which one should read the suggestive introduction which lays the claim to a "psychoanalysis" of Guibert.

51. Zink, *The Invention of Literary Subjectivity*, p. 180.

52. Ibid., p. 171.

53. Ibid., p. 173

54. Guibert of Nogent, *A Monk's Confession*, p. 5.

55. Guibert lost his father eight months after he was born; Augustine lost his when about fourteen years of age.

56. Guibert of Nogent, *A Monk's Confession*, pp. 9–10.

57. Ibid., pp. 33–34.

58. Ibid., pp. 62–63.

59. Ibid., pp. 108–109.

60. Hermannus (Niemeyer), chapter 6, p. 88.

61. Brian Stock, *The Implications of Literacy. Written Language and Models of Interpretation in the Eleventh and Twelfth Centuries* (Princeton, 1983).

62. Augustine, *Confessions*, IX, iii, 5.

63. Ibid., III, xi, pp. 49–50.

64. Ibid., VI, xiii, 23.

65. Ibid., VIII, I, 2, p. 134.

66. Ibid., VIII, vi, 13.

67. Hermannus (Niemeyer), chapter 15, p. 111, line 27 (veritatis confessionem) and p. 112, line 1 (confessus ergo mihi); in both cases this concerns not the author's confession but the confession of the Jews of Cologne. In chapter 16, p. 114, line 6 (si nudam eis veritatem confiterer), Judas wonders whether he should "confess" his Christian feelings to the Jews assembled in the Synagogue of Worms.

68. Ibid., chapter 19, p. 118, line 14 (fidem sancta Trinitatis ex toto corde confessus).

69. Ibid., chapter 5, p. 84, line 16.

70. Ibid., p. 85, line 22.

71. Ibid., chapter 6, p. 90, line 16 (te in toto corde suo exquirentes).

72. Ibid., p. 90, line 12 (ex immo cordis suspiria).

73. Ibid., chapter 20, pp. 121, 123 (de domo cordis mei). Other mentions include pp. 91, 92, 101, 102, 104, 107, 108, 118, etc.

74. Ibid., chapter 21, p. 125, line 17 (velut in ore cordis ruminare).

75. Ibid., chapter 6, p. 92, line 22 (tota mox ad Deum contritione converses). See also chapter 21, p. 125, line 7 (cum vera cordis humilitate et contritione, cum sincere mentis devotione accedere).

76. Ibid., chapter 10, p. 102, line 6 (ad compunctionis gratiam satagebant emollire).

77. Ibid., chapter 11 (clergymen's speech), p. 101, line 13 (et ecce contra spem nostram tuas potius sequi concupiscentias elegisti).

78. Ibid., chapter 19, p. 120, line 18.

79. Brown, *Augustine of Hippo*, p. 160.

CHAPTER 3. THE DREAM AND ITS INTERPRETATION

1. Guillaume de Lorris and Jean de Meun, *The Romance of the Rose*, trans. Charles Dahlberg, 3rd edition (Princeton, 1995), p. 31. *Le Roman de la Rose*, ed. Félix Lecoy (Paris,

1965–1970), I, verses 1–4 and 21–30: "Aucune genz dient qu'en songes / n'a se fables non et mençonges; / mes l'en puet tex songes songier / qui ne sont mie mençonger [. . .] / El vintieme an de mon age / el point qu'Amors prent le paage / des jones genz, couchier m'aloie / une nuit, si com je souloie, / et me dormoie mout forment, / et vi un songe en mon dormant, / qui mout fu biaus et mout me plot; / mes *en ce songe onques riens n'ot / qui tretot avenu ne soit / si com le songes recensoit.*"

2. *The Romance of the Rose*, p. 354. *Le Roman de la Rose*, III, verses 21775–21779: "ainz que d'ileuc me remuasse,/ par grant joliveté cueilli/ la fleur du biau rosier fueilli./ Ainsit oi la rose vermeille/ Atant ju jorz, et je m'esveille.*"

3. Dragonetti, *Le mirage des sources*, p. 35. See also Christiane Marcello-Nizia, "La rhétorique des songes et le songe comme rhétorique dans la littérature française médiévale," in *I Sogni nel Medioevo*, ed. Tullio Gregory (Rome, 1985), pp. 245–259.

4. This is also noted by Jeremy Cohen in *Living Letters of the Law* (p. 271), who brings together, in a chapter entitled "Renaissance Men and Their Dreams," Peter Abelard, "Herman of Cologne," and Alan of Lille because all three authors give their polemical work the form of a dream. In reality, even on the formal level, these works differ considerably. Abelard's *Dialogue* is entirely a dream fiction, like the *Romance of the Rose*. This is also the case with Alan of Lille's *Planctus naturae*, where the poet deplores the decadence of human nature and hopes for its "restoration" in the grace of God, but this is not the case in his polemical treatise *De fide catholica, sive Contra haereticos, valdenses, iudaeos et paganos* (against the Cathars, Waldensians, Jews, and Muslims). Only in the *Opusculum* does the dream *frame* the conversion account so perfectly.

5. Peter Abelard, *Dialogus inter Philosophum, Judaeum et Christianum*, ed. Rudolf Thomas (Stuttgart, 1970), p. 41: "Aspiciebam in visu noctis et ecce viri tres diverso tramite venientes coram me astiterunt. Quos ego statim iuxta visionis modum, cuius sint professionis vel cur ad me venerint, interrogo." See also Peter von Moos, "Les *collationes* d'Abélard et la 'question juive' au XIIeme siècle," *Journal des savants* (July–December 1999): 449–489.

6. Cited in Cohen, *Living Letters of the Law*, p. 284.

7. Joshua Trachtenberg, *Jewish Magic and Superstition* (Philadelphia, 2004 [1939]), p. 231.

8. Chrétien de Troyes, *Le Conte du Graal (Perceval)*, ed. Félix Lecoy (Paris, 1984), v. I, p. 40 (verse 1146). Adapted into modern English by William Kibler: *Arthurian Romances*, ed. and trans. William Kibler (London, 1991), pp. 395–396.

9. Historians who have commented on the *Opusculum* have generally paid little attention to the dream of young Judas. An exception to this is William C. Jordan ("Adolescence and Conversion," p. 85), who sees the dream as an expression of the ritual of knighthood which the young man may have dreamt "in his thirteenth year." It seems to me that the dream also reflects, more generally, the enfeoffment of a new knight, a sort of social revenge on a deposed but once great lord in which the new knight reaps the benefits from the hands of the emperor.

10. Brigitte Bedos-Rezak, "Les juifs et l'écrit dans la mentalité eschatologique du

Moyen Âge Chrétien occidental (France 1000–1200)," *Annales ESC* 49 (1994): 1053, n. 11. Bedos-Rezak also comments on this famous letter of Peter the Venerable to the king of France Louis VII in 1146. Cf. *The Letters of Peter the Venerable*, ed. Giles Constable (Cambridge, Mass., 1967), I, pp. 327–330: "non enim de simplici agri cultura, non de legali militia, non de quodlibet honesto et utili officio horrea sua frugibus, cellaria vino, marsupia nummis, archas auro sive argento (Judei) cumulant, quantum de his quae ut dixi christicolis dolose subtrahunt, de his quae furtim a foribus empta vili praecio res carissimas comparant." See also Jean-Pierre Torelli, "Les juifs dans l'oeuvre de Pierre le Vénérable," *Cahiers de civilisation médiévale* 30 (1987): 331–346; as well as Dominique Iogna-Prat, *Order and Exclusion*, trans. Graham Robert Edwards (Ithaca, N.Y., 2002), p. 282, who insists on another aspect of Peter's accusation: whether by theft or by the effect of their charging interest on loans, Jews sacrilegiously take possession of sacred vases that once contained the body and blood of Christ that they themselves killed. Robert Chazan ("From the First Crusade to the Second," pp. 46–62 [pp. 49–50]) compares Bernard of Clairvaux's attitude to that of Peter the Venerable, both of whom insist on the very long hostility that had existed between Jews and Christians. According to Chazan, however, Peter the Venerable aims to show that the hatred has become stronger in his time.

11. Momigliano, "A Medieval Jewish Autobiography," p. 338.

12. Marcus, *Rituals of Childhood*, p. 17 and passim. See also Jordan, "Adolescence and Conversion," p. 79, who goes even further by saying that "in any case it [the *bar-mitzvah*] is a post medieval ceremony." Jordan adds that this removes nothing from the fact that the age of twelve or thirteen, which cannot be given an exact translation from the Latin *adolescentia*, is a crucial period that also comes up in other cases of conversion. In this case, Jordan shows with good reason (p. 85) how the text itself evokes both a carnal and contradictory moment, since Herman can define himself as "child" (*puer*) at the time of his dream, but then say that despite his age he did not have the "lightness of childhood" (*levitate puerili*).

13. I. Ta-Shema, "The Earliest Literary Sources for the bar-Mitzva Ritual and Festivity (A Review of the Hebrew Translation of Ivan Marcus' *Rituals of Childhood*) [in Hebrew]," *Tarbiz* 68 (1999): 587–598. I am most grateful to Professor Haym Soloveitchik for this reference.

14. Marcus, "Images of the Jews in the *Exempla* of Caesarius of Heisterbach," in *From Witness to Witchcraft: Jews and Judaism in Medieval Christian Thought* (Wiesbaden, 1996), pp. 247–256.

15. Hermannus (Niemeyer), p. 32.

16. Julius Aronius, Regesten zur Geschichte der Juden im fränkischen und deutschen Reiche bis zum Jahre 1273 (Berlin, 1970 [1902]), pp. 71–77, no. 170–171 (c. 1090: privileges of Henry IV for the Jews of Speyer and Worms), pp. 139–142, no. 3142 (privileges given by Frederick Barbarossa). Cf. Chazan, *European Jewry and the First Crusade* (Berkeley, 1987); and Kenneth Stow, *Alienated Minority*, esp. p. 89.

17. Yerushalmi, *"Diener von Königen und nicht Diener von Dienern." Einege Aspekte der politischen Geschichte der Juden* (Munich, 1995), p. 28. The quotation from the book

of Esther is for the author the point of departure in a discussion on Hannah Arendt's *Origins of Totalitarianism*.

18. Amos Funkenstein, *Perceptions of Jewish History* (Berkeley, 1993), p. 171, n. 3. In the Babylonian Talmud, *Berakhot* 56b specifies that "if someone sees in a dream a white horse slowly walking or galloping, it is a good sign. If it is red and walks slowly, it is also a good sign, but if it gallops, it is a bad sign." See also Sanhedrin 93a. I also wish to thank Willis Johnson (of Clare College, Cambridge) for having shared with me his conviction "that this text was indeed written by a Jewish convert," on the basis of a biblical citation that is found in the passage in chapter 7 concerning the brutal death of young Judas's mentor by the will of God: "sicsic iustus iudex" (Hermannus [Niemeyer], p. 93, line 25). Niemeyer relates it (erroneously, I believe) to Paul's Epistle, 2 Timothy 4, 8. W. Johnson traces the expression to the quotation in the Talmud, *Berakhot* 46v, "What do they say in the house of God? [. . .] Rabbi Akiva says: 'blessed is the *true judge*'." In fact, the expression is already found in Psalms 7, 11: "God is a *righteous judge*, and a God who has indignation every day." Thus the idea that the text must have been written by a former Jew. In fact, it is quite difficult to say one way or the other since the Psalms were sacred to both Jews and Christians alike.

19. Jehudah ben Chemouel le Hassid, *Sefer Hassidim. Le guide des hassidim*, ed. and trans. Édouard Gourévitch (Paris, 1988), p. 242, n. 386.

20. M. Förster, "Beiträge zur mittelalterlichen Volkskunde, IV," *Archiv für die Studien der neueren Sprachen und Literaturen* 125 (1910): 54, 56, 57, 69.

21. Pascalis Romanus, *Disputatio contra Judaeos*, ed. Gilbert Dahan (Paris, 1976). On the posterity of the *Key of Dreams* of Pascalis Romanus in Germany until the Renaissance, see *Träume und Kräuter: Studien zur Petroneller "Circa instans"—Handschrift und zu den deutschen Traumbücher des Mittelalters*, ed. Nigel Palmer and Klaus Speckenbach (Cologne, 1990), pp. 121–210.

22. Pascalis Romanus, "Le *Liber Thesauri Occulti* de Pascalis Romanus (un traité d'interprétation des songes au XIIe siècle)," ed. Simone Collin-Rosset, *Archives d'histoire doctrinale et littéraire du Moyen Âge*, 30 (1963): 177 (*De progenie regis*).

23. Anselm of Havelberg, *Dialogues*, ed. Gaston Salet (Paris, 1966), pp. 20 and 68–71.

24. Cohen, *Living Letters of the Law*, pp. 297–298.

25. Around 1444, Firmin Le Ver gives in his Latin-French dictionary the following: "olus, oleris,: ab alendo dicitur, id est quaedam herba ortolana, scilicet caulis, chols, colet. Olus, oleris eciam dicitur cibus inde factus poree." ("olus, oleris, comes from 'to feed oneself' and designates a garden herb, namely cabbage, chols, colet. Olus, oleris also refers to food that is prepared, porridge.") Firmin le Ver, *Dictionnaire latin-français*, ed. B. Merrilaes, CCCM (Brepols, 1994), I, s.v. "olus."

26. Jeremy Cohen (*Living Letters of the Law*, p. 302) has no doubt about this interpretation.

27. *Encyclopaedia Judaica* (Jerusalem, 1972–1981), s.v. "Passover" and "Lettuce."

28. Talmud, *Berakhot* 38b.

29. This is, incidentally, confirmed by the Vulgate and by Christian exegesis which, when speaking of "bitter herbs" in the book of Numbers, does not use the word *olus*, but rather the word *lactuca*, which gives us lettuce. Cf. Rabanus Maurus, *De Universo*, PL, v. III, col. 531D–532A.

30. Marcus, *Rituals of Childhood*, p. 53.

31. Midrash, *Lamentations*, on the treaty *Ma'aser Sheni* 1.1 of the Jerusalem Talmud. Cf. Galit Hasan-Rockem, "Communications with the Dead in Jewish Dream Culture," in *Dream Cultures: Explorations in the Comparative History of Dreaming*, ed. David Shulman and Guy Stroumsa (New York, 1999), pp. 213–232 (p. 219). I thank Ms. Galit Hasan-Rockem for the information she shared with me.

32. Gregory the Great tells the story of a greedy nun who swallowed the devil who was sitting on a piece of lettuce (*olus*) she devoured without taking the time to make the sign of the cross. The account then passed on through medieval *exempla*. See Frederick Turbach, *Index exemplorum: A Handbook of Medieval Religious Tales* (Helsinki, 1969), no. 3503: *Nun swallows lettuce*.

33. *The Life of Christina of Markyate: A Twelfth Century Recluse*, ed. C. H. Talbot, 2nd ed. (Oxford, 1987), pp. 190–191.

34. For more on this during this early Middle Ages, see the pertinent remarks of Philippe Buc, *The Dangers of Ritual: Between Early Medieval Texts and Social Scientific Theory* (Princeton, 2001).

35. Hermannus (Niemeyer), chap. 18, p. 116, lines 16–17 ("I saw a dream that was very sweet to see and to recount").

36. Ibid.: "Ubi dominum Iesum sublimi in solio et paterna maiestate potentissime atque honorificentissime vidi residentem atque sceptri vice triumphalem sue cruces signum super dextrum humerum tenentem."

37. François Boespflug and Yolanta Zaluska, "Le dogme trinitaire et l'essor de son iconographie en Occident de l'époque carolingienne au IVe concile du Latran (1215)," *Cahiers de civilisation médiévale* 37, 3 (1994): 216.

38. Ibid., p. 218.

39. Boespflug, "La Trinité au Moyen-Âge: Visions et images (XIIe–XIVe siècle)," in *Expérience religieuse et experience esthétique: Rituel, art et sacré dans les religions* (Louvain, 1993), pp. 121–152; Idem, "La vision-en-rêve de la Trinité de Rupert de Deutz (v. 1110): Liturgie, spiritualité et histoire de l'art," *Revue des sciences religieuses* 71, 2 (1997): 205–229; *Idem*, "La vision de la Trinité de Christine de Markyate et le Psautier de Saint-Alban," *Micrologus* VI, 2 (1998): 95–112.

40. Guibert of Nogent, *A Monks Confession*, p. 67.

41. For many other examples, see Jean-Claude Schmitt, *Ghosts in the Middle Ages: The Living and the Dead in Medieval Society*, trans. Teresa Lavener Fagan (Chicago, 1998).

42. Shulman and Stroumsa, eds., *Dream Cultures*.

43. Jacques Le Goff, "Christianity and Dreams (Second to Seventh Century)," in his *The Medieval Imagination*, trans. Arthur Goldhammer (Chicago, 1988), pp. 193–231.

44. *Encyclopaedia Judaica*, s.v. "Dreams." *Jüdisches Lexikon*, s.v. "Traum." Leo Op-

penheim, *The Interpretation of Dreams in the Ancient Near East* (Philadelphia, 1956), passim; Franco Michellini Tocci, "Teoria e interpretazione dei sogni nella cultura ebraica medievale," in *I sogni*, pp. 261–290.

45. Brigitte Stemberger, "Der Traum in der rabbinischen Literatur," *Kairos: Zeitschrift für Religionswissenschaft und Theologie*, new series 18 (1976): 1–42.

46. See Maren Niehoff, "A Dream Which Is Not Interpreted Is Like a Letter Which Is Not Read," *Journal of Jewish Studies* 43 (1992): 58–84. For a different approach, see Danielle Storper-Perez and Henri Cohen-Solal, "Toute songe non interprété est comme une lettre non lue: Approche anthropologique et psychanalytique de l'interprétation des rêves dans le traité Berakhot du Talmud de Babylone," in *Le Corps du texte: Pour une anthropologie des textes de la tradition juive*, ed. Florence Heymann and Danielle Storper-Perez (Paris, 1997).

47. Gabrielle Sed-Rajna ed., *Rashi, 1049–1990: Hommage à Ephraim E. Urbach. Congrès européen des Études juives* (Paris, 1993), passim; Herman Hailperin, *Rashi and the Christian Scholars* (Pittsburgh, 1963), p. 22.

48. Hailperin, *Rashi and the Christian Scholars*, pp. 103–111; Beryl Smalley, *The Study of the Bible in the Middle Ages* (Oxford, 1952), pp. 149–172.

49. Rashi de Troyes, *Commento alla Genesi*, introduction and annotation by Luigi Cattani (Casale Monferrato, 1985), p. 333.

50. Jehudah ben Chemouel le Hasid, *Sefer Hasssidim*, pp. 220–245. Harris, "Dreams."

51. Joseph Dan, "Le-Torat ha-Halom shel' Haside Ashkenaz," *Sinaï* XXXV (1971): 288–293. I thank Denise Bonan for having summarized the Hebrew article for me. The article modifies the conclusions of Manfred Harris (see below).

52. Manfred Harris, "Dreams in Sefer Hassidim," *Proceedings of the American Academy for Jewish Research* 31 (1963): 71.

53. Moses Maimonides, *Guide of the Perplexed*, trans. Shlomo Pines (Chicago, 1963), II, pp. 369–373.

54. Thomas Ricklin, *Der Traum der Philosophie im 12. Jahrhundert: Traumtheorien zwischen Constantinus Africanus und Aristoteles* (Leiden, 1998), p. 170.

55. Steven Kruger, *Dreaming in the Middle Ages* (Cambridge, 1992), pp. 45–47.

56. Martine Dulaye, *Le Rêve dans la vie et la pensée de saint Augustin* (Paris, 1973), p. 152, citing Tertullian, *De Anima*, 47, 2.

57. Cited by Jacques Le Goff in *I sogni*, p. 186. English translation from *Origen: Contra Celsum*, trans. Henry Chadwick (Cambridge, 1953), I, 46, p. 42.

58. Dulaye, *Le Rêve*, p. 152, n. 70, citing Augustine, *De catechizandis rudibus*, 6, 10. Augustine, however, remains suspicious about these conversions that are decided immediately after a dream: ibid., p. 153, n. 74, citing letter 80, 3: "most often, it is not because of a voice from heaven, or a prophecy, or the revelation received either in a dream or in the abduction of the mind we call ecstasy, but rather because of the events themselves that call us to somewhere else than where we decided, forcing us to recognize that the will of God is different from our own."

59. Paul Edward Dutton, *The Politics of Dreaming in the Carolingian Empire* (Lincoln, Neb., 1994), p. 37. The Romanesque fresco of the church of Quatre-Saints-Couronnés (thirteenth century) shows the imperial dream and its consequences.

60. Pierre Courcelle, *Les "Confessions" de saint Augustin dans la tradition littéraire: Antécédents et postérité*, Bibliotheque augustinienne, 15 (Paris, 1963), pp. 127–136.

61. Augustine, *Confessions*, III, ii, 19, 13.

62. Ibid., VII, ii, 27, 3.

63. Misch, *Geschichte der Autobiographie*, III, 2, 1, pp. 349 and 430.

64. For more on the difference between immunity and exemption, and on Otloh's actions within the framework of the monastic reform coming from Gorze and Hirsau, see Kassius Hallinger, *Gorze—Cluny: Studien zu den monastischen Lebensformen und Gegensätzen im Hochmittelalter* (Rome, 1950–1951), I, pp. 618–628; and Herman Jakobs, *Die Hirsauer: Ihre Ausbreitung und Rechtsstellung im Zeitalter des Investiturstreits* (Cologne, 1961), p. 10.

65. Hedwig Röckelein, *Otloh, Gottschalk, Tnugdal: Individuelle und kollektive Visionsmuster des Hochmittelalters* (Frankfurt, 1987), p. 28.

66. Ibid., p. 23: it concerns the manuscript in Munich, Bayerische Staatsbibliothek, CLM 14673, f. 1–46 (folios 39–46v are autographed).

67. Autobiographical considerations slip into Otloh's works up until this treaty. Cf. *De doctrina spirituali*, cap. XIV: "De causam meorum relatione, quam hic adjeci ad compescendam pertinaciam cleri" ("On the relation of what happened to me, which I add here to stop the obstinacy of the clergy"), PL, v. 146, col. 278, where Otloh, following the example of Jerome, returns to the dream that turned him away from pagan authors. One finds the same in his *De cursu spirituali*, cap. X, ibid., col. 214–215.

68. Otloh of Saint-Emmeram, *Liber visionum*, ed. Paul Gerhard Schmidt, MGH, 13 (Weimar, 1989), pp. 35–60. The study of Gustavo Vinay makes Otloh into a "neurotic" man who liberates himself of his "psycho-physiological" troubles through his autobiographical writing. This semi-psychiatric diagnosis seems to me unavoidably anachronistic. On the other hand, I fully agree with the author's final remark (p. 37) that conversion allows Otloh to find his balance: "Miracle of conversion? No, miracle of *this* conversion, that is, of a process in which the cultural and psychological givens are inextricably individualized." Gustavo Vinay, "Otlone di Sant'Emmeran, ovvero l'autobiographia di un nevrotico," in *La Storiografia altomedievale* (Spoleto, 1970), I, pp. 13–37. See also Réginald Grégoire, "l'autobiografia monastica," in *L'Autobiografia nel Medioevo*, pp. 87–90.

69. Otloh, *Liber visionum*, p. 34.

70. Jean-Claude Schmitt, "Rêver au XIIe siècle," in *I sogni*, pp. 291–316.

71. I show the systematic characteristic of this distinction regarding the accounts of apparitions of the dead in my *Ghosts in the Middle Ages*, pp. 40–42.

72. Guibert of Nogent, *A Monk's Confession*, pp. 64–69.

73. Brian Stock, *The Implications of Literacy: Written Language and Models of Interpretation in the Eleventh and Twelfth Centuries* (Princeton, 1983).

74. For more on this see the suggestive approach offered in Robert Benton, *Self and*

Society in Medieval France (Toronto, 1984); and Jonathan Kantor, "A Pschoanalytical Source: The Memoirs of Abbot Guibert of Nogent," *Journal of Medieval History* 2, no. 4 (1976): 281–303.

75. It was in this mindset that I elsewhere tried to make use of the notions of "work of mourning" and "repression": Schmitt, *Ghosts in the Middle Ages*, pp. 9 and 12.

76. Cited by Michel Lauwers, "L'institution et le genre: À propos de l'accès des femmes au sacré dans l'Occident médiévale," *Clio, Histoire, femmes et société* 2 (1995): 280.

77. *The Life of Christine of Markyate*, pp. 152–153, 172–173.

78. Guibert of Nogent, *A Monk's Confession*, p. 44.

79. Ibid., p. 54.

80. Ibid., p. 59.

81. Ibid., p. 68.

82. Caroline Walker Bynum, *Holy Feast and Holy Fast: The Significance of Food to Medieval Women* (Berkeley, 1987).

83. See the works devoted to him by Maria Ludovica Arduini, *Ruperto di Deutz e la controversia tra Cristiani ed Ebrei ne secolo XII con testo critico dell'"Anulus seu Dialogus inter Christianum et Judaeum"* (Rome, 1979); and John Van Engen, *Rupert of Deutz* (Berkeley, 1983).

84. On the changes Rupert made to the first *Vita*, see Peter Dinter's commentary in Rupert of Deutz, *Vita Heriberti*, ed. Peter Dinton, Veröffentlichungen des Historischen Vereins für den Niederhein l, 13 (Bonn, 1976), p. 108; and also Van Engen, *Rupert of Deutz*.

85. PL, v. 170, col. 353–358; and Herbert Grundmann, "Der Brand von Deutz 1128 in der Darstellung Abt Ruperts von Deutz: Interpretation und Textausgabe," *Deutsches Archiv* 22 (1966): 385.

86. PL, v. 167 to 170. No Christian author had written as much since Saint Augustine.

87. Rupert speaks of his conversion in his commentary on the Song of Songs as well as in his commentaries on Matthew and the Rule of Saint Benedict. Van Engen, *Rupert of Deutz*, p. 50.

88. Hrabanus Haacke ("Die mystischen Visionen Ruperts von Deutz," *Sapientiae doctrina* [Louvain, 1980]) counts fifteen accounts of visions and dreams, but his list is not complete. Van Engen (*Rupert of Deutz*, p. 50) gave little attention to this aspect of Rupert's personality. However, see Christel Meier-Staubach, "Ruperts von Deutz literarische Sendung: Der Durchbruch eines neuen Autorbewusstseins im 12. Jahrhundert," in *Wolfram-Studien, XVI: Aspekte des 12. Jahrhunderts*, ed. Wolfgang Haubrichs, Eckart C. Lutz, and Gisela Vollmann-Profe (Berlin, 2000), pp. 29–52.

89. Rupert of Deutz, *Vita Heriberti*, pp. 33–34.

90. Other hagiographies place the same amount of importance on the future saint's "dream of the father": take, for example, the *Life of Gerald of Aurillac*, discussed later on (see below, pp. 185–86), written by Abbot Odo of Cluny in the eleventh century. His very chaste father, the noble Gérard, has a dream one night that he assimilates in a certain way

to Jesse: a tree, the symbol of God's blessing on his progeny, comes out of his right foot; he awakens and lies with his wife Adaltrude. During the pregnancy that follows, another miraculous sign occurs: three times the wails of the child are heard from the mother's womb. Cf. Odo of Cluny, *Vita sancti Gerardi Aurilliacensis comitis libri quatuor*, PL, v. 133, col. 643D.

91. The connection is rightly made by Peter Dinter, *Vita Heriberti*, p. 126.

92. Rupert of Deutz, *Vita Heriberti*, pp. 33–34.

93. In chapter 13 it is following a dream that Archbishop Heribert of Cologne founds the monastery of Deutz (see below, p. 185). In chapter 26, a dream dissuades Emperor Henry II from opposing Heribert. In chapters 18, 19, and 20, several personages are miraculously healed following "nocturnal visions." In chapters 29 and 30, dreams announce their death to Emperor Henry II and Bishop Heribert. In chapter 34, Bishop Ebberhard of Bamberg sees in a dream Bishop Heribert's soul arrive in paradise. And in chapter 35 Bishop Heribert appears to the Abbot of Deutz, Folbertus, to announce his imminent death.

94. Rupert of Deutz, *De divinis officiis*, ed. Hrabanus Haacke, CCCM 7 (Turnhout, 1967), VIII, p. 268 (see also PL, v. 170, col. 215–216). For the original passage, see Augustine, *City of God*, XXII, viii, 22.

95. "Epistula Ruperti ad Cunonem Sigebergensem abbatem," in Rupert of Deutz, *De sancta Trinitate et operibus suis*, ed. Hrabanus Haacke, CCCM 21 (Turnhout, 1971), p. 121. Cf. Haacke, "Die mystischen Visionen Ruperts von Deutz," pp. 78–79, regarding this *manumissio*.

96. Rupert of Deutz, *Commentaria in Canticum canticorum*, ed. Hrabanus Haacke, CCCM (Turnhout, 1974), p. 6.

97. Idem, *Super quaedam capitula regulae divi Benedicti abbatis*, PL, v. 170, col. 480.

98. Idem, *Commentaria in Canticum canticorum*, pp. 110–111.

99. Ibid., p. 110.

100. Ibid., pp. 110–111.

101. Ibid., p. 111.

102. Mary Carruthers, *The Craft of Thought: Meditation, Rhetoric, and the Making of Images, 400–1200* (Cambridge, 1998), p. 172.

103. Walter Berschin, *Os meum aperui: Die Autobiographie Ruperts von Deutz* (Cologne, 1985).

104. This is according to Haacke's calculation and refers especially to numbers 6 to 14 (of the fifteen personal visions tabulated by Haacke in the entirety of Rupert of Deutz's work).

105. Rupert of Deutz, *De Gloria et honore Filii Hominis super Matthaeum*, ed. Hrabanus Haacke, CCCM 29 (Turnhout, 1979), p. 377, line 560: "Sed iam redeamus ad rem, propter quam etiam hanc intuli narrationem" ("But let us quickly return to the subject that led me to begin this account").

106. Ibid., p. 374, line 425, repeated on p. 377, line 565.

107. Ibid., p. 367, line 177.

108. Ibid., 368, line 203.

109. Ibid., p. 369, line 242.

110. Ibid., p. 369.

111. Ibid., pp. 370–371.

112. Ibid., pp. 371–372.

113. Ibid. Cf. Boespflug, "La vision-en-rêve," and "La vision de la Trinité."

114. Rupert of Deutz, *De Gloria et honore*, p. 373, line 397.

115. Ibid., p. 373.

116. Ibid., p. 374

117. Ibid., p. 375, line 457.

118. Ibid, p. 376.

119. Ibid., p. 377, line 561.

120. Ibid., p. 377, line 565.

121. Ibid., p. 380, line 659.

122. Ibid., pp. 382–383.

123. Ibid., p. 383, line 779.

124. Ibid., p. 383, line 781.

125. Grundman, "Der Brand," p. 469.

126. Rupert of Deutz, *De Gloria et honore*, p. 383, line 770.

127. Robert Bartlett, *Gerald of Wales, 1146–1223* (Oxford, 1982), pp. 46 and 145.

128. Jean-Claude Schmitt, "Hildegard von Bingen unde die Zurückweisung des Traums," in *Hildegarde von Bingen in ihren historischen Umfeld*, ed. Alfred Haverkamp (Mainz, 2000), pp. 351–374, reprinted in French in Schmitt, *Le corps des images: Essais sur la culture visuelle au Moyen Âge* (Paris, 2002), pp. 323–343. On miniatures that represent Hildegard and even, in the case of the *Scivias*, of miniatures that are inspired by her, see Liselotte E. Saurma-Jeltsch, *Die Miniaturen im "Liber Scivias" der Hildegarde von Bingen: Die Wucht der Vision und die Ordnung der Bilder* (Wiesbaden, 1998), pp. 25–31. See also Madeline H. Caviness, "Hildegard as Designer of the Illustrations of Her Works," in *Hildegard of Bingen: The Context of Her Thought and Art*, ed. Charles Burnett and Peter Dronke (London, 1998), pp. 29–62, illustrations 19 and 20. On Hildegard as prophetess, see Sylvain Gougenheim, *La Sibylle du Rhin: Hildegarde de Bingen, abbesse et prophétesse rhénane* (Paris, 1996), p. 29.

129. Guibert of Gembloux, *Epistolae*, ed. A. Derolez, CCCM 66 (Turnhout, 1988), p. 223: "utrum dormiens in somnis an vigilans per excessum mentis visions tuas contempleris."

130. For more on this correspondence, see Adelgundis Fürkötter, *Hildegarde von Bingen,* "Nun höre und lerne, damit du errötest . . ." *Briefwechsel,* 2nd ed. (Vienna, 1997), p. 227.

131. Rupert of Deutz, *De Victoria Verbi Dei*, ed. Hrabanus Haacke, MGH (Weimar, 1970), p. 342: "Multum, immo incomparabiliter differunt putans homo et putans Deus; multum, inquam, different et procul distant hominis somnium et Dei verba prophetica cuiusque gratia et ipsa summa substantia. Homo putans vel somnians interdum et persepe

nescit quid imagines somniorum suorum significaverint, ut Pharao" ("The thoughts of man and the thoughts of God differ greatly and are even incomparable. The difference is great, I say, between the dreams of man and the prophetic words of God, his grace, and very substance, which is immense. The man who thinks or who dreams often ignores what his dreams signify, such as Pharaoh").

132. Elisabeth of Schönau, *Die Visionen der hl. Elisabeth v. Schönau*, ed. F. W. E. Roth (Brünn, 1884), p. 1. The Migne edition, PL, v. 195, col. 119, is too faulty and incomplete to be used.

133. Ibid., p. 5, iv.

134. Ibid., p. 4, ii.

135. Ibid., p. 6, vii.

136. Ibid., p. 15, xxv: "Tunc ergo ab extasi expergiscens" ("Now, waking from my ecstasy"); p. 16, xxix: "cum solito more essem in extasi [. . .] et ego cum laetitia expergiscens" ("while I was in my usual ecstasy [. . .] and I, awaking with joy").

137. Schmitt, "La 'découverte de l'individu'," reprinted in *Le Corps, les rites*, pp. 213–236.

CHAPTER 4. CONVERSION TO IMAGES

1. This was a usual requirement. Cf. Joseph Shatzmiller, *Shylock Reconsidered: Jews, Moneylending, and Medieval Society* (Berkeley, 1990).

2. Hermannus (Niemeyer), chap. 2, p. 75: "Ubis studiosus omnia perlustrans, inter artificiosas celaturarum ac picturarum varietates monstruosum quodam ydolum video. Cerno siquidem unum eundemque hominem humilitatum et exaltatum, despectum et evectum, ignominiosum et gloriosum, *deorsum* miserabiliter in cruce pendentem, et *sursum* pictura mentiente venustissimum velut deificatum residentem. Fateor obstupui, suspicans huiusmodi effigies simulachra esse, que vario delusa errore gentilitas sibi dictareconsueverat" (emphasis mine). Cf. Morrison, *Conversion and Text*, p. 80: "To be exact, I discerned one and the same man abased and exalted, despised and lifted up, ignominious and glorious. *Below*, he hung wretchedly on a cross. *Above*, by means of painting's lies, he was enthroned, handsome enough to seem to have been deified. I admit, I was struck mute, suspecting that effigies of this sort were such likeness as, by a many-formed delusive error, paganism normally dictated for itself. The Pharasaical doctrine that once was mine easily persuaded me that it was true" (emphasis mine).

In his 1912 French translation (Judas de Cologne, *Récit de ma conversion*), Appoline de Gourlet (p. 21) omitted the two contentious adverbs and provided a translation close to Morrison's: "Je vis un homme, toujours le même, tantôt humilié et tantôt exalté, méprisé et élevé, dans l'ignominie et dans la gloire; suspendu à une croix, puis représenté par une peinture menteuse comme le plus beau des hommes et comme déifié. Je l'avoue, je fus saisi d'étonnement, jugeant que ces images étaient des idoles comme la gentilité avait coutume d'en consacrer à ses diverses erreurs. La doctrine pharisienne ne me permettait pas de douter qu'il en fût véritablement ainsi."

3. Fidel Rädle also recognizes "two clear representations of Christ, a crucifix and a Pantocrator." See Rädle, "Wie ein Kölner Jude im 12. Jahrhundert zum Christen wurde. Hermannus quondam Iudaeus *De conversione sua*," in *Konversionen im Mittelalter und in der Frühneuzweit*, ed. Friedrich Niewöhner and Fidel Rädle (Zurich, 1999), pp. 9–24.

4. Michael Camille, *The Gothic Idol: Ideology and Image-Making in Medieval Art* (Cambridge, 1989).

5. *Kölne, Westfalen. 1180–1980. Landesgeschichte zwischen Rhein und Weser* (Munster, 1981), vol. II, p. 107, n. 293. The Crucifix of Benninghausen is sculpted from oak wood, measures 167 cm, comes from Cologne, and dates to 1070–1180. It is considered one of the major works of Romanesque sculpture in the region. The later influence of the Gero Cross of Cologne (c. 970) is noticeable.

6. Meyer Schapiro, "On the Aesthetic Attitude in Romanesque Art" (1947), in *Romanesque Art. Selected Papers* (London, 1993), pp. 1–27.

7. Jean-Claude Bonne, "Entre ambiguïté et ambivalence. Problématique de la sculpture romane," *La Part de l'oeil* 8 (1992): 147–164.

8. Schmitt, *La Raison des gestes*, p. 183.

9. Bernard of Clairvaux, *Apologia ad Guillelmum Abbatem*, in *Opera*, III, ed. Jean Leclercq and Henri M. Rochais (Rome, 1963), p. 106. See Conrad Rudolph, *"The Things of Greater Importance": Bernard of Clairvaux's "Apologia" and the Medieval Attitude Towards Art* (Philadelphia, 1990), p. 120 and, for the text, p. 282.

10. Anna Sapir Abulafia, "The Ideology of Reform and Changing Ideas Concerning Jews in the Works of Rupert of Deutz and Hermannus Quondam Iudeus," *Jewish History* 7 (1993): 52–53. The author strengthens her argument by an astute reading of the manuscript; see below, p. 206, n. 1.

11. Los Angeles, The J. Paul Getty Museum, ms. 64 (97. MG. 21) f. 85v–86. Cf. Élisabeth C. Teviotdale, *The Stammheim Missal*, Getty Museum Studies on Art (Los Angeles, 2001).

12. Amos Funkenstein cites the Jewish expressions used by the *Tossafists* (commentators on the Talmud in the early twelfth century): Christ is called "hanged," the churches are not "houses of God" (*tefila*), but houses of pleasure (*tifla*), just as the saints (*kedoshim*) are called prostitutes (*kdeshim*), etc. *Perceptions of Jewish History* (Berkeley, 1993), p. 171, n. 3.

13. Joseph Kimhi, *The Book of the Covenant* (Toronto, 1972), pp. 71–72. This *Sefer ha-Berit* was "probably the first anti-Christian polemical treatise written in Europe" according to Frank Ephraim Talmage, *Disputation and Dialogue. Readings in the Jewish-Christian Encounter* (New York, 1975), p. 9.

14. For a discussion of other Jewish authors, in particular Nathan the Official, see David Berger, *The Jewish-Christian Debate in the High Middle Ages: A Critical Edition of the "Nizzahon Vetus," with and Introduction, Translation, and Commentary* (Philadelphia, 1979), pp. 72–73 and 261.

15. Ibid., p. 214.

16. Isidore Loeb, "La controverse de 1240 sur le Talmud," *Revue des études juives* 3

(1881): 49, article XXVIII, which does not, however, appear in either the confessions of Yehiel of Paris or Judas of Melun.

17. Gregory the Great, *Epistulae*, II, x, 10, in MGH (1957), p. 269–272.

18. Schmitt, "L'Occident, Nicée II et les images," reproduced in *Le Corps des images*, p. 63.

19. For a list of these works, see A. Vernet, in *Dictionnaire de théologie catholique* (1925), vol. VIII, col. 1870–1914. Blumenkranz, *Juifs et chétiens dans le monde occidentale, 430–1096* (Paris, 1960); and Blumenkranz, *Les Auteurs chrétiens latins* (Paris, 1963). Gilbert Dahan, *Les Intellectuels chrétiens et les Juifs au Moyen Âge* (Paris, 1990). More recently, see Funkenstein, *Perceptions*, and Cohen, *Living Letters of the Law*.

20. On Agobard's work, particularly his treatises against the "Jewish superstition" and on images, one should see Egon Boshoff, *Erzbischof Agobard von Lyon:. Leben und Werk* (Cologne, 1969).

21. Gilbert Crispin, *Disputatio Iudei et Christiani*, ed. Bernhard Blumenkranz (Utrecht, 1956).

22. On the relation between the two authors in the development of polemical writings, see Cohen, *Living Letters of the Law*, p. 167 (Anselm) and p. 180 (Gilbert Crispin).

23. Guibert of Nogent, *Tractatus de Incarnatione contra Iudaeos*, PL, vol. 156, col. 489–528.

24. Guibert of Nogent, *A Monk's Confession*, pp. 111–116 (massacres at Rouen), pp. 111–113 (another Jewish convert), pp. 89, 193–195 (Jewish magician, mediator, poisoner, accomplice to Count John of Soissons).

25. Guibert of Nogent, *Tractatus de Incarnatione*, III, 9, col. 524B.

26. For medieval Jewish and Christian iconography of the Ark of the Covenant, the Tabernacle, and the decorations of the Temple, see *Monumenta Judaica: 2000 Jahre Geschichte und Kultur der Juden am Rhein: Eine Ausstellung im Kölnischen Stadtmuseum*, ed. Konrad Schilling (Cologne, 1963), vol. 1, handbuch, figs. 75–80.

27. For its date of composition, see Pedro Alfonso de Huesca, *Diálogo contra los judíos*, ed. John Tolan (Huesca, 1996), p. xix.

28. Tolan, *Petrus Alfonsi*, p. 98. Cohen, *Living Letters of the Law*, pp. 201–218.

29. Tolan, *Petrus Alfonsi*, pp. 15–25.

30. Petrus Alfonsi, *Dialogus Petri, cognomento Alphonsi, ex Judaeo Christiani, et Moysi Judaei*, PL, v. 157, col. 670; Pedro Alfonso de Huesca, *Diálogo contra los judíos*, p. 399.

31. Ibid.

32. The legend of the *Volto Santo* claims nevertheless that the shavings resulting from the miraculous sculpture of the crucifix by Nicodemus, then by an angel, themselves fulfill miracles. Cf. Schmitt, "Cendrillon crucifiée: À propos du *Volto Santo* de Lucques," in *Le Corps des images*, p. 217.

33. Rupert of Deutz, *Anulus seu Dialogus inter Christianum et Judaeum*, ed. Hrabannus Haacke in *Ruperto di Deutz e la controversia tra Cristiani ed Ebrei ne secolo XII*, ed. Maria Lodovica Arduini (Rome, 1979).

34. F. W. E. Roth, "Ein Brief des Chronisten Rudolf von St. Trond an Rupert von Deutz," *Neues Archiv der Gesellschaft für ältere deutsche Geschichtskunde*, 17 (1892): 617–618.

35. Rupert of Deutz, *De glorificatione Trinitatis et Processione Sancti Spiritus*, PL, vol. 169, col. 11–14, where Rupert remembers Rudolph's request as well as his own conviction that Jews must first be initiated in the principles of Christian exegesis in order to then understand the Trinity.

36. Rudolph of Saint-Trond, *Gesta Abbatum Trudoniensum*, ed. R. Koepke, MGH, *Scriptores*, vol. X (Hanover, 1852).

37. Let us recall what Rupert says in his *Vita Heriberti* about the "familiarity" between a Jew and Count Hugo, father of the Archbishop Heribert of Cologne.

38. Timmer, "Biblical Exegesis," p. 314.

39. Ibid., p. 316.

40. Ibid., p. 315. Anna Sapir Abulafia, "Jewish Carnality in Twelfth-Century Renaissance Thought," in *Christianity and Judaism*, ed. Diana Wood (Oxford, 1992), pp. 59–75.

41. Rupert of Deutz, *Anulus*, pp. 232–240.

42. Rupert also speaks of the *humaniformi* in his commentaries on Exodus 3, 32 (PL, vol. 167, col. 680D) and on Micah 2, 5, 12 (PL, vol. 168, col. 499B), as well as in the *De divinis officiis*, IX, 9 (ed. Haacke, CCCM, 7; PL, vol. 170, col. 303C). On this heresy, see *Thesaurus lingua latinae* (Leipzig, 1936), III, s.v. "Humaniformianus;" and the *Dictionnaire de théologie catholique*, s.v. "Anthropomorphisme."

43. Gilbert Dahan mentions a number of other Christian authors who use this passage against the Jews. In the *Opusculum*, it is rather surprising to see that the parent in charge of looking after young Judas is named Baruch. See *Les Intellectuels chrétiens et les Juifs*, pp. 444–445.

44. Petrus Venerabilis, *Adversus Iudeorum inveteratum duritiem*, ed. Yvonne Friedman, CCCM, LVIII (Turnhout, 1985), II, pp. 217–226.

45. See above, note 11. Cf. Teviotdale, *The Stammheim Missal*, p. 64.

46. Du Cange, *Glossarium et infimae latinitatis*, s.v. "Adoptari": with the disappearance of the Roman meaning of the term adoption, the verb adoptari took from Saint Boniface (Epist., XV) a baptismal meaning: "Homo quidam alterius filium de sacri baptismatis fonte elevans, adoptavit sibi in filium, cujus postea viduatum duxit uxorem" ("A man, having lifted onto the baptismal font the son of another man, *adopted him as his son* and then married the widow"). The *filius adoptivus* becomes at the same time the godson; thus there comes about—in the present case, where the widow of the godson then remarried the godfather of her former husband—the idea of a "spiritual incest" that forbids a carnal relationship between the two parties. See Bernhard Jussen, *Patenschaft und Adoption im frühen Mittelalter* (Göttingen, 1991), p. 20.

47. Rupert of Deutz, *Vita Heriberti*, cap. 15, pp. 56–58.

48. Many other examples can be found in Schmitt, *Le Corps des images*, passim.

49. Hrabanus Haacke, *Programme zur bilden Kunst in den Schriften Ruperts von Deutz*, Siegburger Studien, IX (Siegburg, 1974).

50. One of the manuscripts of the *De diversis artibus* names its authors as "Theophi-

lus qui est Rugerus." See the presentation given by C. R. Dodwell in *De diversis artibus. The Various Arts*, ed. and trans. C. R. Dodwell (London, 1961), pp. xxxix–xliv.

51. Rupert of Deutz, *De Trinitate*, 2, 3, p. 187 (or PL, vol. 167, col. 248–249): "Sed ea, quae carere non potest homo, facultas rationalitas, instrumentum est sive oculus quidam ad quaerendam similitudinem Dei. Est ergo inexcusabilis, cum ad similitudinem Dei non pervenerit: quia videlicet bono instrumento, ad hoc, propter quod sibi datum est, uti noluit" ("But the faculty of reason, which is the instrument or eye that permits searching for God's similitude, cannot work for man. It is thus inexcusable that he cannot arrive at God's similitude: it is that he did not want to make use of the good instrument that was given to him for this purpose"). On the tradition of the *imago Dei* and its relationship with medieval art, see Gerhart Ladner, *Ad Imaginem Dei: The Image of Man in Medieval Art* (Latrobe, Pa., 1965).

52. John Van Engen, "Theophilus Presbyter and Rupert of Deutz: The Manual Arts and Benedictine Theology in the Early Twelfth Century," *Viator* 11 (1980): 152, n. 28.

53. Ibid., 154, n. 38, and 156.

54. Theophilus, *De diversis artibus*, p. 63: "You have decorated the House of God with such beauty, you have embellished the ceilings and the walls with many colors in order to show the spectator, in a certain way, God's paradise, radiating with various flowers, verdant with grass and foliage, rewarding with multiple crowns corresponding to their merits, the souls of saints."

55. Rupert of Deutz, *Anulus*, p. 242 (provides a list of biblical citations).

56. Inghetto Contardo, *Disputatio contra Iudeos. Controverse avec les juifs*, ed. and trans. Gilbert Dahan (Paris, 1993), pp. 52–53 and 284–285. It is symptomatic that Joshua 22 does not figure in the index of scriptural citations compiled by Gilbert Dahan in his magisterial study of medieval Christian intellectuals' attitudes toward Jews: *Les Intellectuels chrétiens et les Juifs*, p. 615.

57. William of Bourges, *Livre des guerres du Seigneur contre les Juifs et deux homélies*, ed. Gilbert Dahan (Paris, 1981), XXX, pp. 222–225, and commented upon by Dahan, pp. 34–35.

58. I wish to thank Maurice Olender for all the information he has given me regarding Eber, and recommend the early results of his research, especially his "Savoir religieux et genèse des sciences humaines," *Annuaire: Comptes rendus des cours et conférences 1996–1997* (1998): 151.

59. Robert Favreau, "Les inscriptions des fonts baptismeaux d'Hildesheim: Baptême et quaternité," *Cahiers de civilisation médiévale* (1995): 115.

60. "Ad patria(m) Iosue duce flumen transit Hebreus ducimur ad vita(m) te duce fonte (forte?) Deus."

61. Carlo Cecceli, *I mosaici della basilica di S. Maria Maggiore* (Turin, 1956), plate XL, pp. 175–176.

62. From *Aelfric's Paraphrase of the Pentateuch and Joshua* (eleventh-century Anglo-Saxon text. London, British Library, ms. Cotton Claudius. B IV, f. 143). We know that this type of Anglo-Saxon manuscript—*Aelfric's Paraphrase* or *The Bible of Caedmon*—was

variously influenced by Late Antique and Byzantine models. On these latter, see Kurt Weizman, *The Joshua Roll: A Work of the Macedonian Renaissance* (Princeton, 1984). In keeping with the Latin Middle Ages, see the *Pamplona Bible* (Navarre, end of the twelfth century–first third of the thirteenth century), with three Hebrew carrying stones on their back. Cf. François Bucher, *The Pamplona Bible: A facsimile compiled from two picture Bibles with martyrologies commissioned by King Sancho el Fuerte of Navarra (1194–1234). Amiens Manuscript Latin 108 and Harburg Ms. I 2, lat. 4, 15*, 2 vols. (New Haven, 1970), II, plate 164. For another representation of Joshua 4: *Speculum Humanae Salvationis* (Cologne, c. 1370. Cologne, Historisches-Archiv, W. 105). Cf. *Vor Stefen Lochner: Die Kölner Maler von 1300 bis 1430* (Cologne, 1974), p. 140; *Bible Historiale* (in Dutch, c. 1430. La Haye, Koninklijke Bibliotek, Ref. 78. D. I, f. 133).

63. London, BM Add. 15277. Cf. Gianfranco Folena and Gian Lorenzo Mellini, *Bibbia istoriata padovana della fine del trecento: Pentateuco, Giosuè, Ruth* (Venice, 1962).

64. Ibid., f. 69r–69v.

65. Ibid., f. 85r–85v.

66. Rupert of Deutz, *Alercatio monachi et clerici*, PL, vol. 170, col. 537–542. Van Engen, *Rupert of Deutz*, pp. 310–312.

67. Rupert of Deutz, *In Regulam sancti Benedicti*, PL, vol. 170, col. 490–498. Van Engen, *Rupert of Deutz*, pp. 339–342.

68. Anselm of Havelberg, *Epistola apologetica pro ordine canonicorum regularium ad Ecbertum abbatem Huysborgensem*, PL, vol. 188, col. 1117–1140. François Petit, *La spiritualité aux XIIe et XIIe siècles* (Paris, 1947), pp. 56–64.

69. See below, p. 175.

70. Anselm of Havelberg, *Liber de ordine canonicorum*, PL, vol. 188, col. 1097–1099. The thirty-eight chapters of the treaty set out to describe every characteristic of the Premonstratensian canons: their tonsure, their habits, the forms of fasting, the prohibition to becoming a monk. The comparison between Martha and Mary is given a long commentary, especially on Martha, thus privileging the clerics (chap. 35). Concerning another aspect of his activities, relations with the Greek Church, see Anselm of Havelberg, *Dialogues*, ed. and trans. Gaston Salet (Paris, 1966).

71. Pierre Courcelle, *"Connais-toi toi-même" de Socrate à saint Bernard*, 3 vols. (Paris, 1974–1975), I, pp. 276–278.

72. Petit, *La spiritualité des Prémontrés*, p. 132.

73. Philip of Harvengt, *De institutione clericorum*, col. 760A.

74. Ibid., col. 807: a *disputatio* between "a monk that I did not know by face (nequaqum novi) but only by name, and a cleric that I did know well, by face and by name."

CHAPTER 5. BAPTISM AND NAME

1. An excellent synthesis of this evolution is provided in Simha Goldin, "Juifs et juifs convertis au Moyen Âge: 'Es-tu encore mon frère?'" *Annales H, SS*, 54, 4 (1999): 851–874.

2. Elukin, "The Discovery of the Self," p. 66.

3. On Gregory of Tours see Martin Heinzelmann, *Gregor von Tours (538–594): "Zehn Bücher Geschichte." Historiographie und Gesellschaftskonzept im 6. Jahrhundert* (Darmstadt, 1994).

4. Gregory of Tours, *Histoire des Francs*, trans. Robert Latouche (Paris, 1996).

5. See the fine analysis by Peter Brown, *The Cult of the Saints: Its Rise and Function in Late Antiquity* (Chicago, 1981). Jonathan Elukin ("The Discovery of the Self," p. 74) mistakenly confuses Severus of Minorca with his contemporary Sulpicius Severus.

6. Severus of Minorca, *Letter on the Conversion of the Jews*, ed. and trans. Scott Bradley (Oxford, 1996), §11, pp. 88–91.

7. Ibid., §16, pp. 96–97. See Schreckenberg, *Die christlichen Adversus-Judaeos-Texte*, I, p. 471.

8. Schreckenberg, *Die christlichen Adversus-Judaeos-Texte*, I, p. 555; and *Dialogus Judaei cum Christiano quodam ceco cui et visus restituitur*, ed. H. Walter, in *Das Streitgedicht in der lateinischen Literatur des Mittelalters* (Munich, 1920), pp. 230–232.

9. Schreckenberg, *Die christlichen Adversus-Judaeos-Texte*, I, pp. 485–488.

10. Ibid., pp. 84–85; and Bernhard Blumenkranz, "Jüdische und christliche Konvertiten im jüdisch-christlichen Religionsgespräch des Mittelalters," in *Judentum im Mittelalter: Beiträge zum christlich-jüdischen Gespräch* (Berlin, 1966), p. 264. Blumenkranz also evokes the case of another Christian, Wezelin, the deacon of Duke Conrad before 1014 who in 1012 protested against the expulsion of the Jews of Mainz and then converted to Judaism. Emperor Henry II organized the refutation of his arguments.

11. Friedrich Lotter, "'Tod oder Taufe': Das Problem des Zwangstaufen während des ersten Kreuzzugs," in *Juden und Christen zur Zeit der Kreuzzüge*, ed. Alfred Haverkamp (Sigmaringen, 1999), p. 114: all the towns in the Rhineland possessing Jewish communities were affected. Fifty percent of the Jews of Cologne died. The community of Metz was decimated.

12. Ivan Marcus, "Une communauté pieuse et le doute: Mourir pour la Sanctification du Nom (Qiddouch ha-Cham) en Achkenaz (Europe du Nord) et l'histoire de rabbi Amnon de Mayence," *Annales H, SS*, 49, 5 (1994): 1031–1047. See Konrad Schilling, ed., *Monumenta Judaica: 2000 Jahre Geschichte und Kultur der Juden am Rhein. Eine Ausstellung im Kölnischen Stadtmuseum* (Cologne, 1963), p. 61, regarding Jewish witnesses of the crusades: Solomon ben Simson of Mainz, who wrote in 1140, and Ephraim bar Jacob of Bonn, who was thirteen at the time of the second crusade and who likewise evokes the persecutions carried out by the first crusade. For a general treatment see Michael Tock, *Die Juden im mittelalterlichen Reich* (Munich, 1998), p. 123 f.

13. *Westfalia Judaica: Urkunden und Regesten zur Geschichte der Juden in Westfalen und Lippe*, ed. Berhard Brilling and Helmut Richtering (Stuttgart, 1967), I, 3, pp. 24–30 (in Hebrew with German translation). Other famous cases in the Jewish communities of the Rhineland after the massacres can be found in Goldin, "Juifs et juifs convertis," p. 861.

14. Alfred Haverkamp, "Baptised Jews in German Lands During the Twelfth Century," in *Jews and Christians in Twelfth-Century Europe*, p. 261. Bernard of Clairvaux,

Epistola 365 in *Opera*, ed. Jean Leclercq, Charles H. Talbot, and Henri M. Richais (Rome, 1977), VIII, p. 321: "Ad Henricum Moguntinum archiepiscopum, Radulfum monachum, qui fidels in judaeorum necem armabat, arguit" ("For the benefit of the archbishop of Mainz Henry, he criticized Raoul, who armed the faithful in order to kill the Jews"), where he argues that the Church works to convince (*convincens*) and convert (*convertens*) the Jews but without wishing to exterminate them with the sword.

15. In France, the persecutions during the First Crusade were limited to the town of Rouen. In England, persecutions are mainly in the thirteenth century and culminate during the years 1240–1250, which was a prelude to their expulsion from the kingdom in 1290. Cf. Robert Stacey, "The Conversion of Jews to Christianity in Thirteenth-Century England," *Speculum* 67 (1992): 269. See especially the chronicle of Roger of Wendover, *Flores Historiarum*, ed. H. G. Hewlett (London, 1886–89), I, pp. 166–167 (anno 1189), pp. 176–177 (anno 1190), III, pp. 101–103 (anno 1235) regarding the alleged ritual murder of Norwich and its consequences.

16. On Gratian's *Decretum* and the Jews, see the useful list of references compiled by Gilbert Dahan, *Les intellectuels chrétiens et les juifs*, pp. 114–115.

17. Julius Aronius, *Regesten zur Geschichte der Juden im fränkischen und deutschen Reiche bis Jahre 1273* (Berlin, 1902, reissued 1970), no. 314, p. 139: the exact formula is: "Iudeorum in imperio nostro degentium, qui speciali praerogativa dignitatis nostrae ad imperialem cameram dinoscuntur pertinere."

18. Goldin, "Juifs et juifs convertis," p. 856.

19. Haverkamp, "Baptised Jews," p. 267 f.

20. Ibid., p. 273.

21. Ibid., p. 271.

22. Ibid., p. 269.

23. Caesarius of Heisterbach, *Dialogus Miraculorum*, ed. Joseph Strange (Cologne, 1851), I, pp. 92–94: Dist. II, cap. XXIII, "De clerico qui puellam Iudaeam stupraverat: quem cum Iudaei accusare vellent in ecclesia iam contritum, obmutuerunt" ("On the cleric who dishonored a young Jewish girl: and when the Jews wished to accuse him, he who in the church was already full of contrition, they killed themselves"). Ibid., pp. 94–95, cap. XXIV, "Item de virgine Hebraea a quodam clerico impraegnata, quam cum parentes parituram crederent Messiam, peperit filiam" ("On the Jewish virgin impregnated by a cleric: while the parents thought she was going to give birth to the Messiah, she gave birth to a girl"). According to Caesarius, this story happened at Worms. See Marcus, "Images of the Jews," pp. 247–256.

24. Caesarius of Heisterbach, *Dialogus Miraculorum*, I, p. 98, cap. XXVI: "De puella in Linse baptizata."

25. Ibid., pp. 95–98, cap. XXV: "Item de puella Iudaea apud Lovanium baptizata."

26. Thomas of Cantimpré, *Bonum universale de apibus*, ed. G. Colvenere (Douai, 1609), II, p. 295, cap. XXIX, "De Rachele Iudea facta moniali in Parco iuxta Lovanium": "Vidi in Brabantiae partibus Cisterciensis ordinis monialem de Iudaismo conversam." Immediately after the story of Rachel/Catherine, Thomas of Cantimpré describes in the

same chapter the story of another Jewish convert, Sarah/Gertrude, and then elaborates on the question of the ritual murder charged against the Jews.

27. *Bibliotheca Sanctorum* (Rome, 1963), s.v. "Caterina di Loviano, beata." *Acta Sanctorum* (Venice, 1787), pp. 532–534, "De Venerabili Catharina sanctimoniali Ord. Cist. Parci in Brabantia." There is a brief mention in Michael Goodich, *Vita Perfecta: The Ideal of Sainthood in the Thirteenth Century* (Stuttgart, 1982), p. 100; but not in André Vauchez, *La Sainteté en Occident aux derniers siècles du Moyen Âge d'après les procès de canonisation et les documents hagiographiques* (Rome, 1981), which only treats officially canonized saintliness.

28. I translate *genus* with the word "lineage" in order to avoid the anachronism of "race" given its present-day meaning. The medieval word *genus* does not carry any concept of race in the biological sense of the term, but rather signifies birth and attachment to a lineage. This is why Isidore of Seville (Etymologies, IX, 2, 2) relates it to the word *natio*, which comes from *nascere*, to be born. Isidore's modern editor, Marc Reydellet (Paris, 1984, pp. 42–43), can thus declare that he "makes no difference between *genus* and *natio*." I am grateful to Maurice Olender for pointing this out. Furthermore, I translate the noun *loquela* with the word "speak": indeed the text does not target the difference between languages, but language itself, the universal practice of all peoples.

29. Also beginning this way is the famous miracle of the Jewish child who received communion and was thrown into a fire by his father, who was a glassmaker, but was protected from the flames by the Virgin. The *Miracles of Notre Dame* by Gautier de Coinci assures his celebrity beginning in the thirteenth century. It is equally present in Caesarius of Heisterbach, *Die Wundergeschicten des Caesarius von Heisterbach*, ed. Alfons Hilka (Bonn, 1937), pp. 147–148.

30. Saltman, "Herman's *Opusculum*," p. 44.

31. Stith Thompson, *Motiv-Index of Folk Literature*, 3rd ed. (Bloomington, 1975), II, D 1318. 5. 2 and E 231.

32. Haverkamp, "Baptised Jews," pp. 279–282.

33. The expression is cited by Haverkamp, ibid., p. 309, n. 165, taken from another account in the *Annals of Egmond*.

34. Ibid., pp. 277–278 and 283, and *Gesta Treverorum*, p. 190.

35. Guibert of Nogent, *Memoirs*, pp. 111–116. For the reasons I have explained above, I avoid translating *genus* with the word "race" as it is used by E. R. Labande (*Autobiographie*, pp. 246–253).

36. Guibert of Nogent, *Tractatus de Incarnatione* and *Autobiographie*, pp. 424–425. See especially Jan M. Ziolkowski, "Put in No-Man's-Land: Guibert of Nogent's Accusations against a Judaizing and Jew-Supporting Christian," in *Jews and Christians*, pp. 110–122. Curiously, while Ziolkowski is at pains to show convincingly that the Guibert's account of the "Judaizing" Count John of Soissons—about whom we know very little—is a fictional construction, he refuses to offer up the slightest doubt about the "reality" of Herman the Jew in the *Opusculum* (p. 110). According to Guibert, this Christian Count who is a friend to the Jews ends up being *neuter*: neither Jewish not Christian.

37. The stereotype is present in Alfonso the Wise's *Cantigas de Santa Maria*, where the Jewish crucifixion of the wax effigy and the subsequent storming of the synagogue and massacre of the Jews by the Christian mob are represented pictorially.

38. Haverkamp, "Baptised Jews," p. 276.

39. Bernhard Jussen, *Patenschaft und Adoption im frühen Mittelalter* (Göttingen, 1991), p. 239, n. 49, citing Gregory of Tours, *Libri Historiarum*, VIII, 22: the baptism of deacon Waldo, who receives the name of his bishop Berthram.

40. Éric Palazzo, *Liturgie et société au Moyen Âge* (Paris, 2000), p. 46.

41. Hermanus, (Niemeyer), p. 116.

42. Ibid., p. 116 and n. 2: according to Niemeyer's chronology, this would be Sunday, 21 November 1198, or 20 November 1129.

43. Jussen, *Patenschaft und Adoption*, p. 241, n. 62, citing the *Annals of Fulda* (anno 893): the godfathers of Louis the Child (d. 911), the archbishop Hatto of Mainz and the bishop Adalbero of Augsburg, give him the name of his great-grandfather Louis the German (d. 876), who was himself the son of Louis the Pious (d. 840).

44. Christiane Klapisch-Zuber notes that it is the father and more rarely the mother who names the child at birth: *La Maison et le Nom: Stratégies et rituels dans l'Italie de la Renaissance* (Paris, 1990), pp. 83–107.

45. Hermanus (Niemeyer), p. 20.

46. Yvonne Labande-Mailfert, "L'iconographie des laïcs dans la societé religieuse aux XI et XII siècles," in *I Laici nella "societas christiana" dei secoli XI e XII* (Milan, 1968), esp. pp. 489–490, illus. 1: the capital of the Cathedral of Saint Pedro el Viejo de Huesca, after 1096, represents the baptism in an ornate font and mounted on a column in the shape of an adult female; with her hair undone, her bust emerges from the font while the bishop pours water on her forehead. Illus. 2: the bronze door of Gniezo (shortly after 1170); the baptism of a Prussian who converted in a sort of wooden barrel encircled by the evangelizer of the country, Saint Adalbert (martyred in 997).

47. Erhard Dorn, *Der sündige Heilige in der Legende des Mittelalters* (Munich, 1967), pp. 34–36.

48. Schreckenberg, *Die christlichen Adversus-Judaeos-Texte*, pp. 460–461, and *Die christlichen Adversus-Judaeos-Bilder*, illus. 6, after Blumenkranz, *Le Juif médiéval*, p. 15: miniature in a manuscript that comes from the Benedictine abbey of Wessobrunn (Bavaria), dated 814–815. Munich, Bayerische Staatsbibliothek, Clm 22053, f. 16: the immersion of the Levite Judas by two tonsured priests. One of them places his hand on Judas's head, the other waits holding a veil in his hands. See also Ora Limor, "Christian Sacred Space and the Jews," in *From Witness to Witchcraft*, pp. 58–63. Sara Lipton, *Images of Intolerance: The Repression of Jews and Judaism in the Bible Moralisée* (Berkeley, 1999), p. 129, fig. 101.

49. Berlin, Staatliche Museen Preussicher Kulturbesitz, Kunstgewerbemuseum, Inv. No. 33, 25. See also *Die Zeit der Staufer: Geschichte, Kunst, Kultur: Katalog der Ausstellung*, ed. Reiner Haussher (Stuttgart, 1977), I, pp. 394–396, no. 536, and II, fig. 323. Aix-la-Chapelle (?), c. 1160, 24, 4 x 4, 4 cm.

50. See above, n. 48.

51. This practice of reversible writing is very old. The *carmina figurata* of Venance Fortunat, along with the writings of Alcuin and Rabanus Maurus, had great success during the Carolingian period.

52. *Die Zeit der Staufer.* "Otto's will" mentions the two objects, the head that resembles the emperor and the silver font.

53. Hultrud Westermann-Angerhausen, "Zur mittelalterlichen Steinplastik der Freckenhorster Kirche," in *Kirche und Stift Freckenhorst*, pp. 120–133.

54. Wilhelm Kohl, "Die Weiheinschrift auf dem Taufstein der Kiirche Freckenhorst," ibid., pp. 11–13.

55. *Les statuts synodaux français*, v. I, p. 56, art. 9: "Fontes sub sera clausi custodiantur propter sortilegia, chrisma similiter et sacrum oleum sub clave serventur" ("May the baptismal font be protected from spells by a lock and that the holy oil be similarly locked up"). The same formula is found in many contemporary statutes (Cambrai, Bordeaux, Nîmes, Sisteron, etc.).

56. Arnold Angenendt, *Geschichte der Religiosität im Mittelalter* (Darmstadt, 1997), pp. 463–471, who cites (pp. 468–469) the examples of Burchard of Worms and Marie of Oignies.

57. The iconography of baptismal fonts depict Christ's baptism more than the crossing of the Jordan or even the crossing of the Red Sea. One of the most famous examples is the bronze font in Liège, which dates from 1107–1118. See Jean-Louis Kupper, *Les Fonts baptismaux de l'église Notre-Dame à Liège* (Liège, 1994).

58. Simha Goldin ("Juifs et juifs convertis," pp. 863–864) notes the suspicion with which Jewish commentators regard baptismal water, no doubt because of the baptism promised to apostates: Rabbi Itzhak of Troyes went as far as to point out that "in contrast to the other days of creation, the second [in the Genesis account] does not carry the formula: 'And God saw that it was good . . .' That is because this day is completely devoted to water, and that [. . .] God does not want to see evildoers die."

59. Sabine Gäbe (*"Me peperit ecclesia mater,"* p. 97) is alone in making the suggestion, though without going further, that Judas may have taken his baptismal name from Godfried's grandfather and that the latter's reputation might explain the frequency of the name in the vicinity of the abbey during this period.

60. Hermannus (Niemeyer), pp. 12–13.

61. Ludger Horstkötter, "Zweifel an der Gleichsetzung des Propstes Hermann von Scheda mit dem jüdischen Konvertiten Hermann von Cappenberg," *Analecta Praemonstratensia* LXXI (1995): 12.

62. Hermannus (Niemeyer), p. 70: "peccator ego et indignus sacerdos Hhermannus, Iudas quondam dictas, genere israelita, tribu levita, ex patre David et matre Sephora."

63. Ibid., p. 120: "In quo nimirum lavacro sicut vite prioris ordinem, ita et nominis proprietatem mutavi, quique Judas antea appelabor, Hermannus nomen accepi."

64. Eleazar ha-Katan describes himself by evoking his genealogy, one that is as spiritual as it is biological, and by leaving out his maternal line. See *Encyclopedia Judaica*

(Jerusalem, 1971), s.v. "Kalonymus," col. 719: "I, Eleazar ha-Katan, received the true version of the prayers from my father and teacher, Rabbi Judah, son of Rabbi Kalonymus, son of Moses, son of Rabbi Judah, son of Rabbi Kalonymus, son of Rabbi Moses, son of Rabbi Kalonymus, son of Judah . . . etc." On the name in Judaism, see Michael Mitterauer, *Ahnen und Heilige. Namengebung in der europäischen Geschichte* (Munich, 1993), chap. I, "Jacob und seine Söhne. Die jüdische Tradition."

65. Ernst Förstemann, *Altdeutsches Namenbuch* (Bonn, 1900), p. 760 f., especially p. 774. See also Émile Benvéniste, *Le Vocabulaire des institutions indo-européennes* (Paris, 1969), I, pp. III–II5 and 302–303. Henning Kaufmann (*Untersuchungen*, pp. 213–217) notes that the word *Harja* gave rise to the Latinized form *Cari* that one finds in numerous Merovingian names, which in turn yielded *Carolus*, Charles, the favorite name of "Carolingian" rulers. In consideration of its "warrior" meaning, one has to remember the popular beliefs relating to the "furious army" of ghosts (in German: *das wütende Heer*) that the Latin texts of the eleventh century onward name *exercitus mortuorum* and, more specifically, *familia Herlequini*—whence comes, perhaps, the root *Heer. Hellequin* or *Herlequin* eventually yielded *Arlequin*. See my own *Ghosts in the Middle Ages*, chap. 5. In the *Germania*, Tacitus speaks already of a troupe of ghosts or masked warriors called *Harii*.

66. Jacob and Wilhelm Grimm, *Deutsches Wörtbuch* (Leipzig, 1877, reedited 1984), v. 10, col. III3, s.v. "Hermann."

67. Horstkötter, "Zweifel," pp. 69–70.

68. Mitterauer, *Ahnen und Heilige*, p. 275, for the "Hinz und Kunz Phänomen" in German.

69. Ibid., p. 405 f. Monique Bourin and Pascal Charelle, eds., *Genèse médiévale de l'anthroponymie moderne*, vol. III: *Enquêtes généalogiques et données prosopographiques* (Tours, 1995), pp. 219–241.

70. Mitterauer, *Ahnen und Heilige*, p. 253.

71. Tolan, *Petrus Alfonsi*, p. 9.

72. Guibert of Nogent, *Memoirs*, pp. 112–113.

73. William of Bourges, *Livre des guerres du Seigneur*. See the introduction by Gilbert Dahan, p. 7.

74. Chazan, *Barcelona and Beyon*d, p. 25, and "The Letter"; Cohen, *The Friars and the Jews*, p. 129 f.

75. Mitterauer, *Ahnen und Heilige*, p. 473, n. 331: at the Premonstratensian abbey of Steinfeld, Herman, who was born in Cologne in 1150, takes his second name of Joseph in veneration of the Virgin, only indirectly out of veneration for her husband. It is in a vision that she asked him to take the name "ut nomen sponsi pariter cum sponsa accipias" ("so that you receive the husband's name equally with the wife's name").

76. Mitterauer, *Ahnen und Heilige*, pp. 293–294 f. Bourin and Chareille, eds., *Genèse médiévale*, p. 236.

77. These prohibitions extend to the "accomplices," the carnal and spiritual parents of the same child. See Anita Huerreau-Jalabert, "*Spiritus* et *Caritas*: Le baptême dans la société médiévale," in *La Parenté spirituelle*, ed. Françoise Héritier and Élisabeth Copet-

Rougier (Paris, 1995), pp. 133–203; and for later periods see Agnès Fine, *Parrains, marraines: La parenté spirituelle en Europe* (Paris, 1994).

78. Olivier Guyotjeannin, *Salimbene de Adam, un chroniqueur franciscain* (Turnhout, 1995), pp. 120–121; and Guyotjeannin, "Lignage et mémoire généalogique en Émilie au XIIIe siècle: l'example de Salimbene de Adam," in *Media in Francia* (Maulévrier, 1989) regarding Salimbene: "his friends and family" call him Ognibene (*Omnebonum*), which means "all-good." But when he enters the order of the Minors he is given the name Salimbene, which means "ascending-to-good." But Salimbene admits that he would have liked to be called Dionigi (Denis) out of reverence for the great saint and because he was himself born on the saint's feast day.

79. *Vita Godfridi comitis Capenbergensis*, p. 515.

80. In medieval texts the word *quondam* usually means "deceased." But this notion is here expressed by the phrase *bone memorie*: Herman is taken to be already dead when the title and subheading are introduced into the text. The translation "formerly" for *quondam* leaves no doubt.

CHAPTER 6. "A NEW ERA OF CONVERSION"

1. Kaspar Elm, "Norbert von Xanten (1080/85–1134)," in *Theologische Realenzyklopädie*, XXIV (Berlin, 1994), pp. 608–612.

2. *Vita Norberti*, p. 671.

3. A comparison of the two accounts is given in Lefèvre, "L'épisode de la conversion de S. Norbert et la tradition hagiographique de la *Vita Norberti*," *Revue d'histoire ecclésiastique* 56 (1961): 815–817.

4. Ibid. On the conversion of the Apostle, see Marie-Françoise Baslez, *Saint Paul* (Paris, 1991).

5. Hermannus (Niemeyer), chap. 2, p. 75, and again chap. 6, p. 93. The importance of the Pauline model was noticed by Gäbe, "*Me peperit ecclesia mater*," pp. 94–95.

6. *Libellus de diversis ordinibus*, 1, Prologue: "et maxime nostris temporibus diversa monachorum canonicorumve surgat institutio in habitu vel cultu."

7. *Encyclopedia Judaica*, vol. 11, s.v. "Levi." The merging of the "clerics" with the Levites can be justified by several characteristics: the Levites made up the smallest tribe; during the Exodus they distinguished themselves by remaining faithful to the practice of circumcision and by shunning idolatry; they serve the Arc and later on, in the kingdom of David, they become dignitaries of the kingdom; they are granted protection like paupers, widows, and orphans. The distinction between Levites and priests was gradually delineated during ancient Judaism.

8. Godfried of Cappenberg did not wish to go beyond the rank of acolyte. Cf. below, p. 183.

9. *Libellus de diversis ordinibus*, 60–61: "quando et ipsi de populo Dei tamquam levitae assumpti, non aequalitier sacros ordines suscipiunt, sed aliqui eorum ad ministerium sacerdotale attoluntur, aliqui ad diaconatus officium promoventur, nonnulli ad subdi-

aconatus gradum asciscuntur, aliqui etiam in acolitorum, exorcistarum, hostiariorum, lectorum ordine deputantur, vel ad extremum alii minus ad haec agenda idonei in aecclesia tantum ad clericatum suscipiuntur, unde etiam inter suos conversi appelluntur."

10. On the encounter between Bernard and Norbert and their competitive spirit, see Peter Dinzelbacher, *Vision und Visionliteratur im Mittelalter* (Stuttgart, 1981), pp. 69–71.

11. Norbert died in Magdeburg at the age of about fifty. He was buried in the cathedral of Unser Lieben Frauen where his epitaph reads "fundator ordinis Praemonstratensium." Despite the efforts mounted by the brothers, he was only canonized in 1626 when his relics were translated to the abbey of Strahov near Prague. The diffusion of the Prémontré order in Bohemia must explain why the only two surviving ancient manuscripts of the *Opusculum* come from Cistercian monasteries in Bohemia.

12. Jacques Dalarun, *L'Impossible Sainteté: La Vie Retrouvée de Robert d'Arbrissel (c. 1045–1116), Fondateur de Fontevraud* (Paris, 1985), especially p. 176. For the comparison between Robert d'Arbrissel and Norbert of Xanten, see Tadeusz Manteuffel, *Naissance d'une Hérésie: Les Adeptes de la Pauvreté Volontaire au Moyen Âge* (Paris, 1970), pp. 32–37. For a broader comparison with the other "itinerant preachers," see Johannes von Walter, *Die ersten Wanderprediger Frankreichs: Studien zur Geschichte des Mönchtums* (Leipzig, 1906), vol. 2. On the presence of religious women in the Premonstratensian order, a little like those who lived in the double monastery of Fontevraud, see Herman of Laon, *De Miraculis*, pp. 657 and 659, which states that the order included "more than ten thousand." The hagiography of Prémontré also refers to this, notably in the case of the "blessed" Ode of Good-Hope (Hainault; 1120–1158), whose *Vita* was written by Philip of Harvengt. Cf. Petit, *La Spiritualité des Prémontrés*, pp. 71–75.

13. See "Epistola Trajectensis Ecclesiae ad Fridericum Episcopum Coloniensem de Tanchelm seductore," in *Acta Sanctorum*, July III, 832.

14. Guibert of Nogent, *Memoirs*, Book I, chaps. 8–11.

15. Dominique Iogna-Prat, "Évrard de Breuteil et son double: Morphologie de la conversion en milieu aristocratique (v. 1070–1120)," in *Guerriers et Moines: Conversion et sainteté aristocratique dans l'Occident Médiéval (IXᵉ–XIIᵉ siècle)*, ed. Michel Lauwers (Antibes, 2002), pp. 537–557.

16. Guibert of Nogent, *Memoirs*, p. 26.

17. Ibid., pp. 26–27.

18. Ibid., p. 27.

19. Ibid., p. 29.

20. Ibid., p. 30: "hae, inquam, personae *conversionum tunc temporis* extulere primordia" (italics mine). Latin original in Guibert de Nogent, *Autobiographie*, ed. E.-R. Labande, pp. 72–73.

21. Ibid., p. 33.

22. Arnold Van Gennep, *Les Rites de Passage* (Paris, 1909).

23. The *ministeriales* are warriors who are native to the empire and who originally may have come from slave backgrounds. They then became vassals like the others.

24. On the events, see Josef Prinz, "Westfalen und Köln vor 1180," in *Köln, Westfalen. 1180–1980*, pp. 31–41.

25. Franz Mühlen, "Der Dom zu Münster unde seine Stellung in der mittelalter-lischen Architektur," in *Monasterium, Festschrift zum siebenhunderjährigen Weihgedächtnis der Paulus-Kirche zu Münster*, ed. Alois Schröder (Münster, 1966), p. 55 f. J. Poeschke, C. Syndikus, and T. Weigel, eds., *Mittelalterliche Kirchen in Münster* (Munich, 1993), p. 16.

26. Niemeyer, "Die Vitae Godefridi Cappenbergensis," *Deutsches Archiv* 23 (1967): 405–467, after *Der Cappenberger Barbarossakopf und die Anfänge des Stiftes Cappenberg* (Cologne, 1959), pp. 17–26.

27. "statim omnibus abrenunciatis, se et sua omnia Deo per manus hominis Dei disponenda contradidit" ("no sooner, renouncing his possessions, he gave over to God his self and possessions through the intermediary of the hand of the man of God").

28. Religious houses founded after Prémontré (1120) included Floreffe (1121), Cap-penberg (1122), Cuissy (1124), Saint Martin of Laon (1124), and Steinfeld (1130/1140). Each of the establishments that were started following the Prémontré model had their own "daughter" houses. Cappenberg, for example, had Scheda (1139–1143), Bedburg (1138), and several others. See under these different names in *Monasticon Praemonstratense* (1983).

29. *Vita Godefridi comitis Capenbergensis*, pp. 515–516.

30. Ibid., p. 516: "Uterque Paulo post, mutatio seculari habitu, tonsuram religionis cum habitu sacrae professionis assumpsit."

31. Ibid., pp. 522–524. At first, Godfried's renunciation of his castle incites the oppo-sition of his wife and brother, but they eventually support his project. It was viewed as madness by his *ministeriales* and by the bishop of Münster, whose town's military defense now found itself minus an important stronghold. Nevertheless, the bishop supports the archbishop of Cologne's order. The only implacable opponent of the project is Godfried's father-in-law, Count Frederick of Arnsberg. For the foundation of his monastery Godfried obtains, in 1122, a privilege from Henry V, and, in 1126, a privilege from the Pope.

32. *Vita Godfridi comitis Capenbergensis*, p. 525: "pristine dignitatis nomine comitem interdum nuncupabant."

33. Ibid.: "cum seculi pompam vel strepitum sancti viri aegre ferret aspectis."

34. This famous account comes from Bede's *Ecclesiastical History*, I, 30, cited by John Howe, "The Conversion of the Physical World: The Creation of Landscape," in *Varieties of Religious Conversion in the Middle Ages*, ed. James Muldoon (Gainesville, 1997), pp. 63–80.

35. The topic of the "spatialization of the sacred" is currently a subject of numerous studies under the direction of Dominique Iogna-Prat (CNRS, Auxerre) and Michel Lauw-ers (University of Nice).

36. Schmitt, *Le Corps, les Rites*, pp. 360–396. I have discussed elsewhere the legend told in the thirteenth century by the peasants of the Dombes according to whom a castle that was stricken with misfortunes following the criminal actions of the lord was turned over to a pilgrimage site devoted to healing children. Schmitt, *The Holy Greyhound*.

37. Schmitt, *Le Corps des Images*, pp. 199–216.

38. Amy Remensnyder, *Remembering the King's Past* (Ithaca, N.Y., 1995), 68–69. See also Christine Sauer, *Fundatio und Memoria. Stifter und Klostergründer im Bild. 1100–1350*

(Göttingen, 1993), who places less emphasis on these foundation legends than on the liturgical memory of the founders. The case studied by Avrom Saltman ("The History of the Foundation of Dale Abbey," *Derbyshire Archaeological Journal* 87 [1967]: 18–38) is slightly different since it concerns the transformation of a hermitage into a Premonstratensian abbey.

39. Rupert of Deutz, *Vita Heriberti*, chap. 13, 54–55. On the role of dreams in the narrations of the construction of abbeys and churches, see Carolyn Carty, "The Role of Medieval Dream Images in Authenticating Ecclesiastical Construction," *Zeitschrift für Kunstgeschichte* 62 (1999): 45–90.

40. Van Engen, *Rupert of Deutz*, 248, fig. 2: the plan of the castle and the abbey of Deutz.

41. For the sake of demonstration I greatly simplify Gerald of Aurillac's otherwise rich and complex historical significance and the textual tradition that concerns it. On this subject see the work of Iogna-Prat, Lauranson-Rosaz, Cochelin and Facciotto in *Guerriers et Moines: Conversion et sainteté aristocratique dans l'Occident Médiéval (XIᵉ–XIIᵉ siècle)*, ed. Michel Lauwers (Antibes, 2002), pp. 143–233.

42. Odo of Cluny, *Vita Sancti Geraldi*, PL, vol. 133, col. 672A: "Ensis plane, cum equitaret, a quolibet solebat ante eum ferri, quem tamen ipse nunquam sua manu tangebat. Siquidem de balteo vel cinguli apparatus jamdudum crucem auream praeceperat fabricari."

43. *Die Zeit der Staufer*, vol. I, no. 535, and vol. II, 324–325.

44. *Les Trésors des Églises de France*, musée des Arts décoratifs (Paris, 1965), 289–294, no. 534 and pl. 34 and 35.

45. Grundmann, *Der Cappenberger Barbarossakopf*, 7: "Ita etiam crucem auream quam sancti Iohannis appelare solebam, cum gemmis et catenulis aureis, quin et capud argenteum ad imperatoris formatam effigiem cum sua pelvi nichilominus argentea, nec-non et calicem, quem mihi Trekacensis misit episcopus [. . .] ad perpetuum ornatum memorate ecclesie tota devocione inviolabiliter dedicavi."

46. Gerlinde Niemeyer, "Das Prämonstratenserstift Scheda im 12. Jahrhundert," *Westfälische Zeitschrift* 112 (1962): 309–333.

47. In the second half of the twelfth century, the "daughters" of Cappenberg that are duly recognized by the abbot of Prémontré are: Varlar, Scheda, Clarholz, and Quedlinburg. See n. 28.

48. Gerhard von Kleinsorgen, *Kirchengeschichte von Westphalen*, 3 vols. (Münster, 1779–1780).

49. An oil painting of the eighteenth century representing the founding of the priory by Wiltrudis and his sons is still preserved today in the great room of the small manor which was built in the place of the abbey after its suppression (1809) and dismantling (1817). Except perhaps for a grange, there is nothing left of the ancient buildings.

50. Ingrid Ehlers-Kisseler, *Die Anfänge der Praemonstratenser im Erzbistum Köln* (Cologne, 1997), p. 57. See also Horstkötter, "Zweifel," who already questioned (1995) the assimilation proposed by Niemeyer.

51. Hermannus (Niemeyer), 11, 13, and 26.

52. See above, p. 15.

53. Here I distance myself from Gäbe, "Me peperit ecclesia mater," p. 97, who declares that the *Opusculum* completely denies Judas's Jewish identity, a "*Nicht*-Identität." I do not think that Judas is abolished by the Christian identity of Herman. Rather, he remains veiled as an identity that is denied.

54. Bernhard Blumenkranz, *Le Juif Médiéval au Regard de l'Art Chrétien* (Paris, 1966); Sara Lipton, *Images of Intolerance: The Representation of Jews and Judaism in the Bible Moralisée* (Berkeley, 1999); Ruth Mellinkoff, *The Mark of Cain* (Berkeley, 1981).

55. Sander Gilman, *Jewish Self-Hatred: Anti-Semitism and the Hidden Language of the Jews* (Baltimore, 1986), p. 31.

56. Elukin, "From Jew to Christian? Conversion and Immutability in Medieval Europe," in *Varieties of Religious Conversion in the Middle Ages*, ed. James Muldoon (Gainesville, 1997), pp. 171–189.

57. Haverkamp, "Baptised Jews," p. 275.

58. Morrison, *Understanding Conversion*, pp. 73–77.

59. Mellinkoff, *The Mark of Cain*, pp. 92–98.

60. Petrus Abaelardus, *Sermo in circumcissionem Domini*, PL, vol. 178, col. 408D–409A: the comparison is not easy, Abelard explains, except "to convert" my pen into an "allegory" (nisi ad allegoriam stylo converso). Joshua "circumcised with a stone those whom he introduced into the land of promise," just as Christ "led us, we who were regenerated in baptism, to the legacy of the highest vocation, himself imposing upon us the true circumcision symbolized by the stone" (Qui profecto post transitum Jordanis introductos in terram promissionis cum petra circumcidit, dum videlicet nos in baptismo regeneratos, atque ad supernae vocationis haereditatem perductos, veram sibi circumcisionem per semetipsum in petra figuratam tribuit).

61. See Henri de Lubac, *Corpus Mysticum: L'Euchariste et l'Église au Moyen Âge, étude historique*, 2nd ed. (Paris, 1949).

62. See Caroline Walker Bynum, *Holy Feast and Holy Fast: The Religious Significance of Food to Medieval Women* (Berkeley, 1987).

CONCLUSION

1. I wish to thank Patrick Geary for reminding me of this observation made by the great scholar of the Cairo Geniza, S. D. Goitein.

2. I do not entirely share Sabine Gäbe's criticism ("*Me peperit ecclesia mater*," p. 105) of Karl F. Morrison on this point, according to whom Judas/Herman would have addressed Jews on the path to conversion in order to urge them on. In addition, Gäbe relates the *Opusculum* to the more lenient "theological current" toward Jews that is represented by Abelard and Rupert of Deutz as well as, for that matter, Bernard of Clairvaux, in contrast to more determined adversaries such as Peter the Venerable and, we might add, Guibert of Nogent.

HERMAN THE FORMER JEW: SHORT WORK ON THE SUBJECT OF HIS CONVERSION

Translator's notes: The present volume omits Jean-Claude Schmitt's brief summary of translations of the *Opusculum* into German, French, and English and his comments on his own translation into French, as the *Opusculum de conversione sua* has been newly translated into English for this volume.

The new English translation of Herman's *Opusculum de conversione sua* in this volume is based on the text in volume 170 of Jacques-Paul Migne's Patrologia Latina (1854). I am indebted to Gerlinde Niemeyer for her identification of biblical sources of citations in the *Opusculum*.

1. Niemeyer gives the following reading of the manuscript (p. 76): "*Morabatur eo tempore Monasterii Tuitiensis abbas Robertus nomine.*" This should be translated as: "At that time the abbot of the monastery of Deutz, a man named Rupert, was staying in Munster," which is how Karl Morrison renders the passage in his translation. However, even Niemeyer admits that there is no evidence of Rupert's stay in Munster (p. 76, n. 1). Anna Sapir Abulafia sidesteps the difficulty by offering an alternative reading of the manuscript, translating the phrase "*monasterii Tuitiensis abbas Robertus*" simply as "Rupert, abbot of the monastery of Deutz, was staying." Since there is no distinction between uppercase and lowercase words within the Latin sentence, this reading is perfectly appropriate, and I have here adopted it. Thus it is not necessary to have Rupert in Munster for the disputation; it could just as well have taken place at Cologne, especially since, as Sapir Abulafia has explained, chapter 9 and its discussion with the clergy should really be placed between chapters 2 and 3. Her arguments seem fully convincing to me, although there remains the question of why chapter 9 was displaced to begin with. In my translation of the text I therefore preserve the order given in the manuscript.

2. Here in the margins of the Vatican manuscript it reads: "The Jews ought to be treated with clemency."

3. A liturgical formula.

4. Niemeyer cites Ecclesiastes 1:18 and Morrison cites Ecclesiastes 13:18, but neither of these references seems appropriate to me. The closest would appear to be Isaiah 53:3: *virum dolorem et scientem infirmitatem*, "a man of suffering and acquainted with infirmity."

5. A Benedictine convent located in close proximity to the city walls.

Bibliography

The following abbreviations appear in the bibliography.

Annales ESC   *Annales. Économie, société, civilisation*
Annales H, SS   *Annales. Histoire, sciences sociales*
CCCM   *Corpus Christianorum. Continuatio Mediaevalis*
MGH   *Monumenta Germaniae Historica*
PL   *Patrologia Latina*

MANUSCRIPT SOURCES

Detailed descriptions of manuscript sources and old printed editions: Hermannus (Niemeyer), pp. 49–55. I was able to consult in person the manuscript in the Vatican (but not the one in Leipzig) and on microfilm the ones in Brussels and Cologne thanks to Geneviève Contamine (CNRS/IRHT, Paris) and Leopold Schütte (Germania Sacra), both of whom I wish to thank.

Rome, Bibliotheca Apostolica Vaticana, Cod. Lat. 504 (not 507, as was incorrectly indicated by Niemeyer, p. 49.), f. 71 v–93 r. Parchment, late twelfth century.
Leipzig, Universitätsbibliothek, Cod. 220. F. 178–185 v. Parchment c. 1200.
Brussels, Bibliothèque Royale Albert Ier, Ms. 8983–8984 (Collectanea Bollandiana, 3524), f. 114–154 v. Paper, seventeenth century.
Brussels, Bibliothèque Royale, Ms. 18942–18946 (Collectanea Bollandiana), f. 233 r- 270 r. Paper, seventeenth century.
Cologne, Stadtarchiv: Auswärtiges 324. Paper, eighteenth century. Vol. 3, f. 57–61, 64–66: Johannes Gelenius, Farraginis diplomatum historiae ecclesiae coloniensis servientum, vol. 29, f. 449–460: Aegidius Gelenius, Farraginis diplomatum et observationum in usum Historiae, etc. (manuscript copies relating to the priory of Scheda and Hermann "of Scheda," notably his exhumation in 1628; Neimeyer, pp. 28 and 67).

PRINTED SOURCES

Abelard. *Historia calamitatum*. Critical edition with introduction. Ed. Jacques Monfrin. 2nd ed. Paris: J. Vrin, 1962.

Additamenta fratrum Cappenbergensium ad Vitam Norberti posteriorum, in Vita Norberti Archiepiscopi Magdeburgensis. Ed. Roger Williams. MGH, Scriptores, vol. 12. Hanover, 1856 (reprinted 1963). Pp. 704–706.

Annales Egmundani. Ed. G. H. Pertz. MGH, Scriptores, vol. 16. Hanover, 1859.

Anselm of Haveberg. *Dialogues*. Ed. Gaston Salet. Sources Chrétiennes, 118. Paris: Éditions du Cerf, 1966.

———. *Epistola apologetica pro ordine canonicorum regularium ad Ecbertum abbatem Huysborgensem*. PL 188, cols. 1117–1140 (cols. 1119–1120).

———. *Liber de ordine canonicorum*. PL 188, cols. 1093–1118.

Audradus Modicus. *Liber revelationum*. Ed. Ludwig Traube. *O Roma nobilis. Philologische Untersuchungen aus dem Mittelalter, in Abhandlungen der philosophisch-philologischen Klasse der königlichen bayerischen Akademie der Wissenschaften*, vol. 19, 2. Munich, 1892. Pp. 374–391.

———. *Liber revelationum*. Ed. Ludwig Traube. MGH, Poetae Latini aevi Carolini, vol. 3. Berlin, 1896.

Augustine. *Confessions*. Ed. and trans. Pierre de Labriolle. 2 vols. Paris: Les Belles Lettres, 1926 (14th printing, 1996).

———. *Confessions*. Ed. and trans. Henry Chadwick. World's Classics. Oxford: Oxford University Press, 1991.

Bernard of Clairvaux. *Apologia ad Guillelmum Abbatem*, in *Opera*, III. Ed. Jean Léclercq and Henri M. Rochais. Rome: Éditions cisterciennes, 1963. Pp. 63–108.

Caesarius of Heisterbach. *Dialogus Miraculorum*. Ed. Joseph Strange. 2 vols. Cologne, 1851.

———. *Die Wundergeschichten des Caesarius von Heisterbach*. Ed. Alfons Hilka, III. Bonn, 1937.

Gesta Treverorum. Additamentum et continuatio prima. Ed. Georg Waitz. MGH, Scriptores, vol. 8. Hanover, 1848.

Gilbert Crispin. *Disputatio Iudei et Christiani*. Ed. Bernhard Blumenkranz. Utrecht: "Stromata Patristica et Mediaevalia," 3, 1956.

Giraldus Cambrensis, *De rebus a se gestis*. Ed. J. S. Brewer, in *Opera*, "Rolls Series," vol. 1. London, 1861. Pp. 1–196.

———. *The Autobiography of Giraldus Cambrensis*. Ed. and trans. H. E. Butler with an introductory chapter by C. H. Williams. London: Jonathan Cape, 1937.

Gregory of Tours. *Histoire des Francs*. Trans. Robert Latouche. Paris: Les Belles Lettres, 1996.

———. *Liber in gloriam martyrum*. MGH, Scriptores rerum merovingicarum. Ed. Bruno Kusch. Hanover, 1885.

Guibert of Nogent. *A Monk's Confession: The Memoirs of Guibert of Nogent*. Trans. Paul J. Archambault (University Park: Pennsylvania State University Press, 1996).

————. *Tractatus de Incarnatione contra Iudaeos*. PL 156, cols. 489–528.

Guillaume de Lorris and Jean de Meun. *The Romance of the Rose*. Trans. Charles Dahlberg. 3rd ed. Princeton: Princeton University Press, 1995.

Hermannus quondam Judaeus. *Opusculum de conversione sua*. PL 170 (1st ed. 1854, 2nd ed. 1894), cols. 803–836.

————. *Opusculum de conversione sua*. Ed. Gerlinde Niemeyer. MGH, Quellen zur Geistesgeschichte des Mittelalters, 4. Weimar: Hermann Böhlaus Nachfolger, 1963.

Inghetto Contardo. *Disputatio contra Iudeos*. *Controverse avec les Juifs*. Ed. Gilbert Dahan. Paris: Les Belles Lettres, 1993.

Jehudah ben Chemouel le Hasid. *Sefer Hasidim*. *Le Guide des Hasidim*. Trans. Édouard Gourévitch. Paris: Éditions du Cerf, 1988.

Joseph Kimhi, *The Book of the Covenant*. Toronto: Pontifical Institute of Medieval Studies, 1972.

Judah Halevi. *Le Kuzari. Apologie de la Religion Méprisée*. Trans. Charles Touati. Lagrasse: Verdier, n.d.

Judas of Cologne. *Récit de ma conversion*. Trans. Apolline de Gourlet. Paris: Librairie Bloud et Cie, 1912.

Kleinsorgen, Gerhard von. *Kirchengeschichte von Westphalen und angränzenden Orten*. Münster, 1780.

The Letters of Peter the Venerable. Ed. Giles Constable. 2 vols. Cambridge: Harvard University Press, 1967.

Libellus de diversis ordinibus et professionibus qui sunt in aecclesia. Ed. and trans. Giles Constable. Oxford: Clarendon Press, 1972.

Maimonides, Moses. *Le Guide des Égarés* followed by the *Traité des Huit Chapitres*. Trans. Salomon Munk and Jules Wolf. Rev. ed. Charles Mopsik. Lagrasse: Verdier, 1979.

Nahmanides. *La Dispute de Barcelone* followed by the *Commentaire sur Essaï 52–53*. Trans. E. Smilévitch. Lagrasse: Verdier, 1984.

Odo of Cluny. *Vita Sancti Geraldi Aurilliacensis comitis libri quatuor*. PL 133, cols. 639–704.

Otloh of Saint-Emmeran. *Liber de temptationibus suis*. PL 146, cols. 27–58.

————. *Liber visionum*. Ed. Paul Gerhard Schmidt. MGH, Quellen zur Geistesgeschichte des Mittelalters, 13. Weimar: Hermann Böhlaus Nachfolger, 1989.

Pascalis Romanus. *Disputatio contra Judaeos*. Ed. Gilbert Dahan. Paris: Recherches augustiniennes, 1976.

————. "Le *Liber Thesauri Occulti* de Pascalis Romanus (un traité d'interprétation des songes au xiie siècle)." Ed. Simone Collin-Rosset. *Archives d'histoire doctrinale et littéraire du Moyen Âge* 30 (1963): 111–198.

Petrus Alfonsi. *Diálogo contro los judíos*. Ed. John Tolan. Huesca: Instituto de Estudios Altoaragonenses, 1996.

————. *Dialogus Petri, cognomento Alphonsi, ex Judaeo Christiani, et Moysi Judaei*. PL 157, cols. 535–572.

Petrus Abaelardus. *Dialogus inter Philosophum, Judaeum et Christianum*. Ed. Rudolf Thomas. Stuttgart: F. Fromann, 1970.

————. *Sermo in circumcisionem Domini.* PL 178, cols. 398–409.

Petrus Venerabilis. *Adversus Iudeorum inveteratam duritiem.* Ed. Yvonne Friedeman. CCCM 58. Turnhout: Brepols, 1985.

Philip of Harvengt. *De institutione clericorum.* PL 203, cols. 665–1206.

Rashi of Troyes. *Commento alla Genesi.* Preface by Paolo Benedetti. Introduction and annotation by Luigi Cattani. Casale Monferrato, 1985.

Ratherius of Verona. *Praeloquiorum libri VII; Phrenesis; Dialogus confessionalis; Exhortatio et preces.* Ed. Peter L. D. Reid et al. CCCM 46A. Turnhout: Brepols, 1984.

————. "Qualitatis conjectura cuiusdam Ratherii utique Veronensis," in *Opera minora.* Ed. Peter L. D. Reid. CCCM 46. Turnhout: Brepols, 1976.

Raymond Martini, OP. *Pugio Fidei adversus Mauros et Judeos,* cum observationibus Josephi de Voisin, et introductione Jo. Benedicti Carpzovi, qui simul appendicis loco Hermanni Judaei *Opusculum de sua conversione* ex m(anu)sc(rip)to Bibliothecae Paulinae Academiae Lipsiensis recensuit, Lipsiae [Leipzig], sumptibus Haeredum Friderici Lauckisi, Typis Viduae Johannis Wittigav, 1687.

Rousseau, Jean-Jacques. *Les Confessions,* in *Oeuvres complètes.* Ed. Bernard Gagnebin and Marcel Raymond. Vol. 1. Paris: "Bibliothèque de la Pléiade," 1958. Pp. 1–656.

Rudolph of Saint-Trond. *Gesta Abbatum Trudonensium.* Ed. R. Koepke. MGH, Scriptores, vol. 10. Hanover, 1852.

Rupert of Deutz. *Altercatio monachi et clerici.* PL 170, cols. 537–542.

————. *Anulus seu Dialogus inter Christianum et Judaeum.* Ed. Hrabanus Haacke, in Maria Lodovica Arduini, *Ruperto di Deutz e la controversia tra Cristiani ed Ebrei nel secolo XII . . .* Rome: Istituto storico italiano per il medio evo, 1979.

————. *Commentaria in Canticum Canticorum.* Ed. Hrabanus Haacke. CCCM 26. Turnhout: Brepols, 1974.

————. *De divinis officiis.* Ed. Hrabanus Haacke. CCCM 7. Turnhout: Brepols, 1967.

————. *De Gloria et honore Filii Hominis super Mattheum.* Ed. Hrabanus Haacke. CCCM 29. Turnhout: Brepols, 1979.

————. *De glorificatione Trinitatis et Processione Sancti Spiritus.* PL 169, cols. 13–202.

————. *De sancta Trinitate et operibus eius.* Ed. Hrabanus Haacke. CCCM 21. Turnhout: Brepols, 1971.

————. *De victoria Verbi Dei.* Ed. Hrabanus Haacke. CCCM 21. MGH, Die deutschen Geschichtsquellen des Mittelalters, 500–1500, 5. Weimar: Böhlau, 1970.

————. *Super quaedam capitula regulae divi Benedicti abbatis.* PL 170, cols. 477–538.

————. *Vita Heriberti.* Ed. Peter Dinton. Bonn: Ludwig Röhrscheid, 1976.

Severus of Minorca. *Letter on the Conversion of the Jews.* Ed. and trans. Scott Bradbury. Oxford: Clarendon Press, 1996.

Les Statuts synodaux français du XIIIe siècle, précédés de l'histoire du synode diocésain depuis ses origins. Vol. 1: *Les Statuts de Paris et le synodal de l'Ouest (XIIIe siècle).* Ed. Odette Pontal. Paris: Bibliothèque nationale, 1971.

Talmud: Hebrew-English Edition of the Babylonian Talmud. Ed. Isidore Epstein. London: Soncino Press, 1983–1990.

Theophilus. *De diversis artibus: The Various Arts*. Ed. and trans. C. R. Dodwell. London: Thomas Nelson and Sons, 1961.

Thomas of Cantimpré. *Bonum universale de apibus*. Ed. G. Colvenere. Douai, 1609.

———. *Les Exemples du "Livre des abeilles": Une vision médiévale*. Trans. Henri Platelle. Turnhout: Brepols, 1997.

Valerius. *Narrationes memorato patri nostro Donadeo*. PL 87, cols. 421–458.

Die Visionen der hl. Elisabeth und die Schriften der Aebte Eckbert und Emecho von Schönau. Ed. F. W. E. Roth. Brünn, 1884.

Vita Godfridi comitis Capenbergensis. Ed. Philipp Jaffé. MGH, Scriptores, vol. 12. 1856 (1963). Pp. 513–530.

Vita Norberti Magdeburgensis Archiepiscopi. Ed. Roger Wilmans. MGH, Scriptores, vol. 12. 1856 (1963). Pp. 670–704.

Walter Daniel. *The Life of Ailred of Rievaulx*. Ed. and trans. Maurice Powicke. Oxford: Clarendon Press, 1979.

SECONDARY SOURCES

Aarne, Antti, and Stith Thompson. *The Types of the Folktale: A Classification and Bibliography*. 2nd ed. Helsingfors, 1961.

Abulafia, Anna Sapir. "Jewish Carnality in Twelfth-Century Renaissance Thought." In *Christianity and Judaism*, ed. Diana Wood. Oxford: Blackwell, 1992. Pp. 59–75.

———. "The Ideology of Reform and Changing Ideas Concerning Jews in the Works of Rupert of Deutz and Hermannus Quondam Iudeus." *Jewish History* 7, 1 (1993): 43–63.

———. *Christians and Jews in the Twelfth-Century Renaissance*. London: Routledge, 1995.

———. "Twelfth-Century Renaissance Theology and the Jews." In *From Witness to Witchcraft*, ed. Jeremy Cohen. Weisbaden: Harrassowitz Verlag, 1996. Pp. 125–139.

Abulafia, Anna Sapir, and G. R. Evans, eds. *The Works of Gilbert Crispin, Abbot of Westminster*. Oxford: Oxford University Press, 1986.

Angenendt, Arnold. *Geschichte der Religiosität im Mittelalter*. Darmstadt: Primus Verlag, 1997.

Arduini, Maria Ludovici. *Ruperto di Deutz e la controversia tra Cristiani ed Ebrei nel secolo XII con testo critico dell' "Anulus seu Dialogus inter Christianum et Judaeum."* Ed. Hrabanus Haacke. Rome: Istituto storico italiano per il medio evo, 1979.

———. *Rupert von Deutz (1076–1129) und der "Status christianitas" seiner Zeit. Symbolisch-prophetische Deutung der Geschichte*. Cologne: Böhlaus Verlag, 1987.

Aronius, Julius. *Regesten zur Geschichte der Juden im fränkischen und deutschen Reiche bis zum Jahre 1273*. Berlin: Verlag Leonhard Simion, 1902. Reprint, Hildesheim: Georg Olms Verlag, 1970.

Auctor et Auctoritas. Invention et conformisme dans l'écriture médiévale. Acts du colloque de Saint-Quentin-en-Yvelines (14–16 juin 1999). Mémoires et documents de l'École des Chartes, 59. Ed. Michel Zimmermann. Paris: École des Chartes, 2001.

L'Autobiografia nel Medioevo. Atti del XXXIV Convegno storico internazionale (Todi, 12–15 octobre 1997). Spoleto: Centro Italiano di Studi sull'Alto Medioevo, 1998.

L'Autobiographie im Mitttelalter. Autobiographie et références autobiographiques au Moyen Âge. Acts du colloque du Centre d'études médiévales de l'Université de Picardie Jules Verne (30 mars–1 avril 1995). Greifswalder Beiträge zum Mittelalter, 55. Wodan, 55. Series 3, "Tagungsbände und Sammelschriften," 31. Ed. Danielle Buschinger and Wolfgang Spiewok. Greifswald: Reinecke, 1995.

Autor und Autorschaft im Mittelalter, Kolloquium Meissen 1995, ed. Lisabeth Andersen, Jens Haustein, Anne Simon, and Peter Strohschneider. Tübingen: Max Niemeyer Verlag, 1998.

L'Aveu. Antiquité et Moyen Âge: Actes de la table ronde organisée par l'École française de Rome . . . (Rome, 1984). Rome: École française de Rome, 1986.

Baldwin, John. "Jean Renart et le tournoi de Saint-Trond: Une conjonction de l'histoire et de la littérature." *Annales ESC* (1990): 565–588.

———. *Aristocratic Life in Medieval France: The Romances of Jean Renart and Gerbert of Montreuil, 1190–1230*. Baltimore: Johns Hopkins University Press, 2000.

Banniard, Michel. "Vrais aveux et fausses confessions du IXe au XIIe siècle: Vers une écriture autobiographique?" in *L'Aveu: Antiquité et Moyen Âge*. Rome: École française de Rome, 1986. Pp. 215–241.

Bartlett, Robert. *Gerald of Wales, 1146–1223*. Oxford: Clarendon Press, 1982.

Baslez, Marie-Françoise. *Saint Paul*. Paris: Fayard, 1991.

Baslez, Marie-Françoise, Philippe Hoffman, and Laurent Pernot, eds. *L'Invention de l'autobiographie d'Hésiode à saint Augustin: Actes du deuxième colloque de l'équipe de recherche sur l'hellénisme post-classique*. Paris: Presses de l'École normale supérieure, 1990.

Bedos-Rezak, Brigitte Miriam. "Les Juifs et l'écrit dans la mentalité eschatologique du Moyen Âge chrétien occidental (France 1000–1200)." *Annales ESC* 49 (1994): 1049–1069.

———. "Medieval Identity: A Sign and a Concept." *American Historical Review* 105 (2000): 1489–1533.

Benton, John F. *Self and Society in Medieval France*. Toronto: University of Toronto Press, 1984.

Benvéniste, Émile. *Le Vocabulaire des institutions indo-européennes*. 2 vols. Paris: Éditions De Minuit, 1969.

Berger, David. *The Jewish-Christian Debate in the High Middle Ages: A Critical Edition of the "Nizzahon Vetus," with an Introduction, Translation, and Commentary*. Philadelphia: Jewish Publication Society of America, 1979.

Berschin, Walter. *Os meum aperui: Die Autobiographie Ruperts von Deutz*. Koinonia Oriens, 18. Cologne: Luthe, 1985.

Blumenkrantz, Bernhard. *Juifs et chrétiens dans le monde occidentale, 430–1096*. Paris: Mouton, 1960.

———. *Les Auteurs chrétiens latins du Moyen Âge sur les juifs et le judaïsme*. Paris: Mouton, 1963.

―――. *Le Juif médiéval au regard de l'art chrétien*. Paris: Études augustiniennes, 1966.

―――. "Jüdische und christliche Konvertiten im jüdisch-christlichen Religionsgespräch des Mittelalters." In *Judentum im Mittelalter: Beiträge zum christlich-jüdischen Gespräch*, ed. Paul Wilpert. Miscellanea Mediaevalia, 4. Berlin, 1966. Pp. 264–282.

Boespflug, François. "La Trinité au Moyen Âge: Visions et images (XIIe–XIVe siècle). In *Expérience religieuse et experience esthétique: Rituel, art et sacré dan les religions*. Homo Religiosus, 16. Louvain-la-Neuve, 1993. Pp. 121–152.

―――. "La vision-en-rêve de la Trinité de Rupert de Deutz (v. 1110): Liturgie, spiritualité et histoire de l'art." *Revue des sciences religieuses* 71, 2 (1997): 205–229.

―――. "La vision de la Trinité de Christine de Markyate et le Psautier de Saint-Alban." *Micrologus* VI, 2 (1998): 95–112.

Boespflug, François, and Nicolas Losski, eds. *Nicée II, 787–1987: Douze siècles d'images religieuses. Actes du colloque international Nicée II tenu au Collège de France, Paris, les 2, 3 et 4 octobre 1986*. Paris: Éditions du Cerf, 1987.

Boespflug, François, and Yolanta Zaluska. "Le dogme trinitaire et l'essor de son iconographie en Occident de l'époque carolingienne au IVe concile du Latéran (1215)." *Cahiers de civilisation médiévale* 37, 3 (1994): 181–240.

Bonne, Jean-Claude. "Entre ambiguïté et ambivalence: Problématique de la sculpture romane." *La Part de l'oeil* 8 (1992): 147–164.

Bourin, Monique, and Pascal Charelle, eds. *Genèse médiévale de l'anthroponymie moderne*. Vol 3: *Enquêtes généalogiques et données prosopographiques*. Tours: Publications de l'Université de Tours, 1995.

Bourin, Monique, Jean-Marie Martin, and Françoise Menant, eds. *L'Anthroponymie: Documents de l'histoire sociale des mondes méditerranéens médiévaux. Actes du colloque international de l'École française de Rome (Rome, 6–8 octobre 1994)*. Rome: École française de Rome, 1996.

Bowersock, G. W. *Fiction as History: Nero to Julian*. Berkeley: University of California Press, 1997.

Brown, Peter. *Augustine of Hippo*. London: Faber and Faber, 1967.

―――. *The Cult of the Saints: Its Rise and Function in Latin Christianity*. Chicago: University of Chicago Press, 1982.

Buc, Philippe. *The Dangers of Ritual: Between Early Medieval Texts and Social Scientific Theory*. Princeton: Princeton University Press, 2001.

Burgard, Friedhelm, Alfred Haverkamp, and Gerd Mentgen, eds. *Judenvertreibungun in Mittelalter und früher Neuzeit*. Hanover: Verlag Hahnsche Buchhandlung, 1999.

Burnett, Charles, and Peter Dronke, eds. *Hildegard of Bingen. The Context of Her Thought and Art*. London: Warburg Institute, 1998.

Bynum, Caroline Walker. *Docere verbo et exemplo: An Aspect of Twelfth-Century Spirituality*. Cambridge: Harvard University Press, 1979.

―――. *Jesus as Mother: Studies in the Spirituality of the High Middle Ages*. Berkeley: University of California Press, 1982.

―――. *Holy Feast and Holy Fast: The Religious Significance of Food to Medieval Women*. Berkeley: University of California Press, 1987.

Camille, Michael. *The Gothic Idol: Ideology and Image-Making in Medieval Art*. Cambridge: Cambridge University Press, 1998.

Carruthers, Mary. *The Craft of Thought: Meditation, Rhetoric and the Making of Images, 400–1200*. Cambridge: Cambridge University Press, 1998.

Carty, Carolyn M. "The Role of Medieval Dream Images in Authenticating Ecclesiastical Construction." *Zeitschrift für Kunstgeschichte* 62 (1999): 45–90.

Certeau, Michel de. *The Writing of History*. Trans. Tom Conley. New York: Columbia University Press, 1992.

Chartier, Roger. *On the Edge of the Cliff: History, Language and Practices*. Baltimore: Johns Hopkins University Press, 1996.

Chazan, Robert. "An Ashkenazic Anti-Christian Treatise." *Journal of Jewish Studies* 34 (1983): 63–72.

———. "Polemical Themes in the Milhemet Mizvah." In *Les Juifs au regard de l'histoire*, ed. Gilbert Dahan. Paris: Picard, 1985. Pp. 169–184.

———, ed. *European Jewry and the First Crusade*. 2nd ed. Berkeley: University of California Press, 1996.

———. *Daggers of Faith. Thirteenth-Century Christian Missionizing and Jewish Response*. Berkeley: University of California Press, 1989.

———. *Barcelona and Beyond. The Disputation of 1263 and Its Aftermath*. Berkeley: University of California Press, 1992.

———. "The Letter of R. Jacob ben Elijah to Friar Paul." *Jewish History* 6 1–2 (1992): 51–63.

Chenu, Marie-Dominique. "Auctor, actor, autor." *Archivium Latinitatis Medii Aevi (Bulletin du Cange)* 3 (1997): 81–86.

———. *L'Éveil de la conscience dans la civilization médiévale*. Paris: J. Vrin, 1969.

———. *La Théologie au XIIe siècle*. 3rd ed. Paris: J. Vrin, 1976.

Clanchy, Michael T. *From Memory to Written Record: England, 1066–1307*. Cambridge: Harvard University Press, 1979.

———. *Abelard: A Medieval Life*. Oxford: Blackwell, 1997.

Cohen, Jeremy. *The Friars and the Jews: The Evolution of Medieval Anti-Judaism*. Ithaca, N.Y.: Cornell University Press, 1982.

———. "The Mentality of the Medieval Jewish Apostate: Peter Alfonsi, Hermann of Cologne, and Pablo Christiani." In *Jewish Apostasy in the Modern World*, ed. Todd M. Endelman and Jeffrey Gurrock. New York: Holmes & Meier, 1987. Pp. 20–47.

———, ed. *From Witness to Witchcraft: Jews and Christians in Medieval Christian Thought*. Wiesbaden: Harrassowitz Verlag, 1996.

———. *Living Letters of the Law: Ideas of the Jew in Medieval Christianity*. Berkeley: University of California Press, 1999.

Courcelle, Pierre. *Les "Confessions" de saint Augustin dans la tradition littéraire. Antécédents et postérité*. Paris: Études augustiniennes, 1963.

———. *"Connais-toi toi-même" de Socrate à saint Bernard*. 3 vols. Paris: Études augustiniennes, 1974–75.

Dagron, Gilbert. "Judaïser." Collège de France, Centre de Recherche d'histoire et civilisation de Byzance. *Travaux et Mémoires*, 11. Paris: De Boccard, 1991. Pp. 359–380.

Dahan, Gilbert, ed. *Les Juifs au regard de l'histoire. Mélanges en l'honneur de Bernhard Blumenkranz*. Paris: Picard, 1985.

———. *Les Intellectuels chrétiens et les Juifs au Moyen Âge*. Paris: Éditions du Cerf, 1990.

———, ed. *Le Brûlement du Talmud à Paris, 1242–1244*. Paris: Éditions du Cerf, 1999.

Dalarun, Jacques. *L'Impossible Sainteté. La vie retrouvée de Robert d'Arbrissel (v. 1045–1116), fondateur de Fontevraud*. Preface by Pierre Toubert. Paris: Éditions du Cerf, 1985.

Davis, Natalie Zemon. *Fiction in the Archives: Pardon Tales and Their Tellers in Sixteenth-Century France*. Stanford: Stanford University Press, 1987.

Dictionnaire des Lettres françaises. Le Moyen Âge. Ed. Geneviève Hasenohr and Michel Zink. New ed. Paris: Fayard, 1992.

Dinzelbacher, Peter. *Vision und Visionliteratur im Mittelalter*. Stuttgart: Anton Hiersemann, 1981.

———. *Bernhard von Clairvaux. Leben und Werk des berühmten Zistersiensers*. Darmstadt: Primus Verlag, 1998.

Dorn, Erhard. *Der sündige Heilige in der Legende des Mittelalters*. Munich: Wilhelm Fink Verlag, 1967.

Drabek, Anna M. "Hermann von Scheda. *Opusculum de conversione sua*. Ein Beitrag zur jüdisch-christlichen Auseinandersetzung im Mittelalter." *Kairos, N. F.* 21 (1979): 221–235.

Dragonetti, Roger. *Le Mirage des sources: L'art du faux dans le roman médiéval*. Paris: Éditions du Seuil, 1987.

Dronke, Peter. *Poetic Individuality in the Middle Ages*. Oxford: Clarendon Press, 1970.

Dulaye, Martine. *Le Rêve dans la vie et la pensée de saint Augustin*. Paris: Études augustiniennes, 1973.

Dutton, Paul Edward. *The Politics of Dreaming in the Carolingian Empire*. Lincoln: University of Nebraska Press, 1994.

Dutton, Paul Edward, and Herbert L. Kessler. *The Poetry and Paintings of the First Bible of Charles the Bald*. Ann Arbor: University of Michigan Press, 1997.

Eco, Umberto. "Tipologia della falsificazione." In *Fälschungen im Mittelalter*, ed. Horst Fuhrmann. MGH Schriften, 33, I. Munich, 1988. Pp. 69–82.

Ehlers-Kisseler, Ingrid. *Die Anfänge der Praemonstratenser im Erzbistum Köln*. Cologne: Böhlau Verlag, 1997.

Elm, Kaspar. "Norbert von Xanten (1080/85–1134)." In *Theologische Realenzyklopädie*, 24, Lieferung 3/4. Berlin: Walter de Gruyter, 1994. Pp. 608–612.

———. "Norbert von Xanten (1080/85–1134)," In *Reinische Lebensbilder*, vol. 15. Cologne: Rheinland-Verlag, 1995. P. 21.

Elukin, Jonathan M. "From Jew to Christian? Conversion and Immutability in Medieval Europe." In *Varieties of Religious Conversion in the Middle Ages*, ed. James Muldoon. Gainesville: University of Florida Press, 1997. Pp. 171–189.

———. "The Discovery of the Self: Jews and Conversion in the Twelfth Century." In

Jews and Christians in Twelfth-Century Europe, ed. Michael A. Signer and John Van Engen. Notre Dame: University of Notre Dame Press, 2001. Pp. 63–76.

Encyclopedia Judaica. 17 vols. Jerusalem: Encyclopedia Judaica, 1972–1981.

Evans, Richard J. *In Defense of History.* London: Granta Books, 1997.

Favreau, Robert. "Les inscriptions des fonts baptismaux d'Hildesheim: Baptême et quaternité." *Cahiers de civilisation médiévale* (1995): 115–131.

Fine, Agnès. *Parrains, marraines: La parenté spirituelle en Europe.* Paris: Fayard, 1994.

Fleichman, Suzanne. "On the Representation of History as Fiction in the Middle Ages." *History and Theory* 22, 3 (1983): 278–310.

Förstemann, Ernst. *Altdeutsches Namenbuch.* 2 vols. Bonn: P. Hanstein's Verlag, 1900.

Förster, M. "Beiträge zur mittelalterlichen Volkskunde, IV." *Archiv für die Studien der neueren Sprachen und Literaturen* 125 (1910): 39–70.

Foucault, Michel. "Qu'est-ce qu'un auteur?" *Bulletin de la Société française de philosophie* 63 (1969): 73–104. Reprinted in *Dits et écrits, 1954–1988.* Vol. 1: *1954–1969.* Paris: Gallimard, 1994. Pp. 789–821.

———. *History of Sexuality.* Vol. 3: *The Care of the Self.* New York: Vintage, 1988.

Fraenkel, Béatrice. *La Signature: Genèse d'un signe.* Paris: Gallimard, 1992.

Fritz, Rolf. "Die Ikonographie des heiligen Gottfried von Cappenberg." *Westfälische Zeitschrift* 111 (1961): 1–19.

Führkötter, Adelgundis. *Hildegard von Bingen, "Nun höre und lerne, damit du errötest . . ." Briefwechsel.* 2nd ed. Fribourg: Herder, 1997.

Fuhrmann, Horst. "Mittelalter: Zeit der Fälschungen," In *Einladung ins Mittelalter.* Munich: C. H. Beck, 1989. Pp. 195–210.

———, ed. *Fälschungen im Mittelater, Internationaler Kongress der MGH. München, 16.– 19. September 1986.* MGH Schriften, 33, I–VI. 6 vols. Munich: 1988–1990.

———. "Fälschungen im Dienste der Wahrheit." In *Überall ist Mittelalter. Von der Gegenwart einer vergangenen Zeit.* Munich: C. H. Beck, 1996. Pp. 48–62.

Funkenstein, Amos. *Perceptions of Jewish History.* Berkeley: University of California Press, 1993.

Gäbe, Sabine. "*Me peperit ecclesia mater*: Einige Bemerkungen zur Selbstdarstellung Hermanns von Köln in seinem *Opusculum de conversione sua.*" *Analecta Praemonstratensia* 76 (2000): 70–106.

Germania Judaica. Vol. 1: *Von den ältesten Zeiten bis 1238*, ed. I. Elbogen, A. Freimann, and H. Tykocinski. Tübingen: J. C. B. Mohr (Paul Siebeck), 1963.

Gilman, Sander L. *Jewish Self-Hatred: Anti-Semitism and the Hidden Language if the Jews.* Baltimore: Johns Hopkins University Press, 1986.

Goldin, Simha. "Juifs et juifs convertis au Moyen Âge. 'Es-tu encore mon frère?'" *Annales H, SS* (1999): 851–874.

Goodich, Michael. *Vita perfecta: The Ideal of Sainthood in the Thirteenth Century.* Stuttgart: Hiersemann, 1982.

———. *The Other Middle Ages: Witnesses at the Margins of Medieval Society.* Philadelphia: University of Pennsylvania Press, 1998.

Goody, Jack. *Representations and Contradictions: Ambivalence Towards Images, Theatre, Fiction, Relics and Sexuality.* Oxford: Blackwell, 1997.

Goovaerts, Léon. *Écrivains, artistes et savants de l'Ordre de Prémontré: Dictionnaire bio-bibliographiques.* Geneva: Slatkine Reprints, 1971.

Gougenheim, Sylvain. *La Sibylle du Rhin: Hildegarde de Bingen, abbesse et prophétesse rhénane.* Paris: Publications de la Sorbonne, 1996.

Gourevitch, Aron I. *La Naissance de l'individu dans L'Europe médiévale.* Trans. from the Russian. Paris: Éditions du Seuil, 1997.

Graboïs, Arieh. *Les Sources hébraiques médiévales. I. Chroniques, lettres et responsa.* Turnhout: Brepols, 1987.

Graus, Frantisek. *Pest—Geissler—Judenmorde: Das 14. Jahrhundert als Krisenzeit.* Göttingen: Vandenhoeck & Ruprecht, 1987.

Green, Richard Firth. *The Crisis of Truth: Literature in Ricardian England.* Philadelphia: University of Pennsylvania Press, 1999.

Gregory, Tullio, ed. *I Sogni nel Medioevo.* Rome: Edizioni dell'Ateneo, 1985.

Greven, Joseph. "Die Schrift des Herimannus quondam Judaeus 'De conversione sua opusculum.'" *Annalen des Historischen Vereins für den Niederrhein* 115 (1929): 111–131.

Grimm, Jacob, and Wilhelm. *Deutsches Wörterbuch.* Leipzig, 1877 (reprinted 1984).

Grundmann, Herbert. *Der Cappenberger Barbarossakopf und die Anfänge des Stiftes Cappenberg.* Cologne: Böhlau Verlag, 1959.

———. "Der hl. Theodor oder Gottfried von Cappenberg im Domparadies zu Münster." Westfalen. *Hefte für Geschichte, Kunst und Volkskunde* 37 (1959): 160–173.

———. "Der Brand von Deutz 1128 in der Darstellung Abt Ruperts von Deutz: Interpretation und Textausgabe." *Deutsches Archiv* 22 (1966): 385–471.

Guenée, Bernard. *Histoire et culture historique dans l'Occident médiévale.* Paris: Aubier, 1980.

Guerreau-Jalabert, Anita. "*Spiritus* et *Caritas*: Le baptême dans la société médiévale." In *La Parenté spirituelle*, ed. Françoise Héritier and Élisabeth Copet-Rougier. Paris: Éditions des Archives contemporaines, 1995. Pp. 133–203.

Guyotjeannin, Olivier. "Lignage et mémoire généalogique en Émilie au XIIIe siècle: L'exemple de Salimbene de Adam." In *Media in Francia, Receuil de mélanges offerts à K. F. Werner pour son 65e anniversaire.* Maulévrier: Hérault-Éditions, 1989. Pp. 225–241.

———. *Salimbene de Adam, un chroniqueur franciscain.* Turnhout: Brepols, 1995.

Haacke, Hrabanus. *Programme zur bildenden Kunst den Schriften Ruperts von Deutz.* Siegburg. Respublica Verlag, 1974.

———. "Die mystischen Visionen Ruperts von Deutz." In *Sapientiae doctrina, Mélanges Hildebrand Bascour, o.s. B. Recherche de théologie ancienne et médiévale*, special issue. Louvain, 1980.

Hailperin, Hermann. *Rashi and the Christian Scholars.* Pittsburgh: University of Pittsburgh Press, 1963.

Hallinger, Kassius. *Gorze—Cluny: Studien su den monastischen Lebensformen und Gegensätzen im Hochmittelalter.* 2 vols. Rome: Herder, 1950–1951.

Harris, Manfred. "Dreams in Sefer Hassidim." *Proceedings of the American Academy of Jewish Research* 31 (1963): 51–80.

Haverkamp, Alfred, ed. *Hildegarde von Bingen in ihren historischen Umfeld, Internationaler wissenschaftlischer Kongress zum 900 jährigen Jubiläum, 13.–19. September 1998.* Bingen-am-Rhein: Verlag Philipp von Zabern, 2000.

———. *Juden und Christen zur Zeit Kreuzzüge.* Sigmaringen: Jan Thorbecke Verlag, 1999.

———. "Baptized Jews in German Lands During the Twelfth Century." In *Jews and Christians in Twelfth-Century Europe,* ed. Michael A. Signer and John Van Engen. Notre Dame: University of Notre Dame Press, 2001. Pp. 255–310.

Heinzelmann, Martin. *Gregor von Tours (538–594). "Zehn Bücher Geschichte": Historiographie und Gesellschaftskonzept im 6. Jahrhundert.* Darmstadt: Wissenschaftliche Buchgesellschaft, 1994.

Horstkötter, Ludger. "Zweifel an der Gleichsetzung des Propstes Hermann von Scheda mit dem jüdischen Konvertiten Hermann von Cappenberg." *Analecta Praemonstratensia* 71, fasc. 1–2 (1995): 52–76.

Iogna-Prat, Dominique. *Order and Exclusion: Cluny and Christendom Face Heresy, Judaism, and Islam (1000–1150).* Trans. Graham Robert Edwards. Ithaca, N.Y.: Cornell University Press, 2002.

———. "Évrard de Breteuil et son double: Morphologie de la conversion en milieu aristocratique (v. 1070–v. 1120). In *Guerriers et moines: Conversion et sainteté aristocratique dans l'Occident médiéval (IXe–XIIe siècle).* Antibes: Éditions APDCA, 2002. Pp. 537–557.

Jaeger, Michel. *Autobiographie und Geschichte: Wilhelm Dilthey, Georg Misch, Karl Löwith, Gottfried Benn, Alfred Döblin.* Stuttgart: Verlag J. B. Metzler, 1995.

Jakobs, Hermann. *Die Hirsauer: Ihre Ausbreitung und Rechtsstellung im Zeitalter des Investiturstreits.* Cologne: Böhlau Verlag, 1961.

Jordan, William Chester. "The Last Tormentor of Christ: An Image of the Jew in Ancient and Medieval Exegesis, Art and Drama." *Jewish Quarterly Review* 78, 1–2 (1987): 21–47.

———. "Jews, Regalian Rights and the Constitution in Medieval France." *American Jewish Studies Review* 23/1 (1998): 1–16.

———. "Adolescence and Conversion in the Middle Ages: A Research Agenda." In *Jews and Christians in Twelfth-Century Europe,* ed. Michael A. Signer and John Van Engen. Notre Dame: University of Notre Dame Press, 2001. Pp. 77–93.

Jüdisches Lexicon. Ein enzyklopädisches Handbuch des jüdischen Wissens in view Bänden. 2nd ed. Frankfurt: Athenäum, 1987.

Jussen, Bernhard. *Pattenschaft und Adoption im frühen Mittelalter.* Göttingen: Vandenhoeck & Ruprecht, 1991.

Kantor, Jonathan. "A Psychoanalytical Source: The Memoires of Abbot Guibert of Nogent." *Journal of Medieval History* 2, 4 (1976): 281–303.

Katz, Jacob. *Exclusiveness and Tolerance: Studies in Jewish-Gentile Relations in Medieval and Modern Times.* London: Behrman House, 1961.

Kaufmann, Henning. *Unterschungen zu altdeutschen Rufnamen*. Munich: W. Fink Verlag, 1965.

Kirche und Stift Freckenhorst, Jubiläumschirft zur 850. Wiederkehr des Weihetages der Stiftkirche in Freckenhorst am 4. Juni 1079. Warendorf, 1978.

Klapisch-Zuber, Christiane. *La Maison et le Nom: Stratégies et rituels dans l'Italie de la Renaissance*. Paris: École des hautes études en sciences sociales, 1990.

Kleinberg, Aviad M. "Hermannus Judaeus's *Opusculum*: In Defense of Its Authenticity." *Revue des études juives* 151 (1992): 337–353.

Kölmel, Wilhelm. "Autobiographien der Frühzeit." In *Individuum und Individualität im Mittelalter*, ed. Jan A. Aersten and Andreas Speer. Berlin: Walter de Gruyter, 1996. Pp. 667–682.

Köln, Westfalen. 1180–1980. Landesgeschichte zwischen Rhein und Weser, 26. Okt. 1980 bis 18. Jan. 1981, Westfälisches Landesmuseum für Kunst und Kulturgeschichte Münster, Landesverband Westfalen-Lippe. 10. Apr. 1981 bis 15. Mai 1981, Josef-Haubrich Kunsthalle Köln. 2 vols. Münster, 1981.

Kruger, Steven F. *Dreaming in the Middle Ages*. Cambridge: Cambridge University Press, 1992.

Kupper, Jean-Louis. *Les Fonts baptismaux de l'église Notre-Dame à Liège*. Feuillets de la cathédrale de Liège, nos. 16–17. 1994.

Labande-Mailfert, Yvonne. "L'iconographie des laics dans la société religieuse aux XIe et XIIe siècles." In *I Laici nella "societas christiana" dei secoli XI e XII, Atti della terza Settimana Internazionale di Studio, Mendola, 21–27 agosto 1965*. Milan: Vita e Pensiero, 1968. Pp. 488–529.

Ladner, Gerhart B. *Ad imaginem Dei: The Image of Man in Mediaeval Art*. Latrobe, Pa.: Archabbey Press, 1965.

Lagny, Anne, ed. "Autiobiographie et courants spirituels." *Revue de synthèse* 3–4 (1996): 373–484.

Langmuir, Gavin. *History, Religion and Antisemitism*. Berkeley: University of California Press, 1990.

———. *Toward a Definition of Antisemitism*. Berkeley: University of California Press, 1990.

Lauwers, Michel. "L'institution et le genre: À propos de l'accès des femmes au sacré dans l'Occident médiéval." *Clio: Histoire, femmes et société* 2 (1995): 279–317.

———, ed. *Guerriers et moines: Conversion et sainteté aristocratiques dans l'Occident médiéval (IXe–XIIe siècle)*. Antibes: Éditions APDCA, 2002.

Lefèvre, Pl. "L'épisode de la conversion de S. Norbert et la tradition hagiographique de la *Vita Norberti*." *Revue d'histoire ecclésiastique* 56 (1991): 813–826.

Le Goff, Jacques. "Naissance du roman historique au XIIe siècle." *Nouvelle revue française* 238 (1972): 163–173.

———. *The Birth of Purgatory*. Trans. Arthur Goldhammer. Chicago: University of Chicago Press, 1984.

———. *The Medieval Imagination*. Trans. Arthur Goldhammer. Chicago: University of Chicago Press, 1988.

————. *Saint Louis*. Trans. Gareth Evan Gollrad. Notre Dame: University of Notre Dame Press, 2009.

Lejeune, Philippe. *Le Pacte autobiographique*. Paris: Éditions du Seuil, 1975.

Lipton, Sara. *Images of Intolerance: The Representation of Jews and Judaism in the Bible Moralisée*. Berkeley: University of California Press, 1999.

Loeb, Isidore. "La controverse de 1240 sur le Talmud." *Revue des études juives* 1 (1880): 247–261; 2 (1881): 248–270; 3 (1881): 39–93.

Lotter, Friedrich. "The Scope and Effectiveness of Imperial Jewry Law in the High Middle Ages." *Jewish History* 4, 1 (1989): 32–58.

————. "Ist Hermann von Schedas *Opusculum de conversione sua* eine Fälschung?" *Aschkenas. Zeitschrift für Geschichte und Kultur der Juden* 2 (1992): 207–218.

————. "'Tod oder Taufe': Das Problem des Zwangstaufen während des ersten Kreuzzugs." In *Juden und Christen zur Zeit der Kreuzzüge*, ed. Alfred Haverkamp. Sigmaringen: Jan Thorbecke Verlag, 1999. Pp. 107–152.

Lubac, Henri de. *Corpus mysticum: L'Eucharistie et l'Église au Moyen Âge, étude historique*. 2nd rev. ed. Paris: Aubier, 1949.

Manteuffel, Tadeusz. *Naissance d'une hérésie: Les adeptes de la pauvreté volontaire au Moyen Âge*. Paris: Mouton, 1970.

Marcus, Ivan G. *Piety and Society: The Jewish Pietists of Medieval Germany*. Leiden: E. J. Brill, 1981.

————. *Rituals of Childhood: Jewish Acculturation in Medieval Europe*. New Haven: Yale University Press, 1996.

————. "Une communauté pieuse et le doute: Mourir pour la Sanctification du Nom (Qiddouch ha-Cham) en Ashkenaz (Europe du Nord) et l'histoire de rabbi Ammon de Mayence." *Annales H, SS* 49, 5 (1994): 1031–1047.

————. "Images of the Jews in the Exempla of Caesarius of Heisterbach." In *From Witness to Witchcraft*, ed. Jeremy Cohen. Weisbaden: Harrassowitz Verlag, 1996. Pp. 247–256.

Meier-Staubach, Christel. "Ruperts von Deutz literarische Sendung: Der Durchbruch eines neuen Autorbewusstseins im 12. Jahrhundert." In *Wolfram-Studien*, XVI. *Aspekte des 12. Jahrhunderts*, ed. Wolfgang Haubrichs et al. Berlin: Erich Schmidt, 2000. Pp. 29–52.

Mellinkoff, Ruth. *The Making of Cain*. Berkeley: University of California Press, 1981.

————. *Outcasts: Signs of Otherness in Northern European Art of the Late Middle Ages*. Berkeley: University of California Press, 1993.

Mentgen, Gerd. "Jüdische Prosselyten im Oberrheingebiet während des Spätmittelalters: Schicksale und Probleme einer 'doppelten Minderheit.'" *Zeitschrift für die Geschichte des Oberrheins* 142 (N. F. 103) (1994): 117–139.

————. *Studien zur Geschichte der Juden im mittelalterlichen Elsass*. Hanover: Verlag Hahnsche Buchhandlung, 1995.

Metzger, Thérèse, and Mendel Metzger. "Méir ben baruch aus Rothenburg und die Streitfrage zu dem Bildern bei den Juden im Mittelalter." *Aschkenas: Zeitschrift für Geschichte und Kultur der Juden* 4 (1994): 33–82.

Miramon, Charles de. "Embrasser l'état monastique à l'âge adulte (1050–1200): Étude sur la conversion tardive." *Annales H, SS* (1994): 825–849.

Misch, Georg. *Geschichte der Autobiographie.* 4 vols. in 8. Frankfurt: Verlag Schulte-Bulmke, 1949–1969.

Mitterauer, Michael. *Ahnen und Heilige: Namengebung in der europäischen Geschichte.* Munich: C. H. Beck, 1993.

Momigliano, Arnaldo. "A Medieval Jewish Autobiography." *Settimo contributo alla storia degli studi classici e del mondo antico.* Storia e letteratura, vol. 161. Rome, 1984. Pp. 331–340.

Monasticon Praemonstratense. Ed. Norbert Backmund. Straubing, 1949. Reprint Berlin: Walter de Gruyter, 1983.

Moore, Robert I. *The Formation of a Persecuting Society: Authority and Deviance in Western Europe, 950–1250.* Oxford: Blackwell, 1987.

Moos, Peter von. "*Occulta cordis.* Contrôle de soi et confession au Moyen Âge. 1. Formes du silences." *Médiévales* 29 (1995): 131–140.

———. "*Occulta cordis.* Contrôle de soi et confession au Moyen Âge. Suite." *Médiévales* 30 (1996): 117–137.

———. "Les *collations* d'Abélard et la 'question juive' au XIIe siècle." *Journal des Savants* (July–December 1999): 449–489.

Morris, Colin. *The Discovery of the Individual, 1050–1200.* London: SPCK, 1972.

Morrison, Karl F. *History as a Visual Art in the Twelfth-Century Renaissance.* Princeton: Princeton University Press, 1990.

———. *Conversion and Text: The Cases of Augustine of Hippo, Herman-Judah and Constantine Tsatsos.* Charlottesville: University Press of Virginia, 1992.

———. *Understanding Conversion.* Charlottesville: University Press of Virginia, 1992.

Muldoon, James, ed. *Varieties of Religious Conversion in the Middle Ages.* Gainesville: University Press of Florida, 1997.

Niehoff, Maren. "A Dream Which Is Not Interpreted Is Like a Letter Which Is Not Read." *Journal of Jewish Studies* 43 (1992): 58–84.

Niemeyer, Gerlinde. "Das Präemonstratenserstift Scheda im 12. Jahrhundert." *Westfälische Zeitschrift* 112 (1962): 309–333.

———. "Die Vitae Godfridi Cappenbergensis." *Deutsches Archiv* 23 (1967): 405–467.

Niewöhner, Friedrich, and Fidel Rädle, eds. *Konversionen im Mittelalter und in der Frühneuzeit.* Hildesheim: Georg Olms Verlag, 1999.

Noirel, Gérard. *Sur la "crise" de l'histoire.* Paris: Belin, 1996.

Oexle, Otto Gerhard. "Marc Bloch et la critique de la raison historique." In *Histoire comparée et sciences sociales,* ed. Hartmut Atsma and André Burguière. Paris: École des hautes études en sciences sociales, 1990. Pp. 419–433.

———. "Im Archiv der Fiktionen." *Rechtschistorisches Journal* 18 (1999): 511–525.

Olender, Maurice. "Savoirs religieux et genèse des sciences humaines." In *Annuaire: Comptes rendus des cours et conférences 1996–1997.* Paris: École des hautes études en sciences sociales, 1998. Pp. 150–153.

Oppenheim, Leo. *The Interpretation of Dreams in the Ancient Near East*. Philadelphia: American Philosophical Society, 1956.

Palazzo, Éric. *Liturgie et société au Moyen Âge*. Paris: Aubier, 2000.

Palmer, Nigel F., and Klaus Speckenbach. *Träume und Kräuter: Studien zur Petroneller "Circa instans"—Handschrift und zu den deutschen Traumbücher des Mittelalters*. Cologne: Böhlau Verlag, 1990.

Paravicini, Werner. "Rettung aus dem Archiv? Eine Betrachtung aus Anlass der 700-Jahrfeier der Lübecker Trese." *Zeitschrift des Vereins für Lübeckische Geschichte und Altertumskunde* 78 (1998): 11–46.

Petit, François. *La Spiritualité des Prémontrés aux XIIe et XIIIe siècles*. Paris: J. Vrin, 1947.

Poeschke, Joachim, Candida Syndikus, and Thomas Weigel. *Mittelalterliche Kirchen in Münster*. Munich: Hirmer Verlag, 1993.

Rädle, Fidel. "Wie in Kölner Jude im 12. Jahrhundert zum Christen wurde. Hermannus quondam Iudaeus *De conversione sua*." In *Konversionen im Mittelalter und in der Frühneuzeit*, ed. Friedrich Niewöhner and Fidel Rädle. Hildesheim: Georg Olms Verlag, 1999. Pp. 9–24.

Reboul, Anne. *Rhétorique et stylistique de la fiction*. Nancy: Presses de l'Université de Nancy, 1992.

Remensnyder, Amy. *Remembering Kings Past: Monastic Foundation Legends in Medieval Southern France*. Ithaca, N.Y.: Cornell University Press, 1995.

Revel, Jacques, ed. *Jeux d'échelles: La micro-analyse à l'éxperience*. Paris: Éditions du Seuil, 1996.

Ricklin, Thomas. *Der Traum der Philosophie im 12. Jahrhundert. Traumtheorien zwischen Constantinus Africanus und Aristoteles*. Leiden: E. J. Brill, 1998.

Ricoeur, Paul. *History and Truth*. Trans. Charles A. Kelbley. Chicago: Northwestern University Press, 1987.

Röckelein, Hedwig. *Otloh, Gottschalk, Tnugdal: Individuelle und kollektive Visionmuster des Hochmittelalters*. Frankfurt: Peter Lang, 1987.

Roth, F. W. E. "Ein Brief des Chronisten Rudolf von St. Trond an Rupert von Deutz." *Neues Archiv der Gesellschaft für ältere deutsche Geschichtskunde* 17 (1892): 617–618.

Rubin, Miri. *Gentile Tales: The Narrative Assault on Late Medieval Jews*. New Haven: Yale University Press, 1999.

Rudolph, Conrad. *"The Things of Greater Importance." Bernard of Clairvaux's "Apologia" and the Medieval Attitude Toward Art*. Philadelphia: University of Pennsylvania Press, 1990.

Saltman, Avron. "The History of the Foundation of Dale Abbey." *Derbyshire Archaeological Journal* 87 (1967): 18–38.

———. "Hermann's Opusculum de conversion sua": Truth or Fiction?" *Revue des études juives* 147 (1988): 31–56.

Sauer, Christine. *Fundatio und Memoria. Stifter und Klöstergründer im Bild. 1100–1350*. Göttingen: Vandenhoeck & Ruprecht, 1993.

Saurma-Jeltsch, Liselotte E. *Die Miniaturen im "Liber Scivias" der Hildegard von Bingen*.

Die Wucht der Vision und die Ordnung der Bilder. Weisbaden: Ludwig Reichert Verlag, 1998.

Schapiro, Meyer. "On the Aesthetic Attitude in Romanesque Art." Reprinted in *Romanesque Art: Selected Papers.* 2nd ed. London: Thames and Hudson, 1993. Pp. 1–27.

Schilling, Konrad, ed. *Monumenta Judaica: 2000 Jahr Geschichte und Kultur der Juden am Rhein. Eine Ausstellung im Kölnischen Stadtmuseum (15. Okt. 1963–15. März 1964).* 3 vols. Cologne: Greven und Bechold, 1963.

Schmitt, Jean-Claude. *Le Saint lévrier: Guinefort, guérisseur d'enfants depuis le XIIIe siècle.* Paris: Flammarion, 1979.

———. "L'Occident, Nicée II et les images du VIIIe au XIIIe siècles." In *Nicée II,* ed. François Boespflug and Nicolas Lossky. Paris: Éditions du Cerf, 1987. Pp. 271–301.

———. *La Raison des gestes dans l'Occident médiéval.* Paris: Gallimard, 1990.

———. "La question des images dans les débats entre juifs et chrétiens au XIIe siècle." In *Spannungen und Widersprüche: Gedenkschrift für Frantisek Graus,* ed. Suzanna Burghartz et al. Sigmaringen: Jan Thorbecke Verlag, 1992. Pp. 245–254.

———. *Ghosts in the Middle Ages: The Living and the Dead in Medieval Society.* Trans. Teresa Lavender Fagan. Chicago: University of Chicago Press, 1999.

———. "La memoire des Prémontré: À propos de l'"autobiograhie' du Prémontré Hermann le Juif." In *La vie quotidienne des moines et chanoines réguliers au Moyen Âge et Temps modernes.* Wroclaw: Publications de l'Institut d'histoire de l'Université de Wroclaw, 1995. Pp. 439–452.

———. "Les dimensions multiples du voir: Les rêves et l'image dans l'autobiographie de conversion d'Hermann le Juif." *Micrologus* VI (1998): 1–27.

———. *Die autobiographie Fiktion: Hermann des Juden Bekehrung,* 2. Trier: Arye-Maimon-Institut für Geschichte der Juden, 2000. Pp. 5–39.

———. *Le Corps, les Rites, les Rêves, le Temps: Essais d'anthropologie médiévale.* Paris: Gallimard, 2001.

———. *Le Corps des images: Essais sur la culture visuelle du Moyen Âge.* Paris: Gallimard, 2002.

Schreckenberg, Heinz. *Die christlichen Adversus-Judaeos-Texte und ihr literarisches und historisches Umfeld (1.-11. Jh.).* 2nd ed. Frankfurt: Peter Lang, 1990.

———. *Die christlichen Adversus-Judaeós-Texte (11.-13. Jh.). Miteiner Ikonographie des Judenthemas biz zum 4. Laterankonzil.* Frankfurt: Peter Lang, 1988.

———. *Die Juden in der Kunst Europas. Ein historischer Bildatlas.* Göttingen: Vandenhoeck & Ruprecht: 1996.

———. *Die christlichen Adversus-Judaeos-Bilder. Das Alte und Neue Testament im Spiegel der christlichen Kunst.* Frankfurt: Herder, 1999.

Schröder, Alois, ed. *Monasterium. Festschrift zum siebenhundertjährigen Weihgedächtnis der Paulus-Kirche zu Münster.* Münster: Verlag Regensberg, 1996.

Schuster, Beate. "The Strange Pilgrimage of Odo of Deuil." In *Medieval Concepts of the Past: Ritual, Memory, Historiography,* ed. Gerd Althoff, Johannes Freid, and Patrick Geary. Cambridge: Cambridge University Press, 2002. 253–278.

Schwarzfuchs, Simon. "Religion populaire et polémique savante: Le tournant de la polémique judéo-chrétienne au 12e siècle." In *Medieval Studies in Honour of Avrom Saltman*. Ramat Gan: Bar-Ilan University Press, 1995. Pp. 189–206.

Sed-Rajna, Gabrielle, ed. *Rashi. 1049–1990. Hommage à Ephraïm E. Urbach. Congrès européen des Études juives.* Paris: Éditions du Cerf, 1993.

Seeberg, Reinhold. *Herman von Scheda: Ein jüdischer Proselyt des zwölften Jahrhunderts.* Leipzig: Akademische Buchhandlung, 1891.

Shatzmiller, Joseph. *Shylock Reconsidered: Jews, Moneylending, and Medieval Society.* Berkeley: University of California Press, 1990.

Shulman, David, and Sarah Stroumsa, eds. *Dream Cultures: Explorations in the Comparative History of Dreaming.* Oxford: Oxford University Press, 1999.

Signer, Michael A., and John Van Engen, eds. *Jews and Christians in Twelfth-Century Europe.* Notre Dame: University of Notre Dame Press, 2001.

Smalley, Beryl. *The Study of the Bible in the Middle Ages.* Oxford: Blackwell, 1952.

Southern, Richard W. *The Making of the Middle Ages.* New Haven: Yale University Press, 1970.

———. *Saint Anselm: A Portrait in a Landscape.* Cambridge: Cambridge University Press, 1990.

Spiegel, Gabrielle. *Romancing the Past: The Rise of Vernacular Prose Historiography in Thirteenth-Century France.* Berkeley: University of California Press, 1993.

Stacey, Robert C. "The Conversion of Jews to Christianity in Thirteenth-Century England." *Speculum* 67, 2 (1992): 263–283.

Steinen, Johan Friedrich von. *Kurze Beschreibung der hochadelichen Gotteshäuser Cappenberg und Scheda.* Dortmund, 1741.

Stemberger, Brigitte. "Der Traum in der rabbinischen Literatur." *Kairos. Zeitschrift für Religionswissenschaft und Theologie*, Neue Folge, XVIII, 1 (1976): 1–42.

Stock, Brian. *The Implications of Literacy: Written Language and Models of Interpretation in the Eleventh and Twelfth Centuries.* Princeton: Princeton University Press, 1983.

———. "Lecture, intériorité et modèles de comportement dans l'Europe des XIe–XIIes." *Cahiers de civilisation médiévale* 33 (1990): 103–112.

———. *Augustine the Reader: Meditation, Self-Knowledge, and the Ethics of Interpretation.* Cambridge: Harvard University Press, 1997.

Storper-Perez, Danielle, and Henri Cohen-Solal. "Tout songe non interprété est comme une letttre non lue: Approche anthropologique est psychanalytique de l'interprétation des rêves dans le traité Berakhot du Talmud de Babylon." In *Le Corps du texte: Pour une anthropologie des textes de la tradition juive*, ed. Florence Heymann and Danielle Storper-Perez. Paris: CNRS Éditions, 1992.

Stow, Kenneth R. *Alienated Minority: The Jews of Medieval Latin Europe.* Cambridge: Harvard University Press, 1992.

Talmage, Frank Ephraim. *Disputation and Dialogue: Readings in the Jewish-Christian Encounter.* New York: Ktav Publishing House, 1975.

Ta-Shema, I. "The Earliest Literary Sources for the Bar-Mitzva Ritual and Festivity (A

Review of the Hebrew Translation of I. Marcus's Ritual of Childhood)." [In Hebrew.] *Tarbiz* 68 (1999): 587–598.

Teviotdale, Élisabeth C. *The Stammheim Missal.* Los Angeles: Getty Museum Studies on Art, 2001.

Thomas, Yann. "*Fictio legis*: L'empire de la fiction romaine et ses limites médiévales." *Droits. Revue française de théorie juridique* 21 (1995): 17–64.

Thompson, Stith. *Motif-Index of Folk-Literature*, 3rd ed. 6 vols. Bloomington: Indiana University Press, 1975.

Timmer, David E. "Biblical Exegesis and the Jewish-Christian Controversy in the Early Twelfth Century." *Church History* 58, 3 (1989): 309–321.

Toch, Michael. *Die Juden im mittelalterlichen Reich.* Munich: Oldenburg, 1998.

Tolan, John. *Petrus Alfonsi and His Medieval Readers.* Gainesville: University Press of Florida, 1993.

Torell, Jean-Pierre. "Les juifs dans l'oeuvre de Pierre de Vénérable." *Cahiers de civilisation médiévale* 30 (1987): 331–346.

Trachtenberg, Joshua. *Jewish Magic and Superstition: A Study in Folk Religion.* 1st ed. 1939. Philadelphia: Jewish Publication Society, 1961.

Tubach, Frederick C. *Index exemplorum; A Handbook of Medieval Religious Tales.* Helsinki: Folklore Publication Society, 1966.

Ullman, Walter. *The Individual and Society in the Middle Ages.* Baltimore: Johns Hopkins University Press, 1966.

Valvekens, J. B. "Hermannus quondam Iudaeus, praepositus in Scheda." *Analecta Praemonstratensia* 40 (1964): 158–165.

Van der Sterre, Johann Christof. *Natales Sanctorum candidissimi Ordinis Praemonstratensis.* Antwerp, 1625.

———. *Lilium inter spinas. Vitas B. Joseph presbyteri et canonici Steinfeldensis Ordinis Praemonstratensis.* Antwerp, 1627.

Van Engen, John H. "Theophilus Presbyter and Rupert of Deutz: The Manual Arts and Benedictine Theology in the Early Twelfth Century." *Viator* 11 (1980): 147–163.

———. *Rupert of Deutz.* Berkeley: University of California Press, 1983.

Van Gennep, Arnold. *Les Rites de passage.* 1st ed. 1909. Paris: Mouton, 1969.

Vauchez, André. *La Sainteté en Occident aux derniers siècles du Moyen Âge d'après le procès de canonisation et les documents hagiographique.* Rome: École française de Rome, 1981.

Vernet, F. "Autobiographies spirituelle." *Dictionnaire de spiritualité*, vol. 1, cols. 1141–1159. 1937.

Veyne, Paul. *Comment on écrit l'histoire: Essai d'épistimologie.* Paris: Éditions du Seuil, 1971.

Vinay, Gustavo. "Otlone di Sant'Emmeran, ovvero l'autobiografia di un nevrotico." In *La Storiografia altomedievale.* Vol. 1. Spoleto: Centro Italiano di Studi sull'alto Medioevo, 1970. Pp. 13–37.

Walter, Hans. *Das Streitgedicht in der lateinischen Literatur des Mittelalters.* Munich: Beck, 1920.

Walter, Johannes von. *Die ersten Wanderprediger Frankreichs: Studien zur Geschichte des Mönchtums.* Vol. 1: *Robert von Arbrissel.* Leipzig: T. Weichert, 1903. Vol. 2: *Bernard von Tiron; Vitalis von Savigny; Girald von Wales. Bemerkungen zu Norbert von Xanten und Heinrich von Lausanne.* Leipzig: G. Böhme, 1906.

Westfalia Judaica. Urkunden und Regesten zur Geschichte der Juden in Westfalen und Lippe. Vol. 1: *1005–1350,* ed. Berhard Brilling and Helmut Richtering. Stuttgart: W. Kohlhammer Verlag, 1967.

White, Hayden. *Metahistory: The Historical Imagination in Nineteenth-Century Europe.* Baltimore: Johns Hopkins University Press, 1973.

Wiesemann, Falk, ed. *Zur Geschichte und Kultur der Juden im Rheinland.* Düsseldorf: Schwann, 1985.

Wood, Diana, ed. *Christianity and Judaism.* Oxford: Blackwell, 1992.

Yerushalmi, Yosef Hayim. *"Diener von Königen und nicht Diener von Dienern": Einige Aspekt der politischen Geschichte der Juden.* Munich: Carl Friedrich von Siemens Stiftung, 1995.

Zak, A. "Zur Biographie des Probstes Hermann Judas von Scheda (Westfäl.)." *Zeitschrift für vaterländische Geschichte und Altertumskunde* 78, 1 (1920): 69–76.

Die Zeit der Staufer: Geschichte, Kunst, Kultur. Ed. Rainer Haussherr. 5 vols. Stuttgart: Würtembergisches Landesmuseum, 1977–1979.

Zink, Michel. *Roman rose et rose rouge: Le roman de la rose ou de Guillaume de Dole de Jean Renart.* Paris: A. G. Nizet, 1979.

———. *La subjectivité littéraire: Autour du siècle de Saint Louis.* Paris: PUF, 1985.

Zumthor, Paul. *Essai de poétique médiévale.* Paris: Éditions du Seuil, 1972.

———. *Langue, texte, énigme.* Paris: Éditions du Seuil, 1975.

———. *Introduction à la poésie orale.* Paris: Éditions du Seuil, 1983.

Index

Acknowledgments

The long years of gestation resulting in this book have led me to accumulate many debts of gratitude toward colleagues and friends for their help with bibliographic references and ideas. In Paris, I have benefited from the opinions of Jérôme Baschet, Gisèle Besson, Denise Bonan, Jean-Claude Bonne, Gilbert Dahan, Aline Debert, Dominique Iogna-Prat, Maurice Kriegel, Beate Schuster, Haym Soloveitchik, and Lucette Valensi. Several stays in Germany have allowed me to deepen the regional aspects of this study. There my gratitude is extended principally to Joachim Ehlers and Kaspar Elm in Berlin, Otto Gerhard Oexle, Martial Staub, and Pierre Monnet in Gottingen, and Arnold Angenendt, Thomas Lentes, Leopold Schütte in Munster, from where Hagen Keller guided me all the way to Cappenberg. I was honored to be invited by Alfred Haverkamp to participate in 1999 in the second Maimonides conference at the University of Trier, which allowed me to sketch a preliminary version of this work. I am grateful to his generosity as well as that of Gerd Mentgen and Christoph Cluse. Other encounters were useful to me, here or there, at one moment or another: with Gadi Algazi and Aviad Kleinberg in Tel Aviv, William Chester Jordan and Natalie Zemon Davis at Princeton, Willis Johnson at Cambridge, Joseph Shatzmiller in Lyon, and Patrick Geary on either side of the Atlantic. Shortly before his death Avrom Saltman generously responded to my letters from Jerusalem. I should also finally like to thank Maurice Olender, whose careful reading and insightful comments had no equal. Two research trips abroad were especially useful for completing this study: one at the Warburg Institute in London in September 2000, at a critical juncture in my thinking; the other at the Getty Research Institute in Los Angeles, where I completed the writing of this book in the spring of 2002.